Also by Phil Crossman

Away Happens

OBSERVATIONS
A Maine Island, a Century of Newsletters
and the Stories Found Between the Lines

OBSERVATIONS

A Maine Island, a Century of Newsletters
and the Stories Found Between the Lines

Phil Crossman

Vinalhaven, Maine

To Ray Blaisdell who, forty years ago, had the fortitude and foresight to give us a Wind that would blow forever.

Table of Contents

Acknowledgements ix

Preface xi

1883-1890 1

1937-1939 15

1974 23

1975 27

1976 29

1977 31

1978 33

1979 35

1980 39

1981 41

1982/1983 43

1984 45

1985/1986 49

1987 51

1988 53

1989 57

1990 61

1991 65

1992 68

1993	75
1994	77
1995	81
1996/1997	83
1998	87
1999	89
2000	93
2001	97
2002	105
2003	123
2004	143
2005	153
2006	161
2007	169
2008	173
2009	179
2010	197
2011	229
2012	258
2013	283
2014	309

Acknowledgements

When I began to paw through the records at the Vinalhaven Historical Society I always found a big bowl of Peanut M&M's in the office to nourish my research, but toward the end, after repeated visits, the quantity and quality of snacks diminished until I eventually found nothing but a long-since opened box of stale cookies. Clearly they'd grown weary of me. Otherwise, though, the Society has been very accommodating, helpful, and supportive and I thank them for it. Sue Radley, in particular, took the time to read the entire manuscript. The result is a much clearer and more accurate compilation. Loretta Chilles was also a tremendous help but she is my cousin and used to tease me as a child so I don't feel I need to lavish thanks on her. Certainly, however, this exercise would have been a waste of time without the Society's generous cooperation.

When I began this long process, knowing my eye for detail and accuracy was not very well suited, I asked Colleen Conlan if she would help me. I knew she had some related experience, and I supposed she might be helpful. That was something of an understatement. She agreed eagerly, her efforts fueled by her faithful adherence to the Chicago Manual of Style and a passion for clarity. I could have done this without her but the result would have been of no interest to anyone

PREFACE

VINALHAVEN IS THE LARGEST OF SEVERAL ISLANDS IN PENOBSCOT BAY, offshore by a dozen miles from mid-coast Maine, home today to twelve hundred or so people engaged directly or otherwise and in about equal numbers in lobstering and tourism.

Since 1974 the island has been served by the *Wind*, a little weekly newsletter/newspaper. Beginning in 1981 the *Wind* featured a column called "The Observer." Although the column's appearance was a little sporadic to begin with, and then disappeared altogether for a few years around 2007, it was a regular component of the paper for most of the next thirty-three years, and for the last several of those I've been the author of that feature. This year I had the audacity to think it might be of interest to readers to have the opportunity to purchase and peruse a volume of my "Observer" columns, and so I resolved to collect them all in a book, sell them here on the island, and become wealthy.

The Vinalhaven Historical Society has copies of nearly every issue of the *Wind*. I was not sure I'd kept copies of every "Observer" column I'd written so I visited their museum to be sure I didn't miss any. Once I'd tucked myself into their archives, though, I became absorbed with the forty-year history of the *Wind,* and then with its several predecessors, most from the late 1800s, and by the broad range of perception and sentiment expressed by folks who'd preceded me. I resolved to produce an account of what has happened in Vinalhaven during the last century and a half as reflected in the letters, reports, opinions, and remembrances — funny and otherwise — of others. Over the next year or so I reviewed each issue of our *Wind* and of earlier newspapers spanning those hundred plus years.

Many of the individuals, organizations, businesses, or events referred to in this assemblage have such locally historic significance I find I have referred to them, perhaps too often, as "institutions." On the other hand, I haven't found many suitable synonyms that convey that iconic sense, so I hope you'll join me in forgiving the redundancy.

Nearly everyone named is familiar to those of us who've lived or summered here for long and so no attempt has been made to explain who many of them are. Thus when you read that Ginny Snow came to Ray's rescue as editorial assistant you will either know who Ginny was or, I trust, find comfort in knowing that most of us do.

This book is arranged chronologically and throughout, when the flow of history has not been clearly reflected by the contributions of others, I have offered concurrent news and items of interest to keep things in perspective.

A few of the contributions to the early papers or items of interest have been photographed and reproduced here. Most, because the font was too small or the museum copy too mangled to read comfortably, have been reprinted for legibility. In those instances I've been generally faithful to the language, grammar, and spelling conventions of the time during which they were written. I've taken the liberty of correcting typos and obvious spelling errors, and have made other minor changes for clarity. Now and then, when it seemed prudent, I've changed the names of folks who might otherwise be left feeling uncomfortable.

Contributors to the *Wind* and to the many short-lived papers that preceded it expressed a wide divergence of interesting opinion and sensitivities. Still, they and I have one thing in common. We are islanders — Vinalhaven Islanders, in fact — and while we certainly do not speak with one voice we do generally speak with one passion: this unique island community and environment and our place in it.

Phil Crossman
Vinalhaven, Maine
February 21, 2015

Volunteers Cynthia Dyer and Sue Radley (Editor) at work on the Wind.

Photo by: Mike Seif

"Let it be known that the Editor rarely knows what he is doing and therefore accepts no responsibility for anything. What appear as errors are put there on purpose so those who need something to complain about will find it easily."

— *Ray Blaisdell*

OBSERVATIONS

1883-1890

IN THE LATE 1800S VINALHAVEN WAS A BUSTLING GRANITE QUARRYING TOWN. The population was nearly 3,000 people, most of whom were simply trying to keep their heads above water, and all of whom kept abreast of developments by listening to what others had to say or reading announcements posted in shops around town. There were, of course, no radios, but neither was the island served by a newspaper. Although a mainland paper or two now and then found its way to the island on a regular basis, few of the islanders, through no fault of their own, were well-informed about what was going on in their own town.

On November 7, 1883, Owen P. Lyons and Charles H. Healey got together over a cup of tea at Lane & Libby General Store and agreed that the island was in need of a newspaper of its own and that such an undertaking could be made profitable. Accordingly, on January 5 of the following year, the *Wind*, calling itself fittingly a "Mid-Ocean Journal devoted to Home News," made its first appearance with this welcoming announcement:

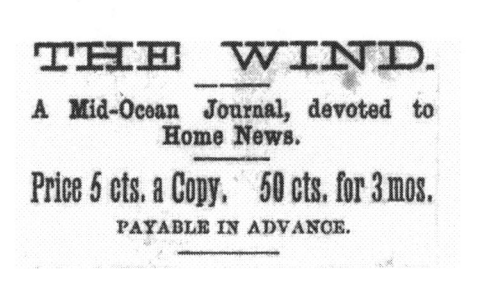

GREETING

'Once more this world has traveled its three hundred sixty and five days' journey, and as eighteen hundred and eighty-four commences its pilgrimage, so does the *Wind*; and through its columns' we offer our friends and patrons our kindly greeting for the New Year. We desire to make this little sheet worthy of home patronage, and give to our readers the best home news we can obtain. If our friends will kindly help us in the way of correspondence, and oblige us with their suggestions, they will aid us greatly in its future. A little difficulty in its attainment will sweeten our success. Too much difficulty will sour it. However, future experience shall be our guide, and whatever can be made available for the benefit of its patrons and the success of the *Wind* we shall endeavor to supply. If our humble abilities and earnest endeavors can give satisfaction and consequent success, we shall feel much pleasure in our labor. The sudden appearance of this modest sheet will be a surprise to many. We think that a town like ours, with its business and financial interests excelling, its population larger, and its means of supplying news none the less than many other towns that boast with pride and pleasure of their local sheet, ought also to have its weekly newspaper. We have decided to attempt the experiment, and our chief object shall be to make the *Wind* an interesting and intelligent local paper, worthy of our town and the respect of all its readers. Whatever comments may appear in its pages will be made in the most friendly spirit, for the best interests of all, and our motto shall be, peace, harmony, and goodwill towards all.

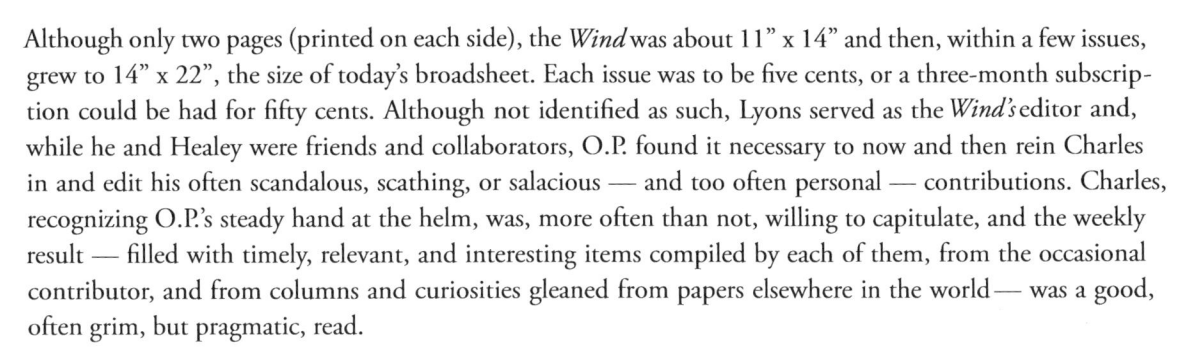

Although only two pages (printed on each side), the *Wind* was about 11" x 14" and then, within a few issues, grew to 14" x 22", the size of today's broadsheet. Each issue was to be five cents, or a three-month subscription could be had for fifty cents. Although not identified as such, Lyons served as the *Wind's* editor and, while he and Healey were friends and collaborators, O.P. found it necessary to now and then rein Charles in and edit his often scandalous, scathing, or salacious — and too often personal — contributions. Charles, recognizing O.P.'s steady hand at the helm, was, more often than not, willing to capitulate, and the weekly result — filled with timely, relevant, and interesting items compiled by each of them, from the occasional contributor, and from columns and curiosities gleaned from papers elsewhere in the world — was a good, often grim, but pragmatic, read.

Our Sick List

It is said that at present there are nearly a hundred cases of measles in town and our doctors say it is the most malignant type with which they ever had to contend. So far there have been two deaths, and several cases that were almost given up were brought back, as it were, from the very verge of the grave. The disease is confined principally to the younger portion of our people, and it is hoped will leave us without claiming another victim. Aside from this, several of our older people are suffering from various diseases. M.Y. Hall, who several years ago had one of his arms paralyzed, the use of which he has never fully recovered, was stricken down about two months ago with bilious fever and at times it was thought he could not possibly live, but tender care and the best of medical treatment have kept the spark of life burning, and although very low at present, it is hoped by everyone that the battle between life and death will end in a sure victory for the former. Mr. Leroy Lane, a highly respected young man, has been suffering for several weeks with chronic rheumatism, which has rendered him almost as helpless as a child, and several times his life has been despaired of; we are glad to learn that he is recovering and hope ere many days to see him again. Mrs. William Smith has been a sufferer for several years, but was able to get round until nearly a year ago, when she received a shock of paralysis which completely prostrated her and she has been confined to her bed most of the time since. At present writing she is very low, and it will not surprise her friends to learn at any moment that she has passed away; being now about 74 years old, and this coupled with her severe illness, make it extremely doubtful if she ever recovers. Mrs. Smith is a kind and benevolent lady, and her loss would be very much regretted in this community. Mrs. Thaddeus Smith, a lady now in her 79th year, has been failing very fast of late, and her death is looked for at any hour. She is receiving every care, and if the kind wishes and good will of those who know her could be of any aid, she would live for many years to come. She has lived a life of extreme usefulness and is completely worn out in mind and body. No hopes are entertained of her recovery, although she may rally and live many years to grace the family circle.

Fish Shipment

Lane & Libby, fish dealers, shipped on Monday last, about eight tons of dry fish as follows: Ten 450-pound boxes of large shore cod, and one hundred and nine 40-pound boxes of boneless cod to Chicago. One hundred and twenty-eight 40-pound boxes of boneless cod to Philadelphia, and ten 100-pound bundles of large Cape Shore cod to Portland.

OBSERVATIONS

LITTLE CYCLONES
[excerpt]

Oh, the hand that rocks the cradle
Is the hand that rules the world;
And the hand that feels a buzz-saw
Is the hand that will get hurled;
And the hand that shirks the shovel
Is the hand the farmer hires;
And the hand that fools with matches
Is the hand that kindles fires.
And the hand that picks up horseshoes
In a smithy will get hot;
But the hand that holds a "straight flush"
Is the hand that scoops the pot.

Pay day was last Tuesday.

Next comes the Fourth.

Last Wednesday was a scorcher.

'Skeeters have made their appearance.

The measles die hard — still some cases.

Shall we have a celebration the Fourth?

It is said that snow fell on the outskirts of the town, last Friday.

Schooner *P. M. Bonnie,* Capt. Burgess, arrived from Belfast Tuesday.

It is reported that six small boys were drunk on the street Memorial Day.

We understand that Ernest Jones has sold his place and intends moving out of town.

If you don't believe that Capt. Rufe can run, just turn that bull and horse loose again.

Agents for fireworks are abroad in the land, and the heart of the small boy waxeth warm.

Some of the girls have given up cigarettes. Three for a quarter is the kind they use now.

Two of the large horses belonging to the Bodwell Granite Company Store (B. G. Co.) were shipped to Spruce Head on Thursday last.

The Roberts Harbor Granite Co. is the title of the Company that is working Duchane Hill and other places in that vicinity.

Rev. Theodore Gerrish delivered the oration here on Memorial Day last year, and Rev. C. A. Southard of Rockland this year. It is said that both gentlemen were private soldiers in the late war.

There have been several arrivals at the Ocean House this week, and more are expected every day. This house is delightfully situated, a half mile from the village proper. A fine ocean view, with unexcelled advantages for boating, fishing, etc.

There is some talk of moving several buildings on the bridge back on a line with the B.G Co.'s store. This would be a move in the right direction. It can be done at comparatively small expense and would add greatly to the beauty of our principal thoroughfare.

The schools in several of the back districts commenced last Monday.

Dr. Austin will be at his rooms in Vinalhaven Thursday, June 12.

Lyford & Ginn's new canning factory is being painted; the color is sky blue.

Sloop *Yankee Girl* sailed Friday for Jonesboro, after stone for this place.

Schooner *J. R. Bodwell* loaded this week at Robert's Harbor with paving for New York.

The financial depression has not affected Merriam. The rush for latest styles in millinery continues. Call early if you want to be up with the times.

Mr. W. Sands arrived in town last week, and will stay through the hot weather. He is occupying the house near Lane's Bridge that he bought of Benj. Kittredge last year.

Besides the new work secured by the B. G. Co. for this place, mentioned in last week's *Wind,* they have secured an additional contract to furnish stonework for the first story and trimmings for the nine upper stories of the Gaf building, Chicago. Part of this work goes to Charleston, Mass. It is to be of Jonesboro granite.

We understand that a man, supposed to be a lawyer, came from Rockland in a small boat one night last week, arriving here about midnight. After getting a lunch at the McDonald House, he went at once to the schooner *M. A. Achorn,* lying at Sands wharf, and calling one of the crew, informed him that he had fallen heir to $500,000, and wanted him to sign certain papers, but the sailor lad, not in the least excited at his supposed good fortune, refused to sign, saying that if there was money left for him, he would get it all right. The supposed lawyer failing to get the man's signature left as he came, in the night. It is thought by some that there is a much larger amount than the sum mentioned above, and that the lawyer was scheming to get some of it.

Calderwood's Neck

School commenced Monday, with Miss Annie Talbot as teacher.

Capt. O. B. Ames sailed on his first voyage of fishing for the season, Tuesday last.

Measles have vanished; no more cases at present.

Observations

One of our industrious farmers, upwards of 70 years of age, has finished planting and must be all through hoeing, for he is now at work haying. We do not see where he finds any grass.

Shoot that gol darned old crow, F—, and stop him from catching those young turkeys.

Johnnie H — will soon start out with his trained bull frogs, and will favor us with his first entertainment, providing he can have our schoolroom.

There is a farmer in North Haven who makes a specialty of raising the well-known herb, catnip, and we extend him our thanks for a sample package just received. This herb is recommended very highly for numerous diseases, and our physicians prescribe it for small infants. Cats, from whence it derives its name, delight to nip its leaves when it first appears in the spring. Even hogs will root it from the ground and devour it savagely. However, this farmer cultivates it on a small tract of land that was once occupied by our red brethren, as the soil has a very clam shelly appearance, so much so that the cats cannot eat the weed for fear of cutting themselves, therefore it grows unmolested and yields abundantly. Hundreds of pounds can be gathered annually. A rare chance for herbalists. A sample package will be forwarded by mail to anyone addressing, T—, North Haven.

The Codfish
Its Value as Food — How the Grand Bank was Formed

What a marvelous influence upon civilization and human progress the humble but nutritious codfish has had. He has been a mine of wealth to a vast population. It seems that good mother nature, foreseeing the needs of humanity, has made special preparations for a good supply of this very necessary article of food for body and brain, she floated her icebergs, which were filled with the sandy bottom of northern seas, down to the Gulf Stream, where they melted and deposited their debris, formed the Grand Bank of Newfoundland. It was the work, the slow and toilsome work of ages. Every spring thousands of these bergs, one-third above the water and two-thirds below, the upper part clear, sparkling and translucent, reflecting the sunshine and giving it back to the enraptured eye with that prodigality and brilliancy of coloring which only nature can afford, the lower part mixed with the coast bottom of Greenland or Labrador, to the extent of thousands of cartloads, came floating down majestically through Davis strait, and meeting the warm air and warm water of the Gulf Stream, melted and deposited their contribution, until those immense shoals were formed, where the cod and haddock swarm. And it is said that these sand banks have huge depressions, like vast valleys, which serve as aquaria, and that when a vessel is lucky enough to anchor over one of them, it can fill its hold and deck with as many as it can carry. For generations, the inhabitants of Newfoundland and the venturesome folks who live all along the New England coast, got their daily bread, or lay up a competency from this never-failing source of wealth. What a vast number of people on the globe get their living out of and subsist principally on the invaluable cod, and what vast quantities have been landed by the fishing fleet of Gloucester, since her fishermen first engaged in the business.

from *Fisherman's Own Book*

EXPELLED

Mr. Editor: —We would like to mention in your columns the circumstance of our being expelled from the Good Templars' Lodge.

Of course you have read the lines,

"Into each life some rain must fall,
Some days must be dark and dreary."

Well, that is our case now. We have been expelled from the Good Templars for 60 cents dues, without even being notified, or without any action taken on it by the lodge whatever. It is the first time in the history of the lodge to our memory that the financial secretary could alone take the responsibility of expelling its members — more especially those that have always paid their dues regular. It may be, however, that the by-laws have been changed. If they have, it is news to us, and if they have not, the secretary would do well to post himself as to what the duties of his office are.

We claim that if we were behind with our dues, we should have been notified, and that the secretary had no right to strike our names off as expelled, until we had been notified and some action taken upon it by the lodge. However, we accept it in the best grace possible, knowing that it was either a lack of knowledge of his office duties, or an insulting illustration of his natural domineering disposition. We thank the gentlemanly secretary for his gallant conduct in the matter, while we remain,

—Back Dues

WE ALL HAVE FAULTS

He who boasts of being perfect is perfect in his folly. I have been a great deal up and down in this world, and I never did see either a perfect horse or a perfect man, and I never shall until I see two Sundays come together. You cannot get white flour out of a coal sack, nor perfection out of human nature; he who looks for it had better look for sugar in the sea. The old saying is "lifeless, faultless." Of dead men we should say nothing but good, but as for the living, they are all tarred more or less with the black brush, and half an eye can see it. Every head has a soft place in it, and every heart has its black drop. Every rose has its prickles and every day its night. Even the sun shows spots, and the skies are darkened with clouds. Nobody is so wise but he has folly enough to stock a stall at Vanity Fair. Where I could not see the fool's cap, I have nevertheless heard the bells jingle.

As there is no sunshine without some shadows, so all human good is mixed up with more or less of evil; even poor-law guardians have their little failings, and parish beadles are not wholly of a heavenly nature. The best wine has its lees. All men's faults are not written on their foreheads, and it's quite as well they are not, or hats would need wide brims; yet as sure as eggs are eggs, faults of some kind nestle in every man's bosom. There's no telling when a man's faults will show themselves, for hares pop out of a ditch just when you are not looking for them. A horse that is weak in the knees may not stumble for a mile or two, but it is in him, and the rider had better hold him up well. The tabby cat is not lapping milk just now, but leave the dairy door open, and we will see if she is not as bad a thief as the kitten. There's fire in the flint, cool as it looks; wait till the steel gets a knock at it, and you will see. Everybody can read that riddle, but it is not everybody that will remember to keep his gunpowder out of the way of the candle.

THE NET BUSINESS

Perhaps not the least important branch of our industry in this place today is its net knitting. At one time, before the application of machinery was introduced into the business, and the granite industry was developed here, net knitting was one of the chief employments of nearly every inhabitant of the island, and to many it was their only employment and one of the necessities of their existence. To-day, however, it does not assume such gigantic dimensions, yet it is the almost sole dependence of many. Its present management is under the control of Mr. E. L. Roberts of this place, who has conducted it for about 18 years and thoroughly understands the business in all its minutest details. Comparatively the force employed in the business at present is small compared with former years. Mr. Roberts tells us that his present force — knitting nets of different descriptions — are over four hundred, and the number of girls employed weaving them together is seventeen. His weekly shipments of horse nets and tips amount to about eighteen hundred in number, making his season work amount to about 43,000 horse nets and ear tips, besides other knitting of lesser magnitude. The nets are all made for the American Net Company, Boston. In the summer season the business is generally at a standstill, resuming early in the fall again, and continuing until late in May. It is expected, however, that in the future knitting will continue the year-round.

FISH ARRIVALS

Following are the fish arrivals the past week: To Lane & Libby, Sch. *Grace Lee*, Capt. Burgess, 9,059 pounds cod, 9,023 pounds hake. Sch. *David Osier*, Capt. Smith, 19,060 pounds cod, 7,000 pounds hake. Sch. *Champion*, Capt. Young, 805 pounds cod, 2,000 pounds hake. Sch. *Morning Light*, Capt. Ames, 866 pounds cod, 3,800 pounds hake. To Lane's Island Fish Co., Sch. *C.W. Grey*, 2,200 pounds cod, 1,800 pounds hake. Sch. *Conqueror*, 1,000 cod, 3,000 pounds hake. Sch. *Water Sprite*, 2,000 pounds cod, 5,000 pounds hake. Sch. *Seaside*, 1,000 pounds cod, 4,000 pounds hake. Schooner *Eliza Ellen*, 4,000 pounds cod. Sch. *Jennie Gilbert*, 25,000 pounds cod, 5,000 pounds hake. To F. M. Brown, Sch. *Petrel*, Capt. Barton, 3,000 pounds mixed fish. Small boats, 2,000 pounds mixed.

THE VALUE OF A WOMAN

A woman is a handy thing to have in a house. She does not cost any more to keep than you will give to her, and she will take a great interest in you. If you go out at night she will be awake when you get home, and she will tell you all about yourself and more, too. Of course she will know where you have been and what kept you so late. Yet after she gets through telling you that, she will ask you where you have been, and what kept you so late. And after you tell her and she won't believe you, you must not mind that. And if, after going to bed, she says she has not closed her eyes the whole night, and then keeps up the matinee two hours longer and won't go to sleep when she has a chance, you mustn't mind that, either. It's her nature.

Unfortunately, and uncharacteristically for the partners and for the otherwise prosperous O.P. in particular, the "little sheet," as they liked to call it, was not a profitable undertaking. Since each of them was simultaneously pursuing lucrative enterprises elsewhere, the 32nd and last issue of that first *Wind* appeared a few months later, on August 8, 1884, under a somewhat more tumultuous masthead.

With this issue we wind up our journalistic career. The *Wind* has not been a paying investment and therefore to continue its publication any longer, we feel, would necessitate an outlay of labor and money which we can ill afford. The complimentary notices from our many bright exchanges and words of approval from people at home and in different parts of the Union have led us to believe that, although not financially a success, our little sheet has met the requirements of what a home paper should be. We therefore have done our part, but not having sufficient encouragement to remain with you in the capacity, we are obliged to close. And now "Good-bye, and may you all live long and prosper."

In the month of December of 1884, O.G. Dinsmore, about whom we know little else, arranged to have the *Vinalhaven Review*, a little paper he edited, printed on the press of the *Thomaston Herald*. Hardly any information about this enterprise has survived except that it, too, was short-lived.

The next year O.P. tried again, this time partnering with James Grant, W.W. Freeman, and Herbert Lovejoy, and on February 6, 1885 the *Messenger* made its debut. It referred to itself as a "desirable family journal, desirous of promoting harmony and good feeling among its readers," and like the *Wind*, it sold for five cents.

Friday, February 6, 1885

The attempt to once more establish a newspaper in this town, and successfully carry it on, will appear to many to be very unwise, and doubtless certain failure will be predicted to the enterprise. The reasonableness of this conclusion will be very apparent, from the fact that the first enterprise was

OBSERVATIONS

not successful, although conducted with much ability and judgment. It was a matter of regret to many that the editor of the *Wind* was compelled to stop that journal, for its usefulness as a medium of news was recognized by all, and to many who have been connected with this town, but who are now scattered in various parts of the country, it was a welcome visitor to their firesides. However, it could scarcely be expected that Mr. Lyons could devote his time and talents to its continuance, when it had proved a financial failure. But although his effort to maintain the first newspaper established in this town was not successful, he may be consoled with the fact that the value of his effort was fully appreciated by his townsmen, and the esteem and respect which he is held by them cannot be overestimated. In commencing this journal we do not presume ourselves to be superior in talent or ability to our worthy predecessor, nor do we think we can more successfully conduct the paper, as far as its contents are concerned, but we have consented to undertake this business by the advice of a number of gentlemen who have agreed to support us in its management and otherwise, and who are anxious to have a weekly sheet again established here. We think that a town such as this, whose inhabitants can be counted by the thousands, whose trade matters and business relations excel other towns who pride themselves in their weekly newspaper, and also the consideration of our isolated position, ought to have a newspaper in our midst.

In starting this enterprise we do not do so with great hopes of success; we are aware of the great amount of work we have to perform in order to make this an ordinary success, but it shall be our endeavor to make it as bright, original, and interesting as we can— worthy of our town and its interests. Its purpose shall be to collect and present the news of the town and vicinity in a brief and interesting manner, and shall be entirely devoted to the interests of the town and neighborhood. To give this work necessary justice, and make it worthy of its object, would require more time than we could afford to bestow upon it, but with the spare time after our daily employment, and with the proffered assistance of a few friends, and the leniency of the public, we expect to attain a fair degree of success. We propose to have our columns free to all, and all communications addressed to us will receive due attention. It shall be our endeavor to prevent the appearance of personal, slanderous, or abusive matter, and our chief end will be to promote harmony and good feeling among our readers. Whatever comments we may chance to make on public or social afairs will be made in an independent spirit, with true regard to facts, and without sectional or personal consideration. If we should touch on any political or religious questions, our action shall be equally indcpendent, and should we conflict with the opinions of any of our readers, it shall be done in the most unbiased spirit. Our opinions shall be expressed with a just regard to what we believe to be right. With constant devotion to our work, we shall hope to receive a fair share of public support, and with friendship and good will towards all we will continue our task.

Unhappily, the *Messenger* lasted even fewer months, the last issue appearing on July 17 of the same year, although with the assurance that the editors, finding their energies then required elsewhere, would return with the *Messenger* again soon. Alas, they did not.

OUR LAST ISSUE

With this issue the second three months of the *Messenger* is ended, and its existence terminates. In commencing to publish the *Messenger* , it was our intention to only run it three months during the winter, but the support we received was so strong and the encouragement so great that we were impelled under the circumstances to continue it another quarter. The support and encouragement has in no manner lessened, and our circulation is as large as it has ever been, with a steady increase, yet in spite of this prosperous condition of affairs we are reluctantly compelled from outside circumstances to discontinue its publication. To those who have helped and encouraged us in our humble effort to furnish a newspaper in the town we are exceedingly grateful. Our task has in many respects been very congenial. The contributions and assistance given us by several ladies and gentlemen have in a great measure helped us to present weekly a small but interesting and intelligent paper, which has received the compliments and praises of our many exchanges, and whose matter has been copied weekly by a large number of contemporaries. The original talent which our contributors have displayed is highly credible to the town. In such an undertaking it is easily seen that it would be an impossibility to satisfy and please all parties, and in commencing this paper we declared it to be our intention to honestly and uprightly declare what we believed to be right, in whatever we published. We have endeavored to hold by this intention. Where in our judgment praise and approval justly belonged we have rendered it, and where we believed it just to condemn and disapprove we have not hesitated to do so. We hold that honest condemnation is better than false flattery, and whatever we have condemned or censored we were satisfied honestly deserved it. We have always tried to respect the good sense of our intelligent readers, and presented our work as best we could, for their satisfaction and approval, regardless of the opinions of the unfriendly few. The approval of the intelligence of the town is of more importance to us than the recrimination of a few who if they be not strewn with the sweetest flattery must disapprove and sneer at all things. Although we discontinue the Messenger just now, we intend at a future time to commence again, but we have other work to do in our spare time at night, and we are compelled to give it up at present. For what favors we have received from our many friends we are highly thankful. To those who may think us unreasonably severe towards them, we are ready to apologize if we can be proved wrong. But we have criticized because it was right in our judgment to do so. He is our friend who will tell us of our weakness and not keep it back from our view. Whatever we have said or written has been done in the best spirit, with the best intention, believing it always best to express reasonable conviction at all hazards. We finish our task, our labors are ended, and if we have unjustly done anyone an injury we are sorry. With the best wishes towards all, with malice towards none, we wish you all farewell.

Like O.P., Charles Healey remained enthusiastic about an island paper and optimistic about its chances and on October 7, 1887, he edited and produced the *Vinalhaven Echo*. It did a little better than its predecessors, lasting fifteen months, ending with a note of thanks for those who supported it and a somewhat bitter acknowledgment of those who did not.

Observations

We have decided to attempt the experiment of issuing a weekly paper in this place, not only giving the Island news but furnishing an especially marked feature in the state, general, and county news as fresh as can be obtained by any weekly paper of like pretentions. Owing to our Mid-Ocean situation, previous attempts to do this have been considered impossible, but the matter has now been overcome and in this our advance copy will give you an idea of what has been done in that respect. Past experience has given us a clearer recognition of what the public most desires in a home paper, and if our experiment is successful, shall endeavor to give the best possible satisfaction to all. In order to make this paper a success we must ask the favor of any and everyone securing a copy to solicit a few subscriptions that we may start the regular issue soon.

Men of Vinalhaven

H. Y. Carver

Very few people understand or know the identity of this interesting individual who keeps his name before the public through the medium of the *Echo* advertising. This individual was born sometime during the present century. He is neither rich nor handsome. In appearance he is not one bit feminine but there is an expression on his face that casts vague suspicions that he would take the upholstered chair if there was only one in the room. The only assurance that the good natured lad is making money is that his not over handsome face is always wreathed in smiles. If he is not making money as fast as he wants to he can make it faster by dexterously counting both ends of dollar bills when making change with customers.

I. C. Glidden

This good looking clerk is familiar to everybody in Vinalhaven, and in his youthful days was a bashful country boy. Time and accident worried him along to manhood and as he reached the wooing stage of life his bashfulness disappeared and with his verdant country ways from the farm he pushed himself into his present prosperous condition and became a public waiter in the Bodwell Granite Co. store. He is an indispensable civilized man for the firm that employs him. Although he is fat and bulky the law of gravitation would balance his body even if he did not wear a No. 11 boot.

Everybody Sees Water Poured from Reuben's Nozzle

Decoration day, Fourth of July, and Barnum's circus are all old chestnuts, and so not more than 10,000 people get out here to see the sights and enjoy the day when they make their appearance, but when James P. Teller and his assistant E. M. Byington made their appearance with the new steam fire engine Monday of this week the washboards were laid on the shelf and business was of no account whatever. Men and women, boys and girls, cripples and invalids with their dogs were all out to see and be seen. Even millinery stores and tailor shops closed business that the girls might have time to scratch their heads and see Reuben. Women advanced in years, weighing nearly 200 lbs. in their stocking feet, were seated in easy graceful positions on top of surrounding houses watching every trifling incident with a wonderful fascination. Nothing ever moved this community at house cleaning time as the advent of this "Ingine." People that have been sick for a long time have been fortifying their systems with graham bread and oat meal, developing some weak muscle or trying to create an appetite to obtain strength to be on deck and witness Monday's program.

He Left Town Taking $1,000

Wilson Harris, bookkeeper and clerk for J. P. Armbrust at this place, left town on Friday, the 16th day of November for Rockland, where he said he was going to have some teeth extracted, Mr. Armbrust was at this time in New York on business. Harris closed the store, leaving the key with a young man at this place. Several days passed and he did not return. A gentleman, knowing the store to be closed, telegraphed Mr. Armbrust in New York, who immediately returned here. When Armbrust went away he left $1,000 in cash and checks, telling Harris to pay off his men and discharge some of them. Mr. Armbrust, upon examination, found all the money and checks missing and the cash register cleaned out with the exception of a few cents. He telegraphed to Fort Fairfield, the home of Harris, and received a reply that he had been there about three hours and nothing had been heard of him since. Mr. Armbrust had always put perfect confidence in Harris. He came here in April of this year from Fort Fairfield and is a man of the following description: About 28 years old, 5 feet, 8 inches high, light complexion, blue eyes, weighs about 145 pounds, nearsighted, wears nose glasses and when he left had sandy mustache. A warrant for his arrest is now in the hands of the sheriff.

Joshua Dyer

This is Joshua Dyer's account— as told to a mainland reporter — of first arriving on these islands:

In the fall of 1812, I, with my wife and family consisting of four children named Timothy, Jane, Joshua and Hannah, left Provincetown, Cape Cod, and arrived here all right. Leaving my family for a few weeks, I went to the White Island and built a camp out of such material as I could find there. I moved my family there taking for provisions, two bushels of meal, half bushel of potatoes and a few dry fish. The winter was a severe one and our principal article of food was clams. I had hard work at times to procure enough to keep my family from being hungry; having some powder and shot and an old Queens Arms flint-lock gun, I managed to bring down 48 wild ducks in two shots. I salted the birds and we managed to get through the winter. One day in spring my oldest boy and I went in a small boat fishing and got quite a few. On our return we found a sloop of war at anchor. On going alongside, the commander invited us aboard, telling me that peace had been declared, the first news I had heard since the fall before. The men on shipboard were glad to exchange pork and hard bread for my fish. Feeling pleased with my trip, I went out again and got a good haul carrying them to Castine to exchange for provisions, about $40 worth. I returned home happy in the thought that I had some good food for my family.

Joshua later bought Dyer Island and settled there where he lived to be more than eighty years old.

A few years later, around 1890, a fellow named Daniel Monro of Rockland undertook to produce a paper there that would be of interest to the residents of both Vinalhaven and neighboring North Haven. The *Islander* looked promising to some but production was mysteriously and suddenly ended. No good reason was given or has been offered. No examples have survived.

Vinalhaven, Maine, January 24, 1889

We have been requested by many to continue the *Echo* after this month, but it's utterly impossible with its present subscription list and small amount of advertising. If the list could be increased a few hundred — say three more — and hold its present number, it could be done, and if Vinalhaven people want a paper they should exert themselves to increase its subscription list, and the best method to do it is to form a publishing association and each member use their influence to increase its circulation. In forming an association there is not one penny invested or one involved. The association can at any time the paper is not self-sustaining, stop it. If an association of 20, more or less, make themselves interested and use their influence to get subscribers and make the list three hundred more than at the present time, a paper could be run successfully here, but at its present list it cannot live beyond the present month. We have done our level best to give the town a lively local paper for fifteen months, but are compelled to abandon it on account of insuffcient support. If other parties have any desire to take up the paper thinking it a bonanza as a source of revenue, they are welcome to it and all the work involved. There is no more work for a subscription list of five thousand than for five hundred and whoever at any time runs a paper will find it no pleasant task, unless he has the support to make it a booming success.

With this issue of the *Echo* it fulills its contract with subscribers to the letter making 65 issues for the fifteenth months' run. There are only eight subscribers that have paid beyond this date, and they will have the balance due them returned or we will furnish them the *Courier Gazette* for the balance of the time — just as they wish. The *Courier* will contain the local news of Vinalhaven from a correspondent employed here that will be just as interesting as the *Echo* besides getting a larger amount of general news.

With this issue of the *Echo* it gracefully retires from circulation. We regret such a step has to be taken but our interest in other business which is more remunerative demands it. There is not support for a local paper in Vinalhaven. We have given it a faithful trial and find the task a hopeless one. We have worked hard to give a good local paper as was within the limit of our ability, and fifteen months struggling convinces us that there is not suffcient support to make a paper successful, at least under its present management. There are many who have rendered us all possible assistance and many who have not. To those who have done their mite and more too we thank you and wish you a prosperous 1889, and to those who have not helped to support it we also wish a pleasant year's journey and may they always have the $2.50 that they have saved in not subscribing for the *Echo*.

Photo: Provided by the Vinalhaven Historical Society

Observations

1937-1939

MANY YEARS WENT BY, years during which folks were born, died, married, had yard sales, had quarrels, came and went, ran businesses, suffered tragedies or loss, enjoyed success, received congratulations, and sought employment, but if the islanders knew, they knew only by word of mouth or signage. Then, in June of 1937, John Gordon created a little press from junk material and, calling it "The Smallest Press" produced a volume of the *Vinalhaven Pilot,* offered as a "Home Magazine-Newspaper for Business, News and Entertainment." It had an unusual format, that of a little magazine, about six by eight inches, but it too, didn't last long.

Greeting

To the Vinalhaven Public:

In my estimation the Town of Vinalhaven, with its lovely harbor and adjacent bays and islands, is the most beautiful spot in the wide world that I ever saw. Vinalhaven, "The Gem of the Ocean," is okay.

It is inhabited by a quiet, industrious, home-loving people, who give a stranger a hearty welcome, and if in trouble do something more practical to take the sting out of worldly misfortunes.

Now, as the Town has not had a local newspaper for several years, and as I have had several years of editorial experience, I decided to publish this magazine-size newspaper, as a medium for business, news, and sociability.

To conclude, I may say that if the townspeople and businessmen desire it, I would be pleased to publish the "PILOT," with eight or more pages, every Saturday, at 5c. per copy.

As Time rolls by, births, marriages and deaths, accidents, fires, parties, dances, etc., will occur and they would all be faithfully recorded in the "PILOT." So that the 52 numbers, bound yearly, would be practically a history of Vinalhaven to tuck away in the family library for coming generations.

—the Editor

Alumni Banquet
Again Old Pals Meet

On Tuesday evening, June 29, a most enjoyable event will occur — the Annual Banquet of the Vinalhaven Alumni Association, at the Union Church Vestry, at 6 p.m.

From all over the U.S.A. will come the students of bygone years to renew old happy friendships and recall the carefree days of youth.

Here's hoping that Time, as it endlessly slips by, has dealt kindly with them, and that they enjoy to the utmost their visit to their lovely Old Home Town, and return to their homes reinvigorated for another year of hurry and hustle in this modern world of strenuousness.

With Our Fishermen

This spring the Vinalhaven fishermen have had about average luck up until the last two weeks of May when an extraordinary run of pollock came in quite close to Isle au Haut, in fact all over the bay.

When someone tried a hand line and found them hungry as shedded lobsters and he couldn't haul them up fast enough, most all fishermen laid aside their trawls and got out their hand lines, and then the boats came ashore with record hauls.

Soon the Bay State Fish Company was handling over 100,000 lbs. of fish daily, and employing a maximum crew to dress and salt them, working until 2 o'clock a.m.

This run of luck may continue several weeks yet, and it is a gladsome break in the monotony of dull times. A fisherman, while yarning with the PILOT news hound said, "Oh boy! Those big pollock are sure hungry fighters. Many times I've hooked two 15-pounders and it sure was a man's job to land them."

The PILOT wishes to extend to our many summer visitors its sincere welcome to Vinalhaven, "The Gem of the Ocean," hoping that they enjoy to the limit the perfect, peaceful quietness, invigorating, sunny days and cool, restful nights and, on leaving, determine to come again next summer.

Some time ago, as in most everywhere, the clocks were put ahead an hour, Vinalhaven followed suit. A couple of weeks was enough, enough is plenty, and plenty is too much, so on May 17 the Town voted to go back to sensible time.

There's no such thing as time saving. It's just like taking a dollar out of one pocket and putting it in another. Ridiculous idea!

A month ago Henry Ford made the statement, "I will never have anything to do with any Unions." By-the-by, George III, of England said something very similar in 1775 when he was told the news of the slaughter of his crack troops at Bunker Hill. He said, "Never will I treat with those damn rebels."

So not the least doubt Henry will eventually have to eat humble pie like King George did when the great American Union was established. What would be the workingman's condition today if there had never been Unions or strikes? Collective bargaining is the only fair, practical way of ironing out problems of Capital and Labor.

By the time the Spaniards get fed up on killing each other there won't be many left, and their famous old cities only heaps of junk. O well, they're only getting what they handed out to the millions of South American natives for 350 years. Listen to this horror:

OBSERVATIONS

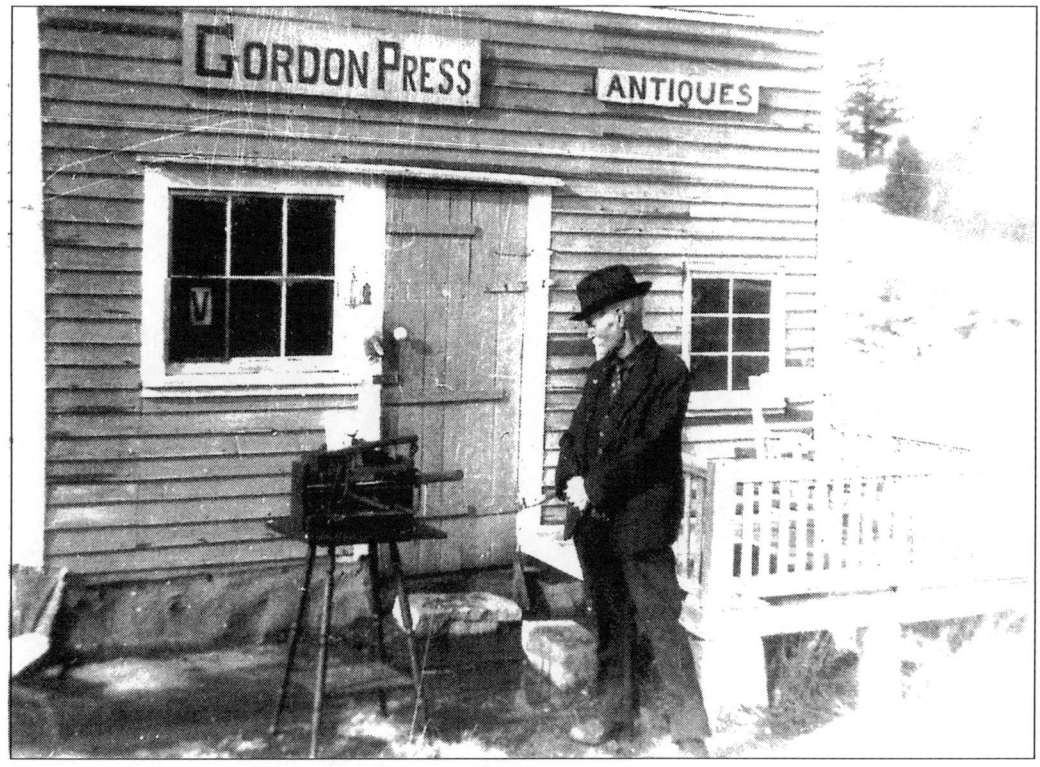

John Gordon, the Smallest Print Shop, and the press he created from junk.
Photo: Provided by the Vinalhaven Historical Society

Los Angeles, May 25 — Maj. F. I. Lord, 38-year-old veteran of six wars, who recently served with the Spanish Loyalist forces, said: "I've seen the rebels set fire to hospitals and then lie in wait outside and shoot down patients and wounded soldiers as they staggered from the buildings."

Late in the Depression and just in time for the town's sesquicentennial, favorite and native son Sidney Winslow, author of *Fish Scales and Stone Chips*, made a herculean effort to write, edit, publish, and personally deliver 650 copies of the *Vinalhaven Neighbor* each week.

THE VINALHAVEN NEIGHBOR

Concerning the Picture on the Cover
The James Pierce House–
Birthplace of Anna Coughlin

Appearing as our frontispiece in this "sesqui" edition of the *Neighbor* is a picture of the James Pierce place at Old Harbor, birthplace of Anna Coughlin, author of the official Vinalhaven Centennial and Sesqui-centennial poems.

The house stands at the foot of Pierce's Hill, at the left and close to the road that leads to Granite Island, just before you come to the bridge that spans the picturesque inlet known as the Dyke, where the salt ocean water mingles with that of Old Harbor Pond. The James Pierce house is known today as "Windy Cottage."

We have been unable to learn in what year it was built but the original owner was Mr. James Pierce, who resided there for a number of years. He later became interested in Mormonism and a few years after the death of his first wife he married again, sold the house to his son Mr. Allsbury Pierce, and went to Salt Lake City to live. It was during Mr. Allsbury Pierce's ownership of the house that Mr. and Mrs. Garret Coughlin occupied it, and it was here that Miss Anna Coughlin first saw the light of day.

In 1889 Miss Coughlin, who was then a young lady, was asked by the Vinalhaven Centennial Celebration Committee to write the official Centennial Poem. It is reported that she was very much overcome by the invitation, feeling that the task was quite beyond her ability and was almost inclined to refuse the honor, but through the urgent plea of her mother she at last consented to write the poem, and in lieu of the manner in which Vinalhaven folk have remembered and treasured it down through the years, there seems to be no doubt but that the Centennial Day Committee of 1889 made a wise move when it appointed Miss Coughlin as official poet.

> "Clasped in the arms of the loyal old ocean,
> Fair has the hamlet grown to the town,
> Long have they slumbered, our sturdy forefathers
> Careless alike of fame and renown.
> Builders! thy work shall endure till the trumpet,
> Calling the nations from east and from west,
> Sounds its wild notes through heaven's vast arches
> And summons earth's tribes to their last long rest!"

Interesting Items of Vinalhaven History

Leon W. Sanborn and Everett Libby were the first Vinalhavenites to cross the bay in an aeroplane May 1929.

Thursday July 2, 1932 — Steamer *North Haven* made her first trip to Vinalhaven.

Sat. May 30, 1933 — Big forest fire at northern end of the island. Vinalhaven's most destructive forest fire within the memory of oldest inhabitants.

OBSERVATIONS

Sunday May 28, 1933 — Owen P. Lyons, Vinalhaven's Grand Old Man and most beloved citizen, died.

Tuesday, July 25, 1933 — General Italo Balbo, the Italian Aviator, and his fleet of 24 planes, passed near Vinalhaven on their way back to Italy after a visit to this country and the World's Fair at Chicago. One of the planes stopped at Rockland for repairs.

Sunday, Aug. 13, 1933 — First game of legalized Sunday baseball in Vinalhaven. A contest between Vinalhaven and Clark's Island.

October 1933 — Work began on Federal Aid at northern end of island. John Gardner of Rockland was superintendent.

1932, May 30 — Hon. Leroy T. Carleton delivered Memorial Day address in Memorial Hall.

Mr. Carleton was a past commander of the G.A.R.; he was 85 years old at the time he delivered this address which is probably the last that Vinalhaven folks will hear delivered by a G.A.R. veteran.

Aug. 16, 1888 — A new gallery was being put in the town hall, capable of seating 100 people.

Also in a copy of the *Echo* dated Aug. 16, 1888 we read the following:

> "The black spook that has been sitting on the cemetery fence in the dim twilight has given up its ghostly wanderings, after frightening everybody in the neighborhood."

On July 2, 1939 Winslow reported:

> At 8:30 on the evening of our 150th birthday 800 people assembled at the ball ground and listened to the reading of an original poem by its author Miss Anna Coughlin of Rockland, the well-known educator and former Vinalhaven resident. Miss Coughlin was introduced by W. A. Smith, former representative to legislature. Miss Coughlin's poem revealed the fact that though she had been away from Vinalhaven many years, she had kept in close touch with what was transpiring here. It was understandably epochal; each era being so accurately portrayed in her word picture that the listeners caught the spirit of hope, progress, joys, and sorrows, of former Fox Islanders and the determination of present day citizens to carry on and match the achievements of their noble ancestors.

Each issue of the *Neighbor* comprised eight or ten mimeographed pages. It was a mighty effort and lasted longer than any of the others, even at ten cents, but it, too, folded after holding on for nearly two years. The Depression years were tough on readers as well as entrepreneurs.

These early papers contained items we might consider odd today. Personals, for example, were not the tawdry solicitations we find now in big city newspapers. Rather, they were recitals of who'd come and gone and for what purpose.

PERSONALS

Benj. Lane arrived home last Monday.

Charles Lovejoy visited Rockland this week.

E. B. Smith left for Quincy, Mass., last Monday.

Capt. Reuben Carver went off Monday morning.

Mrs. Charles Thompson is visiting friends at Liberty.

John Frohock left for Boston last Monday on business.

G. M. Reed visited Rockland Monday, and returned same day.

Mr. E. P. Walker arrived home from Montville last Monday.

Dr. P. J. Conroy made his usual trip to Hurricane last Monday.

J. F. Gerrity arrived in town Tuesday and left for Eastport on Wednesday.

John Chadwick made his usual business trip to the Island on Tuesday.

L. M. Crockett and wife left for Camden Friday morning to attend the trot.

J.J. Lane has been visiting friends at this place, and left for Canton Thursday morning.

John Green returned from the main on Tuesday where he has been visiting during the week.

Miss Dora A. Stone left last Saturday morning for Warren, where she will teach a term of school.

F. E. Roberts has been confined to the house for the past week. We are glad to see him out again.

Miss Jennie Hopkins will attend the fall term of the Eastern State Normal School at Castine.

Mrs. Charles Littlefield and Miss Nellie Newcomb have arrived from Boston with a large and select stock of spring millinery.

Mr. and Mrs. L. T. Lovejoy left Monday morning. Mr. Lovejoy will attend the Hotel Keepers' Union at Augusta. Mrs. Lovejoy went to Waldoboro.

The papers never wanted for editorial comment from all quarters on all topics and many were critical of the behavior of one group or another:

Going to Church

A great many people only go to church to show their new clothes. We all know this to be a fact. They may profess religion or not. They may come home pleased with the sermon or not. They may go to church when they have clothing on, remarkably good or not. But mark you, they never fail to go when they have new clothing on. They never fail to when they have anything on they fancy will excite the envy of others, or shed a little glory on themselves, and when they go to church, they may not recollect the text, but they will be certain to remember what kind of a bonnet Miss So-and-So wore, they will not fail to recollect who was in Mrs. So-and-So's pew, and whether the lady's nice-looking gown was made of new silk, or was only an old one, "turned for the sake of economy." What good does going to church do such people? They would do less wrong to remain at home. They may flatter themselves that their devotions are as sincere as other people's, but the mind, which, in church, can be so occupied with the frivolities of this world, can have little room in it for the serious things of the next.

Observations

Interesting, too, were the advertisements. Vinalhaven's economy in the late 1800s and early 1900s was vibrant and healthy; downtown was swarming with retail activity and the ads in all these papers reflected the vitality of that critical element of island life.

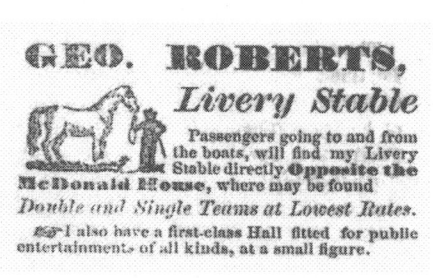

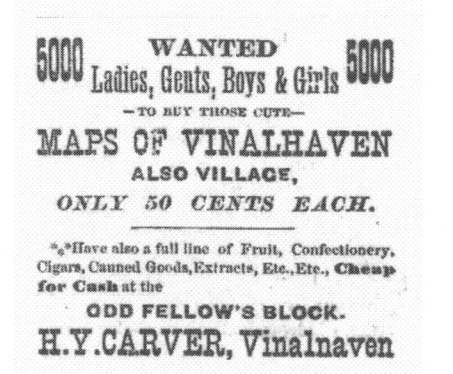

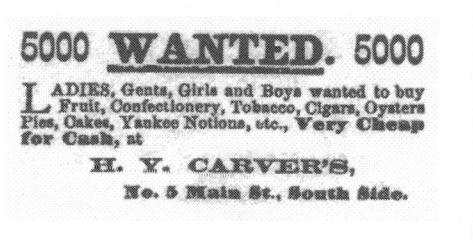

Intemperance Among Women

There is much said about the growing habit of intemperance among women, perhaps more than the facts would warrant. If this habit exists it is owing to the fact that women are often forced to perform domestic and social duties under great physical suffering, and by partaking of liquors for temporary relief or a little protraction of strength, the habit becomes a necessity. If all ladies who suffer with the complaints peculiar to their sex would take Dr. Pierce's Favorite Prescription, they would find nature's restorative, and the evil results of pernicious drugs and liquors would be avoided. For all cases of nervous and general debility, sleeplessness, spasms, periodical pains, suppressions, and irregularities, it is the only medicine so certain in curative action that it can be guaranteed to benefit or cure, or money returned.

The original *Wind* and the several efforts that followed it had one thing in common: they were intended to be profitable. None were, however, and none lasted more than a couple of years. For over three decades Vinalhaven had no paper of any kind. We learned what we needed to know by stopping in at Tibb's Pool Hall or the bowling alley or the hardware store (I.W. Fifield's) or any of the several other busy retail establishments along Main Street, or by lingering around the waterfront.

Ray and Judy Blaisdell
Photo: Provided by the Vinalhaven Historical Society

OBSERVATIONS

1974

VINALHAVEN GOT ITS SECOND WIND, so to speak, in may of 1974. Ray Blaisdell had come to Vinalhaven the year before on behalf of the Maine Seacoast Mission, a remarkable organization that has provided nondenominational spiritual and health-related services to Maine coast islands for over a hundred years. Ray succeeded John Mingus as minister of the Union Church and quickly brought his enormous energy, determination, and good will to bear, not only from the pulpit, but throughout the community. In particular he decided the town needed a newspaper. He did not intend that it be a profit-making venture, and it was not. Now, forty years later, it still is not, and that probably spells the difference between the clear success of this *Wind* and the lack of success that attended its half dozen predecessors.

Over a thousand weekly issues of the *Wind* have rolled off the presses, with only a handful of exceptions, since that first issue in 1974. That undertaking was conducted under the auspices of the 501(c)(3) that is the Union Church, and the paper has always been assembled and distributed by volunteers. The first issue was one 8" x 11" page, printed on both sides, but before long it became two pages, each printed on one side only, much easier to read since the paper was so flimsy that, when printed on both sides, the information from one side bled through to the other. Interestingly, the first issue called our attention to a public discussion of alternative power, primarily wind, and a subject that would find its way back into the pages of the *Wind* thirty years later in a big way.

Initially the *Wind* accomplished distribution by leaving copies of each new issue in selected stores and in a few *Wind* boxes hung in conspicuous places around town. Those boxes are still used. A few newsletters were mailed first class to folks in town who couldn't get around, and to rural box holders and others, particularly summer residents, elsewhere. Readers were asked to contribute a suggested amount to offset the costs of producing the paper, and advertisers were similarly encouraged to contribute in proportion to the amount of space consumed. At one point, Ray found himself at the waterfront and encountered a fellow who remarked, "You know, I'd like to sell my skiff," whereupon he gave Ray a contribution and asked him to put an appropriate notice in the *Wind*. A little farther along on his walk, he came across another guy who said, "You know, I'd like to buy a skiff," and gave Ray a similar contribution.

23

Ray provided him with the necessary information from the first gentleman whereupon they accomplished the trade, and he brought the two contributions home to the *Wind*.

The *Wind's* masthead was composed of four capital block letters spelling WIND. Within those four letters or nearby was found the caption: *John 3:8*. This was presumably Ray's suggestion that the reader turn his attention to that passage in the Bible which reveals itself to be:

"The Wind blows wherever it pleases. You hear its sound but you cannot tell where it comes from or where it is going. So it is of everyone born of the Spirit."

Although not a newspaper in the fullest sense of the word, as will be revealed, a great deal of news could be gleaned, albeit a little late, from reading the invitations and announcements, help wanted ads, thank-yous and acknowledgements, advertisements, committee reports, obituaries, reports of hospitalization, birthday and anniversary congratulations, and the occasional complaint or editorial comment. With a couple of exceptions, we got a lot more news from examining the aftermath — the consequences found in the *Wind* each week — than from nose-to-the-ground reporting. Those two exceptions were Vinal's News Stand (aka the Paper Store) and I. W. Fifield's, where two critical announcements, those of births and those of deaths, were scrupulously acknowledged. Jerry and Carlene Michael had years before continued the practice of installing a basket on the counter in the Paper Store whenever someone, an islander or someone associated with the island, died, and affixing the name of the deceased to the basket. The tradition, over a hundred and fifty years old, had begun even before Vinal's News Stand had come into existence in the mid to late 1800s. Donations were then and still are collected in the basket and after a few days, the money and the signatures of those who made contributions are given to the family of the deceased. Many patrons are compelled, no doubt, to visit the store on the pretense of buying a paper, but in fact are equally interested in keeping abreast of comings and, so to speak, goings. The practice continues to this day. Additionally, until I.W. Fifield's successor, Port O' Call, regrettably closed a few years ago, the equally prompt announcements of births — name, sex, weight, height — was accomplished with a sign in the window and a great deal of fanfare.

During this first year of its existence we learned or deduced from reading the *Wind*, among other things:

Our old power plant, which had generated electricity for Vinalhaven and North Haven for years, was on its last legs. It was feared that we'd have to share what little power we generated with North Haven: them for a few hours, then us for a few hours. Before long it happened. A Vinalhaven gentleman put a lasagna in the oven and, when the power was shut off down here, he ran it up and rowed it over to relatives on North Haven to finish off. We all called it "hour power." The Fox Island Electric Cooperative (FIEC), formed of representatives of both islands, was charged with finding an alternative source of power. Meanwhile they issued regular bulletins in the *Wind* urging conservation of electricity — Christmas lights were to be on for only so long each night, for instance — to prolong the life of the old generators for as long as possible.

In 1974 kids were still attending record hops, dinner was being served at the Bridgeside, a lovely inn right at the Lane's Island Bridge on Indian Creek, in town at the Islander, and at The Three Fishermen.

Seasonal property owners and caretakers were alerted to a rash of burglaries.

The Old Drug Store became the first real Main Street gallery and also the first business to put an emphasis on natural foods, and the Island Players undertook to present *Showboat*.

OBSERVATIONS

Elliott Hall, an indubitable native, instrumental in starting the Vinalhaven Historical Society, died in January of 1975, and Dr. Ralph Earle, our legendary island physician for as long as any of us could remember, passed away the following month. By April, Ralph's replacement had been found and the eighteen-year tenure of Dr. Gregory O'Keefe began.

Dr. Ralph Earle
Photo: Provided by the Vinalhaven Historical Society

In 1974 sixteen million pounds of lobster were landed in Maine by 10,500 license holders, and the price was $1.41 per pound.

1974

Home of the Wind
Photo: Provided by the Vinalhaven Historical Society

OBSERVATIONS

1975

RAY WORKED TIRELESSLY TO INVOLVE EVERYONE IN THE LIFE OF THE COMMUNITY, the community in the life of the Church, and both in the lives of the island's youth, a demographic which, in the seventies, was more than a little troublesome. Before long Ray had begun penning editorial comments and, as the first papers were quite literally cranked out on a mimeograph by him personally, he signed them "Will Crank." Now and then those ellicited responses, which prompted him to acknowledge that sometimes his commentary was "three sheets to the *Wind*." In fact, most of the very few negative reviews had to do with grammatical errors, the inevitable result of Ray's one-man push against the clock and his other responsibilities to get the paper out on time. By the end of 1974 the *Wind* was still two pages but bigger, each page now 11" x 14". It was being mailed to five hundred islanders and ninety off-islanders. At about the one-year anniversary he published the *Wind's* editorial policy in response to complaints about errors or omissions:

> "Let it be known that the Editor rarely knows what he is doing and therefore accepts no responsibility for anything. What appear as errors are put there on purpose so those who need something to complain about will find it easily."

After one particularly frustrating effort with a malfunctioning press feed he called a mainland printer acquaintance who reminded him that now and then even the best editors could do no more than go out and get a bottle, to which Ray responded, "I'd be happy to do that but a bottle of what and where do I pour it into the press?" Eventually he succumbed to the insistence of Ginny Snow that she be allowed to proofread and type. It was, in Ray's words, a great leap forward. About this time production was improved further by the acquisition of an offset press.

There was no *Wind* in August of 1975. Looking back, one could easily conclude Ray's frustrations had overwhelmed him for a few weeks. In September a column, entitled "Observations of a Crank," lamented the difficulties of dealing with underage drinking and behavior. This and another like it the following week might be considered the first two "Observer" columns.

OBSERVATIONS OF A CRANK (WILL)

We took a tour of duty last Saturday at the Recreation Center at the VFW hall and had a most interesting evening. While a friend kept the lid on inside, we spent most of the evening outside; that is where the kids are. First, around back we informed two young men of 18 that drinking in the Center or on the grounds outside was not allowed — and why. By observation it seems to be a common practice for some 18-year-olds to buy beer and other alcohol for those not yet able to buy it themselves (I have even observed 11- and 12-year-old girls being given drinks). Supplying alcohol to underage youth is illegal. Next we spent some time meeting and observing each car and truck that pulled in and as a result discouraged the usual practice of drinking in the vehicles. Following the sound of voices proved educational as three boys ran away as we approached the summer home where they had been drinking. Conversations also proved interesting as one young person confided that some kids came to the Center in order to smoke and drink without their parents' knowledge. NOW YOU KNOW! We are convinced that it is impossible for any one person to control these problems. Exclusion of 18-year-olds might help. Requiring everyone to stay inside might help. A telephone for communication with the parents might help. At the same time the rules would mean less contact with the youth the Center seeks to serve. A word of thanks to the parents that have been helping at the movies (especially to the two fathers who came last Friday). YOU DO MAKE A DIFFERENCE!

Vinalhaven Harbor, 1975

In 1975 seventeen million pounds of lobster were landed in Maine by 10,500 license holders, and the price was $1.61 per pound.

OBSERVATIONS

1976

As it had been from the beginning, the Wind's first page was primarily an announcement of all the church activities. Within a couple of years the paper began carrying a notice alongside the masthead describing the *Wind* more particularly as a ministry of the Union Church, and inspirational pieces, most submitted and signed by Ray in his own name, appeared frequently. The press, by then installed in the second floor of the church's belfry, was referred to as the Bell Tower Press. The three active congregations—the nondenominational assembly at the Union Church, The Reformed Latter Day Saints (RLDS), and the Catholics—were given as much front page space as needed. The same courtesy was extended to the occasional less familiar denomination, such as Christian Scientist, Episcopalian, or the New Covenant Fellowship. The paper otherwise remained a collection of want ads, announcements and acknowledgments, thank-yous, obituaries, descriptions of items for sale, notices of meetings or of lost pets or personal items, reminders of those in nursing homes or otherwise needing attention, and so forth.

Ray wanted to encourage local businesses to advertise, commonplace elsewhere in the world, of course, but these island businesses had not relied on advertising in anyone's memory and, while the value would seem obvious, it took a little persuasion. Ray approached my Uncle Vic of Shield's Grocery on Skin Hill and persuaded him to run an ad announcing a "hamburger special." Before that week's edition had been out only a day Vic had sold out. He agreed to do the same thing the following week and other retailers followed.

A tide calendar for the relevant week was soon included, first as a sidebar and later in a more abbreviated form, and, though it seemed practical, it disappeared after a few years. Ray also put a note in the *Wind* inviting public comment or letters to the editor, intending to broaden its appeal.

About that time Chris Heddericg, a longtime summer resident who'd retired here, became Ray's eager assistant, helping with assembly and distribution. Chris adopted the pen name "The Printers Devil," and authored numerous lengthy and interesting columns, most having to do with the injustices visited on us by the state and federal government, but some taking us to task for not doing something about it.

VOTER APATHY

For the past twenty years, the number of people participating in voting throughout the nation has declined. With the exception of a few cities, voter apathy has increased. In the recent Maine special election, less than 40% went to the polls to vote on the important issue of the Uniform Property Tax and eight referenda questions affecting their pocketbooks.

Two hundred thirty-seven Vinalhaven voters went to the polls on Dec. 5. More people should have exercised this most precious of our political rights — that of voting. Allied with this voter apathy is the failure of taxpayers to attend and to participate at meetings concerning town afairs. Parents should attend the monthly meetings of the Board of Education (ten persons were at the November meeting); there were thirty present at the annual school budget meeting held last June, a budget involving thousands of dollars. Taxpayers should be present at the annual town meeting and special town meetings to express their opinions. It was Voltaire who said, "I disapprove of what you say, but I will defend to the death your right to say it." There are too many Sunday quarterbacks who should be in there playing instead of criticizing the quarterback's calling of the plays.

Why don't people vote? Many non-voters distrust government. One hears such remarks as: "they are a bunch of crooks; Washington is run by a few interests as shown by their powerful lobbies; they don't care about the little guy, and my vote won't count."

The core of the apple might be in the attitude of the people who say that their vote will not count. How wrong they be! If people want to change the governmental policies or they want to remove an incompetent official from office, they can do this through their votes. Suppose Senator Hathaway and Congressmen Cohen and Emery were to receive an avalanche of mail concerning state and national problems. Would they have a reaction? You bet they would, especially as an election year is coming in '78. They are counting on your votes to elect them to office.

Until people realize that their votes and their participation in local affairs do INDEED matter, the voter apathy and the failure to attend and to participate in local political meetings will steadily go downward and, therefore, there will be fewer and fewer voices in YOUR government.

In 1976 nineteen million pounds of lobster were landed in Maine by 9,000 license holders, and the price was $1.54 per pound.

OBSERVATIONS

1977

FOX ISLANDS ELECTRIC COOPERATIVE, in concert with the Rural Electrification Adminstration, arranged for an underwater cable to be installed, just in the nick of time, from the mainland to the islands, and the old power plant closed on its last legs.

Following one issue's revelation that islanders had once voted unanimously against seceding from Massachusetts, a libertarian spirit seized the publisher. The *Wind's* masthead suddenly carried the bold exhortation, "Long Live the Republic of Vinalhaven," and its return address reflected the same change.

Ray petitioned to vote the town dry after a failed effort to stop the licensing of Harbor View Lanes (now Carver's Harbor Market) for the sale of beer.

> Again we have witnessed a most horrible example of the utter disregard of majority public opinion in the Liquor Commission's hearing. The Harbor View Lanes is the only place of recreation that the townspeople, and especially our youth, have. Now it is obvious that the commission is interested in revenue only. Now there can be no middle ground where the consumption of alcohol is concerned. Our only alternative is to vote the town dry at the next opportunity. Toward this end a petition will be circulated requesting that the liquor question again be voted upon. R. P. Blaisdell

Roadside and town park cleanups were annual events and all involved or were initiated by Bodine Ames, just as they are now, forty years later, as this astonishing island tradition of gathering volunteers each year to clean up after some of the rest of us continues.

Ray was determined that nothing appear in the *Wind* that could be considered slanderous or hurtful. Often an odd announcement would find its way in, perhaps because, while unclear, the piece was at least not offensive. A piece submitted by a gentleman in New Hampshire and provided with a return address asked simply:

> Cultured well-educated gentleman desirous of learning new position, resume on request.

In 1977 eighteen million pounds of lobster were landed in Maine by 8,800 license holders, and the price was $1.74 per pound.

1977

Captain Bobby Warren aboard the Seabreeze
Photo credit: Photo by Cindy O'Dell

OBSERVATIONS

1978

ALTHOUGH OPINION PIECES BY NOW SHED SOME LIGHT ON WHAT WAS GOING ON, as did fairly comprehensive reports of board of selectmen and town committee meetings, no news was being "dug up" and reported and, as before, off-island subscribers often only learned of major events when acknowledgements of one kind or another appeared in subsequent issues. Often, that was the result of the compassionate nature of the editor who, when grievous news presented itself in time for publication, thought better of further burdening the bereft. Young Marc Bradley was lost at sea but the uninformed only learned of it when a heartbreaking note of thanks from the family to those who searched in vain appeared in a later issue. Sadly, in the midst of this tragedy, vandalism, robberies, arson, and misconduct continued to plague the community, prompting this editorial:

> Many persons have expressed concern about the senseless acts of destruction against both public and private property this week. This is no isolated occurrence. The latest attack is but one more item in a series of equally disturbing events. Businesses are repeatedly robbed; shoplifting is a growing cost; homes have been threatened, abused and robbed; citizens receive obscene and threatening calls; property is vandalized and our people threatened and attacked. It happens over and over again. Vinalhaven's cherished freedom has depended upon the historic code of "Live and let Live." That freedom has been defended by an equally important element of "Don't Tread on Me." In this situation when we are under an attack by a group who act without regard for the rights of others, we can only survive by helping one another. Be your brother's keeper. (Will Crank)

A Crime Prevention Committee was formed and a police department was consequently established. The new chief promised a weekly report, which became, for several years, a regular feature.

In January of '78 a tremendous storm pushed the tide so high that folks were paddling around in the town parking lot and the water level reached the center of Main Street before beginning to recede.

Alcoholics Anonymous and Al-Anon (a support group for the families of alcoholics) were heavily promoted and testimonies published.

Alcoholism the Family Disease

> It is about three years since I entered Al-Anon. The miracles wrought, the adventure of changing, the release of suppressed emotions, are only some of the experiences I feel I must share with others. When I started with the group I was ill, physically and mentally. My life was one mad obsession — my husband's alcoholism. The neglect of my children and myself was a frightening thing. Fear is contagious and our home was full of fear. I was aware of it, but could do nothing. The shame, the fear of the future — I need not explain! In utter despair I reached out at my first Al-Anon meeting, and a room full of people grasped me, lifted me up and gave me hope, love, and faith. They quieted me with their "easy does it" manner. They explained the disease of alcoholism to me and, best of all, they taught me detachment. I reached hungrily for their twenty-four hour philosophy, and I learned to let go of a problem over which I was completely powerless, in a healthy and constructive way. Gradually, I became aware of the change in my children. The emotional energy I had been wasting in trying to sober up my husband I could give constructively to them.

Curious announcements continued to appear regularly. This one was found right below the touching testimony preceding and, in that context, was terribly startling until the more cognizant among us identified it as unrelated to the Al-Anon column but rather a plea to find homes for kittens.

Because of tragic family breakup due to desertion by father, mother is forced to give up children for adoption.

In 1978 nineteen million pounds of lobster were landed in Maine by 8,700 license holders, and the price was $1.77 per pound.

OBSERVATIONS

1979

THE PERIWINKLE TAKE-OUT BECAME THE HARBOR GAWKER (IT IS NOW ISLAND SPIRITS). The Gawker then froze a banana and dipped it in chocolate and nuts. Someone on staff ate it, and described the decadent experience that others might come in and try one.

Weight Watchers coalesced on the island in 1979 and began meeting in the Old Engine House.

A committee was formed to investigate the possibility of constructing a nursing home on the island.

Another landmark vanished as an arsonist burned the Islander Inn in February.

Peaslee's Garage, an institution for everyone my age or older, changed hands (it is now the town garage). I was administered my driving test there and provided a permit by Carl Williams, the stern and intimidating proprietor, in 1959.

The police chief resigned, citing lack of support, as did the school principal/superintendent, citing school board interference.

We learned from an islander returning from a trip to England that Martin Pring, credited with having discovered these Fox Islands, was buried at St. Stephen's Church in Bristol, England.

A column of "School News" became a regular feature.

My grandparents wrote a letter of gratitude to those who helped save (most of) their house. The uninformed thus learned of the fire that nearly destroyed it.

I began writing a sports column describing softball games:

> The Sweat Sox continued their league domination, taking a Sunday doubleheader from the No Sox 8-4 and 9-5. Coach Tibbetts reactivated veteran Cy Davidson as a gesture of contempt for the opposition and in a locker room interview after the game, boldly announced he would claim the championship for himself if his "best of five" challenge drew no takers. Unfortunately for Tibb, takers abounded.

Construction began on Harborside Apartments, a federally subsidized housing project.

Meals on Wheels got underway.

R. E. Candage Grocers opened up on Skin Hill at the former Shield's Grocery site in November. The grocery E.G. Carver, another in a long line of island institutions, succumbed to the changing tide of island economics and was sold. It retained its name but for the first time its owner was not a Carver. The Haven opened the following month, and this notice appeared from our resident telephone man:

> While awaiting the outcome of contract negotiations Abe Knowlton will receive nuisance calls to relieve the boredom.

Ivan Calderwood, whose *nom de plume* was Uncle Dave, in the first of many more columns over the next several years, made an impassioned plea to keep and restore the old ballground, the repository of so many happy memories for us all. The effort went nowhere, however, because a new ballground was being built at the school and there was a great deal of enthusiasm for its completion. Chris Heddericg, "The Printers Devil," ill-advisedly belittled Ivan's column and earned a moderate tongue-lashing from an islander who called his attention to the unacceptability of criticizing a native, particularly one of long and respected standing, before himself having quite settled in here to everyone's satisfaction.

Opposes Purchase

I will be unable to attend the annual Town Meeting so I am expressing my opposition to the town's purchase of the Old Ball Park. A plea has been made that the youngsters and the "oldsters" need an area to play ball, and the children, in particular, need a place to skate. It is also stated that the Park should be purchased to preserve the memories of old-timer baseball players who "could hit the ball across the street." Starting in April, the school will construct a ballfield. We hope that the children and the twilight league players will be able to use the field. A portion of the new field could be set aside as a skating area. The town voted to appropriate a sum of money as its share of the new field, so why pay for another site? The town now leases the property for one dollar for one year.

If the town did not purchase the field, youngsters would still continue to play ball, and to skate. Knowing the condition of the field and the cost that would be entailed to make a suitable use of the park, what single individual would purchase the site?

Many times the Old Ball Park is unsuitable for play; the area is flooded for days. The high school baseball team cannot practice daily and play an entire schedule in this park.

$20,000 is a considerable sum of money to pay for this park. There are many worthwhile projects that are more imperative.

Chris Heddericg

I understand that the ballground issue is stirring a lot of controversy. It seems as though the "nostalgic" dreamer has been shunned and the question of $20,000 spent for the old ballground is wrong.

Sadly enough, the nostalgic dreamer is fast becoming one in a dozen. I'm not advocating living in the past, but the truth is: the past is the backbone of our existence.

I've regretted seeing the Memorial Hall torn down, but was a silent watcher. The Islander Inn now, too, is but a memory, and now the ballground has the chance of being sold. For anyone who has not lived on Vinalhaven all his or her life, this may seem grossly exaggerated and a waste of money. But there's something that stirs, even within my young heart, that just can't seem to let go of the old ballground. It must be especially hard on those who are a product of the "old time" ballplayers and all that the ballground has stood for and represented.

In short, it's easy for some off-islanders not to understand the sentiment involved in losses such as this, and even a few natives may not give a hoot either way. But as the old saying goes, "Doesn't it always seem to go that you don't know what you've got until it's gone."

I'm especially aware of the changes on Vinalhaven since I'm a native who's moved away and can look back and see the things that at one time meant so much just fall to the wayside.

OBSERVATIONS

I've done my share of complaining about island living, but you can't turn your back one hundred percent. And he who moves to Vinalhaven from another place must try to look through the eyes of the native. An off-islander has as much right to live on Vinalhaven as anyone else, but there are certain things that cannot be understood unless you live it every day! The ballground issue is no exception. We must have a hold on some part of the past and for once do as our hearts tell us. That's why Vinalhaven is so loved — it makes few demands for progress, and I hope it stays that way! (Think about it!) Comments?

Barb Dyer   and
University of Maine   Sue (Dyer) Radley
Farmington, Maine 04938   Bucksport, Maine
Box 46, Rm. 404 Dakin Hall

Ray and Judy Blaisdell left for a new ministry in Cherryield, Maine and their departure, and his in particular, as editor of the *Wind*, was marked by several poignant tributes. Ray and Judy had undeniably given the island and this ministry their all. The community was certainly the better for their efforts and the *Wind* was thriving, popular, and had already lasted twice as long as any of its predecessors, due entirely to Ray's indefatigable determination. Grant Duell took the helm as editor.

A new and very useful regular column called "The Reporter's Notebook" by one "Town Hall Tommie," otherwise unidentified, appeared. Here is a typical offering:

> Our assessor, Olga Carleton, indicates the new tax rate is 16 mills for the current tax year. While town appropriations have remained the same, the 1978 school deficit of $30,000 and current increases in the cost of education have jumped the rate from the previous 13 mills. There were also changes in the tax base of the town. More veterans became 62 years of age making them eligible for exemptions of $4,000 to $6,000 of taxable value on their homes. The Electric Co-op is also off the tax rolls and more taxpayers are utilizing the "tree growth law." With everything on the way up, it appears that Vinalhaven is no exception. Dave Moyer III, representing the lobster and fishing co-ops, Bronson Clark, First Selectman, and Olga Carleton as an alternate member of the Ferry Service Advisory Board, continued ongoing meetings with the DOT about a freight boat or freight trip. The meeting held last Friday in Augusta involved Governor Brennan and DOT Commissioner Roger Mallard. The DOT indicated that they would undertake a study of freight requirements and freight fares, especially in view of the new fish plant requirements next spring.

The *Wind* sported a new masthead created gratis by my brothers David and Matthew Crossman.

1979

Cardiopulmonary resuscitation (CPR) training and certification was offered at the Medical Center.

Clams, historically a plentiful resource, were becoming scarce, and a "Clamittee" was formed to address the issue.

The Finest Kind String Band, consisting of Kilton and Cissy Smith, Perry and Annie Boyden, Bob Tolman, Charlie McCabe, and Fred Swanson, was a big hit at the Evening Festival of Maine Vaudeville.

And this:

"To: Bullet: There ain't gonna be another time. Moose."

Annie and Perry Boyden bought the building at the top of the hill next to the Historical Society and aggressively sought supporters to create there a new Arts and Recreation Center (ARC).

The Police Report remained an irregular feature:

Police Report (Jan 1 – June 30): Officers responded to 319 complaints up from 291 filed over the same period last year. Arson 1, attempt to locate 7, auto accidents 20, assaults 5, property damage $9,010, fires 6, personal injury 1, boating accident 1, burglaries 26, larceny theft 17, criminal trespassing 3, criminal mischief 31, property stolen $3,681, property destroyed $3,255, restitution made $400, disorderly conduct 4, domestic complaints 11, drunkenness 3, juvenile complaints 6, liquor violation 5, public service calls 47, obstructing a public way 10, prowlers 4, rescue calls 6, unattended deaths 1, traffic summons 16, and one complaint each for driving to endanger, helicopter crash, indecent exposure, joy riding, and negotiating a worthless instrument.

(That last legalese is a wonderful characterization, not unlike my high school band leader Norman Guidiboni's description of me and my clarinet.)

Vandalism peaked around this time with issue after issue announcing rewards for information leading to the arrest of miscreants slashing tires, siphoning fuel, and burning property. In one issue two homeowners thanked the fire department and others who provided assistance when their respective houses were torched. Eventually an anonymous columnist (I think it was me) wrote:

The people of Vinalhaven apologize to Roy Ames, Frank Farnsworth, and the many others who've suffered from the pitiful behavior of a handful of mental cripples. It's really the vandals that deserve pity. These flagrant acts of cowardice testify to their inability to deal with life. The Ames, Farnsworths, and others will replace their tires and their rage will run its course but there is no patch job that can fill the void where the culprit's brains and heart should be. They are all re-treads.

In 1979 twenty-two million pounds of lobster were landed in Maine by 8,600 license holders, and the price was $1.80 per pound.

OBSERVATIONS

1980

In a rare piece of real news from elsewhere, we learned from the *Wind* that the state had adopted the first of many shameful policies providing for balancing the state's budget on the backs of the less fortunate and the less disciplined by putting forward a proposal that it license slot machines. The door was thus nudged open for the state to lavish encouragement and subsidies on a wide array of gambling venues, in turn creating opportunities for us to ease our burdens by bankrupting and ruining those with a weakness for gambling or simply desperate to improve their own circumstances.

"Aunt" Caddie Vaughn turned 101.

A public shore access study was undertaken with Del Webster doing the research for the town, the old power plant was demolished, and a contract for operating the dump for a year was ill-advisedly awarded to someone without the wherewithal to fulfill the inherent obligations.

The ARC was in full swing with movies, field trips, theater, skateboarding, surfboarding, courses of instruction in all sorts of things such as chair caning, dancing, and cooking, and undertook fund-raising to build an addition that would more readily allow for theatrical productions.

The town ignored an odd demand from Milford, Massachusetts that we return the eagle we'd installed in the parking lot, claiming it was rightfully theirs.

Robert Indiana applied for (and was eventually granted) landmark designation of the International Order of Odd Fellows building — the Star of Hope — and undertook its restoration.

A group of fifty or so living within the downtown area published a plea that noise and offensive behavior in the town parking lot stop.

Shore Land Zoning was adopted.

Ivan Calderwood, now in his eighties, author of *Uncle Dave's Fish House,* and a compelling historian, continued regular, lengthy, but very interesting columns under the heading "Uncle Dave Says." The contributions, nearly always more than an entire column in length and often serialized, were uniformly wonderful, intriguing and detailed accounts of people, places, or events from our island's past. In one issue he gave an account of how the town got by when its only ferry, the *W. S. White*, was sold and we were left with no connection to the mainland. In another he described the gas lights that lit the town for ten years or so at the beginning of the twentieth century. Memories were the bread and butter of "Uncle Dave Says."

Early Morning on Main Street

I see Sid Winslow walking along the street carrying his bucket of paste, his long handled brush, paint can, and etching brushes, with a rill of paper under his arm. He was getting ready to give the Old Billboard across from the Old Memorial Hall, where the movie hall was, a face lifting. Along comes Gene Hall, who was the state agent for the Steam Boat Wharf, with his little pack of spirits. "You know, Gene, our old timers are passing beyond the sunset," said Sid. "I know, Sid; time marches on and remember we are the old timers now," replied Gene. How true! Any morning you might have

1980

seen: E.G. Carver, O.P. Lyons, L.R. Smith, C.B. White, Frank White, our druggist, Harry Carver of the Spa, Babbin Fifield of the hardware store, sweeping out the dirt onto Main Street. They all wore their linen dusters, each greeting the other, happy with their lot, doing business in our little town of Vinalhaven. They didn't want recession or depression. They sold their wares at a reasonable price to fit their customer's pocket books. My friend Staffy Smith would say, "Don't that settle it." May God keep them and love them as we did. A tear drop falls. Says Uncle Dave.

And another of Uncle Dave's contributions:

Joseph S. Black came to this country as a very young man from Scotland, almost too young to get in. He was preceded by an older brother and sister (William and Jennie). He married Annie Calderwood, a descendant of one of the earliest settlers of the Fox Islands. Of this union there were seven girls and two boys and Kenneth Black was one of them. Joseph Black, the first to become interested in paving cutting on Vinalhaven, quarried stone off Main Street where Sheridan's Garage [presently the town garage] is now and where the Net Factory and the old Gas House used to be. He was very thrifty and planned his operations so not to waste any stone that would block out as paving. Every part of cutting was done by hand as there were no air compressors or steam drills for channeling the big sheets of stone. At first they used Lewis holes drilled by strikers and a man to hold the drill, to start the sheets of stone. To be a good striker, you had to have rhythm like Granddad's clock—tick-tock. The trade was passed down from father to son. All the grout (waste stone) was leveled off into the tidewater. That made the foundation for our Main Street— so Joe Black made our Main Street. Later, Joe had quarried at Dushane Hill and other places where he manufactured paving for many years. Another early quarry was at Armbrust Hill near the present Medical Center. The waste from the quarry, which the Englishmen would call "hode and hens," was dumped along the shoreline. When my grandmother was a little girl, she said there were two logs at the Cascade where the Main Street Bridge is now for people to cross the falls, and the horses waded across. The contract to build a bridge made of stone with the blocks twelve feet in length and six feet wide was awarded to John Carver in 1849 at a cost of $300. Mr. Black was also involved in other quarries such as Dark Brook and the Swamp. It took brains and much hard work to be successful in the stone business. Hard work never hurt anyone. Says Uncle Dave.

Ivan Calderwood
Photo: Provided by the Vinalhaven Historical Society
In 1980 twenty-two million pounds of lobster were landed in Maine by 9,200 license holders, and the price was $1.90 per pound.

1981

IN 1981 *WIND* CIRCULATION REACHED ONE THOUSAND, and by then thirteen folks, all volunteers, were involved in its production and distribution.

The Vinalhaven High School girls' basketball team won the state championship, beating Buckfield 40-37.

We adopted the town manager/selectmen form of government. Until then we'd been governed by a board of selectmen. One among them, the head selectman, had served as a sort of mayor, but increasingly critical issues were clearly not getting the attention they deserved.

The Penobscot Bay Fish & Cold Storage plant (PFCS) was dedicated in April.

"The Observer" column, unsigned, appeared suddenly, and then regularly in every issue for years. Its focus was whatever issues were being addressed by the board of selectmen, the results of committee meetings, and so forth, not unlike the "Town Hall Tommie" column that preceded it but with many more specifics.

The ARC caught fire and was badly damaged, leaving all involved quite discouraged, but not for long. They began fund-raising and rebuilding, finished quickly, and a regular column of "ARC Happenings" appeared, an accompaniment to its progress.

A new police department employed radar to nab speeders and closed the town parking lot from 11:00 p.m. till 5:00 a.m. Vandalism continued to plague the community. The bandstand was nearly destroyed by one night of such behavior.

A local mom and her infant son survived the crash of Flight 30H which overshot the runway at Logan airport and landed in the frigid January waters of Boston Harbor.

A note appeared from the selectmen thanking Fred Swanson, who was retiring from his authorship, for having produced the "Observer" column. Until then the author hadn't been acknowledged. The column continued, however, and the identity of the new reporter was again not made public, although we all knew it was Bill Minor.

In 1981 twenty-three million pounds of lobster were landed in Maine by 8,500 license holders, and the price was $2.09 per pound.

1981

Winter Harbor

OBSERVATIONS

1982/1983

THE *WIND* BECAME A LITTLE DULL. "Uncle Dave Says" gave it a little color and the "School News" and "ARC Happenings" added interest but, otherwise, in a typical issue one might find one page lamenting instances of vandalism; announcing committee or group meeting times, including AA and Al-Anon; inviting attendance at an open house for new arrivals; and posting the hours of a new animal clinic. The next page featured several real estate ads (there were three realtors at the time), a list of rental properties, services offered, a report of the progress being made by the Law Enforcement Study Committee, and so forth. The third page announced births, deaths, restaurant hours, things for sale, and lost and found items. And it published the names of those hospitalized or who'd fallen on hard times, and the thank-yous from those same people and from others who'd been helped or befriended. No issue was without thank-yous, often several, and one didn't have to read too many of them to conclude that while living in a small community might mean everyone knew what you were doing, sometimes that wasn't a bad thing.

Brown's Head Light was one hundred and fifty years old and appropriate observations were undertaken.

Bob and Lois Candage visited the Holy Land, presenting a program of slides when they returned.

The town began negotiations with a cable TV provider.

A program of dances was cancelled due to the bad behavior of a few but *Take Joy* was produced around Christmas in 1983 and was a huge — legendary, even — hit.

A proposal was considered to build a loading dock at the north end of the island so overflow traffic from the Vinalhaven ferry could be routed to the North Haven ferry when necessary.

A big summer home, formerly the Harrowers', but then belonging to Andrew von Hirsh, was torched, and a local fellow arraigned and eventually incarcerated as a result.

A first step toward recycling, accepting bundled newspapers in a separate container at the landfill, failed for lack of cooperation. The vast quantities of plastic trash on our own shores, most of it discarded by fishing boats, was brought to our attention and efforts to clean up and educate were undertaken.

And this:

> An intellectual is someone who
> Can listen to the William Tell
> Overture without thinking of
> The Lone Ranger

Lawson's Quarry was purchased by the town for nine thousand dollars.

We began to adjust to having to get a permit each time we wanted to build new or to create an addition.

The Town Band folded for lack of enthusiasm, and I, with no lack of enthusiasm whatever, married Elaine Austin.

A Seafarer's Monument was erected on Lane's Island. It's still there, but unattended, and can only be found by careful search.

1982/1983

The Sands Cove Lobster and Clam Bake, only a year or two old but a wildly popular and exceedingly informal waterfront restaurant, announced it was closing, but intended to reopen elsewhere in the vicinity.

Sand's Cove drawing by Rusty Gibson

Priscilla O'Keefe originated the "Evening with the Artist" series at the ARC.

**In 1982 twenty-three million pounds of lobster were landed in Maine by 8,900 license holders, and the price was $2.21 per pound.
In 1983 the price was $2.33 per pound.**

Observations

1984

THE NATIONAL HEALTH SERVICE CORPS RECALLED DR. O'KEEFE, resulting in an uproar of opposition from us all, including Dr. O'Keefe, who wanted very much to stay right here.

The school property was posted to keep hell-raisers out after hours.

The planned restoration work on the Odd Fellow's Hall was completed and congratulations extended to its owner, Robert Indiana, for having essentially saved the building.

PFCS reported shipping product to sixty-five countries in addition to cities throughout the U.S.

A moving obituary was composed in memory of the pathetic 1983 Red Sox.

An island cookbook, *Fish Scales and Chocolate Chips*, quite some time in the making, appeared with an impressive 502 recipes.

My grandfather, Ted Maddox, collapsed and died while leading the 1984 Fourth of July parade, and a very nice tribute, penned by Chris's wife, Bea Heddericg, appeared in the next *Wind*.

With His Boots On

The flags were waving in the sea breeze. The Town Band was playing spiritedly. The annual Fourth of July parade began, led, as usual, by the Police Chief flashing blue lights on the patrol car and followed by the First Selectman, standing in an open Jeep waving to the hundreds of Vinalhavenites and visitors. It always began this way, as far back as I can remember. The personnel in the cars, floats, and on foot naturally varied from year to year. This year of 1984 our First Selectman was Ted Maddox, a tall, handsome man of about three score and twenty. I remarked to a friend beside me, "How handsome he looks." Indeed, he did — standing with one foot on the running board of the Jeep and the other resting on the floor of the vehicle. He wore white slacks and a navy blue jacket; his crisp gray/white hair perfectly groomed, and a warm, happy smile spread over his firm jaw. If ever there was a Town Father, Ted was it. Although not a native Vinalhavenite, he had served his adopted town in so many ways for so many years, that his actual birthplace mattered little to anyone here. He had been a member of the Board of Selectmen several times before. Many buildings in our town had known the heft of his hammer; he represented our legislative district in Augusta for term after term, and was a talented amateur actor. His long list of credits will appear elsewhere. It is enough now to say he cared — he gave the utmost anyone can contribute — himself! Even with the slow pace of a parade, it takes but a few minutes to cover the length of our Main Street. As the patrol car and the Jeep reached the last of the stores, Ted Maddox, with his arm raised in greeting to the assemblage, suddenly collapsed and fell. A large heart had given out. And so, with the flags waving, the band playing, and most of the townspeople gathered, Ted made his final exit. Way to go, Ted!

Grant Duell and Chris Heddericg retired nearly simultaneously from their critical posts at the *Wind*, leaving the paper in rather desperate circumstances. Jean Wetherbee stepped into the breach and became the new editor and other volunteers took up the slack.

1984

Fox Islands Concerts presented its first program and has since been a regular and welcome cultural feature of summer life here on the island.

The ARC continued to thrive and their weekly column was an open invitation to join in all sorts of appealing activities.

The flea market, which had been held in the town parking lot, moved to Ray's Field, across from the bandstand, where it has since become an institution.

The prestigious Maine Printmaking Workshop, under the guidance of Pat Nick, moved into the Washington School and became the even more prestigious Vinalhaven Press. We were reminded that the Washington School had been built in 1896 for $6,621.

The Vinalhaven Historical Society building, once a church in Rockland but brought to Vinalhaven in 1878 and improbably moved (rolled?) up the hill to its present location, was completely repaired and repainted and, in 1984, its museum hosted 1,359 visitors from 378 states and 10 countries.

Chris Heddericg passed away only a few months after leaving the *Wind*.

The Town Band re-formed and we were reminded that it had formed originally one hundred years earlier and made its first appearance in a Fourth of July parade on a float being towed by seventy-two yoke of oxen (that's one hundred forty-four animals).

The State of Maine Department of Education announced that Vinalhaven had, during the preceding years, Maine's highest percentage of graduates going on to higher education.

My great-grandmother, Rena Johnson, known to all who loved her as Gram J, celebrated her ninety-eighth birthday and was presented with the Boston Post Cane. The *Boston Post* newspaper, in 1909, distributed these canes, made from African ebony, to over six hundred New England towns, asking that they be bestowed, in perpetuity, to the oldest resident in each town. It was a great publicity stunt and did wonders for the *Post's* circulation. Still living at home and taking care of herself, Gram J was the matriarch of five island generations, all of whom gathered with her each Saturday for her own baked beans and homemade rolls.

The town was given the land on which the bandstand and galamander are situated, which it had been leasing from the owners for one dollar a year.

We were going through police chiefs at better than one a year. The town finally decided to forego trying to maintain a police department and put itself under the auspices of the Knox County Sherriff.

The ARC sailing program got underway and has been a thriving enterprise ever since.

A tombstone that read "Sarah, wife of Chaney Noyes, died Mar. 10, 1865, aged 35 years" was uncovered when tearing down some derelict buildings behind the stores on the Carver's Pond side of Main Street. That same night an unsuspecting babysitter, alone with a sleeping child (ours) in the Carver Street house that, in the nineteenth century, belonged to Chaney Noyes, watched an apparition, a young woman in a lovely red dress, come in through the front door, walk down the hallway in front of her, and disappear up the stairs. Presumably the unearthing of the tombstone had liberated her. She remains liberated but companionably with us today.

OBSERVATIONS

Uncle Dave's columns became a little shorter and began to appear a little less regularly. Then, at eighty-six years of age, Ivan published his seventh book of island recollections, *Uncle Dave's Memoirs*. Copies of it and of Ivan's other books, and of similarly invaluable volumes of island history, remain available at the Historical Society today.

In August a fledgling osprey chick fell from its nest on the microwave tower. Roy Dyer provided a blanket to prevent injury from its talons and the FIEC guys, using their bucket truck, put it back in the nest to join its two siblings. The same bird fell out once more the following week and was again returned home. When it fell out the third time it was taken to a mainland sanctuary with the intention that it be kept there till it learned to fly, which it did.

A new airstrip, or an extension of the existing runway, was under discussion, and a meeting was called in late September to discuss whether to form a Vinalhaven Land Trust.

Teenage drinking continued to plague activities and the island in general. The school grounds were again placed off limits after 7 p.m. to prevent vandalism and an accumulation of broken beer bottles and other debris. Destruction of the bandstand continued. Young people gathered there at night, smoked and drank, and smashed out the spindles that were the upper and lower rails. The Vinalhaven Lions Club announced its intention to make repairs and put a stop to that sort of behavior.

The warrant for the '85 town meeting was to include an article asking whether the town would allow the sale of liquor. Volunteers were sought to serve on a committee responsible for developing a Comprehensive Plan.

A new eighty-nine-foot water tower was built to replace the failing original.

In 1984 twenty million pounds of lobster were landed in Maine by 8,700 license holders, and the price was $2.52 per pound.

1984

Murch's Brook

OBSERVATIONS

1985/1986

THE *WIND* OF AUGUST 11, 1985 was easily the most heart-wrenching with the acknowledging thank-you from the parents of little Thomas Getman, who drowned at Booth's Quarry in spite of the efforts of so many people. The lives of many of us were changed that day, some, more than just the family, irretrievably.

Another young man, Gary Small, was lost at sea in April of 1986.

A contract was awarded in 1985 for construction of a new ferry, and controversy over its size, which island would then be assigned which boat, who would park where at each terminal and under what circumstances, consumed the town for the next year.

The new water tower was completed, then condemned, torn down, and replaced with another.

The seventieth annual Alumni Banquet took place.

In response to a petition begun by my brother Dick, the name of his classmate Owen Webster was added to the Vietnam War Memorial seventeen years after he died from injuries suffered during that idiotic conflict.

The Vinalhaven Land Trust (VLT) was incorporated in July of 1986 and our new ferry, the *Governor Curtis,* was commissioned at about the same time.

Coot Eaton, himself an island institution, died in July of that year. In 1958, having escaped from the local constabulary at fourteen years of age, I had holed up at Coot's, until, after enjoying a heaping plate of his famous flapjacks, I was persuaded to turn myself in.

The library support group known today as The Friends of the Library (FOL) was formed.

The town began negotiations to acquire or lease Geary's Beach from the state.

Alfred Osgood's *Starlight*, now a bait provider and a fixture on the waterfront, emigrated here from her home in Florida.

1985 twenty million pounds of lobster were landed in Maine by 4,800 license holders, and the price was $2.24 per pound. In 1986 the price was $2.34

1985/1986

Betty Roberts
Photo: Provided by the Vinalhaven Historical Society

OBSERVATIONS

1987

THE VINALHAVEN LAND TRUST ACQUIRED ITS FIRST PROPERTY AT PERRY CREEK. The town voted to allow liquor to be served in local eating establishments, and negotiated a lease of Browns Head Light, now automated, from the U.S. Coast Guard.

Gram J celebrated her one hundredth birthday at my home.

The RLDS Church decided to give up its historic but way too demanding building on Atlantic Avenue and announced plans to build anew at Pleasant River on land donated to them by the family of Curtis Webster.

E. G. Carver, the grocery we'd all grown up with, closed on March 14, 1987, and Cy and Barb Davidson's Carver's Harbor Market opened a few doors away.

Kim Smith, another of those institutions, retired as town clerk after twenty-four years.

The newly constructed ferry, the *Margaret Chase Smith,* was assigned to Islesboro but it wouldn't fit in that island's pen, an interesting oversight.

Negotiations began with Blue Rock Industries to build a sidewalk from the ferry terminal to town.

Raymond Alley was selected to be a part of the *Sunday Telegram* Dream Team after having averaged twenty-nine points per game.

A public hearing was scheduled in early 1988 to consider the application of Atlantic Salmon, Inc. to lease twenty five acres around the White Islands and in Hurricane Sound in which to farm salmon.

A Plea for Our Future or Say No to Salmon
by Marguerite Adair

The hardy pioneers who lived here for many years, enduring privations but successfully making homes for their families on the island, were true examples of strength, spirit, and endurance *plus* a resourcefulness that still prevails on the bay today. In 1989 we celebrate our Bicentennial. It will be a sad commentary on our times if this period in our history must be remembered as the year the White Islands were polluted and contaminated and a region of impressive beauty was lost to us and to the wildlife. There are so many reasons to deny this proposed lease. This multi-million dollar company which sees only dollar signs would do untold harm in the future to our clear salt waters, harm that would be beyond restoration. On the West coast, contamination and barren sea bottom have been the result, the filtering down of residues of medication used to treat young salmon. This can also remain in lobsters and be dispersed by tide and current into other areas. Human consumption of contaminated shellish could be at risk. Our dismay could easily turn to horror. There is no justification for a lease to be issued which would be so detrimental in all respects and would prevent our fishermen from using a vital water route. Vote "NO" at Town Meeting March 22 and attend the public hearing April 4.

Betty Roberts, who'd recently offered Armbrust Hill to the town as a gift, passed away.

1987

Raymond Alley
Photo: Provided by the Vinalhaven Historical Society

Raymond Alley, on his way to becoming a local basketball legend, scored his one thousandth point.

OBSERVATIONS

1988

THE OBSERVER OF APRIL, 1988, signed by Bill Minor, informs us that the selectmen had voted to ask that the column no longer carry the news from town hall. Bill was a selectman himself and his signature was the first official confirmation that he was and had been the "Observer's" author for some time, which, of course, we all knew. The town, in a separate announcement said that it — the town, that is — would henceforth take responsibility for providing relevant news from town hall in a regular piece titled "Public Notices." It was certainly an interesting situation; the selectmen seemed to think it was OK to insist that their activities, clearly a matter of public record, not be independently reported and further, to claim that prerogative for themselves. As it happens, they did go on to report weekly as promised but it wasn't as interesting. A few weeks later the board made a more strident disavowal of the "Observer" column, stating unequivocally that the column "is not an official town information outlet." Bill Minor resigned from the board of selectmen, citing the difficulty of working with certain members, but continued the column. Clearly there was more to this story than could be gleaned from reading the *Wind*.

Our first Comprehensive Plan, thoughtfully drafted in response to the state's mandate, was adopted in March of 1988. Every Maine community had been mandated to develop such a document whose purpose was to establish long-term public policy in the areas of, for example, transportation, utilities, land use, recreation, natural resources, and housing.

The Maine State Ferry Service (MSFS) continued to grapple with line-up and parking procedures and enforcement of the same. All sorts of amusing solutions were promulgated and given the force of law.

The town acquired the State (Geary's) Beach property, and the application for constructing a salmon farm in Hurricane Sound was rejected 357-29.

Math teacher Pete Pedersen contributed a long and worthy column detailing math team progress from last place in 1987 to first place in 1988.

The Vinalhaven Fire Department celebrated one hundred years in service on July 2, 1988.

Fishermen's Friend, a business whose success I forecast at the time as unlikely, opened. Today it is something of an institution and I am no longer asked for my predictions.

That spring — every spring, for that matter — the *Wind* again announced the annual roadside and shoreland clean up, organized by Bodine Ames, during which island youngsters were — and are still — enlisted to form little road gangs whose responsibility it was to pick up the litter that had accumulated over the winter. In the following issue those kids were thanked for picking up after those of us who, confident, I guess, that the children would take care of it, had chucked our trash and, especially bottles and cans, out our car and truck windows all fall and winter. Likewise, the young volunteers from Hurricane Island or Outward Bound or from the Holy Family Life Team of Rockland, Massachusetts, were — and some still are — regularly enlisted to clean up after us or paint and care for town property that we ought to have been taking care of ourselves, and they've done — and do — it eagerly and very well. This has happened every year and probably will for years to come, and while it seems to be an arrangement everyone finds satisfactory, it's a mystery to me.

1988

Bodine Ames and friends
Photo: Provided by the Vinalhaven Historical Society

OBSERVATIONS

The town gratefully accepted Betty Roberts's gift of Armbrust Hill.

Penobscot Bay Fish and Cold Storage (PFCS) was ordered closed following an ammonia leak, and the town broke its lease with the plant citing its failure to pay rent or to meet its other obligations, many of which the town was forced to assume.

Actor Cesar Romero graciously declined an invitation to be our Grand Marshall at the following year's (1989) bicentennial celebration, but recalled fondly the time he spent here in 1947 filming *Deep Waters*. Broadcaster Walter Cronkite subsequently accepted an invitation to serve as Grand Marshall.

Gram J passed away on August 25, 1988 at the age of one hundred and one. In her eighties and nineties she was one of only a few practitioners of the nearly lost art of knotted netting, an art form that now resides with her great-granddaughter-in-law, Stephanie Crossman, who developed the medium to such an extraordinary degree that she was later invited to the Smithsonian Craft show in Washington, D.C. and appeared there in 2013.

A couple of land owners, whose property fell within the recently created Water District Reservoir Zone and who consequently lost the right to build, sued the town for damages, and a public hearing was scheduled to discuss the need for a municipal sewer.

The original Observer, Bill Minor, died in October of 1988, just after publishing his last column. Less than a month after Bill passed away his wife Gert took up the gauntlet and began authoring "The Observer" herself.

The sad circumstances that often required our elderly to spend their remaining days off-island in a mainland nursing facility prompted a group of us to again discuss the creation of an eldercare facility.

A way to remove an embarrassing and enormous accumulation of junk vehicles from the island was finally found and, during the course of 1988, much of that eyesore was removed.

The fire department and town office staff, occupying the same building, were beginning to feel crowded and discussions were undertaken to find solutions.

The Nighthawks, a ladies' social club that had been meeting in Vinalhaven since the 1930s, undertook to get the town's two granite fountains operational for the Bicentennial.

Another institution, Barton's Store, closed in November.

As 1988 drew to a close, North Haven and Vinalhaven prepared to celebrate the upcoming Bicentennial year with a one-hundred-shot salute from Smith Point on New Year's Eve.

In 1988, twenty-two million pounds of lobster were landed in Maine by 5,600 license holders, and the price was $2.79 per pound.

1988

Mill River

OBSERVATIONS

1989

IN COMPLIANCE WITH THE NEWLY ADOPTED COMPREHENSIVE PLAN, the town applied (successfully) for a Coastal Planning Grant to study public access to the shore. No mention was made of a similar survey undertaken by Del Webster several years earlier however.

Barbara Morton authored a book on knotted netting, *Downeast Netting: A History and How-to of Netmaking.*

PFCS, having overcome its financial and compliance difficulties, asked the town to allow it to establish a relationship with a "sister" city overseas. The lucky sibling hadn't been chosen but we were assured it would be somewhere in Europe.

An application from the town to the Department of Environmental Protection (DEP) resulted in the area beneath the island being designated a sole source aquifer.

I.W. Fifield was put on the market, eliciting laments from every quarter. Fifield's had, for years, been the place to go for nearly everything, particularly opinions, as the island's self-appointed sages gathered around the wood stove to dispense advice and counsel to everyone, whether or not called for. It was an institution, perhaps *the* institution, plain and simple.

Photo: Provided by the Vinalhaven Historical Society

From left to right: Bert Porter, Paul Christie, Kim Smith and Bruce Grindle (proprietors), and "Mouse" Lloyd. Note the Wind box. Photo: Sally Thibault.

1989

Raymond Alley scored his two thousandth point in a January game with Buckfield, becoming only the third high school player in Maine's history to do so, and boys and girls teams headed for the tournament with the boys in first place and the girls in third. At the same time our cheerleaders won a state competition. It was a great year for Vinalhaven basketball.

Our public library, built in 1906 with a grant from Andrew Carnegie, was entered into The National Register of Historic Places.

I was elected to the board of selectmen.

A Spiritual Thought for the Day began a weekly appearance, authored by Rev. Roland Arno.

> Hebrews 3:12-13 (NIV) "See to it, brothers, that none of you has a sinful, unbelieving heart that turns away from the living God. But encourage one another daily, as long as it is called 'today,' so that none of you may be hardened by sin's deceitfulness." What have you done to encourage someone? Don't miss the opportunity to encourage someone.

The bicentennial parade, with Walter Cronkite as Grand Marshall riding on our antique steam fire engine Old Reuben, was memorable for us, but also for Walter who, while attending the annual Lions Summer Visitors Night a few nights before, had lost a Walter Cronkite look-a-like contest to Luke Dorr. Luke's Lion chums always thought he looked more like Cronkite than Walter did himself, and we were right.

The first *Breaking Wind* appeared on the occasion of the Bicentennial. The satirical take-off sold for one dollar with the proceeds contributed to the *Wind*.

While a few deer ticks were found in a statewide sampling, none were found on the twelve deer selected here for testing.

Heron Neck Lighthouse burned in May. The cause was never determined.

Penobscot Bay Fish and Cold Storage closed, insolvent and $950,000 in debt.

The 1989 math team excelled in state competition and was chosen to participate in the national equivalent in Florida.

The Schwans (purveyor of fast or nearly fast, frozen, and ready-to-eat or ready-to-cook entrees) truck put in its first appearance.

The fraternal Marguerite Order of the Eastern Star surrendered its charter.

OBSERVATIONS

The Nighthawks succeeded in restoring our two fountains, and my grandmother, Phyllis Maddox, read a speech she'd written for the occasion at the christening of one of them.

> If you were to walk up Main Street seventy years ago you would stop and look at a park which was right here, green and lovely. It went from the Block to within a few feet of the curb around the Libby House. Beautiful trees and shrubs enclosed by a fence, our bandstand right here, and this beautiful fountain which was given to the town by Moses Webster.
>
> I lived in this Block from the time I was five years old until after I was married. I looked out on this park from my bedroom window, played in it, and went to sleep with the music from the running water.
>
> This fountain deserves to be cared for and cherished. Bill Clayter had a great idea when he suggested that the Nighthawks make this our project for the Bicentennial.
>
> We are all so grateful for the donations and enthusiasm, not only from our townspeople, but from those who love Vinalhaven just as we do.
>
> Now once more we can rejoice and rededicate these memorials to the granite industry of Vinalhaven.

The fountain at the "Block"
Photo: Provided by the Vinalhaven Historical Society

1989

A permit to build a home on Sheep Island was granted to the owners and caused such an uproar among those who regarded the island a bird sanctuary (or a pristine and special place that ought to be left alone) that the issuance was immediately appealed and a fund set up to finance that process.

A public hearing was held in September regarding whether to undertake the construction of a municipal sewer. The voters were against it, 201 to 137.

In October of 1989, islanders found themselves pondering a proposal from an Oklahoma company to build an ethanol plant at the site of the town dump, a proposal for which they tried to make a strong case, but my recollection is that the degree to which they hoped to sell the proposition to a population they felt ill-informed was a little transparent. The proposal was rejected by the selectmen.

The year 1989 ended with the town in some turmoil. The town manager, two years on the job, had resigned, citing difficulties with members of the board. The Sheep Island controversy was raging. Our roads had been neglected for too long and were in terrible shape. We had no licensed plumbing inspector, and the issuances of some building permits were stalled as a result. The town was faced with deciding whether and where to build a new airstrip or extend the existing one. The fish plant many of us had been very enthusiastic about had gone belly-up, leaving the town embroiled in its residual obligations and trying to find a new and solvent tenant, and the suggestion that we needed a municipal sewer struck some as irrefutable and others as outrageous. At a town meeting to discuss the subject, we selectmen who supported the idea were imaginatively characterized by someone as Nazis.

In 1989 twenty-three million pounds of lobster were landed in Maine by 6,200 license holders, and the price was $2.55 per pound.

1990

A LOCAL GROUP CALLING ITSELF SEAFARE negotiated a deal with the town to reopen the fish plant. They intended to cook, peel, freeze, and ship shrimp, but those plans fell through before they even got off the ground.

A Thanksgiving storm paralyzed the island for days, leaving us without power. Hundreds of trees came down in and around town and volunteers fanned out to provide firewood and assistance to those needing it.

A proposal for a municipal solar aquatic sewer treatment plant, the most comprehensive yet, was pitched to the town, but again voted down.

Reverend and Mrs. Roland Arno announced plans to leave the island. Their contributions to the church and to this community were compared favorably to those of Ray and Judy Blaisdell, a high and well deserved compliment.

The most recent town manager having only lasted for a few months of turmoil, the board of selectmen found itself again considering applicants for that position and, coincidentally, for that of fire chief. Additionally, the board's plate was full of other pressing matters. More proposals for the cursed town-owned fish plant and for the waterfront lot it occupied were being considered, as was the question of whether to again forge ahead with plans for a municipal sewer. The State Bureau of Water Quality Control had sent a letter giving the town till January 5, 1990 to comply with its directive that, one way or another, we address the issue of a municipal sewer and treatment facility, but the town didn't even publish the letter in the *Wind* until January 24. In February the voters finally approved the most recent proposal. We'd also been dealing, for some time, with the issue of overcrowding at the municipal offices, which were being shared with the fire department. Things were so tight that the town clerk was doing business from her home, the only place where room could be found. In February the suggestion was first heard that the town offices move to the Washington School to make more room for the fire department.

A joint caucus of the Republicans and Democrats was held, a first.

Sixty-eight islanders petitioned the selectmen to drop the appeal against the owners of Sheep Island and let them proceed with their plans, contending that pursuit of that action was costing the town too much, whereupon the VLT submitted an open letter to the *Wind* explaining that, notwithstanding that petition, the selectmen did not have the luxury of overturning a decision of the planning or appeals board or of stopping an appeal mid-process.

John Spear was hired as town manager. When asked during the interview how he viewed his responsibilities, he memorably replied, "I am a servant of the board of selectmen."

1990

In April of 1990 the bandstand was knocked off its foundation by a drunk driver, and a subsequent "Observer" column lamented its destruction and reminded us of its history.

Photo: Provided by the Vinalhaven Historical Society

OBSERVATIONS

A lengthy column called "Save the Earth," unsigned but full of useful information, much of it ahead of its time, began early in 1990 and ran for a while.

SAVE THE EARTH

If just 25% of American homes used 10 fewer plastic bags a month, we'd save over 2.5 BILLION bags a year. The kitchen is a good place to start integrating an environmental consciousness into your everyday life. By substituting environmentally sound kitchen products and practices for unsound ones, you can help conserve resources and play a part in changing America's habits.

DID YOU KNOW Coffee filters, paper towels, etc., are white because they're bleached? The process of bleaching is responsible for creating dioxin, a deadly toxin which has been dumped into American waterways. To make plastic wrap cling, manufacturers add "plasticizers," potentially harmful chemicals that can work their way into your food.

Tuesday Music Nights at the Mill Race were ongoing and wildly popular.

Fox Islands Seafood, comprised of some local entrepreneurs, was granted a five-year lease of the old fish plant. They hoped to be in operation by May.

A pink flowering crabapple tree was planted in the Earth Day Garden at the school in memory of Billie Jo Littlefield, who'd recently passed away at the age of seven.

The Coast Guard offered a thirty-year renewable lease to whichever serious and reliable candidate could be found to restore Heron Neck Lighthouse.

Jim Grumbach, responding to an earlier "Observer" column that addressed his having purchased two used fire engines from the town's fire department, sent the following explanation to the *Wind*.

> I would like to comment on your recent report that I was the successful bidder on the two older fire trucks. "Success" is a difficult word to qualify. If I bid on two trucks in the hope of getting one, am I doubly successful if I get two, especially when my wife wants neither? Since I now own both trucks and, although it is clear that I am a fire truck buff, others, including some close relatives, have concluded that I'm still crazy after all these years. Concerning the report that the trucks will return to my home in Pennsylvania, I would very much like to see the trucks continue their residency on the island and I hope they will be welcome at parades and picnics. However, if I don't sell one of them soon, neither they nor I will have a home in Pennsylvania.

Thank you for allowing me to set the record straight, and I hope you will observe the trucks on the 4th of July as I have for the last 20 years. It was that memory and my love for the island that prompted me to throw marital and fiscal caution to the wind (get it) and bid on the trucks.

From the sofa, Jim Grumbach

Tim Sample performed at the Union Church in August. Before he was to come up on stage the phone could be heard ringing downstairs in the vestry where he was waiting. A moment later Tim came out of the wings, scanned the audience inquiringly, and asked in his very best Downeast drawl, "Is Franklin Philbrook here?" Franklin was there, and very, very shy. He raised his hand hesitantly and Tim said, "Look heah. Corrie…," "She's the sitter," he explained to the rest of us, by way of an aside, and then continued, "Corrie wants to know if little Alice can stay up and watch *Peter Pan*." Franklin nodded his red-faced acquiescence and Tim went downstairs to deliver the message before returning to be introduced.

In September one of our own young men, critically ill and hospitalized, wrote a stirring and mindful thank-you for the attention he'd received.

> Thank you! To everyone for all the nice cards, thoughts, prayers, encouragement, flowers, and gifts that I received due to my recent illness. It has meant a great deal to me. If all of you could see your-selves as I've been privileged to, then perhaps there would be more self-love here. I wish there were more words to convey my feelings, but they elude me at this time. Anyway, take care and God Bless.
> — Dana Thomas.

Now that the town had finally adopted a plan for constructing a municipal sewer, the Environmental Protection Agency announced it had run out of money in the 1991 budget. Talks were underway to find a resolution.

Pastor Bob Genovicz and family arrived on island and began another popular ministry.

Ivan Calderwood, over ninety, published *Patchet, the Country Boy*, his ninth book about Vinalhaven.

A Superior Court judge ruled that the owners of Sheep Island could, without disturbing nesting birds, build on a half-acre portion of the thirty-three acre island and occupy it except for the period from April 1 through June 30.

A proposal having been presented for expansion of the existing airstrip facility, four hundred islanders petitioned the town to reconsider the airport issue, revealing that most were not in favor of an expanded facility, particularly one not owned or controlled by the town.

The Community School Enrichment Committee began a popular program of cultural events.

A very scary and remote nighttime fire destroyed the year-round Green's Island home of a family of four, all of whom escaped.

In 1990 twenty-eight million pounds of lobster were landed in Maine by 6,600 license holders, and the price was $2.20 per pound.

1991

THE OBSERVER BEGAN TO TAKE ON AN HISTORICAL FLAVOR, with interesting columns describing boat building, formation of the Maine Lobstermen's Association, ice harvesting, cooking, the mental hospital at Widow's Island, and myriad other items of interest, some having no connection to Vinalhaven, i.e., the history of Valentine's Day and of Groundhog Day. It also reported in March that three local fellows, under the watchful eye of a half-ton bull (dad?), rescued a baby seal from a shallow well it had fallen into, and that the math team, under teacher/coach Pete Pedersen, was in third place in Maine and on its way to the New England Math Meet.

The board of selectmen issued this travel advisory:

"Don't park in the middle of the road to take pictures, pick flowers, or pick up litter. It's dangerous."

The Boy Scouts had by now planted a hundred disease-resistant elms, and were intent on planting that many again in 1992.

The ARC, ahead of its time since inception, began a series of programs called "Solid Waste Solutions," each featuring practical solutions to a growing problem.

Captain Ambrose Peterson offered pleasant day cruises to see the puffins on Matinicus Rock, to Isle au Haut, or around Vinalhaven aboard the *Lively Lady*, later named the *Capn's Lady*.

A local guy, quiet, humble, grounded, dry as a rasp, won a $3.5 million lottery. We all knew, of course; the news spread like smelt rushing upstream, but after a few initial congratulations and only very moderate acknowledgements in return we stopped talking about it. We knew he was uncomfortable with the whole business. After a few months he had one side of his house vinyl sided, and after a decent interval, one that would not leave anyone thinking he was extravagant, he bought a new second-hand truck with naugahyde seat covers. A few months later he invited the whole town to attend a concert featuring the Old Time Radio Gang, provided free admission, paid the band's expenses, and provided soft drinks and refreshments. That was over twenty years ago. We haven't heard anything since and don't expect to, but he suddenly passed away, far too early, and then more heartache settled in as a daughter died after a long illness, and a grandson died unexpectedly.

The issue of Tree Growth exemptions and the resultant additional tax burden got a lot of press.

Artificial bait, promised to last two weeks, was introduced.

A dental clinic opened at the Medical Center.

The usual coastal cleanup, accomplished, as always, by youngsters recruited for the occasion, yielded, in a certain quadrant, four bags of trash, half of what had been collected a couple of years earlier in the same area and thus a cause for celebration.

The fish plant had a new tenant by year's end: Claw Island Seafood. It wasn't clear what happened to Fox

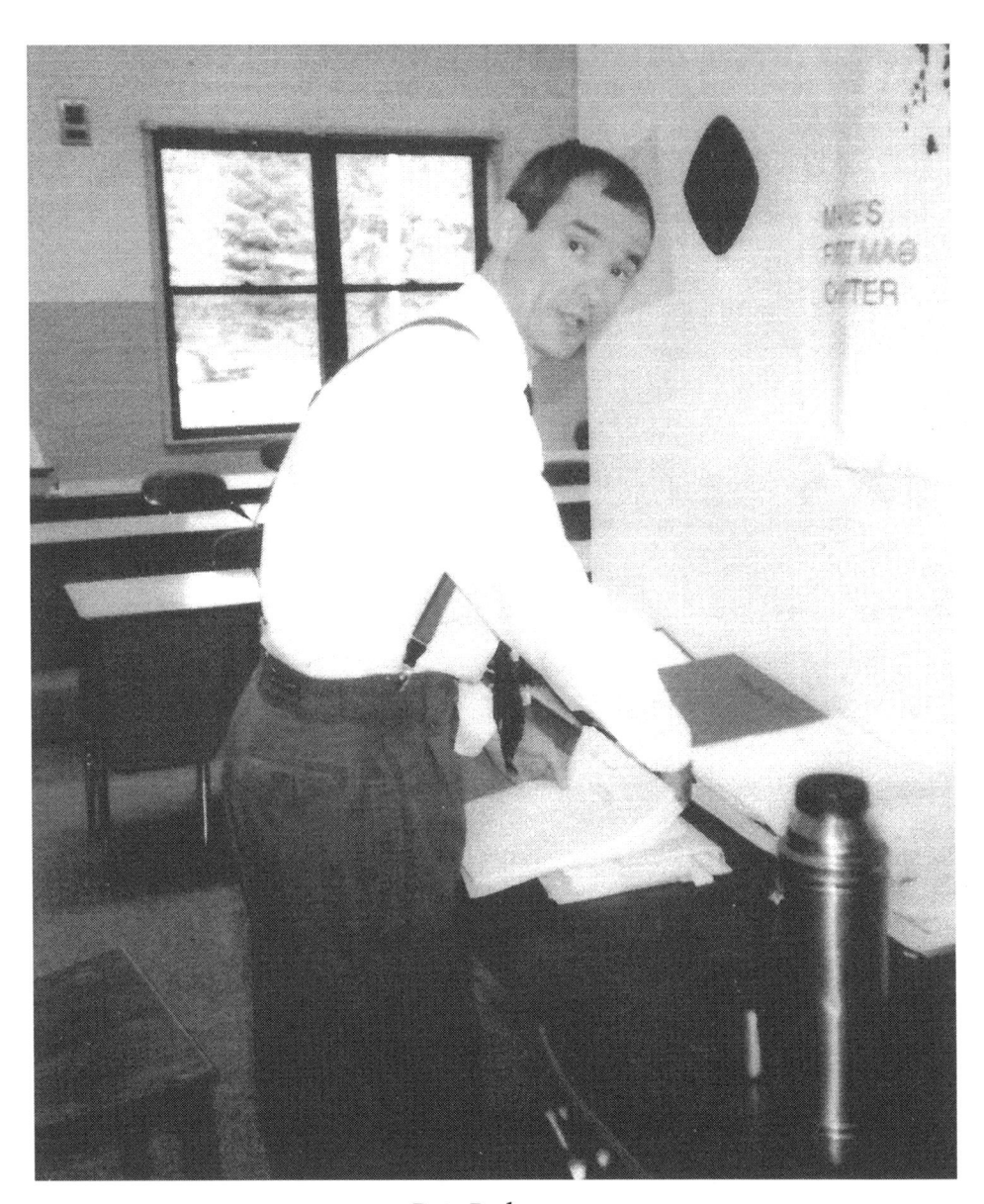

Pete Pedersen
Photo: Provided by the Vinalhaven Historical Society

The math team continued to astonish, beating schools twice their size or more, being invited to meets all over the country, and setting individual records left and right. Teacher Pete Pedersen was invited to Washington D.C. to receive the prestigious Escalante Award for great achievements in math instruction.

OBSERVATIONS

Island Seafood, but Claw Island appeared a lot more stable than its predecessors.

The state, involved in difficult negotiations with its Department of Transportation workers, announced plans to furlough ferry service employees and to forego fifty-four days of ferry service in the upcoming six months.

The "Public Notices" column that had been authored by the selectmen or by someone at their behest became the "Town Report," and labor and management continued to play brinksmanship with the impending furlough of ferry workers and the expected fifty-four days without ferry service.

A state-ordered mandate to shut down grandfathered landfills, including our own, was put off till December 31, 1992.

Touch-tone telephone service arrived on island but there was a big price to pay. Henceforth all seven digits (!) would need to be dialed for local calls instead of only the last four we'd been long accustomed to. It seemed an enormous hurdle.

The folks who live around Old Harbor issued this apology to some visitors who were shamefully treated:

> The residents of Old Harbor would like to apologize to the owners of the S/V *Safari* for their unfortunate and regrettable experience while spending a few nights moored in our beautiful harbor. They came ashore in their dinghy and tied it up at the float on Pierce's Point and went bicycling to the Thorofare. Upon their return they discovered their boat had been removed from the float, their oarlocks were gone, and the boat had a hole in it. We hope the *Safari* owner's conversation with one of Old Harbor's lobsterman conveyed the outrage we feel at the treatment they received.

In 1991 thirty-one million pounds of lobster were landed in Maine by 6,800 license holders, and the price was $2.35 per pound.

1992

IN 1992, AN INTERESTING BIT OF HISTORY was given more than two pages when Bill Chilles offered a letter he'd received from Ted Maddox, his great uncle and my grandfather, ten years earlier when, as a boy, Bill had inquired about Ted's experience as a fireman aboard the early steamers that had served these islands.

Dear Bill,

I promised you I would dredge up some of my recollections and experiences in the steamboat service on Penobscot Bay. I hope the following will be of use to you in the research you are doing.

I will not attempt to account for all the steamers that have served our island of Vinalhaven, beginning with the doughty little *Pioneer* and ending with the *William S. White,* a history of service spanning nearly 100 years.

Instead, I will relate some of my experiences as fireman on the two best known ships, with the longest service records, namely: the *Vinalhaven* and the *Governor Bodwell*.

Our present ferries are practical and utilitarian, pared down to load cars and people in as efficient a way as possible. But the two above-mentioned steamers were designed to serve the public with grace and dignity.

Picture, if you will, the scene at Tillson's Wharf in Rockland in the early 1920s, as the deckhands manhandle dollies loaded with freight down water-slicked ramps to the main deck where crewmates swiftly pack cartons, boxes, bales, and crates of merchandise, feed, groceries, and small livestock into the roomy freight storage area.

The cavernous roofed-over wharf is alive with the smell of brine, tar, and salt water. Passengers are arriving from the railway station after an all-night trip from Boston.

The ticket agent with his stiff black-visored cap is passing out tickets stamped *Vinalhaven-Rockland Steamboat Line*, and the deckhands are wrestling some of the larger travelling bags and trunks down the ramp for storage below.

With their hand luggage and smaller suitcases the passengers cross an elevated gangway to the salon deck, the second deck above the water line. Here they can relax in genuine comfort in the largest room on the ship, popularly called "the saloon."

Surrounded by windows, it boasts oak chairs with velour upholstery, fine carpets, paneled walls, spanking white paint, and highly polished brass fittings.

If any of the ladies become indisposed during the voyage, they can retire to the "Ladies Cabin" on the main deck, aft of the galley and mess room.

A private retreat much appreciated by lady voyagers, this comfortable room is furnished in wicker, colorfully upholstered; there are plenty of chairs and a sofa or two, tables, curtains to draw over spray-flecked windows or portholes, and wall-to-wall carpeting. Adjacent is an immaculate lavatory with all the essential fixtures.

Two more restrooms for both gentlemen and ladies open off the "saloon" on the deck above.

Just outside the Ladies Cabin, and aft of the mess room, a wide carpeted stairway with polished brass handrails leads up to the saloon. Passengers pass up and down, investigating the ship, greeting friends from previous trips, conscious of the mounting excitement as sailing time nears.

The purser in his smart uniform emerges from his office aft of the saloon. His stateroom is there, too. Soon he will be fulfilling his unofficial duty as purveyor of good will to the sea-going public. In fact, he is the ticket collector, but in practice, he recalls names, voyages, marriages, deaths, college-bound offspring, and those unfortunate few among the passengers who are inclined to be seasick.

The activity below on the main deck reaches a peak. The deckhands are working against the clock. Unlike the travelers now climbing to the open top deck for a better view of the harbor and wharf, these men are unconscious of their picturesque surroundings.

They work, eat, and sleep on the freight deck. Here in the bow is the chain locker with its anchor chain and towing cable. Just aft of that dark compartment is the forecastle with racks of bunks where the crew can stretch out for a well-earned sleep, separated from the noise and heat of the boiler room by a water-tight bulkhead.

On either side of the great boiler are the coal bunkers, each holding six tons of the black fuel. I am shoveling it at top speed as the engineer watches the gauge, bringing the pressure up in preparation for sailing.

If we are on the *Vinalhaven*, the shoveling is hard but not exhausting because this vessel has a Roberts boiler and a compound engine. The large boiler and 120-horsepower engine make a very easy steaming unit.

If, however, we are on the *Bodwell* today, I have already worked up a fine sweat, because she has a small Almy boiler and a large 220-horsepower engine, demanding the best I can give.

It is essential, even crucial, that we keep the steam pressure up, because the ship depends on that pressure to run the compass courses at the required speed and precisely on time.

I know that in the galley there are smells rising now other than coal, steam, and sweat. The cook will be preparing a hearty meal for the crew accompanied by a hot biscuit and a rich Indian pudding or Plum Duff.

As soon as we sail, the deckhands will crowd into the mess room to chow down. The galley is just beyond this boiler room and the mess room is between the galley and the luxurious Ladies Cabin.

As soon as the crew is finished, the tables will be scrubbed down and reset, and those passengers who wish will be fed the same delicious meal in a more leisurely fashion.

High above, on the top, or boat deck, a crewman has just run a quick check on the two lifeboats hanging from their davits. Nearby is a sturdy workboat and a canvas life raft. Everything is in apple pie order, and ready for instant use.

Forward of the saloon the deckhouse stands like a detached structure, its interior divided by the pilot house across the front and two fine staterooms at the rear. These lofty perches belong to the Captain and his First Mate.

Both are in the pilot house now; both are in uniform. They are figures to inspire confidence.

Today will be a fine crossing; it is summer, just a little Southwest haze, but good visibility. We will hit our compass marks dead on.

It is not always so.

I have fired this ship in fog and gales when our pilot had nothing to rely on but his own skill as a navigator and my strong back feeding coal in to keep the pressure up in the boiler.

The Captain has never heard of Radar, Loran, or Radio. In a fog he sets his course by compass and by the time elapsed between buoys. For example, from a certain bell buoy on a course of NNE ¼ E it would take twenty minutes at a constant speed of 12 knots to reach bell buoy number two.

You can see how, at night, or in fog, that sustained speed is essential to insure safe navigation.

Today we are making our second trip across the bay from Rockland to North Haven, then on to Vinalhaven. It is now four o'clock as we pull away from the Maine Central Wharf with a deep blast of our whistle. It will be after six before we tie up in Vinalhaven.

We have been on board since six this morning when we came down to the island dock and woke the sleeping deckhands in their forward berths.

For this summer run we need a Captain, Mate, Engineer, fireman, three seamen, a cook, and a mess boy. In winter we take on an extra fireman and a quartermaster.

In spring and fall I will be on the *Vinalhaven*, making one round trip a day between Rockland and Vinalhaven, while the *Governor Bodwell* makes the North Haven run.

But I mentioned winter a minute ago. It's the winters that make or break you. From December until April I will be firing on the *Bodwell* as she takes over the entire Island run from one end of Penobscot Bay to the other.

Our winters in these early '20s are the coldest on record.

We will come aboard in darkness at Swan's Island in that bitter cold, fire up and get the boiler hot, load our freight and passengers, and head out at six o'clock before the sun comes up. On, then, to Stonington, North Haven, Vinalhaven, and Rockland.

We take pride in keeping pretty much to schedule, fair weather or foul. But when the Thorofare freezes we can't land at North Haven. So when that happens we come direct from Swan's Island to Vinalhaven, load on freight and passengers, then swing out around the treacherous ledges of Lane's Island and run down the eastern bay to Stonington.

More often than not we find that harbor ice-locked, too. So we stand off and put our freight and passengers down on the ice, where horse-drawn sleds come out to carry them ashore.

OBSERVATIONS

One February morning in 1923, the *Governor Bodwell* left Swan's Island and couldn't get back for three weeks. That's how brutal the cold was. During that time only Vinalhaven and Stonington had service and much of that over the ice.

As a matter of fact, on one of those trips that winter we were three days making the circuit, because the ice caught us two miles from Stonington and there we sat for twenty-six hours, prisoners of the cold.

Still, we gave it our best, all year-round, concerned for the comfort and safety of our passengers.

Those trim ships with their commodious interiors, quiet, dependable steam engines, and skilled pilots offered an experience many Mainers recall with affection today.

It's not 1924, is it, Bill? Now the bay is full of diesels and outboard motors.

With the passing of the steamboat from Maine coastal waters an interesting era in our maritime history came to an end, an era that diesel engines cannot revive. The blast of a deep-throated steam whistle and the jingle of the pilot's bells, as those white ships slid gracefully into the landing, are sorely missed by those of us who were part of it.

Good luck and best wishes, Uncle Ted

The town had some time ago placed trash barrels strategically in the town parking lot and on the sidewalk but, because a few individuals continually stopped at those to drop off their household trash, the selectmen voted to discontinue them, a dubious move which, while denying those few individuals the freedom they'd abused, left the rest of us, particularly our summer visitors, with no choice but to pocket rubbish or throw it on the ground. Main Street quickly became a mess.

The town entered into an agreement with the owners of the airstrip property to acquire twenty-six acres, including the strip, and voted to name the new ferry the *Captain Charles Philbrook*.

Claw Island began hiring, a promising sign.

In late November the Union Church Trustees, mindful of some controversy regarding content, harmoniously ended their formal relationship with the *Wind*. Henceforth the paper, while it continued to be prepared and edited in the church vestry, would be an independent organization.

An AIDS awareness program got underway.

The Vinalhaven math team beat all contending east/west conference schools on their way to securing a place in the New England Tournament scheduled for May of 1993.

The Island Community Ambulance Service, independent from the town and from the Islands Community Medical Services (ICMS), and the first iteration of today's EMT service, was organized.

Right after Christmas, Bruce Grindle, another institution, passed away at ninety-three. When the Memorial Hall was torn down years earlier, the single most ill-considered and grievous action this town has ever undertaken, Bruce had written a little memorial of his own, lamenting:

Gay times, show times, operetta, dances, graduations, fairs, town meetings (including dinner), every event held there was perfect material for fond memories. It is with a heavy heart that I watch the

1992

destruction of the Memorial Hall, a building that has meant so much to so many. Its like we will never see again.

The following tribute to Bruce had been penned six years earlier by my mother and published in the *Island Journal.*

> It seems incredible that in a few short years we have seen the passing of the old-fashioned soda fountain, quickly followed by its revival as an expensive boutique. Along with soda fountains went the old-fashioned drugstore, the place where some fast-talking kid could get a hold of sulfur, saltpeter, and a test tube — a day or two before word about it filtered down (or up) to the folks. And nearly gone, too, are the real hardware stores. You know the ones — if you're old enough. They stocked forged tools in bins, nails by the keg, raw duck (canvas) by the roll, iron stove parts, and, somewhere in back, a box of buttonhooks, a rack of scythe, and newel-post stops. Not seldom would there be a large, round coal stove encircled by deeply polished chairs of assorted vintage, regularly occupied by the experienced and wise. Though the coal stove (and the spittoon) are gone, the rest of the ancient picture remains true to type at Fifield's Store, on Vinalhaven. Here, in an age of reproductions, originals hide in the inventory with the old trade secrets as to their care and use. Here are advice and history and a piece of mandatory candy. Pass by the store and your passing will be remarked. Pass into the store and you will be in a remarkable place.
>
> One morning last winter I was awakened in predawn darkness by the sound of whistling. I shoved my feet into my slippers and padded through the silent apartment to a front window overlooking Vinalhaven's Main Street.
>
> Overhead the stars wheeled in their courses, cold and distant. Black water boiled under the Main Street Bridge, rushing into Carver's Pond from the sea. My indoor-outdoor thermometer told me it was six above, and my ship's clock struck three bells: 5:30 a.m.
>
> As I watched and listened, a familiar figure stepped into the pool of light under a nearby telephone pole: Bruce Grindle, eighty-six years old and legally blind, was whistling himself to work at Fifield's Hardware Store, as he has every workday morning since 1946.
>
> A handknit scarf fluttered behind him as he leaned into the wind, punctuating each step with a jaunty swing of his cane. And as he walked, he whistled.
>
> Suddenly the cold morning seemed much warmer.
>
> Diagonally across the street I could see the welcoming lights of the hardware store spreading a glow over the icy sidewalk. A few minutes earlier, Bruce's younger cousin and partner, Clinton "Kim" Smith, seventy-one, had unlocked the front door to admit the first visitor of the day, Louis Martin.
>
> I watched until Bruce was safely inside, then crept back to the comfort of my bed. But I didn't sleep. I thought about that store, about the two men who ran it and how they came to be there. Fifield's has no affiliation with big-name hardware conglomerates. It is a bastion of a vanishing institution, the family-run emporium.

OBSERVATIONS

A liberal sprinkling of handmade posters adorns the two plate-glass show windows. A perusal of these announcements will keep the interested passerby current on most events in town. From the impressive front door with the store name in dignified gold to the dim reaches of the windowless back room, every conceivable item an islander might need is stacked or hung.

The visiting summer artist is surprised to find aspiring local painters as well outfitted with brushes, oils, or watercolors as he himself, courtesy of Fifield's. The gardener comes for potting soil, fertilizer, and advice from this town clearing house.

For everything from canning kettles to ice skates, breadboxes to picture hooks, customers old and new come to browse and buy, confident that owners Smith and Grindle will be holding court as usual.

From 1929 until 1946, their uncle, Irving "Babbin" Fifield, owned the store and operated it with an occasional assist from his sister-in-law. The war years were hard. Babbin was growing older, new merchandise was hard to come by, and he had no sons to follow in his footsteps.

True, there were nephews. His wife had two sisters, each of whom had a son. But they couldn't help. The elder, Bruce, was working in a defense-related electronics firm in Southbridge, Massachusetts, while Kim, who had worked for four years at the Bath shipyard, was drafted in 1943 and went overseas to Europe.

When the war ended, Kim found himself routed through Fort Devens on his way to civilian life and home. On impulse, he decided to detour to Southbridge to see Bruce before heading back to Vinalhaven. To his surprise, he found his cousin packing up, too. He had just given his notice at the electronics plant, with no particular plans for the future except to yield to the inner call to return to the island he loved. The two men, separated by sixteen years but joined by their longing for home, returned together to find their uncle in failing health.

Bruce went into the store at once, and was joined by Kim a few months later. In June 1946, the two bought I.W. Fifield's store from Babbin's widow, and a Main Street institution was born.

Alone and childless, the two men, different in temperament and personality, have gradually made the residents of the island community their family. Since 1963, Kim has been town clerk, his cramped office at the rear of the store a Mecca for anyone researching a family genealogy or curious about local history. Customers know they may have to wait if Kim is "out back" issuing a hunting license or registering a birth.

While they wait, Bruce will extend the hospitality unique to Fifield's. From a cast-iron skillet he dispenses an assortment of candies, heavy on butterscotch drops and candy corn. If the wait is a long one, he may suggest that the customer pull up a chair and peruse the dozens of photo albums filled with Polaroid pictures of townspeople, summer residents, grandparents and children, baby-sitters and their charges, all in living color and all with a look of special pride at being included in Bruce's "Rogues Gallery."

The most current crop of snapshots is always displayed on a makeshift bulletin board just inside the front door. As each batch is taken down, it goes into an album. Every one of these hundreds of pictures was taken inside the store.

From his customary chair [second from the right in a row of six that march down the right-hand aisle of the store, see photo on page 57], Bruce waits for the daily visits from dozens of island children. They come for a pat on the head or a hug, a new winter cap, warm mittens, or a bag of oranges, raisins, and pantry cookies, dispensed with heartfelt comments on the child's special nature and attributes.

The row of chairs, which effectively blocks any use of the right-hand aisle for shopping purposes, is referred to by Kim and Bruce as "the pecking order." A recognized forum has been established here for individual opinion, social exchange, and current information on any subject.

Except when the weather is foul, Bruce delivers cookies and candy to the clerks and secretaries working in Main Street businesses. If a storm keeps him in, he sends a younger man to deliver the tokens of his esteem.

Kim reads, watches TV, and putters in his workshop when he's home. The puttering led to a sideline he now pursues with enthusiasm: framing. Townspeople and summer people bring him their artwork, diplomas, cartoons, and mementos to be preserved.

Bruce used to play the saxophone; he was an avid reader and enjoyed discussing the nonfiction he preferred, but his loss of sight has made him turn outward for interest and stimulation. Daily he makes a morning visit to all the Main Street restaurants, for breakfast, or muffins, or just a cup of coffee.

Coming and going, he whistles. Everyone who passes him greets him by name. But his real joy is to be in the store, to meet people there, and to wait for the children.

"Who's this?" he cries, as a mother urges a small child forward. "Who's this little darling?"

Someone asked Kim what has meant the most to him during these 40 years in business.

His answer required no thought.

"Why, just to be here; to be able to be here, at home."

Pat Crossman continues her freelance writing career as an avocation, a call to wordsmithing in the midst of a busy life. Since her work last appeared in these pages, she has been published again in Good Housekeeping and the National Baptist Magazine. Currently Pat serves as chairman of the Vinalhaven Library.

Courtesy of the *Island Journal*, Vol. 3, 1986

In 1992 twenty-seven million pounds of lobster were landed in Maine by 6,100 license holders, and the price was $2.68 per pound.

OBSERVATIONS

1993

GRANT DUELL ANNOUNCED THAT HE WAS FED UP with the continuing destruction of the bandstand and was retiring as the person who voluntarily replaced spindles day after day. The board of selectmen then published an appeal for a replacement volunteer to "replace spindles in the bandstand as they are destroyed."

Our new ferry, the *Captain Charles Philbrook*, arrived in May.

Conlan Plumbing received an interesting congratulatory note having to do with an oil-burnerman exam, but nothing in the note made it clear he'd passed.

Our math team, having placed first or second in countless Maine and New England competitions, was headed for a major Hawaiian tournament in August.

A subscription to the *Wind* was now twenty dollars, personal ads, three, and business ads were five.

Lawson's Quarry closed when it was found to harbor e-coli and reopened a month later when tests revealed it to be OK.

"An Evening with the Artist" was now in its tenth popular year at the ARC.

Heron Neck Lighthouse was transferred to the Island Institute.

Pete Pedersen was named the top math teacher in Maine and invited to Washington D.C. in April when the nation's top teacher would be announced.

The *Wind* published its balance sheet relecting a $1,037 loss, and reprinted an essay I'd written for the *Inter-Island News* (now the *Working Waterfront*).

A Season of Upheavals

Usually it's March before island communities find their nerves on edge. By that time rough ferry rides, isolation, endless winds, cold, and the strain of making ends meet have taken their toll. But it's only the beginning of December, and a lot of folks here on Vinalhaven are edgy already. Too much is changing all at once.

In the last few months we've lost a town manager and hired a new one, lost a school principal and hired a new one, acquired a new ferry untested in winter weather, and similarly an untested new pilot on our air route. We are losing our doctor and getting a new one, and the new occupant of the town-owned fish processing facility is so upset with the town that it has threatened to abandon ship. Too much of what is familiar is vanishing too quickly, and too much of what is not is arriving too quickly.

The loss of our doctor, who's been with us for nearly twenty years and has delivered or been involved in the births of over three hundred babies, tended thousands of mishaps, and who is intimately familiar with most of our frailties, has submitted his resignation. More telling, the board of trustees of the Medical Center has accepted it, and, perhaps more telling still, he has not withdrawn it. This loss is affecting the town in a very emotional and heartfelt way. It wasn't too long ago that Vinalhaven made such noise over the fact that the National Health Service planned to withdraw Dr. Greg O'Keefe from the island against his wishes that the whole nation helped us rally a defense against the ill-conceived action of the Federal Government. Senator Bill Cohen responded to our pleas for assistance and Dr. Greg left the NHS but stayed with us. Many in the community, and especially the older members, have grown very comfortable knowing that this doctor, this "known quantity," is here and knows their health so intimately. So why is he going? No one is telling. The several members of the 20-member board of trustees with whom I've spoken have politely declined to talk about specifics, but offer assurances that they are acting on behalf of us all. Several have intimated that the "whole story" will be made public eventually. These are people whose opinions, especially in such numbers, carry some weight. There is, in fact, a time and place to accept our representatives at their word and not go after the truth at all costs in blind pursuit of the "right to know." I'm just not sure this is one of those moments. Unfortunately, neither am I sure it isn't.

Meanwhile, just when Vinalhaven appeared to have an economically viable occupant in the town-owned fish plant, Claw Island Seafoods notified the town that it is withholding rent and the board of selectmen has responded by unanimously voting to evict them from the premises at the expiration of the thirty-day grace period called for by the lease if they have not by then cured the default.

Claw Island appears to have built a potentially profitable business here at the plant which stood vacant and/or unprofitable for so long. Now, for the second time in a year, they are at loggerheads with the board of selectmen over the issue of responsibility for major repairs or replacements to the plant. Last year, the roof was discovered to be failing. Claw Island insisted the town fix it at town expense. The town refused, claiming it was clearly the intent of the lease that in return for the exceedingly low monthly rent ($1,200), Claw Island has assumed responsibility for all repairs: regardless of the extent. A petition was circulated which compelled the board to make the roof repairs in the "spirit of good will and cooperation" which was called for in the lease. A subsequent town vote cemented that initiative.

Unhappily, neither the town nor Claw Island took any subsequent steps to negotiate the clear difference of opinion that created the dfficulty in the first place, and now the boiler has failed. Claw Island again maintains that this is the responsibility of the town; the town has denied it. Claw Island has notified the town that it intends to withhold rent and to take action to compel the town to assume the approximate $25,000 cost of replacing the boiler, the $230 a day rental of a temporary unit and the $8,000 cost of its installation. The board of selectmen, in turn, voted to have them evicted if the rent deficiency is not cured within the 30-day grace period.

In the last few days, common sense has reappeared and cooler heads have begun negotiations that may culminate in Claw Island eventually acquiring title to the plant thus eliminating the touchy subject of responsibility for repairs. Such an eventuality would require a vote of the town. Let's hope this effort is successful. The level at which the two parties now conduct their affairs testifies to the speed with which this relationship, which was conceived in a spirit of mutual economic cooperation, has soured. If the marriage can be saved, let's save it. We can all only benefit as a result.

In 1993 thirty million pounds of lobster were landed in Maine by 5,800 license holders, and the price was $2.47 per pound.

OBSERVATIONS

1994

TRUE NATIVES are those who can claim to have been born and brought up on the island, and who have only ventured far-afield long enough to realize what a mistake it would be not to return quickly. Until now island doctors had routinely conducted home deliveries but the last such intended birth took place in 1994. Since then, while there have been plenty of midwife assisted home deliveries, those involving discerning moms who know what a blemish a mainland delivery is to a child's later claim to pedigree, no children have been born at home by pre-arrangement with the medical center.

Although I've neglected to acknowledge it thus far, a column called "Weather on Carver's Pond" had been a regular weekly feature for several years. Unsigned, it was more than a simple recital of conditions but rather described, often taking an entire column page length, the behavior of wildlife, circumstances incidental to the weather, sea conditions, and the author's personal relationship to the climate.

> On Christmas Day we awoke to find about an inch of snow on the ground. It was a pleasant day, some sun, temperature in the 30s. More snow on Sunday plus wind. Monday was frigid, 0 degrees low, 10 degrees high. Sea smoke shrouded the harbor. Got out the hair dryer to thaw out freezing pipes. Stoked up the wood stove. Went to bed early to get away from the howling sound of wind. Tuesday, some improvement. Wednesday 0 again. On Thursday morning we found 5 to 6 inches of snow and high winds. The first ferry was cancelled. The temperature on New Year's Eve Day was 16/32. A beautiful full moon that night. On New Year's Day the temperature rose to 39 degrees and on Sunday there was an early "January thaw." When we awoke the snow was all gone and the high was 47 degrees! That didn't last. Monday was gray and bitter cold. The final "blow" of this period was a Nor'easter that roared in at 35 to 50 mph early Tuesday morning bringing several inches of snow plus sleet, stopping the ferry (12' to 20' seas), and making the roads almost impassable despite the efforts of the highway crew. Some gusts of 70 mph shook the house and blew wood smoke back down the chimney.

Yearning to brighten a bleak winter, a group of enlightened locals gathered for an evening with poet Ruth Fox. It was a delightful time, and the "Hunker Down Cultural Society" was born. Two island authors, my brother David Crossman and Wendy Lord, each published first books. David wrote *Murder in a Minor Key* and Wendy penned two children's books, *Pickle Stew* and *Gorilla on the Midway*.

Brud Carver and Jack Waterbury were out on the ice with their iceboats early in the year.

Raymond Alley, then a senior at Husson College, broke that school's scoring record by racking up 2,481 points during his four-year career.

The Vinalhaven Vikings won the division basketball championship and were headed for the March state championship tournament in Augusta.

Wildlife observer Marcia Davis began authoring "Nature News."

> Sunday a broad-winged hawk was attacked by a flock of crows at the Lobster Pound on Lane's Island. Dick Bennard rescued the hawk, and his wife Juanita took the bird to the Animal Rehabilitation Station run by Ray Perry of Lincolnville. Despite the rough treatment by the crows, upon

1994

examination, a sore wing was the only injury discovered by Perry. The bird is being fed mice and may be released on Saturday.

Sam Bickford, First Honor Essayist, class of 1994, wrote an extraordinary tribute to his grandfather, Clyde Bickford.

> Some of my earliest and fondest memories are of the wonderful times I spent with a man who means all the world to me. His example and influence have caused me to develop a love for the water and an interest in pursuing lobstering as a career. The hard work and enthusiasm I saw in his life have, hopefully, rubbed off on me. He has gone out of his way to help me to prepare myself for my choice of occupation. Together we have spent many, many hours repairing old wooden pots to fish with. He has been there to teach me, to guide me, and to work with me as I have expanded my business. Growing up, I can remember the hours of stories he told me about his life's experience: seining, lobstering, playing baseball for the Vinalhaven Chiefs, working on a lobster pound down east and last but not least, fighting the fire in the old Masonic Hall. These memories that he has shared with me have given me great appreciation of his life and for my heritage as a Vinalhavenite. How do I describe this man? Words seem so inadequate. But I will try, by using some that come to my mind and some that I have heard other people use to describe him. Kind, caring, thoughtful, generous, industrious — some of my words. A gentleman, a gentle man, a man of integrity, helpful, strong, honest, fair, a good citizen — words I have heard others use to describe him. He is a Mason, a faithful Lion, an active member of the Union Church, serving as both Trustee and Head Deacon for many years. He has lived an exemplary life. I can never recall hearing a cuss word or swear word come from his mouth. By now you probably have figured out that the person I am talking about is my grandfather, Clyde Lawrence Bickford. He has truly been a wholesome influence on my life as well as on many other lives. I wanted to share with all of you and with him my deep appreciation for his support, encouragement and contributions to my life. Grandpa, you're one of a kind, and always remember, I love you very much.

Bodine Ames, long a champion of the island's less fortunate and protector of our town parks, of the Lane's Island Nature Conservancy, and many of our historic artifacts, was presented a Jefferson Award for Public Service at a Bangor ceremony on March 11. Surplus food, clothing, and other assistance for those in need, such as HEAP (Home Energy Assistance Program) were steadily available thanks to her selfless efforts. They still are and the credit is still hers.

The ARCoffee House got underway in their building next to the Historical Society.

The math team and teacher Pete Pedersen were honored at the House of Representatives in Augusta in recognition of their extraordinary achievements.

Seasonal resident Scott Hamilton transmitted a real-time report of his attempt to climb Mount Everest. At the time he was still a few days from the summit. He was ultimately deprived of reaching the top due to circumstances beyond his control, those being weather and fellow climbers who were injured and had to be evacuated.

A questionnaire appeared in the *Wind* asking for suggestions about whether the town should retain ownership of the Washington School and how it might be used.

OBSERVATIONS

The MSFS published a new "Line-up Policy for Non-reservations" that included this admonition: "You can substitute one car for another but no ends sticking out."

Plans were underway to raise money to send twelve island students to Russia. They were selected from among those submitting competitive essays as part of a cultural and student exchange program. The scheduled departure date was October 3.

The July *Wind* carried an announcement that the landfill as we knew it was going to be closed, covered, and thence operated as a transfer station. Subsequent issues of the paper introduced us to and began to acquaint us with recycling and the degree to which that practice was about to become a singular issue in the life of this community and communities everywhere.

We were also alerted to an upcoming musical theater project being organized by Helen Handley and Annie Boyden, a production about the ferry. Interested parties were invited to a brainstorming session the following week. Before long everyone was recording memorable ferry experiences, material for the upcoming show, a performance that would eventually set a very high bar for island entertainment. Rehearsals for *Ferry Tales* began soon after.

The water level at Round Pond was dropping precipitously.

The generosity of many was acknowledged in an "Observer" column leading up to the October departure of students for Moscow.

> October is fast approaching and our students will be on their way to a new and unforgettable experience. Randy Knowlton reports that the preparations are completed. The down payment has been made on the air fares and the visas are all in proper order. More than half of the tickets for the car raffle have been sold. Harold Ralph, the donor of the 1988 Chevy Celebrity, has been selling the tickets at his place of business in Waldoboro. Incidentally, the car was an outright gift and has cost nothing. The young people have worked hard to earn money and have planned two more suppers, one on August 6 and one on September 2, both at the Union Church. Annette Philbrook has knitted a large, beautiful afghan and two local fishermen have donated a total of fifty pounds of lobsters to the cause. Raffle tickets for these are now available. The twelve students are studying Russian with three qualified tutors and will be able to converse easily with their host families come October. They are also being indoctrinated in the food and accommodations they will find in Russia. They will be staying in normal Russian homes, on the outskirts of Moscow, in a small village. The auction, which was all profit, brought in more than $3,000. Merchants on the island and on the mainland were more than generous in their donations, as were other islanders. Randy said all the youngsters are grateful to all who have helped, for the moral support and the unstinting financial aid from both Islanders who make their homes here and those who are here only in the summer and to Carlene Michael who has given so much of time and material to the cause. Everyone is excited about the trip and hope that it will be one of many cultural exchanges, and that a group of young Russians will be visiting Vinalhaven.

1994

The town found itself in violation of state DEP-mandated recycling guidelines and the Town Report urged everyone to pick up a copy of *The How-To's of Recycling* and to work together to get the town in compliance by the time another review was conducted.

In October several calls were received from Moscow to confirm the kids had arrived safely.

Full service dental care became available at the medical center.

My sports column continued to appear sporadically.

> The mighty Dogtown Draggers ended their relentless drive for the pennant Sunday night in a stunning defeat of the Pequot Puffins. Puffins "Drool Ball" pitcher, Mark "Wet N Wild" Candage, was moderately effective through regulation play, holding the normally overpowering Draggers to a 5-5 tie in extra innings. However, the Draggers cashed in on their considerable reserve of offensive skills and uncanny hitting. Second baseman Sharon Philbrook, cool through the early season and plagued by injuries, warmed to the task, turning double plays like pancakes and throwing out one after another of the Huffin' Puffins. Clearly a dynasty in the making, the Draggers' superb mix of power hitting, incomparable fielding, and skillful pitching gave them this final 10-5 victory and the pennant.

The PTA hosted a forum, an evening featuring candidates for state and local office, a tradition that has continued but which has since been due to the singular efforts of retired history teacher Karol Kucinski.

Our students returning from Russia and the Russian kids simultaneously arriving here enjoyed a festive reception at The Haven.

The Vinalhaven Community Council became the Vinalhaven Chamber of Commerce (VHCoC).

Dr. Donahue, at a public forum, discussed the extraordinary findings of Dr. Ralph Earle who, years earlier, had documented the unusual incidence of diabetes on Vinalhaven and had, well ahead of his peers, demonstrated that it could be cured.

Longtime summer resident Eleanor Campbell gifted the area at the head of Polly Cove to the VLT.

In 1994 thirty-nine million pounds of lobster were landed in Maine by 6,200 license holders, and the price was $2.59 per pound.

OBSERVATIONS

1995

PORT O' CALL (FORMERLY I.W. FIFIELD) AND THE CROW'S NEST (NOW THE HARBOR GAWKER) OPENED. Port O' Call continued the Fifield tradition of dispensing hardware and advice, and of announcing island births. The Crow's Nest, a restaurant serving three meals a day, returned the popular music night of yesteryear with Bob Tolman, the Boydens, and Louise Bickford, and expanded that musical venue every weekend with a slate of appearances by well-known artists such as the Boneheads, Erica Wheeler, Cormac McCarthy, and Anne Dodson.

The town had been notified that it could no longer dispose of raw sewage at the landfill site formerly designated for that purpose (hard to believe isn't it?).

The Maine DOT accepted a bid for replacing the old Rockland ferry terminal.

John Ward went through the ice on Carver's Pond while on his iceboat and was rescued none too soon.

ABC Sports cast local fisherman Walter Day as a "typical Maine lobsterman" and his dog as "Old Blue" and filmed a fifteen-second spot at the Browns Head Lighthouse for a Super Bowl promo.

The math team continued their winning ways, beating all comers.

"The Observer" began to morph into a column of remembrances or the retelling of historical events, which were to remind us of how much better things were once upon a time.

[Excerpt]

School opens this week, bringing memories to some of other days, other school openings: memories of the first day of school in the little neighborhood schools, wood stoves, a communal water bucket and teacher greeting each child by name, the beautiful sunny rooms in the Washington school. The consolidated school did not come on the scene until the seventies. One hundred years ago the Supervisor of Schools was concerned about the arithmetic book being used. He announced that he had purchased White's Arithmetic and recommended disposing of the Common School Arithmetic, which he considered out of date. How his eyes would light up to see the computers in the school rooms and the library in the school building today. Support of schools was sporadic in the early days and though the 1880s. Some years the question of support for schools was "passed over." One year $752.25, and another year $800 was approved. An appropriation of $200 for the North island and $200 for the South island was proposed and a year or two later, in 1870, "$1.00 per capita for the support of schools" was included in the town report. In that period it was voted to approve the "amount required by law," although the sum was not mentioned. One supervisor mentioned the truancy problem and complained that "attendance at horse trots for one class of pupils was bigger than the attendance at school." He wanted a truant officer to be hired. Supervisor E.H. Lyford would be pleased to see parents taking an interest in the schools and what the children are learning today. In his 1877 report he noted that the schools where parents frequently visited were more interesting and prosperous. He would probably have a bit of a stroke if he could walk into the school today. He demanded in his report that the "houses in which our children spent so much time be kept in good order, well whitewashed each year and well ventilated." His quaint phrasing, to me, was caring. "Let us economize when we can, but let us not be penurious to the education of our children." He would approve of Vinalhaven's school system today. Many go on to good schools and make a good showing. Any teacher will agree with his concerns that "being assured of the best books and other tools" is of the same concern today. Old time teachers and administrators would be astounded at the strings attached to teachers wishing to maintain discipline today. Many of the older school annual reports noted that the teacher in one district "taught a very good school, her only failing being a lack of discipline. In order to gain the highest success as a school teacher she must *insist* on the most perfect quietness and order." In the very early 1880s one administrator wanted the town to employ only local residents as teachers. Staffing one-room district schools was a minor task compared to the staffing of the schools today. One admonition, "give them a good education, fit them to become good citizens, honored by the town, the state and the nation," a century ago, holds true today. Local young people have done well in mainland competitions and in colleges throughout the country. I believe that the amount of money spent through scholarship today in Vinalhaven would probably stun some of those old time educators. People who have a deep interest in young people do not change much.

John Wulp, not yet an institution locally but soon to become one, had moved to the island in 1992 and in August of 1995 he directed a staged reading of *The Gin Game* for the Friends of the Library. John was an award-winning director who'd been recognized with, among many accolades, a Tony Award for his production of *Dracula* on Broadway in 1978.

The first annual Seal Bay Festival of Music, including a concert at the Union Church, took place in early June.

Kim Smith, the other half of I. W. Fifield, and instrumental in creating the Vinalhaven Historical Society in 1965, passed away at eighty on June 27th.

Sunset Rock was gifted to the town by the Dal Molin family, and the first of several Granite Block Parties, events sponsored by the VHCoC and which occupied the town parking lot with music and games, took place in late August.

Ferry Tales proved to be a legendary event, an enormous hit.

In October the *Wind,* perhaps under pressure from some quarter, let it be known they would not print opinions or anonymous items, although for years they'd been doing precisely both things, and although Gert's "Observer" had by now become quite clearly an opinion column. It was a good column still, an interesting one, but certainly opinionated.

The VLT's Perry Creek holdings had grown to over 600 acres.

In 1995 thirty-seven million pounds of lobster were landed in Maine by 7,500 license holders, and the price was $2.74 per pound.

OBSERVATIONS

1996/1997

THE JANUARY ISSUE carried a lovely and certainly fitting anonymous tribute to the Union Church organist Louise Bickford, who'd been an accomplished fixture at the keyboard for as long as I could remember.

> She sits down at the organ.
> Her fingers touch the keys —
> And from out of the depths
> Of that old instrument
> Come the stirring notes of
> *The Lost Chord.*
> They fill the church and a
> Lump fills my throat — always
> For this is my favorite piece.
> I am not a musician, but I
> Know a good one, when I
> Hear her play — she plays for me.

The island's School Enrichment Program began its second year. Its purpose was pretty much what the name implied and it had by then offered, or would offer in the very near future, instruction in gymnastics, workshops with or lectures by successful writers, artists, scientists and professionals, and would involve students in an African immersion project that allowed them to experience the culture of that part of the world.

The Island Institute extended an invitation to artists and artisans from its fourteen constituent islands to take part in the creation of a mainland cooperative gallery. Co-chairs were Herb Parsons of Vinalhaven and me. With a great many enthusiastic participants, the effort got underway very quickly and "The Island Arts and Crafts Co-operative" now Archipelago, scheduled an opening for June 1.

"Library Activities" and "Health Center News" had become a regular column, and the Medical Center offered group vasectomies on February 16 promising a new and "gentle technique."

The math team continued apace winning the Central Maine meet. Kurt Lazaro scored a perfect 60, the first such perfect score in league competition. Only the much larger schools of Bangor and Oxford Hills had higher overall scores.

Bodine Ames was presented the Giraffe Award, given to those who, further than others, stick out their necks for children.

The new ferry terminal in Rockland was finished and open for business.

On May 27, the town switched from an "over-the-log method" of waste disposal (essentially only requiring that one toss refuse beyond a log positioned for that purpose) to a pay-per-bag system and we began to deal with the state-mandate that we permanently and effectively cover our old landfill.

The "Vinalhaven People: Lives and Work" summer programs, sponsored by the ARC that year, featured Emily

1996/1997

Lane, Helen Greven, and John Wulp.

Jean McDonald, a familiar face and confidant to us all, retired from the Medical Center after thirty-two years.

The DEP was again leaning on the town to develop a municipal sewer, but now were willing to consider several small plants instead of one big sewer facility.

Marcia Davis continued her brief, but very interesting and informative "Nature Notes."

> 9/15 A hummingbird with a snow white bill flew into the yard, checked out the feeder, which was empty, and went over to flowers in a nearby garden. My son, hauling traps off Roberts Island and Lane's Island way, saw an adult and an immature eagle. A large deer has been feeding on lettuce in the next door neighbor's garden! With most dogs under "control," deer are living right along the wooded back yards of neighborhoods along Carver's Pond and East Boston areas. Walking in the woods on a late August day one notices many partly eaten mushrooms. Isn't it wonderful how deer, mice, and squirrels know which fungus are edible! Thinking of fungus, many people used to cut the large shelf fungus off birch trees, dry them, and according to their talents paint scenes on them. Song sparrows are still feeding one large fledgling at the window feeder. Baby is as big as Mama and Papa! Monday at sunset a man was fishing beside the bridge over Indian Creek. When I asked what he hoped to catch he said there were striped bass coming in on the rising tide! He had caught one before I came along. People have also been fishing for these bass down by the motel. Some people saw an eagle far off on the mudflats up by Sparrows' farm. The bird seemed unable to take off. The tide began to rise and the people worried; after calling several sources for "official help" and having no luck they decided to do what they could. Putting on layers of thick clothes, they set off on a rescue mission. When they reached the spot the eagle was gone but the remains of a good sized cormorant partly imbedded in the mud were found, also signs of the bird's futile attempt to disengage and carry off his prize!

The town entered into an agreement with the Nature Conservancy whereby we assumed responsibility for the care and maintenance of Lane's Island Nature Preserve.

Reverend James and Donna Wood moved into the parsonage. Rev. Wood began services on December 8.

One of our own kids — actually one of the Green's Island kids — headed out for Thailand that spring for an academic year of American Field Service sponsored education.

Thousands of dollars' worth of school windows were smashed on several different occasions. Apparently someone was upset with school or with someone or something having to do with school and this sort of thing has, historically, been the end-all of conflict resolution among a tiny, in more ways than one, few.

The VLT began offering guided monthly nature walks of specific trails and continued sponsoring bird walks with ornithologist John Drury.

The Junior class, back when we had to line up our cars for ferry departure twenty-four hours in advance and had to have posted a scrap of paper with our desired departure time in the windshield, had the brilliant idea to create and market the "Ferry Flipper," a loosely hinged little tablet displaying days of the week and the various departure times, that could be flipped open to readily communicate to the line attendant which

OBSERVATIONS

departure time was intended. Before long each of us was in possession of one and the Junior class had raised a lot of money.

Gert's "Observer" columns sometimes consumed an entire page and continued to cover a tremendously wide range of topics: an allegedly bogus "save the whale" campaign, corporal punishment, the creation and history of the American flag, kindness, ancient trees, the end of the British empire, Margaret Chase Smith, the foolish and counterproductive behavior of our elected representatives, and so forth. It was always an entertaining surprise.

Teacher Randy Knowlton, who'd worked to organize the exchange program with Russian students, among other things, died unexpectedly just as this year's Russian kids were due to depart their homeland. They came anyway, just as Randy would have wanted.

Winnie Ames celebrated her 106th birthday in a mainland facility, and Ivan Calderwood, at ninety-six, became the oldest person living on island.

An interesting program meant to more fully acquaint youngsters with their island heritage was begun by Annie Boyden and students. Rehearsals for *Island Voices* got underway with the beginning of classes in 1997.

Vassar College prudently chose freshman Rebecca Drury, who'd spent much of her youth rowing a mile or so back and forth to school every day from her home on Green's Island, to be a member of their rowing team.

The math team, now nine years old, turned in its best performance ever at the nationals in Seattle, Washington.

Claw Island shipped lobster to Hong Kong on the occasion of the English handing that enclave over to the Chinese.

Vinalhaven Eldercare Services (VES) organized into a 501(c)(3) for purposes of finding solutions to the health care concerns of the elderly.

The Vinalhaven Lions Club raised $20,000 to purchase new computers for the computer lab at school.

In 1996 thirty-six million pounds of lobster were landed in Maine by 7,000 license holders, and the price was $2.96 per pound. In 1997 the price was $2.94.

1996/1997

Phil 'n' the Blanks, a devilishly handsome six-man a cappella group focused on gospel and doo-wop, made its first public appearance.

Yesteryear

Today

OBSERVATIONS

1998

SCHOOL BUS DRIVER FRANNIE FLAGG DIED SUDDENLY IN MAY. I took over his route temporarily. Nick Barton, then a youngster who rode just behind my driver's seat so he could provide directions and advice on how to drive, was quite concerned about what he clearly saw as my limitations and was very vocal about it. As I drove by the landfill one morning a kid in the back of the bus asked Nick what he would do if I were to have a heart attack like Frannie. "I would call in (there was a bag phone on the dashboard) and tell them I was bringing the bus in," he answered responsibly. "What about Phil? What would you do with Phil?" "There's the dump," said Nick jerking a thumb toward the debris and without missing a beat.

Frannie Flagg
Photo: Provided by the Flagg family

1998

VES broadened its activities a little further by offering free transportation to the elderly.

Sunday morning Men's Fellowship Breakfasts began. Lobsterman Bobby Warren was the first speaker.

Vinalhaven's math team, mid-season, was #1 in Maine, lording over schools like the Maine School for Science and Mathematics.

Three pages of an eight-page *Wind* were now quite customarily consumed by ads from the three local real estate agencies.

Key Bank became Camden National Bank.

Island Voices, a musical celebrating the connections of islanders to their heritage and to those who preceded them, was presented to rave reviews. It involved over 130, nearly all, of our students.

The selectmen again invited a committee to study the feasibility of constructing a sidewalk from the downtown area to the ferry terminal.

John Wulp's passion, a musical he'd co-written called *Red Eye of Love*, opened on North Haven.

A scholarship was established in the name of dearly departed former teacher Jerry Michaels who, with his wife Carlene, had run the Paper Store since his retirement.

Reverend Jim Wood and Donna announced the end of his ministry here on the island.

The Medical Center took on its first Physician's Assistant (PA) in the person of Barbie Brittell, a remarkable woman who has since gone on to leave her compassionate mark around the world.

A School Assessment Committee, having been at work all year, hired a firm to study the condition of the school, educational programming, future needs, and how to meet them.

OBSERVATIONS

1999

FRANCIS CHANDLER PASSED AWAY, and the indefatigable cooking duo known to Lions, Masons, every other nonprofit on the island, and every class who ever raised money for one thing or another, as Dottie and Francis, became just Dottie and, while Dottie was really never "just" Dottie, a cherished institution had been halved.

Francis Chandler and Dottie Young
Photo: Provided by their family

1999

The *Wind* continued to be the place, the only place, for folks to publicly acknowledge one another and the many gestures of kindness shown. Consequently, one could nearly always count on one or two of those notes in each issue thanking certain people for helping "after my fall" or "after my accident," thereby prompting everyone who wasn't already in the know to wonder what happened and how serious it was. One issue carried this interesting expression of gratitude:

> Thanks for that thing you did for me the other day up at you know where. It was a big help. Signed: You know Who.

Twenty-seven volunteers had worked on the *Wind* at one time or another in 1998.

Sisters Lindsay and Samantha Carter each scored their one thousandth point, a first for each in Vinalhaven girls' basketball history.

Several undersea cable failures, each caused by careless boating activity, prompted FIEC to issue a plea for those likely to anchor or drag in the area to give the cables a wide berth.

The RLDS youth group, over the course of the preceding two years, raised $21,000 towards the purchase of a thermal imaging machine for the fire department.

Mainely Girls, a state-wide nonprofit founded to work with rural communities to assist them in focusing on the needs of girls, was doing just that and to great effect.

VES accepted Ivan Calderwood's gift of property and buildings — his own home — for the purpose of creating an assisted living facility for aging islanders.

Guys and Dolls was such a success that accolades poured in from all over. I was in it — just sayin'.

At school, the Marine Technology Class undertook the construction of a Cornish Pilot Gig, a long rowing boat of the type used to take pilots out to escort ships approaching the English Channel.

Serious consideration of building a new school was now underway, and math teacher Pete Pedersen was presented with the prestigious Tandy Award.

Just before she died, Jamien Morehouse, a young, courageous, and irrepressibly vibrant woman struck down by cancer, urged everyone attending her service to wear an interesting hat.

The *Wind* was barely able to make ends meet and implored readers to be more forthcoming with contributions.

Bodine was honored by her fellow islanders by being asked to lead the Fourth of July parade, and Gert penned a terrific tribute for the occasion.

> It was with great pleasure that I heard that the Health Council had persuaded "Bo" to be Grand Marshall for the last 4th of July parade of this century. Although Bodine was born on North Haven, her name had become synonymous with Vinalhaven. She has raised her three children here and helped many more young people. I remember when youngsters who got out of line were sent to Bodine. I recall several young boys washing the police car and others clearing the snow from Main Street. They told us they were doing this for Bodine. When we first met, Bo and Randy were picking up trash on the State Beach; we had such a fun afternoon that I thought of her only as a fun

person. Her true character soon became apparent when we went to take pictures of the kids from Hurricane Island who were working with Bo, cleaning the State Beach of all sorts of debris and then going to the quarry, where they cleared brush and picked up litter. They all seemed happy to work with her. Her "saving of the old Fire Hall" with the late wonderful Ann Carver is well known and she still keeps an eye on it, maintaining the old building. Many times I have seen her, down at the Fire Hall, boxing and distributing free food, all by herself. She has never been able to garage her car; it is always filled with clothing and furniture for the many people who would have nowhere else to go for assistance. Bodine has been honored by several Maine State Committees for her hard work and her compassionate regard for every person. When I met her father, Argyle McDonald, he said that from the time she was a very little girl, she was anxious that everyone be helped. She just loved humanity, he said. She still has that philosophy, she keeps track of everyone who may need help, and she has always taken care of her own mother on North Haven, who has been ill for many years. When my furnace blew up, just before Christmas, I was devastated, never having even purchased a winter coat myself. But, without any fuss, Bodine appeared with a man who made arrangements for a loan to replace the furnace. This was a traumatic experience; we had never even had a mortgage, on several houses, but when Bodine quietly and firmly explained just what could be worse than a loan to replace the furnace, like frozen pipes and a frozen old lady, it did not seem so awful. Nobody works as hard on the 4th of July as does Bodine. She collects all year for the booths at the big day celebration.

Taking care of the less fortunate on Vinalhaven means many trips to the mainland to attend conferences and to beg for more help for her people. She also keeps our Library and Medical Center spotlessly clean, in addition to the many hours she devotes to the maintenance of the Old Fire Hall. We will really have a Grand Marshall at the 1999 Independence Day celebration.

The Jerry Michael Scholarship began hosting annual roasts. Each event featured dinner catered by the Haven, entertainment by Phil 'n' the Blanks, and a roast by me of someone chosen and surprised for the good things they've done for this community. PA Barbie Britell left Vinalhaven to help provide medical relief in Haiti, but before she departed she was the subject of one of those roasts and it was great fun. A few months earlier, she and I had occasion to be alone in one of the examining rooms, I the patient, she the physician. Something startled her and she slipped off her chair and onto the floor. Equally startled, I moved to help her but tripped over the cords of my hospital gown and fell on top of her. That's where we were when the nurse came in and that's where my roast began.

A notice appeared that I was to speak at the Men's Fellowship Breakfast, a notice that characterized me as controversial.

? ?

1999

Kurt Lazarro, who'd been a member of the Maine All Star Math Team each of his four years in high school, was presented with the 1999 Sobol Award for Noteworthy Achievements in Mathematics.

And this:

> I would like to thank whoever was responsible for the recent ad announcing my Pogus Point Escort Service. I'm sorry to say I am completely booked through November and, till then, have all the business I can handle. Thanks again, though. What a great community!

My mother wrote a note to the *Wind* protesting that, although I had reported in a piece for the *Working Waterfront* that she'd been born in Massachusetts, she was, in fact, born right here on Vinalhaven and would certainly straighten me out on that critical point. She subsequently did. My brother David Crossman, the most prolific among us, eventually authoring more than fourteen books, appeared at the Paper Store for the first of many book signings.

Telling the Story, a history of the Union Church, written by Rev. Harry Shirley, was released.

The Washington School Committee hosted an open house at the premises for the purpose of discussing what they expected to do with the building and to invite comment.

Pete Pedersen was given the prestigious Milken Family Foundation Award, which includes a sum of $25,000.

The newly formed Partners in Island Education (PIE), whose goal was to secure funding for school facilities and programs not otherwise funded, began comprehensive discussions with the public about school priorities. A subsequent survey revealed that most of those responding thought the school needed an expanded library and a decent auditorium. Toward the end of the year the state announced that the list of communities to receive funding for new construction would be announced in January.

VES set a target of $446,500 for remodeling and new construction required to transform Ivan Calderwood's homestead into a compliant assisted living facility, and a $93,000 grant quickly reduced the fund-raising target to about $353,000.

Although several big fund-raising projects were in full swing elsewhere, and the appeal for contributions was great, the *Wind* ended the year in the black.

In 1999 fifty-three million pounds of lobster were landed in Maine by 6,800 license holders, and the price was $3.45 per pound.

2000

A BENEFIT CONCERT WAS PRESENTED IN FEBRUARY. The range of performers was pretty impressive, a range that was commonplace at the time.

Planning something else for Wednesday, one week from today? Cancel it!
Ten island music makers performing rock, classical, blues, gospel, country, pop, folk, and doo-wop
Will perform for the benefit of Isles Wentworth.

Appearing will be:

Dallas Anthony

The CanAreys

George and Tammy

Indian Creek Ensemble

The Lights Out

Phil 'n' the Blanks

The Squid Cove Trio

Raggyroad
(Jamie Thomas Band)

Sonic Gale
(Jim Conlan Band)

The Woodcocks

Tickets on sale at Port O' Call or the Paper Store – $10.00

The town approved a proposal to renovate the Washington School building intending that it then house the town offices.

A petition was circulated to protest the dredging and subsequent dumping of bottom material from Mack Point in Searsport, material that would have been dumped at a disposal site 3.3 miles northeast of the Rockland Breakwater. It was a precursor to a similar proposal fourteen years later.

The Tidewater Motel filed an application for a permit to install an in-current hydroelectric generator. Eric Davis objected that it would interfere with navigation, with small boats getting back and forth under the Tidewater, thereby continuing a memorable feud between Eric and me, a litany of disagreements that readers had enjoyed for some time and would for some time to come.

During one of those exchanges Eric memorably rejected my offer to show him around the support structure and waterways under the motel. He wrote, "knowing Phil's feelings toward me, taking a guided tour under the Tidewater Motel didn't seem like a wise thing to do."

2000

The *Vixen*, the thirty-two-foot pilot gig built by the Marine Technology Class, was launched to great fanfare at high tide on May 6. The rowing team then took the gig on to victory in a race at Lake Champlain a month later.

Fund-raising for the Vinalhaven Eldercare Facility was going well; construction had begun, and folks were invited to leave their empty redeemable containers piled behind the Old Engine House. Volunteers picked up the accumulation every few days and transported it to the barn at VES where the stuff was sorted by more volunteers, later to be trucked to a mainland redemption center by still another volunteer, and the profits given to VES.

After a great deal of study and input from all quarters a monumental decision was made to build a new school, inclusive of all grades.

Deer ticks arrived and Lyme disease followed.

A concerned veteran called our attention to the need to demonstrate our patriotism:

Independence Day and Patriotism

What a spectacular fireworks display and what a great Parade! The hearts of all who were there must have beat a little faster.

HOWEVER, what has happened to our once-fierce pride in our country and our sense of patriotism? Of course, I couldn't see everyone who lined the route of the parade in Vinalhaven, but I didn't see a single man doff his cap or hat as the American flag went by, carried by a veteran in uniform at the head of the parade. In my youth I was taught to take off my hat and hold it over my heart as the colors passed, and one of the general orders I was forced to memorize in the U.S. Marine Corps was to "salute… all colors…"

Our national aims may not always have been right in the views of some of us, and some of our leaders from time to time may not have been worth our admiration; but it is still our Country, and it is still our flag, and both deserve our full-time support and respect.

"'Tis the star spangled banner long may it wave o'er the land of the free and the home of the brave"

—Joe Ewing

Islands, a musical written by Cindy Bullens and directed by John Wulp, opened on North Haven on August 20.

Wayne Cooper penned a series of columns as he and Carol Petillo enjoyed an off-season road trip.

America in the Off-Season
by Wayne Cooper
with editorial assistance from Carol Petillo

From Ocracoke (correct spelling!) on the Outer Banks, we took a 2¼ hour ferry ride across the Pamlico Sound back to Cedar Island and the North Carolina mainland. Our next big objectives were Savannah, Georgia (to visit my sister) and from there, Key West via the east coast of Florida. We decided to follow the coastal roads to Savannah, well to the east of I-95, the N-S speedway to Florida.

OBSERVATIONS

In North Carolina, our route took us across the eastern edge of Camp Lejeune, the county-sized U.S. Marine training base. As an armchair warrior, I was eager to get a glimpse of it. My excitement increased after we crossed the checkpoint onto the base. There a sign informed us that live shells sometimes passed over the roadway (NC state 172). We also saw frequent signs alerting us to tank crossings. Oh boy, maybe we would see some action — a kind of virtual reality drive! Alas, it was not to be. All was peaceful in our sector; we saw not a single tank or a solitary shell. After a 22-mile drive, a very proper, but probably bored, young Marine waved us through, back to civilian life.

In South Carolina, we passed through Myrtle Beach, the popular seaside playground, but stopped at Beaufort's lovely old historical district full of antebellum homes and live oak trees.

In Savannah, the dogs got a break in the form of a huge back yard completely enclosed by an eight-foot concrete wall which my brother-in-law had constructed in response to a small public housing project the city had built directly behind his property. The housing project and the neighborhood long ago learned to accommodate one another, and our dogs now became the beneficiaries of Johnny's heroic attempt to insure his privacy. For four days they became outdoor dogs. Their presence in the yard at night, however, set off intermittent choruses of barking on all sides. "Who are these strange dogs behind the concrete wall?" other dogs seemed to say. "Well, who are you!" our dogs replied. Ma stopped the barking by bedding our dogs down in the van at night. Aren't relatives wonderful to endure such antics?

Town Manager Sue Lessard announced she was leaving the island to take a job elsewhere.

Gert Minor, "The Observer" for twelve years, was hospitalized, then recovering in a mainland nursing facility. During her convalescence I wrote my first "Observer" column, signing it "Yitzhak" after the dog for whom the column was penned.

I was born ready, ready to love without condition. So simple were my needs that to be adopted thirteen years ago by a human family represented complete fulfillment. Over the years I found a real home on this island. This is a real Dog Town. From the beginning I went to work with someone almost every day, carpentering with Katie's dad, gardening with Linnell, or in the woods with the Ames Brothers. I lived for the moment and the moments always came: running down a dirt road following the van, retrieving sticks, peeing on everything, catching balls, playing rough, welcoming company. Early on I picked out some real softies. Betsy Bates, Gigi Baas, Linnell Mather were some of my favorites. Betsy kissed me all the time, right on the nose. I think Gigi saved my life once when I wolfed down a tasty D-Con patty. I didn't think much of her at the time; Clorox isn't much of a chaser. I'd be invited for sleep-overs, often at Linnell's. She introduced me to the Ames Brothers who took me working in the woods with them. That was where I had my closest call. A felled tree struck me on the head and only the efforts of Linnell and Martha Reed saved me. I flew in a plane to the hospital.

I had a great spot in my own front yard from which I could see all who approached from either direction. I had kind of a funny spell there for a while and couldn't get entirely clear just what my responsibilities were when strangers came to the house. I tried to bite Ed Conway one day and I did manage to get ahold of Mary Hurtubise, actually got her twice. Thank goodness she had a sense of humor. For years I was my most ferocious when other dogs went by. Those on leashes, like Dixie or Kobe or Betsy, just got a warning shot barked across their bow but those unaccompanied got the full force of my fury and kept a respectable distance. Except, that is, for Jeff and Donna's dogs who were a little too much for me: charging down the road, unleashed, and jumping right over my head as I lay napping. Embarrassing! By the time I got to my feet they'd be all the way to the library. Lucky for them. Galling young squirts.

Early this year I began feeling a little poorly, had a lot of discomfort in my mouth, couldn't eat easily, lost weight and strength. Elaine had to feed me by hand. I was anesthetized for an examination that revealed an inoperable tumor surrounding my jaws and moving down my throat. At the time my family was driving to Massachusetts to take Katie away to school. And so her dad asked the vet to administer a fatal dose and on the same day they let Katie go they let me go. Although he made the decision quickly and without coming back to say goodbye I don't have to forgive him. I'm a dog and don't have to deal with all that baggage. There is no room in my heart for anything but devotion.

—Yitzhak

It was a big year, perhaps the biggest ever, for fund-raising: VES, the new school, Union Church, the ARC, and School Enrichment. All placed huge demands on the largesse of the community.

In 2000 fifty-seven million pounds of lobster were landed in Maine by 6,900 license holders, and the price was $3.28 per pound.

Observations

2001

PARTNERS IN ISLAND EDUCATION, having announced a goal of raising two million dollars for construction of a new auditorium and comprehensive library to augment the anticipated new school, reported having already accumulated $1.5 million toward that goal.

My mother, Pat Crossman, penned an "Observer" during each of the first several weeks of Gert's convalescence; the first was an interesting reflection on Main Street in the early part of the 1900s.

In 1932, interesting distinctions prevailed concerning the area we know as Main Street. Those distinctions had to do with the location of one's residence. If you lived in the general vicinity of Main Street, between Leo's Lane and the library, you went "overstreet" to grocery shop and pick up your mail. From Shields Hill, Pequot, and Dogtown, you would go "downstreet." Those who dwelt near Lane's Island bridge, Round the Mountain Road, and Pogus Point headed "upstreet" to do their daily errands. But on Saturdays, of a summer evening, the distinctions all melted away, as Vinalhaven folk from every neighborhood set out for downtown to meet and greet, to see and be seen.

In 1932 I was eight years old, living for the summer with my great-grandmother in the boarding house she ran for Scandinavian quarry men. We were in the six-family building still known as "the Block."

To this day the words "Saturday Night" can bring those special evenings vividly to mind. A week's worth of anticipation preceded the event. As soon as supper was over, I was whisked off to the pantry, where the only sink in the house was waiting like a sacrificial altar. There I was scrubbed to a fare-thee-well, and my best dress pulled over my toweled and tingling body. White ankle socks resisted my great-aunts' efforts to get them on my damp brown feet. But as always, the two great-aunts prevailed, and in only moments my feet were neatly subdued in polished Mary Janes.

There was only one more impediment to their task. The boyish bob my parents had decreed I should have before coming to Maine, had, from the moment I stepped out of the Massachusetts barber's chair, defied taming. Still, the persistent aunts strove to secure a taffeta bow to the crown of my head. It was a hopeless task, given the fact that my hair was fine, very short, and as straight as a stick.

An air of haste, a sense that not a moment should be lost, permeated the proceedings, so they pronounced me satisfactory, and with my great-grandmother, attended to their own attire. Discreet suggestions were made as to embellishment. Gloves? Brooch? A little rose-scented talcum about the neck?

As soon as those vital matters were dispensed with, we joined the pedestrian flow moving down the block sidewalk, crossed over Main Street by the fountain, and were at once transported to a world of light and sound. Overhead, the first stars came faintly to the twilight sky.

Our progress was slow. The stores spilled bright pools of light onto the Main Street sidewalks. Gathered in those circles of light were neighborly groups with whom the affairs of the day might be discussed. Children clinging to father's hand or mother's skirts shuffled impatient feet, eager to move on.

An occasional wagon or motorcar passed, the occupants alert for a chance to park and join the town folk on foot. Indoors, those who had the means paid their weekly grocery bills, and received a bag of candy in return. Even a dollar or two paid on account assured a stick of licorice or a lollipop for the children of a struggling family.

In the hardware store men lingered to exchange individual views on politics, local concerns, and the deepening national depression. Women and children, however, had little patience with such somber topics. It was Saturday night, for heaven's sake, a bright island of cheer in a week of uncertainty and toil.

As the women and younger children came to the millstream bridge, their teenage sons lagged behind to peer in the windows of the Cascade poolroom, and to encounter, with any luck, teenage girls similarly widening the gap between themselves and the older women making up the vanguard.

By eight o'clock, the sound of talk and laughter had diminished. Sleepy children with sticky fingers drowsed on their fathers' shoulders, as families headed home, each to its own neighborhood. But in Will Lincoln's bakery, a handful of celebrants still lingered, scooping up the last spoonful of rainbow ice cream, as one by one the lights went out downtown.

The state reminded the town of the need to develop an updated Comprehensive Plan for Vinalhaven by 2003 or suffer serious consequences, including the loss of most state funding. Accordingly the board of selectmen asked for volunteers to serve on a committee to accomplish that.

I wrote my second and third "Observers" before Gert passed away on May 5. She had authored the column for thirteen years and had transformed it into a piece more of opinion or reflection than had been the case when her husband Bill was responsible for it. Many of my own efforts were in the same vein.

Winter wears on us out here. No doubt it does on others elsewhere. Regular winter gatherings help sustain increasingly irregular islanders through these long and airy cold months. Bean suppers, bingos, club meetings, book or poetry readings, concerts, committee meetings are among our diversions. So is an annual gathering, about a decade now, of scotch drinkers who gather to, ostensibly, celebrate the life of Scottish poet Robert Burns (1759-1796) whose thirty-seven brief years gave life, beyond literature, to a popular tradition of assembling on or about his birthday to taste and quantify good scotch whiskey and sample the culinary contributions, anything remotely Scottish, of the attendees. This year's connoisseurs were a grocer, a freight hauler, five lobstermen, a lobsterman/urchin fisherman, a nurse, a librarian, a photographer, a pianist, an innkeeper, an artist, the town manager, the banker, two teachers, a sales clerk, and an assistant to our state's likely next governor. All were married. Eleven were men; six from here, one almost from here, four from away. Of the six from here, four had wives who were from here; the one almost from here — his wife was from away. Of the twenty, nine were women — the quicker among you figured that out; three were from here, six from away. Between them all they had nineteen children and four grandchildren. Nine were the offspring of parents from here, seventeen were parents of kids from here. Two from here were parents of one of the others from here who, in turn was married to another from here and between them they had three kids from here. One was a parent of kids not from here, two were grandparents of kids from here, one was a stepmom of a child not from here, seven were Democrats, five, generally the more attractive, were Republicans, eight were independent, six had been to college, five had bachelor degrees, two had masters. Twenty had a good time.

OBSERVATIONS

For most of my life, the last forty-five years or so, I've been taller than Ethel Doughty. It wasn't always so. One day last year she came to the Islander for her strawberry pancakes and there were no empty tables. Many spoke up, inviting her to join them. She seemed to hear only us and approached our table, stooped and listing precariously to port, but steady and purposefully leaning on her yardstick. Did I say her yardstick? I meant her cane. She was at eye-level with me even though I was still seated. It wasn't hard to recall, however, how she towered over me when I summoned the courage to walk into the Gulag, the third grade, the maw of hell about which surviving upperclassmen had tortuously harangued us for two years. She stood at the door like a dare and with my eyes only open enough to keep me from falling over something, I cast a furtive glance at her companion yardstick whose brass tip top stood at just about my eye level and I bravely passed through.

That was a great year. Mrs. Doughty deployed a complicated plan to see that a particular bully never had the opportunity to accost me on the way home from school. She made me sit up front where she could keep an eye on me. She took me, now and then, to the little room that separated our grade from the second grade and hit my hand with her cane giving me the chance to emerge in the presence of my classmates, brave, flushed, eyes brimming, but a survivor. Did I say her cane? I meant her yardstick. Above all, she taught us the fundamentals and we learned them, and she taught us to be good kids and got us ready to be good fourth graders. Earlier I said she was at eye level with me in the restaurant even though I was seated. I hope my memory is faulty and that I stood in her presence. Certainly I should have because with any luck I may not have seen the last of her.

Construction of the proposed new school was put out to bid.

Policing continued to be woefully inadequate.

A new Comprehensive Plan Committee formed with twenty-nine members. I was chair; Bill Alcorn was vice-chair. We promptly embarked on an ambitious program intended to produce a finished plan within two years and keep everyone in the loop with continual updates. The committee announced early on that the plan would focus on seven areas of concern: Marine Resources, Other Natural Resources, Historical and Archeological Resources, Growth and Development, Tourism and Housing, Public Facilities, and Economics.

Jean Wetherbee retired as editor of the *Wind* after sixteen years, and Linda LaPoint took the helm.

A debate about a proposed cell phone tower raged and got kind of ugly.

A very complicated ferry line up procedure was proposed requiring, for example, those planning to leave on the 7:00 a.m. departure to be at the terminal the previous afternoon between 3:30 and 4:00 p.m. to secure passage.

For the first time, registered Democrats outnumbered Republicans 255 to 217. Still, more Republicans turned out at the polls.

Ground-breaking ceremonies for the new school were held on October 14.

"The Observer" column continued fairly regularly, although with nowhere near the reliability it knew when Gert was responsible. Various of us took up the slack.

One time we, the Staples boys and I, decided to go over to Smith's Island, which was near the island of Bluff Head and we knew August Peterson had a camp on Smith's so we had to investigate it. We knew August had died, so thought we could maybe claim it. So when we arrived there we found, under the porch, some lobster traps all ready to be set out. We figured August didn't need them anymore so we went to Benny's Cove and caught us some lobster bait and came back and loaded our dory with traps and set them out.

After a couple of days we went to haul our traps but some were missing. We thought we must have set them into deep water and sunk them. So the next time we hauled the same thing happened. Some more was missing. This kept on until all the traps had disappeared, and we had never seen a lobster. After a while we found out the traps belonged to the Murch boys and they wondered who set their traps for them.

After this episode, we found out we could dig clams for the Black and Gay factory for thirty-five cents a bushel. Sometimes I managed to get a bushel to a tide with a little help from the older boys.

One time we were caught in the middle of the bay in a thunder and lightning squall. I don't think a speed boat could have caught us as we made for land and home.

by Woodrow Bunker

From the mid-1950s to the mid-1970s, my grandmother's nearest neighbor in the six-unit "Block" was May Lawry. They shared a common wall, which made communication much simpler than a telephone call. If one rapped on the wall, the other would rap back, then proceed to the front door, where her neighbor would be peering from her own door, just a few feet away. Sometimes the exchange was short and sweet, covering an assessment of weather prospects, plans to get together and knit nets later in the day, or an offer of one of May's original poems, gifts she bestowed on all her neighbors in an unending flow.

In her 80s, widowed and childless, May had infinite love to share. Her one sister, Elsie Calderwood, was the constant recipient of that complete and uncomplicated devotion. But so were May's fortunate neighbors in the block, on Water Street, and along Atlantic Avenue. Then, too, there were the people who passed along the block sidewalk, coming or going on their daily errands.

At any moment, as May hailed a passerby from her front door, the one hailed might find a penciled poem pressed into her hand, along with a modest disclaimer that the gift was "certainly not much, but when I saw you, I thought, 'now, she might like something cheery to think about today,' so here it is, and you just have a joyful day!"

As one blessed by May's precious and prodigious outpouring of love, I now have a treasure of fading penciled poems, some that May gave my grandmother, some she gave to me.

This is my favorite:

OBSERVATIONS

I Will Love Deeply
by May Lawry

I will love deeply
the sea and the sky,
mountains and stars,
and the flowers close by,

Children and birds
I will love more and more,
the cat on her cushion,
the dog on the floor.

I will love deeply,
for I have been told
that those who love deeply,
will never grow old.

Such a priceless gift, yet so simple, and so lovingly bestowed!

by Pat Crossman

Many years ago, when I was in my teens, my family came to Vinalhaven each August. Much has changed since then. Our first trip to the island was on board the steamship *Vinalhaven*. It had a luxurious ladies cabin below decks with comfortable chairs and sofas. Later we sailed on the *W. S. White*.

We stayed in various rented cabins with oil lamps, dug wells, and outhouses. In bare feet we dug clams, picked mussels from the beach while dodging sea urchins with their painful spines.

We bought fish and lobster from neighboring fishermen. A small grocery store on Main Street supplied other needs.

The island had its own telephone system operated by two women who sat in a second-floor room on Main Street over a men's barber shop and a small drug store.

The Memorial Hall, a handsome building also on Main Street, towered over the town. It was the scene of many concerts, plays, and dances. The post office was located on the ground floor.

There was also a movie theater on Main Street, the Gem Theater, where I saw *Captains Courageous*.

I got to know several island teenagers and begged my parents to let me stay and go to the island school. Not surprisingly, they said no. Obviously, I've never gotten over my liking for Vinalhaven and have been coming back year after year — and now I live here year-round!

by Jean Wetherbee

The sidewalk around Carver's Market slopes severely toward the road, and for that reason is a bad place for those of us not entirely steady on our feet. The sidewalk in front of the Port O' Call, home of the mid-morning misanthropic irregulars, is a bad place to suffer misfortune of any kind if you're thin-skinned. Woody is not and, new knee and restored youthfulness notwithstanding, this is where he, eighty-three but not looking a day over eighty-two, took an ill-considered swing with an imaginary sand wedge.

He'd done this before; that much was clear. His header was graceful and, breaking his fall as he did with his nose, practiced. Alerted by Kimmy who, driving by, had seen him tumble, the brain trust spilled out of the hardware store and ran, to the extent they could execute that dim memory, to Woody's assistance. "What happened?" asked Woody after he'd regained consciousness. "Kimmy run you over 'cause you was in the way," was the reply. "What are you doin' down there, Woody, lookin' for change?" asked someone. "Your pirouette's a little rusty, ain't it?" came another query. "Kimmy don't want you lying here in front of the store, folks might stumble over you on their way in and hurt themselves." "We better drag you outta here 'fore Bob starts sweepin'. Litter's litter as far as he's concerned."

Woody was helped to his feet, a little dazed, hearing aid hanging down next to his chin, finger badly gashed and bleeding profusely, cheek sliced open, shoulder wrenched, and glasses bent. A white resin chair was produced; Woody settled down in it to regain his composure and in no time it was covered by blood. "I guess you know you bought that chair," admonished Bobby.

Phil Crossman

The Vinalhaven Farm Project, undertaken a few years earlier, and involving site visits to old Vinalhaven farms, continued under the leadership of Jeannette and William Lasansky, along with builder Andrew Creelman, and with Joel and Wendy Greenberg photographing each example.

Vinalhaven Farm/Cape Project Resumes

Jeannette and William Lasansky, aided by Andy Creelman, have resumed site visits to island farms and farmhouses that flourished on Vinalhaven in the late 18th to early 20th centuries. Last year, twenty-five of these farms with still standing farmhouses and outbuildings were visited and the Lasanskys took measurements of rooms, noting arrangements, chimney supports, attic timber construction, and substructure. This summer and fall about half as many remain to be done. In August, Joel and Wendy Greenberg will resume the photography of the buildings' important architectural elements as well as the homes' relationship to outbuildings and important land features.

Most of the 114 island farms enumerated by the census taker in 1870 were of modest size but there were a number totaling 100 acres or more and they were scattered. Among the largest were Samuel Young's near the Thorofare with 300 acres, a third of which was cultivated; Jesse Calderwood, Jr. on Calderwood's Neck had 250 acres, while William Combs had cleared 140 acres near the end of Coombs Neck and Joshua Calderwood had 200 acres on the eastern shore. They were generally raising wheat, Indian corn, oats, peas, beans, Irish potatoes, barley, and hay. Most sold butter, with Jesse Calderwood, Jr. at Eastholm producing the most at 600 pounds.

Observations

Farm homes in this period were capes, and while there was uniformity with variations, each house seen to date has had details in construction and trim that make it stand apart from the others. Many of these farms were photographed by an island photographer, Will Merrithew, and his extant glass plates are owned by the Vinalhaven Historical Society. They can be viewed there, as can all of the agricultural statistics compiled by the Lasanskys to date. Please call 863-9331 or leave a message at the Historical Society if you have any information on any of the island farms that you care to share.

The first season of a two-year lobster tagging study was undertaken by the Island Institute with the help of several participating island lobstermen. The results were expected to shed light on lobster development and movement/migration, and help with stock assessment.

The musical production *Islands* was taken to the New Victory Theater on 42nd Street in New York City for a prestigious one-night engagement.

The work of the Comprehensive Plan Committee continued apace as they regularly kept the scope of their business in the public eye.

Marine Resources

Obviously this is an area of vital concern to our island community. Fully half of the people who live here year-round sustain themselves directly or indirectly from fishing of one kind or another. The state's charge to the town of Vinalhaven as it relates to marine resources is to develop, within our Comprehensive Plan, a means of protecting the town's marine resources industry, ports, and harbors from incompatible development and to promote access to the shore for commercial fishermen and for the public. Because the sustainability of marine resources is so very critical to Vinalhaven's economic health and to our quality of life in general, the state has further defined our responsibilities in developing the marine resources section of our Comprehensive Plan. Accordingly we must give particular consideration to the cumulative effects of development on coastal resources while giving preference to water dependent uses. More striking, we, the Comprehensive Planning Committee, are directed to develop a strategy for managing the marine environment and its related resources, for preserving and improving the ecological integrity and diversity of our marine communities and habitats, and for expanding our understanding of the productivity of the Gulf of Maine and coastal waters.

There are about thirty members of the Comprehensive Planning Committee. Only two or three of us can claim even a remote connection to the fishing community. We know we are not a representative group when it comes to debating issues related to marine resources. We know we need to attract the participation of men and women who make their living from the sea. We know the eventual Comprehensive Plan will be a less effective instrument if it is developed and adopted without the support of the people most familiar with marine resources. That said, though, Vinalhaven's Comprehensive Plan, expected to be complete by 2003, will be binding and will dramatically affect us all for the foreseeable future, including those of us who make the greatest use of marine resources.

We urge you, even though you're tired and overextended already, like many of the rest of us, to join the efforts of the Vinalhaven Comprehensive Planning Committee, particularly as it relates to marine resources.

The next regularly scheduled meeting of the committee is August 14. Watch the *Wind* for details.

A local businesswoman, having been taken to task for not flying the American flag, penned this pointed response:

> After I complimented his building, the gentlemen commented back on my own and its lack of signs (American Flag and business). With a hurried stammer, my usual response, I crossed the street wondering about this symbolism. Patriotism is also in the heart and mind; between citizenship, volunteerism, and belief, it can be as strong (or stronger) than those who display the American Flag and business sign. With many other demands and expenditures, it's not a priority. A flag or sign does not make person or business who or what they are. It is what's inside that matters.

In 2001 forty-nine million pounds of lobster were landed in Maine by 6,800 license holders, and the price was $3.17 per pound.

Observations

2002

THE WIND CONTINUED, as it had since its inception, to be a vehicle for announcements of births and deaths, for condolences, and for notes of appreciation to those who were responsible for those gestures of kindness and compassion. More often than not those acknowledgements began with something like "words cannot express…" and then went on to express eloquently as if the proscription were never voiced. The sentiment—and similar wording—continues today.

The effort to reclaim and restore the old ball field ground to an unhappy halt.

Update on Ball field Restoration

The DEP has withdrawn the permit it gave the town to work on the old ball field. The claim of the DEP is that the town did not apply for the correct permit, and that no matter what the ball field was, it currently is a wetland and has special legal protection.

For remedial action, the town has been instructed to do one of two things: fill in the ditches, or stabilize what has been removed by putting four inches of straw over it and mesh to keep the straw from blowing away. The selectmen voted Monday night to fill the ditches back in.

For punitive action, the town has agreed to consider a consent agreement. This will include an as-yet undetermined fine. If the town agrees to the consent agreement there will be no further legal action by the DEP.

The selectmen also voted Monday night to apply for the more difficult application, which the DEP has assured the town is very expensive and which we have no possibility of obtaining. The selectmen understand that the majority of the citizens of this town want the ball field to be restored, and are doing what is most reasonable to achieve that end.

Construction of the new school was underway, and PIE was only $40,000 from their $2 million goal to finance the inclusion of an auditorium and expanded library in the project.

An acquaintance passed away, prompting my own fourth "Observer" column.

Last Sunday the church was full of people paying their respects to Joel Morton and to his family. Many of us have no idea of the reach and impact of the lives of others among us. It takes a funeral or memorial to illuminate the breadth of a lifetime spent right here in our midst. Joel and I worked together for a few years and have known one another for years and yet I knew precious little about him or about his life.

I did know a couple of things. He was terrified of ghosts. Once I asked him to go up to the big Reynolds place on the Thorofare in late spring to do some painting. He didn't want to go because he was sure those places were all haunted, but he went, reluctantly. A young lady, a member of the Reynold's household, had arrived the previous night, unannounced, on the last North Haven ferry. Foy had run her across the Thorofare and she'd settled in for the night. When she heard Joel down in the foyer the next morning she came out of her upstairs bedroom in a long white flannel nightgown that wafted gently in the breeze of an open window, and stood, in the early morning dark, at the rail on the upstairs balcony until Joel, sensing a presence, looked up. The effect was wonderful.

I also remember his smirk, an expression which, when I encountered it always seemed to say, "I know something about you that you think no one knows." Often it was true, but whenever I encountered that smirk and took the time to interact with it I could count on enjoying a good restorative laugh. It's been suggested more than once that we take the time to celebrate the lives among us before they are departed.

Other contributing Observers wrote of times past.

A "Bang-up" Celebration

by Patricia Crossman

The news broke over the island like a rogue wave from the sea: The war was over! After four years of rationing, blackouts, V-mail, and lonely nights, we would see loved ones long absent, resume our lives, and look to a future bright with possibilities! It was the afternoon of August 14, 1945 when word of Japan's surrender crackled over island radios.

With my nine-month-old son, Phillip, I was spending the last few weeks of summer with my aunt Cleo Shields, and four-year-old Lauretta, in her snug home at the end of Frog Hollow road, on Indian Creek. Cleo's husband, Victor, had been wounded in the Italian campaign. Recovered, he was sent back to the front, and was still on active duty there when the European phase of WWII ended, with Germany's surrender in May of 1945.

But now, at last, Japan, too, had given up the dream of world domination. It was over! Bud, a gunnery sergeant with the 516th Field Artillery Battalion in Germany, would at last see his son, born on October 8th, 1944, and Vic could watch his daughter go to school, grow up, and give him grandchildren!

Feelings too overwhelming for words called for action! It wasn't long in coming! People, long dutifully holding their posts on the homefront, spilled out into the streets. Someone got into the church belfry and tolled the bell.

From Cleo's doorstep, we heard the sound of voices on School Street, calling back and forth, corralling children who ran and jumped and cheered, just out of our sight. Lights, long-banned, came on; doors were thrown open and neighbors gathered in clusters. Every few moments a cheer would go up, snatches of song, laughter. Above us, on Armbrust Hill, we heard shouts of celebration that suggested the celebrants might have fueled their enthusiasm with a nip or two.

Shadows were lengthening; in Frog Hollow twilight had already come. It was time to feed the children and put them down for the night. We herded them inside, but left the doors and windows open. The neighborhood was quieter, but the exuberant voices still sounded from above. They seemed to be coming from the flat area where the old wooden merry-go-round stood.

"They'll run out of steam before long," Cleo said, as we tucked the children in. They fell asleep almost immediately, prompting us to realize that we, too, were ready to call it a day. We stepped out on the sun porch, and before closing the door, listened once more to the diminished sounds of jubilation, a laugh, a call, a firecracker.

In that settling quiet, we were jolted by a thundering blast that reverberated across the hill, the creek, the town, and rumbled away like cannon fire. Debris rained down around us, rocks and dirt peppered the waters of the creek, smaller pebbles pattered on the grass. Incredibly, the children slept through it! It proved to be the grand finale to a memorable day.

Cleo had her suspicions about who set off the dynamite, but stopped short of naming names. I'm still speculating.

LIVING FREE
by Jean Wetherbee

My early memories are of life in a Salvation Army Service Center on 48th Street in New York City. My father ran the Center where trucks canvassed the city and brought contributions to the Center where they were sorted and later sold to the needy. The center was a six-story building that also housed homeless men. My family had an apartment in the building. I attended PS 48. As a Salvation Army officer, my father was never paid much but we always received free living quarters.

Living in the city was boring for me and I enthusiastically inspected the large racks of books that accumulated as trucks came in with donations. My lifelong love of reading began then—along with the need for glasses, which I disliked.

My father's enthusiasm for the social center work led him to take a course at the New York School of Social Work. County officials had been seeking a qualified person to run the Westchester County Penitentiary. My father was chosen and again we moved into a rent-free apartment over the prison offices. The penitentiary was located in the country near White Plains. My brother and I were driven to a nearby public school. My schoolmates were fascinated by the idea of living in a prison and loved to visit. As I got older I went out on dates. However, there was no opportunity for a loving farewell when I returned home. The moment a car pulled up, a guard would dart out and shine a bright flashlight on us. I did manage to meet young men approved by my parents and eventually "escaped" from prison by getting married.

From Seal Bay and the Town Farm
by Woodrow Bunker

My writing today is about the Town Farm and people who were there from 1925 to 1936. I always felt, growing up there, that the term "Poor Farm" was a derogatory term. The inmates were people whose families had passed on or had the misfortune of growing old and unable to work and care for themselves. At one time they had walked the streets as you and I, had families, knew happiness and sadness, and worked for their living. Through no fault of their own, they had to have help.

I would like to list their names as I remember them, as they will probably never be mentioned again. When I was a young boy growing up, they were my friends and I would visit them and listen to their stories.

George Emery had only one arm but he was always ready to go with us boys smelting.

Nellie Beverage, confined to a wheelchair. The poor soul could not talk so one could understand her.

Hannah Collamore — her room was next to Nellie's and they were good friends for a long time.

Rita Gourd was another lady confined to a wheelchair.

John Emery was a brother to George. He was in and out at different times.

"Hunky" Beverage was Nellie's husband. He also was in and out as he found work.

Frank Pease was a big man — he must have weighed at least 300 pounds. He always drank a quart of tea with every meal.

"Shine" Lawry was at the Farm only a short time, as was Charles Abbott.

Samantha Grant used to smoke a T.D. pipe. This was a clay pipe, which I imagine could get quite hot!

Frank and Charles Collamore were there and both died there. I think Frank was buried in the Town Cemetery, which is across the road from the dump.

Ike Merrithew was an inmate for a short time.

Fanny Dyer cured the warts on my hands. I was always grateful to her but don't know how she did it!

Edie Beverage was one of the younger ones and she would help my mother in the kitchen. Mother showed her how to make cookies and she was very proud of that chore! One spring when I had come in from milking, a bolt of lightning struck and exploded in the kitchen. Poor Edie was so scared she spit her false teeth into the stove!

I think that I have listed all of the people who were at the Farm as I grew up. I am grateful that I had these people touch my life for a few short years.

The Comprehensive Plan Committee, now with its own logo, continued to keep folks informed with weekly progress reports in the *Wind*. The "Vinalhaven School Project Update" column also appeared faithfully each week as construction of the new school progressed, and the "Vinalhaven Crime Report" became a weekly feature, as well.

Vinalhaven's Comprehensive Plan

The next regularly scheduled meeting of the Comprehensive Planning Committee will be on Tuesday, February 26 at our usual berth, the Union Church vestry.

On Friday, February 8, we'll host our second monthly public chowder after which we'll hear an interesting talk on island forestry issues by Chuck Gadzik. In March, Ben Neal of the Island Institute will talk to us about lobstering as a sustainable fishery.

The Marine Resources subcommittee is busily considering such important issues as aquaculture and how to control its development; shellish harvesting, seeding, and policing; mooring assignments; and a harbor ordinance.

OBSERVATIONS

Did you know that fifty-four people live in Upper Dogtown, twelve on Granite Island, sixty-eight in Lower Dogtown and fourteen on the Reach? Twenty-five are lobstermen and six are sternmen.

Vinalhaven School Project Update

In an effort to keep the public informed, CPM Constructors will provide a monthly update on the status of the Vinalhaven School Project.

The foundation placement is 95% completed. There will be a few remaining placements for small miscellaneous items. The site contractor, George Hall & Sons, has been backfilling the interior with crushed stone. The plumbing contractor, Warren Mechanical, and the electrical contractor, Elco Electric, will be on-site to begin under slab rough-in. CPM Constructors has been erecting the structural steel in the gymnasium, locker room, and janitor area. We will begin erecting steel for the auditorium next. Shortly, our suppliers will be delivering the panels, roof insulation, and smaller joists.

The long span bar joists for the gymnasium were delivered on-site. It was discovered that they were one foot short. The supplier took responsibility for the error. The architect, Oak Point Associates, approved a field extension modification. This is not unusual since joists often come in sections, and it does not affect the integrity of the product. The modifications were inspected and approved by an independent testing agency. CPM Constructors strives to provide a quality product that we, too, can be proud of. If you have any questions please don't hesitate to call our field office at 863-4879.

Vinalhaven Crime Report

The selectmen have appointed a Police Task Force, charged with the task of evaluating the effectiveness of our current policing and crime prevention system.

One of the most significant problems identified is the lack of people willing to go on record, i.e., give a statement with their name when reporting a crime.

In the first month that Deputy Welch has been on Vinalhaven, there have been fifty-one complaints. Of those, nineteen needed statements in order to be prosecuted. Only six were given.

We have to bear witness! Officers cannot simply throw people in jail without evidence, or because "everyone knows who did it." The law requires that a witness provide his or her name.

The freedoms of law-abiding citizens are limited when crimes are committed against them that go without punishment.

You can call in a complaint, and be a valid witness, without having your name broadcast on the radio. Simply inform the switchboard operator that, although you are not making an anonymous call, you do not want your name broadcast over the air.

If you do not give your name because you fear retaliation, think twice. Let the officer know of your fear. And if someone does "retaliate," report this, too. We cannot allow crime to continue because we fear the criminals.

The municipal sewer was finally about to become a reality. Phase I was to cost $6 million, all but $625,000 coming from various government grants.

Our new town manager, Marjorie Stratton, began work in June, and VES began a weekly column titled "Homestead News." "Medical Center News" and "Library News" remained regular features.

Homestead News

As winter ends, life at the Homestead continues to be cheerful and full! Last week, in addition to Jennie's welcome regular visit, Dot and Harvey cooked on Thursday night. From all accounts, the meal was wonderful, and everyone had a good time! Thanks so much, both of you! On Friday, Tracy and Ashlyn spent two hours healing bodies and souls. Tracy gave all the residents and one of the staff soothing massages. Ashlyn gave out smiles and cuddles. Mother and daughter were very much appreciated and everybody is hoping for another visit soon.

As spring approaches, we're all eagerly awaiting the flower gardens that Colleen is planning and has promised to put in. What joy she will bring!

Don't forget, anyone who wants to volunteer as a guest chef, or for anything else you can think of, please call Carol at 2706.

Medical Center News

For your convenience, we have set up a voice mailbox for prescription refills. If you need a refill on a medication, you may now call 863-4965 at your convenience and leave us a message. Please state the following information on your message:

1. Name of the patient.
2. Patient's date of birth.
3. Medication and dosage.
4. Number of days requested.
5. Pharmacy where you want your prescription sent.
6. Would you like your prescription mailed to you or will you be picking it up on the mainland?

We will check the voice mailbox at least twice a day and will fax your prescription on the next business day to the pharmacy of your choice.

Please be sure that we have your current prescription insurance as well, if applicable, including a copy of your Medicaid card each month.

Because we now have a contract with Camden Drug for pharmacy services, all prescriptions given out at the Medical Center are processed through Camden Drug. With our new dispensary set up, when you get a medication at the Medical Center, we send your insurance information to Camden Drug. They in turn submit the request to your insurance and you may get a bill from Camden Drug for your medication co-pay. ICMS does charge an administrative fee when you get a medication at the Medical Center. If you have any questions, please contact Dinah Moyer at 863-4341.

OBSERVATIONS

Library News

Last week was the final "Reading is Life" Summer Saturday Reading program. With the Favorite Books theme we went on a bear hunt; we jumped on the bed; we sold gray, brown, blue and red caps; and we took a ride with a cow down a canal. Those attending received books donated by the Friends of the Library, who sponsor the summer program. Thank you to everyone who helped this year and, again, a special thank-you to Pat Bunker for tending the library circulation during summer and all other Saturday Story Times. Next Saturday we resume our Saturday Story Time at 10 a.m. — no bells and whistles — just reading and caring.

School starts soon whether you are on Vinalhaven or elsewhere. EBSCO will go with you as long as you are a state of Maine resident. Access EBSCO via: http://libraries.maine.edu/miainedatabases and enter as a patron of this library. EBSCO recently added more sites including poetry search— browse the offerings — it is a great resource provided by the state.

We have the new *Lord of the Rings* video.

If you are leaving the island, call and we'll help you check that all your books are in the library. In the future, if you prefer, family members could have their own cards or have a visitor card for $10. Just tell us. Library Hours: T&T 1-5, 6-8 p.m.; W&F 9-12, 1-5 p.m.; Sat. 9-1 p.m.; closed Sun. and Mon. 4401.

Most, if not all, of us who have lived on this island all our lives harbor an understandably proprietary regard for it. A handful manifest that prejudice badly, contemptuous of visitors and of folks who move here "from away," that dreadful place where it is assumed lesser people breed for the sole purpose of coming hither and destroying our way of life. Some of us are barely aware of our partiality. Most of us are mindful and keep it largely to ourselves or temper it with an honest and conscious regard for those others, our equals except for their having come from elsewhere. Now and then a real rant has appeared in the *Wind*. I won't reproduce any of those here. Suffice to say they were forthcoming in their scorn and unforgiving of a visitor or new resident who mustered the wherewithal to voice an opinion about nearly anything. More often the bias was more subtle, politely framed but clear in its disapproval. Now and then, too, a respondent will have mustered the same civil restraint.

> I have really enjoyed reading Woodrow's and Pat Crossman's articles about growing up on Vinalhaven. Although from a different generation, I, too, was born and raised and have lived here my entire life of forty-two years on Vinalhaven.
>
> I can remember the days when "we" were only outnumbered by those that came to soak up the summer sun, swim in our quarries, and eat cheap lobsters.
>
> I recall the day in 1968 when we took delivery of the *Governor Curtis*. My grandfather, Charles Philbrook, was captain at the time. He spent much of his younger life on Hurricane Island, which was a thriving granite town of about 1,200. My Philbrook ancestors were some of the last inhabitants to leave after the island was sold. As a high-schooler, I remember making the trip to George Wright's sawmill every spring to truck sawdust to the old ball ground so we could dry it out enough to have a baseball game. I'm not old enough to remember the Vinalhaven Chiefs, but I remember

well going down for Tibb's Softball league, complete with its own lunch wagon. Swenson Granite was here at about the same time, quarrying some of the now-famous Vinalhaven granite that has gone to destinations all over the country and probably the world. Some of the granite used in the Washington Monument was actually quarried on Hurricane.

The granite industry was "booming" in the early 1900s to sometime in the 1930s, I have been told. The town itself was built on the back of the granite industry — most of Main Street and the waterfront is all man-made land. With time comes progress and with progress comes change. We now have two large ferries which make six trips a day. These summer "sun-soakers" have now become property owners and Vinalhaven residents. I understand that a local group has approached the idea of fixing up the old ball ground since our ball field has been displaced by the new school construction. Bill Mills generously donated his time and equipment to help with the drainage problems. After digging a drainage ditch around the perimeter, the project was halted, apparently by a complaint to the DEP that a wetland was being disturbed. I doubt this complaint came from a Vinalhaven resident who can remember the good old days at the ball ground.

A new granite industry has been launched on the north side of the island, this too drawing complaints to state and federal agencies. I doubt these complaints came from a Vinalhaven resident who can appreciate what the granite business has meant to this island.

We, as Vinalhaven residents, have voted at least twice to construct a cell phone tower on the island; again we are met with opposition. Do those that oppose this tower use a cell phone on the mainland? My guess is you betcha! The traditions that I grew up with on Vinalhaven are rapidly slipping away. It seems that the old ball ground is gone, the granite industry is in peril, and now we can't use our cell phones. What's Next — Bean Suppers??

John C. Hildings

I'd like to thank John Hildings for his "Observer" column last week. Though I don't agree with everything he wrote, it opens the door for discussion of a very important topic, and for that I am grateful.

Quarrying is a time-honored way to make a living, and is part of our town's history. Many of the families living here now are descended from those original quarry workers, many of whom were immigrants who came to this country, and this island, with not much more than their skills and their families. I value living in a place with such a rich history, and very much appreciate the fact that granite, and the men who worked the quarries, literally helped to build this town.

Something important to keep in mind, though, is that an operating quarry changes a place. The usual neighborhood sounds are swallowed by the noise of trucks, back-up beeps, hammer drills, and occasional explosive blasts, which rumble through the earth. Take a look at the old photos to see what a working quarry looks like. There's no mistake that you are looking at an industrial site.

When the quarries of old were in operation, there was no thought to a Land Use Ordinance. And when our town adopted a Land Use Ordinance, I believe in the 1970s, there were no quarries in operation. There are huge gaps in the ordinance, which could potentially affect any of us. For instance, our ordinance does not require notifying neighbors of a quarry permit application, which would undoubtedly affect them. There are minimal regulations regarding setbacks from abutters, from wells, or from the road. There are no regulations regarding possible impacts on neighbors' wells, or on the municipal water supply (which would require an on-site survey by a hydro geologist). There are no regulations at all regarding blasting. These are important issues, which must be addressed. We all need to take the long view, and have a voice in deciding how quarrying will be allowed to affect our lives here, in terms of our health, our safety, our well-being, and our land values.

The truth is, I'd rather not have a quarry operating across the street from my house and my family. But I recognize the fact that quarrying appears to be making a comeback, and we need to co-exist. Nobody is trying to regulate the quarry industry out of business, but we all need to have some regulations in place to protect us. If everything is spelled out, it protects quarry owners, as well.

At our town meeting on June 24th, we will all have the chance to vote on a six-month moratorium on new quarry permits. This gives the planning commission time to thoughtfully address the ordinance, suggest any necessary changes, and give the people of Vinalhaven the chance to vote on them. This past month has been very difficult for all parties involved. I wouldn't wish it on anyone. Yet without sensible regulations in place, it can happen to anyone.

Please let's not muddy the waters by turning this very real issue, which can potentially affect any of us, into an "us" vs. "them" issue. The people affected by the North Haven Road quarry are all working class families. We have given birth here, are raising our kids here, work hard, volunteer at school, and pay taxes here. We are part of this community. Maybe our ancestors aren't buried in Vinalhaven granite, but this is our home.

And by the way, I'm all for bean suppers, but I'll pass on the jello-and-mayonnaise salads!

Colleen Conlan

Call me sunsoaker
I'm proud to be one
It takes real persistence
with so little sun
When fog shrouds the harbor
And ice coats the trees
I still keep on soaking
With others like me
Who serve at bean suppers
Who doctor the sick
Take care of the elderly
Work at the library
Sit on commissions

> And listen all day
> To endless discussions
> Without any pay
> Who sing in the choir
> And play in the band
> Volunteer at the Homestead
> And work on the WIND
> Who are plumbers and painters
> Who work at a store
> Who build houses, plant gardens
> And do many things more
> So I'll keep right on soaking
> Whatever the weather
> For this is my home
> And we're in it together
>
> Nans M. Case

The first Duathlon and Family Fun Run, an annual fund-raising event for the ambulance service, was held on August 10.

The weekly "Raven Report" detailed the accomplishments of our junior baseball team each season.

RAVEN REPORT

Thursday saw our playoff hopes come to an end and with that the end of the season losing to last year's champs 5 - 0. The season was an exciting one with a lot of close games, a season which saw the home team win seven games, the most ever by a Ravens team allowing only 4.2 runs per game, by far the best ever, while averaging 5.8 runs per game. They clearly have emerged as a highly competitive team. The team will be losing four players this year: Brandon Osgood, Phillip Hopkins, Ethan Watt and Ethan Warren. Osgood, Hopkins, and Watt have played all four years for the team amassing over 300 at-bats combined, quite an accomplishment! You will all be missed; thanks for the memories, guys! The team, at this time, would like to thank everyone for their support on and off the field. Special thanks to Charlotte Goodhue for the use of the field, which was immense. Once again a huge thank-you to all. We'll be back! Guys, you did a great job — be proud!

An ambitious art project was undertaken in August. *Site Specific* invited participating artists in all mediums to develop and present works at and particular to selected sites designated to have historical significance by the Historical and Archaeological Resources arm of the Comprehensive Plan Committee. It proved to be a memorable event.

The first annual Parade of Lights took place before Christmas.

Kris Osgood's journalism class became regular contributors to the *Wind*.

Observations

Beyond the Grave in Vinalhaven

by Delwyn Webster, Class of 2003

The candle was lit and placed carefully in the center of the table. All present gathered around and joined hands to concentrate on the moment. Then…it happened…the séance had achieved its desired end. A fluttery blue form became visible to a few of those who dared to open their eyes. A terrified scream from one of those present shattered the heavy silence, and the lights were turned on. However, the figure had vanished! Thus the question must be asked, "do you believe in ghosts?"

As can be seen in the previous description, one island resident, Susan Radley, does. She said the event occurred in 1966 when she was about sixteen years old. A friend had invited Radley over to her house on Brighton Avenue to investigate the rumors of a haunting that had long surrounded the residence. They would do so through a séance with the participation of her friend's family. In fact, her friend's mother, who had experienced strange events in the house before, had looked into the house and found that it had a troubled history. At one time, long ago, two young sisters had lived in the home. One was beautiful, named Elsie, and the other was ugly. Of course, the ugly sister was jealous of the sister with beauty and she decided to solve the situation by throwing acid on her sister's face. This emotionally and physically scarred Elsie, so she lived in miserable seclusion for the rest of her life in the house. It is her spirit that many claim to have met.

Radley further elaborated on the séance: "After we were all gathered around the table, my friend's mother began to chant. I felt something diferent about the room, so I decided to open my eyes. I looked over my shoulder towards the pantry and I saw a willowy shape." The rest is history, as her friend's little brother opened his eyes at around the same time and let out a shriek of terror as he saw the same apparition.

These two accounts are not the only ones telling of sightings in the house, as two other townspeople also claim the same. The residence has been home to several other owners since that spooky night, including one of Vinalhaven's previous town managers, who claimed that the house did not seem quite right. But for all those who read this and are skeptical, perhaps you could do a little investigating of your own. The acid was supposedly thrown at Elsie in the garden, and several people have claimed that there is a certain spot in that garden that just will not allow for growth.

My wife Elaine and I each undertook new and additional enterprises. Elaine opened the New Era Gallery and I christened Island Spirits.

Geographic Information Systems (GIS) mapping of the island was undertaken and concluded.

Hannah Pingree of neighboring North Haven announced her candidacy for the Maine House of Representatives, thus beginning her meteoric rise to the House leadership.

The Comprehensive Planning Committee completed year one of its work.

Vinalhaven Fuel announced, quite proudly and with great enthusiasm, the opening of a small slot next to the door of their West Main Street office. The innovative little opening was created to receive payments.

About this time the *Wind* began including photos of children in the early grades, first and second, from the early 1960s. They were not the best quality photos and suffered further in being transposed to the *Wind*.

The editor had invited guest columnists, hoping to continue "The Observer" as a regular feature. My mother had become a frequent contributor, and Woodrow Bunker and I less often.

> Did anyone notice, in the busy-ness and bustle of Christmas, that the calendar took a quiet turn toward spring?
>
> It happened, without fanfare, on December 21st, while you were wrapping that out-of-town gift for mailing, and someone you know was just pulling the last zucchini bread out of the oven.
>
> For one split second, the sun lingered longer above the horizon; for the blink of an eye we were not so abysmally light-deprived. Our spirits rose in ways that were totally unassociated with our Christmas euphoria.
>
> Given how brief the moment was, its importance may seem exaggerated. But is it? Something primal in us takes note, even as we tie the bow on the package, string the lights on the tree.
>
> Someone preceded us, many centuries ago, someone whose blood runs in our veins, and that person, peasant or king, felt it, too. It was a stirring that went unidentified, but not unnoticed.
>
> Now, twenty-four days past the turning of the sun toward spring, we lift our faces, straighten our backs, and begin our own journey toward that subtle promise of December 21st, that on March 21st, less than ten short weeks away, we will arrive, refreshed and restored, at spring.
>
> by Pat Crossman

> Basketball fans who had earlier questioned the wisdom of negotiating a long-term contract with rookie coach Mike Johnson were hushed somewhat after Friday's victory at North Haven. Before his appointment, allegations had flown that Johnson's athletic credentials were, at best, questionable. His resume proved to be a little inflated when it was revealed that the years during which he purported to have honed his athletic skills were really spent partying hard on what can only be considered the fringes of athletics, i.e., golf and running hard round and round the island trying to catch or even keep up with his wife, an activity he fruitlessly pursues to this day. Few, however, could dispute the observation, heard more than once, that if Johnson had spent even half as much time polishing his skills as he did buffing his dome, the season might have gotten off to an even more auspicious start. That said, however, his rapidly evolving technique of deflecting harsh gym lighting of his skull into the eyes of officials is gaining admirers.
>
> Phil Crossman

> How many remember all the stores and gas stations we had back in the '20s and '30s? I will try to remember the places I can think of growing up by the area they were in.
>
> Starting off in Arey Harbor we had John Smolander's store, selling canned goods, tobacco products

OBSERVATIONS

and candy. One of the candies I remember was Mary Jane, and oh yes, golf balls, which were coconut covered with chocolate.

Moving right along, we are in Pequot and Jim Webster's store. Jim was the grandfather of the Jim Webster we know today. Jim's store was a little bigger than Smolander's as he also sold fruit. All these small neighborhood stores sold cigarettes for a penny to anyone who had a penny back then.

Moving along to the flat, we have Sophfrania "Frania" Tolman and Nell Rolf. They were a little bigger than Jim Webster's, as they sold ice cream and they had a gas pump out front of the store. Down the street a bit we had Tat Mills's store; this is where Frannie's Frills is today. Tat's was a little bigger than Frania's and Nell's, as he sold groceries and meats. I think one spell he delivered to the houses.

Now we are at the ball ground and have Nellie Hall's store. Elizabeth worked there evenings for fifty cents a week. Now we are in East Boston at Christy Young's. She did great business with all the East Boston workers coming from the quarry for tobacco products and candy.

Back on Main Street, first was Peaslee's garage and gas station, which Carl Williams owned at one time. Next was Beatrice Ewell's twine and net business. A good many of the ladies in town knit nets for her. One I remember was called eel noggles and I think they got three cents for them. Next we had Frank White's drug store. A good many thought Frank was as good as any doctor. Oh yes, Staffy (Langtry) Smith had a barbershop above Beatrice's store. Next to the drug store was a small building that was Will Fossett's casket storage and Casey Snow's barbershop. Casey's hands were always ice cold when cutting your hair. Maybe he was too close to the casket storage. His building burned down.

Moving across the street in what is now the Masonic Hall, we had Jimmie Carver's barber shop, Russell Arey's shoe repair, and Artie Johnson's pool room. Next to this was Bill and Hannah Lincoln's Bakery. Then was the Order of Moose Hall. Downstairs was a pool room run by Bill Fossett and upstairs was the Moose Hall.

Back across the street we had L.R. Smith, in later years run by Tim Lane and his father before him. They sold clothing and shoes and boots. I think I am wandering a little as I was just listing neighborhood stores but I guess I am into a history lesson. Next to L.R. Smith was Burt Smith's Plumbing and Tin Knocking shop. Across the street again was Hill Dane's drugstore, and the A&P was in there at one time. This building burned down one foggy night. Next to this was Ed Carver's grocery store, which was later moved across where Burt Smith and Tom Saranto's ice cream and popcorn place was. These places were torn down and Carver's was built up new and the old store was torn down also. Next to Tom Saranto's was Ernest MacIntosh's grocery store and across the street was the Vinalhaven Grocery. These three stores were the largest in town and handled all meats and groceries.

In the Odd Fellows Block we had Vinal's News Stand and H.Y. Carver's Spa ice cream parlor. In the G.A.R. Hall was the C&C Restaurant. The A&P was in the old Masonic Block at one time; in fact it was there when the Masonic Hall burned. Next was Fifield's Hardware Store, later run by Bruce and Kim. Barton's Store sold dry goods and knickknacks. Bob Candage's mother ran this store after her mother retired. Homer Gray had a restaurant called the Gray Gull and Joe Kit (Kittridge) had a barbershop next to him. Cascade Lanes was run by O.V. Drew, and had pool and billiard tables, and two bowling lanes. Young boys got two or three cents a string for setting up pins.

Across the Mill Stream the building that is now the Paper Store had various tenants. One time it was a restaurant and a grocery store run by Ralph "Hebo" Clayter. After that it was a garage for auto repair run by Bruce and Duncan. The little building next had various projects. What I remember was the Red Light Cafe run by Penny Coombs. All the sales as I remember was beer on draft, ten cents a glass. The next building was Bill Merrithew's photography shop and his son Louis sold ice cream and tobacco products. This was torn down to make room for the bank.

Capt. Kent had a restaurant about where Bob Oakes's house is now. Jim Calderwood sold candy, tobacco products, and ice cream. Most of his customers were the fishermen, as he stocked also all the gear they needed to fish with. He also handled gas and oil and fuel oil. Plato Arey was next, and he sold about the same as Jim C., but he also bought lobsters and sold firewood.

Going up High Street we come to Bert Shields's store across from Carver's Cemetery. I guess Bert did great business with the kids from Washington School. Moving on down to the Sands we had Lettie Nelson's store. Going toward Dog Town, there was the George Lawry Store across the road from Capt. Frank Thompson. Crossing the bridge by Old Harbor we came to Frank Walls's store. It also had a gas pump.

I think that completes my memory of neighborhood stores and large stores in the '20s and '30s. There may be more that I don't remember. There was one by the ball ground that was never occupied and one in Shirley Guilford's yard that was never open in my time.

These stores were very necessary back in the '20s and '30s, as there were very few automobiles then, and if you forgot to get a can of beans for supper, without these stores meant a long walk back and a late supper.

In reading my notes, if the *Wind* prints these, they may have to make a novel of them. Anyway it's nice to think back when life was a little calmer than it is now.

P.S. I neglected to mention Creed's Garage. They sold gas and did car repair and had a taxi.

by Woodrow Bunker

At one time in his life, what male worth his salt hasn't hankered to build a camp, a clubhouse, a place exclusively for fellas: "No Girls Allowed!"

Back in the late 1930s, my grandmother's family rented space in the Moses Webster house, on the end toward the former L.D.S. church.

Beyond the other end, toward School Street, loomed an elegant two-story carriage house, with a slate mansard roof and a bulbous cupola.

Gram's youngest child, Bob Johnson, was fourteen, a prime candidate for a self-made getaway. When he broached the subject to his mother, she was at a loss to comprehend.

"Build a clubhouse? Why on earth would you go to all that trouble, when there are two lovely big rooms upstairs in the carriage house for you to use, all plastered, big windows, and empty, too?"

OBSERVATIONS

"That might be okay for girls playing house, but Ma, a guy wants a place to suit himself, a place for secret meetings and stuff."

My grandmother's Swedish husband, Andrew Johnson, was brought in for consultation. He listened to his wife's common sense viewpoint, and his son's heartfelt plea for autonomy. There was no contest; he sided completely with a young man's need for self-government. Furthermore, he reminded my grandmother of the ruins of a collapsed shed heaped behind the carriage house.

"There's a lot of good wood there, if you dig for it." Bob had himself an enthusiastic ally.

"All right," Gram said, "but it's full of nails and splinters; there may be a nest of snakes under there, for heaven's sake! Don't you bring one into this house! And you be careful!"

The architect was left to his own devices, in spite of ominous noises begging parental investigation. The sound of construction went on through late March and ended during April vacation.

I was on the island then, ten years old, visiting with my Gram during my school vacation. We were the only female persons invited to view the finished structure. Neighborhood boys, his father, and a few of his father's friends were there to lend solemnity to the occasion.

Bob knocked aside the sheaths of cardboard covering the facade, and stood back, tingling with pride.

It was maybe 5½ feet high, six feet square, and windowless. None of the four sides was perfectly aligned to another, but it was reasonably straight, had a door with real hinges that bore a warning, ominously black: "Girls Keep Out!!"

The door was opened by the proud builder, the boys trooped in, and the door was closed. The bumps and bangs of many bodies in small space threatened to undo the work of many weeks.

I wanted to be in there so bad I could taste it!

"I wouldn't go in there if you paid me," I said.

by Pat Crossman

The Vinalhaven Round the Island Duathlon debuted this past Saturday and is expected to be an annual event for the foreseeable future. The remarkable coordination was due to the leadership of Burke "Pain is Just Weakness Leaving Your Body" Lynch, who quickly transformed a ragtag bunch of slackers hoping for free food and drink into a demoralized and cowering company of volunteers so desperately seeking his approval that everything could only go smoothly.

The event was not without controversy, however, thanks, as many expected, to the dubious participation of Jay "The Shortest Distance Between Two Points is a Straight Line" Carlson, whose disappearance at the Pequot/Round the Island Road junction coincided suspiciously with the arrival of his sternman's pick-up headed for the dump. "He seemed to come out of nowhere," observed several competitors at the junction of the Poor Farm and Round the Island Road, as Jay burst, so to speak, from the underbrush with a Harbor Gawker container snarled up with one sneaker and three dump stickers clinging to the other.

Close behind and gaining steadily on a startled pheasant with an injured wing, Jay gasped to his dubious contenders that he'd rounded a corner so fast he'd been unable to negotiate a sharp turn and wound up in the puckerbrush. A nasty scene marred the otherwise noble and sportsmanlike behavior at the Finish Line as Bob "Short Legs Just Means I'm Closer to the Action" Candage questioned Jay's achievement and challenged him to a grudge mud wrestling match at Squid Cove to be refereed by Sid "The Best Mussels Are Over by the Discharge Pipe" Smith. A large turnout is expected.

Phil Crossman

The Return of the Native

In November, 1948, we arrived in Vinalhaven to stay. We moved into a three-room apartment, upstairs in the Carver block, on the corner of Main Street and Water Street.

It was an unusual accommodation, and took some getting used to. The tiny kitchen was in what used to be a dressing room, adjacent to the stage (or platform) of a roomy meeting hall.

A similar dressing room on the other side of the platform had been converted into a bathroom. We credit our strong legs to the continual up and down three steps from kitchen to platform, and from platform down to what had been the floor of the meeting hall, but was now a windowless inner room where our two sons slept, along with a lion (so they vowed) which had taken up residence under Phil's bed.

That room was without heat, but the former resident, Dr. Ralph Earle, had installed an interior window between the dark room and the living room. So when we cranked it open, some of the heat (and smell) from the gawky kerosene heater in the living room seeped through and kept our sons from freezing to death. Another kerosene burner that heated the water tank in the bathroom had a tendency to explode, spewing greasy soot over every exposed surface in our three rooms.

Since we had no refrigerator, we took advantage of the cold provided by Mother Nature. Bud built a plywood shelf outside our 2nd floor kitchen window, where milk, margarine, and eggs defied botulism, salmonella, and all heat-loving organisms. This worked fine until the late fall moved into early winter. Does anyone remember how frozen milk looks, pushing its tubular tongue of cream four inches above the bottle? And truly, there's no help for a frozen egg!

We had to get a refrigerator. Two years before, in Weymouth, Massachusetts, we had bought a pre-1941 G.E. secondhand. A friend freighted it up to Rockland, and onto the *Vinalhaven II*. It arrived on the island with all the pomp and huzzahs usually reserved for some great Poo-bah (and was our sole source of refrigeration until 1979!).

So, warm, or a facsimile thereof, cleaned to a paler shade of gray, and safe from food poisoning, we felt ready to face our first full winter on Vinalhaven. But, no. Innocently, we harbored a serpent in our midst, ready to strike when we least expected it. Having now mastered cooking on an iron stove (black on top, white enamel on the sides) I was ready to branch out into baking.

A gauge on the oven door provided constant information about the temperature inside. 350°, it said. Perfect! I opened the door, inserted the pan full of chocolate cake batter, and closed the door gently. I was confident. I was serene. The apartment smelled wonderful!

About twenty minutes later, I walked past the stove and glanced at the temperature gauge. 260°!! What's worse, it was dropping moment by moment! 250°! 245°! I was paralyzed with indecision; then I got mad. I grabbed a pot holder, pulled the pan out of the oven, and drop-kicked it across the kitchen (Bud considers this a signature moment in our marriage). Out of curiosity, and to mollify me, he began a search for the culprit and found it lurking in the attic and chimney.

The chimney was vulnerable to massive up and down drafts during high winds. Our stove-pipe, soaring more than ten feet above the stove before it disappeared through the ceiling, was actually hung on wire hangers all the way across the vast attic before it joined the chimney, a distance of over forty feet. The forces at work in that circumstance are awesome. Henceforth, I baked only on calm days, and we enjoyed our first ever pudding-cake, with a dollop of Dream Whip.

by Pat Crossman

~

My grandmother, Rena Johnson, died in 1989, two months before her 102nd birthday, so you can see that the following long-ago experience didn't frighten her to death. Just almost.

When Gram was a girl she had friends who were spiritualists. That is to say, a playmate of hers was part of a spiritualist family. From her young friend Gram heard accounts of meetings held in darkened rooms where the spirits of the departed returned to tip tables and deliver cryptic messages to the loved ones left on this plane. The two girls remained friends through school, but eventually marriage and families took them in different directions.

Many years passed, and then in the mid-1930s, Gram, newly married a second time, was looking for a house to rent with her half-grown family. The house she found suited her needs in every way. It had fruit trees, garden plot, berry bushes, a dock and fish house. In fact, considering its sunny exposure, it was difficult to find any logical reason to hesitate.

But Gram had reservations, all the same. She remembered all too vividly the years when her school chum's family had lived there, and how the house had seemed strange and mysterious to an impressionable girl. Nonetheless, good down east common sense prevailed. With her sensible Swedish husband and three teenage sons, she moved in.

If medals were awarded for turning houses into homes, Gram would win the Congressional. Her kitchens have always expressed a special joy in the housewifely arts.

Those first busy days in the new house were uneventful and pleasant. Gram's uneasiness dissolved and disappeared. But not long afterward, she was awakened in the darkest hours of the night by the sound of heavy knocking coming from the depths of the house. From her bedroom on the second floor she could hear the slow, deliberate sound of one blow after another, then a cascade of them, tumbling over one another frantically. She shook her husband awake.

"Andy, Andy! Wake up! The spirits are rapping in the cellar!" Her boys came stumbling in from their rooms, rubbing their eyes.

"What's up?"

"Come with me," Andy said. "We'll get to the bottom of this." Together they trooped downstairs, while Gram lay frozen in the bed, her head under the covers. An eternity passed before she heard them returning, talking in hushed voices. She sat up in bed.

"Well? Well? What was it?!"

"Spirits, all right," her oldest son said.

"Yes, ma" the younger son agreed, "and we've brought one to show you." As he spoke, he had his hands behind his back.

"It's horrid!" he said, "all wrinkled and old and shriveled up." He held his closed hand out over the bed and let the "spirit" drop. It was a large apple, part of a forgotten bagful that had tipped over in the cellar stairway, and rolled down the cellar stairs.

by Pat Crossman

In 2002 sixty-four million pounds of lobster were landed in Maine by 6,800 license holders, and the price was $3.32 per pound.

Observations

2003

THE WIND ENDED 2002 $8,400 IN THE BLACK, and, as things now and then heated up a little, the editor cautioned that submissions would be subject to editorial review.

The municipal sewer construction began and the 9-1-1 system for emergency calls was instituted.

"Viewpoint" became a column. I think the title was chosen to put a little distance between the kind of innocuous topics normally found in "The Observer" and the opinions about controversial issues that were suddenly finding voice. A "Viewpoint" column, for example, criticized a handful of folks who'd stationed themselves on the Mill Stream Bridge to protest our country's impending involvement in Iraq, prompting quick responses from me and another Vietnam veteran, the latter having experienced the extremes of combat.

Another Patriotic Note

I confess that as a serviceman back in the '60s I was not particularly aware of my duty to God and country. I didn't really carry the banner of patriotism to Vietnam. Like other guys, I was just full of myself and wanted to go where the action was. After my return home it became clear very quickly that America's involvement in Vietnam had not been a noble exercise and my role in it was even less so. During the ensuing forty years I've remained enthusiastically supportive of those who serve. In particular, I've grown increasingly appreciative of our nation's role in WWII and grateful for those who fought that good fight. I've been less and less enthusiastic, though, about some of our country's subsequent digressions and about our often mindless flag-waving in support of those ill-conceived ventures. At the same time I've become more and more aware of the sacred right we have as Americans to speak our mind and of our obligation to find fault, when conscience requires it, with our government. I've never, for even a moment, equated the exercise of those precious hard-won freedoms with a lack of patriotism. The sight of a few people willing to walk the walk (so few of us are) is an inspiring one to this veteran, regardless of which side of the bridge they're on.

Phil Crossman

Viewpoint: Another Patriotic Note

Protesting the stupid actions of our government is not a slap in my face. I have personally experienced one stupid war and do not want our servicemen in another. Everyone, including protesters, support our troops. Many do not support our government's reasons for this war (which has already begun). To suggest that protest is unpatriotic is wrong. It is this policy of "If you are not with us, you are against us" which is polarizing the world.

Our government says this war is the moral thing to do, the Pope says it is not. What bothers me most is the idea that we can attack another country because we think they may be thinking of doing something to us. Iraq did not do 9/11, and despite all the B.S., is not a direct threat to us. Preemptive war is a bad example for the rest of the world. Going to war in Iraq will not make us more secure. Perhaps many Americans need a slap to wake up and look at what our country is doing.

P.S. I would be happy to talk with anyone about this issue.

Patriotically, Jim Seawell

I began submitting columns more regularly, some as "The Observer," some under a different heading. My mom also contributed now and then but not as regularly. On one occasion we shared a page.

> The government came to Vinalhaven first in the sixties, and more frequently in the seventies, for the purpose of impressing upon us the need to deal in an acceptable way with our municipal waste. They concluded — even though only one shamelessly conscientious person responded to an invitation to come forward at a public meeting and acknowledge that he was discharging sewerage directly overboard — that Vinalhaven must, one way or another, provide for an acceptable means of waste disposal. At the time the prospect of installing pipes in all this rock was so daunting that the Feds invited us to come up with alternatives on our own. Pressured, we finally called a Town Meeting for the purpose of discussing our options and entertaining some new ideas. Entertain was an appropriate term. One suggestion given serious consideration was that we install an enormous catapult down around the harbor and periodically heave the waste from the village toward Matinicus. A similar machine, less powerful given the shorter distance, would reside up near the Thorofare and would loft a more highly refined product toward North Haven.
>
> Another proposal we all digested that night was one that would have our sewage transported to industrial lawn sprinklers throughout the community that we might all enjoy the fruits of our labors over and over.
>
> Now we are installing a conventional municipal sewer system through some very unconventional and resistant terrain. Our ancient and delicate municipal water delivery system lies closely parallel to the sewer pipes presently being installed and there is real concern that the fragile old pipes will be damaged, or worse, by the invasive excavation and blasting. Accordingly, we recently heard it suggested that we simply abandon the fragile old water system and instead let the pipes now being laid do double duty, carrying water in an easterly direction in the morning and our communal byproduct westerly in the afternoon. Innovatively speaking, I think, we continue to be way out in front.
>
> Phil Crossman

Dear Mr. Substitute School Bus Driver:

I am just a little kid. I have bounced around now in this bus, each morning and each afternoon, for several months. For a long time I worried about whether I'd get to school in one piece and then worried all day about whether I'd be returned home safely. Finally, after having ridden with the same driver for a few weeks, my concerns began to subside. And now this. I get to the top step, look to the driver's seat for the small assurance of seeing his familiar face and find instead, under a mop of gray hair, an old man, certainly too old to be driving anything, let alone a bus. You are peering over your glasses and seem unaware not only of me but of pretty much everything. I search your face for an indication that there is even the remotest chance you are capable of delivering me

OBSERVATIONS

home. There is none. Then I glance despondently down at the note in my fist, instructions from my mom that I be delivered to Grammy's, and I realize that all hope is lost. You don't know who I am or, or perhaps who you are; you certainly don't know who my Grammy is. I stall at the top step, remembering now that you are the same old guy who buried the bus in the ditch over at East Boston last fall during your only other substitute appearance. Panicked, I try to retreat but there are others piling up behind me, all urged on by the gentle albeit persistent nudge of the teacher on duty. I want to cry out "there is a comatose person at the wheel" but no one can be heard on the bus of Babel. Imploringly I pass you the note and you regard it blankly. It might as well have read *My name is Phil Crossman; if found wandering please return me home.*

To my astonishment you did complete the route safely and deliver us each to the correct destination, keeping your wits about you just long enough but apparently no longer. I understand you abandoned the bus at the motel with its flashers on and that during the fifteen minutes or so during which you were blissfully and typically unaware, six westbound cars and twenty-seven eastbound (the ferry having just unloaded) vehicles, one of which contained my mom, dutifully piled up waiting for permission to pass. If you are going to continue to be a substitute driver could you please give us a little notice so we can make alternative arrangements??

Signed, the little kid who sat right behind you and who wanted to stop at Roberta's to pee but you wouldn't let me.

The Depression years, 1929 to 1939, required new and ingenious methods to provide recreation, at low cost, for most American families. One particularly successful scheme for such a provision was "Ladies Day" at Fenway Park. Despite their devotion and fervor, Red Sox fans, like everyone else, were hard put to come up with the cost of tickets.

For thousands of the faithful, "Ladies Day" was the answer. On that day, dads paid full price, moms paid nothing, and kids under 12 were free, too. Over 12, half price.

So, as often as circumstances would allow, a sunny summer day (or spring, or fall!) would find me clutching a parent's hand on both sides to boost me up the steps of the trolley car, on my way to a day-long outing in bustling Boston.

The trip was long, the trolley crowded, but there was much to observe on the way. Hamlets were supplanted by suburbs; suburbs gave way to tenements at the city limits.

On the crowded car, men stood, and women sat. Sometimes I stood with my dad, but more often I perched on my mother's lap, a viewpoint from which I could observe the other riders and the passing landscape.

We had to change at Neponset, and at Columbia Circle we changed once more, to a subway. The swift, swaying trip underground, through black tunnels punctuated by flashing lights was fearsome, but thrilling, too.

When we exited on the elevated platform near the great brick structure that surrounded the ballpark, a tide of people swept us up, and moved us along as if we were on a conveyor belt.

As my father neared the ticket window, a young man standing by the turnstile gave my mother a pink carnation. Being a girl, I was not eligible for the folio, in which boys could keep their baseball card collections. But that was not a major disappointment, since I was much more into Shirley Temple than anything else. Besides, I knew Dad would buy a program, and everything I ever wanted to know about the Red Sox would be inside.

As long as I could remember, my father had been pitching for a twilight league team sponsored by Jordan Marsh department store. One of his teammates was a fellow from Vinalhaven named Carrol Burns. He was an employee of Jordan Marsh, an avid Red Sox fan, and, as an upper echelon member of the staff at J.M, had access to the Boston team's dressing room. Sometimes he took my father with him. Those visits provided my dad with some memorable moments.

I never saw him approach the ballpark with anything but anticipation of a wonderful time. Sometimes we got to see pre-game practice, an opportunity for Dad to explain to me the finer points of the game. As I grew older, those pointers instilled in me an appreciation for the game that has remained constant for more than seventy years.

My enthusiasm for our ballpark outings went way beyond the peanuts, hot dogs, and soda pop. What could surpass the home run that brought us to our feet with thousands of our fellow fans in full-throated acclamation? Not much!

There was just one downside to the experience. It occurred on the subway platform as we waited for the train that would bear us homeward. I wore a red beret to the game. It was my personal show of support for the team. Inevitably, as my mom and dad discussed the game, batting their opinions back and forth over my head, Mom would reach down and adjust my beret so it covered my ears. A few moments later, Dad reached down, grasped the little tab on top of my hat, and pulled it up till my ears popped out again. This continued until the train arrived, and ended my bewilderment.

For years I wondered what it all meant. It was no impediment to their conversation, usually a re-hash of the game we had just seen, but it had me looking from one of them to the other in anticipation of the next move.

As an adult, I asked one day why we had to have the "red hat ritual" on the subway platform. They looked at me as if I had lost every brain in my head.

"Who ever heard of such a thing?" Mom said.

"Why would we do that?" Dad asked.

Anyone got any ideas?

by Pat Crossman

Observations

The Reporter

A person can get advice in this town from almost anyone, and the fact that hardly anyone is qualified to give it doesn't slow either the seeker or the giver down a bit. We all know how much trouble can result if we take advice from just anyone and then run with it. With that in mind please take note of the following procedure for soliciting advice. You might tape it to your fridge.

Only three people have been officially authorized by the selectmen to offer advice. They take their places at the hardware store weekday mornings around nine. They do not include the proprietor who, although he offers advice freely and may seem knowledgeable, is much too young to be relied upon and is not authorized. Those of you who seek advice may have to wait for the Council, as they like to be called, to assemble, and they often arrive with issues of their own that need to be dealt with or otherwise resolved before their attention can turn in the direction of the lesser among us who seek their opinions. There is an accepted procedure for addressing the Council and a supplicant is well advised to follow it or risk getting bad advice. The established procedure requires only that you show up. You don't have to speak. Just stand there respectfully. The Chief Counsel, the one on the left with the attitude, will tell you what your problem is. Whether you are in agreement is of no consequence. He will then give advice freely and at length. Advice from the other two Council members may erupt sporadically or they may simply slump in their chairs and look irritated. Reliable advice has historically been that upon which all three agree. Don't hold your breath. If the Chief Counsel determines that you have conducted yourself respectfully he may offer you a cookie. If you are particularly deferential and if the tide was right the night before he may offer you a fried mussel. In either event don't take more than one. Advice can be withdrawn.

A similar group gathers in the afternoon. Don't be fooled. These are trainees and may include women.

Phil Crossman

Lost

I'm driving a long way tomorrow in the face of growing objections from Elaine, who seems to think I'm slipping a little; specifically, she thinks I'm getting forgetful, enough so as to make my driving alone for long distances risky. She cites examples. During a long drive, for instance, to ease the discomfort of being folded up for so long, I often undo my pants. Once, a young woman, already burdened with a car full of unruly kids, lurched to the shoulder with a flat tire. She was out of her car, quite pregnant, and glaring suspiciously when I pulled up behind her to help and got out of my van. Her apprehension was not diminished much when, having forgotten my unassembled condition, my pants fell down. "Don't even think about it," she hissed.

Headed to Hartford once, with something on the radio more interesting than the landscape, I stayed on I-495 and was all the way to Providence before I realized I'd forgotten to exit at the Mass Pike.

Today I walked home from an event wondering, as I approached my vacant drive, who might have taken my van. Elaine took, it seems to me, excessive pleasure in pointing out that I'd forgotten I had driven my van to the very event from which I'd come and where I'd probably find it. Personally I'm sure these modest instances of minor forgetfulness are nothing more than the by-product of an engaged mind. Incidentally, my bike is missing. It's a nice new white and blue 24-speed Raleigh. It's quite big and was last seen between myself and the road on each of several spring days around the end of March. I know some of you saw me because many commented on my graceful style.

Now I can't find the bike. It is missing. I had intended to compete with it in this summer's Duathlon and, while I have no proof, I can't help viewing with suspicion a certain short-legged hardware store proprietor who doubtless and understandably feared the competition. Or, as Elaine reminds me, I may have simply forgotten where I dismounted.

If anyone knows where it is please call me at 863-4917.

Phil Crossman

The Enlightenment

For much of the past decade, we four men — one tall and youthful, three otherwise — who are the a cappella group Phil 'n' the Blanks, have, by generously sharing our gifts, enriched the lives of this deprived indigenous population, and have occasionally brought a measure of enlightenment to the lackluster existence of our culturally challenged summer residents, too. During this time we have performed at nearly every island venue. Usually we come because we are invited but, with a mind toward the heavy mantle of social responsibility that comes with being a cultural icon, we have nonetheless had to crash the occasional event to which we'd not been extended an invitation but whose attendees, we knew, could only profit from our presence. Thus it was that our tenor heard of an upcoming private soiree at which the host had neglected to ask us to perform. This was to be one of those franchised events, in this case, he joyfully reported, a Body Mighty Party and, while the syntax seemed a little odd, even for auto repair enthusiasts, we all agreed it must be a rust-proofing workshop. So we rushed through a couple of rehearsals of "Maybelline," "Hot Rod Lincoln," and "The Ballad of Thunder Road" and set out on the appointed evening full of ourselves and of the happy anticipation that comes with knowing one is about to bring joy to others. Unfortunately, or fortunately, depending on your frame of reference, our tenor is, among his other shortcomings, a little deaf and we found ourselves not at a Body Mighty Party but rather a Naughty Nighty Party. The lusty nature of the hostess, a fact that had not entirely escaped our attention as we prepared for this gig, now made a little more sense. Still, the ladies were, indeed, appreciative; we each came away with little outfits and we've been asked to come again next year.

Phil Crossman

The Revelator

Last week someone busted out all the windows in my van and slashed all its tires. In narrowing down the list of suspects by eliminating those who are not responsible, I have determined it was not a woman. 676 women live here and only 34 are capable of heaving a fifteen-pound boulder with enough force to cause it to pass through the window on one side of the vehicle and out through a window on the other. Of those 34 women 6 are relatives with whom I am on good terms, 8 are Republicans and thus incapable of criminal behavior, 5 are evangelical Christians and so equally unlikely, 6 have demonstrated a fondness for me, one works for me now and then and I don't owe her any money, and the other 8, while admitting they do not like me, all say they think I'm funny and they wouldn't do such a thing, and I believe them.

So it's a man, or at least a male pretending at manhood. Of the 606 males in residence, 151 are children and 82 are retired, and no one in either group is a candidate. Of the remaining 373, I am close friends with 16, on good terms with 237, casually and pleasantly acquainted with 41, and happily doing business with another 74. The remaining five are openly hostile to me. Four would not have resolved their differences with me like this, however. One even said, "I don't wave or speak to you, but if I did I would say I didn't do it." The fifth, the male who has not achieved manhood, who is wavering mightily in its pursuit, and who is farther from the goal line now than he was when he started, did it. The *Wind* has a policy against personal attacks so I can't name him, but I can describe him. He is small.

Phil Crossman

Coming Again Soon

Running the motel, I've wandered in and out of Hair Haven over the years and, unlike similar exposures elsewhere and at other times, the lessons learned have not been entirely lost on me. On the contrary, I have assimilated a great deal, not only as an observer of the cutting and styling techniques employed, but also as an unintentional eavesdropper on the other side of the skimpy wall that has separated Hair Heaven and its exceedingly talkative patrons from the motel lobby. Accordingly, because Hair Heaven is leaving, and because I can't bear the thought of a summer without the unmistakable aroma of a perm in progress wafting through the lobby, I've decided to become a part-time hairdresser. Further, I expect to retain Hair Heaven's former clientele, and I suggest to those among you who may feel otherwise that you think carefully before making a hasty decision to abandon ship. You might, for example, consider the consequences of an accidental spillage, as it were, of the surreptitiously shared secrets, knowledge of which I innocently acquired during the aforementioned unintentional eavesdropping. Enough said. Suffice my assurance that your intimacies will continue to be safe with us here at Hair Hell as long as you remain our faithful patrons.

Special this week: Men's Back to Summer Whiz bangs, $6.99. Please line up outside next to the hose. The attendant (probably Dave Wooster) will tend to your shampoo. You can speed things along if, after your wash, you towel dry and arrange one of the nearby Cool Whip containers on your head in such a way as to expose only what you'd like removed, and then come on inside. But prepare yourself: many of the former luxuries have been removed in favor of mechanized cutting stations I've created here in my own shop. These may seem intimidating at first, but rest assured: I've tested them on my employees. *Remember: from automation flows affordability.*

Phil Crossman

Shades of 2000

Some may wonder why, following last week's elections, I have not conceded defeat. It's not simply because my loss astonished me, which, of course, it did. It's because with each passing day I'm growing more and more skeptical of the results. Why was I not called on election night to inform me of my defeat, as is customary? Why was I not called first thing the following morning or the results not posted on the town office door as they customarily are? Those oversights implied to me then and, as whispers of voting and vote counting irregularities grow stronger, imply to me now that this election was stolen from me, that Bodine's narrow victory and Carlene's significant margin are, at best, suspect.

Consider how many folks in this town, perhaps vote counters among them, are indebted to Bodine for her generosity and kindness over the years. My sources report that they and their friends and relatives were coerced to vote, that it was made clear they could be easily forgotten if things did not go Bodine's way.

Carlene may have similarly snatched victory from where it might otherwise not have been. Highly placed sources from within her organization report that she and her employees abandoned subtlety in communicating to Paper Store patrons that if the election results were not favorable, the time might come when one or another of them, upon death, might not find the customary basket on the counter, that no donations would be forthcoming, that their passing — their very lives — might go entirely unnoticed.

For these reasons I am, for the moment and while I await the results of an investigation, refusing to concede defeat.

Phil Crossman

Self Defense

I can hardly think of a time when, intending to be serious, it was not assumed I was just kidding, like when I asked Karen Johanson to marry me. Neither has there been a time when, joking, I am not thought to be serious, like when I suggested she might rather marry Gene Herzberg. The *Wind* receives regular complaints regarding my recent columns. For example, I should not have been allowed to write a column critical of the school bus driver notwithstanding that I am and was the bus driver in question. Another complained about my characterization of Bob Candage as a short-legged athletic wannabe. Well, sometimes the truth just hurts. I do confess that I erred in describing the stature (as in developmental) of the misfit — actually there were three of them — who vandalized my van as small. That was thoughtless because there is a family of Smalls on the island and I certainly wasn't referring to them as might have been inferred. One complaint alleged that my column on the Naughty Nighty party was in poor taste. Upon closer inspection of the merchandise I have concluded that everything's relative. In spite of a complaint that I have committed slander, I stand by my claim that the election was stolen from me by Carlene. How else to explain the basket on the Paper Store counter that says Vote Counters?

Phil Crossman

Bad Language

Four-letter words have insinuated themselves into the lives of my family. They've settled comfortably into the fabric of the lives of my wife and our daughters but they're unsettling to me. They use these words—actually there are only two words (so far)—freely. Not only do they use the words without hesitation but they employ both the technique described by one word and the substance of the other freely as well and—this is the troubling part—they are unabashedly trying to introduce these terms and the respective concepts into my life. The offending words are *yoga* and *tofu*.

I sometimes stumble, in my house, over a woman who has assembled herself in an unlikely and uncomfortable looking pose, looking very much like someone who has fallen and who, because she has apparently broken several things, cannot get up again and whose helpless form a devilish passerby has twisted further askew with legs emerging from where arms should be and the reverse. Since they position themselves often and for sustained periods in my path I assume they are subliminally suggesting that I, prompted, no doubt, by my natural grace and flexibility, become a yoga disciple.

We have recently taken to dining by candlelight, a move I coyly suspected was intended to put me in a receptive mood. Not so. Instead it was thought that in dim light I could not distinguish between the tasty morsels I enjoy and those gelatinous blobs trying to pass themselves of as chicken. If God had meant for us to eat tofu, why did He give us teeth? It's like trying to chew the stuff that congeals around a canned ham, like trying to land a punch in a dream; there is nothing there. Why, for that matter, did He give us taste buds? Certainly not so we could more fully appreciate tofu. If it's cooked with chicken it tastes like chicken. If it's cooked with fish it tastes like fish. I have a better idea: chicken and fish.

Phil Crossman

Behold our Leader

A few of you have expressed dismay over my repeated allegations about recent voting irregularities. Ever conscious of your sensitivities, I was prepared to concede defeat. Ready, that is, until last week when Carlene Michael, my former opponent, whose ascent to office could not now be more clearly in question, enticed me to join her in a canoe ride out on the open water and then tried to drown me. By nature a trusting person, always eager to think the best of others, I cast caution ahead of faith, and, although she sat in the bow facing in the wrong direction, and although she clutched a cinder block instead of a paddle, I foolishly assumed she was ready to acknowledge her complicity in the sham election, and I was prepared to offer redemption. How naive of me. Still, I survived the attempt, no thanks to the onlookers gathered at the bridge.

The incident is under investigation by the Knox County Sheriff. An arrest, as always, is expected momentarily.

Phil Crossman

The Reporter

Jeff likes to refer to his jeep as a Babe Mobile. Until the Fourth, however, when Phil 'n' the Blanks made a float from it and attracted, not unexpectedly, a female companion, the only babe I've ever seen in it is the one he struck and knocked unconscious last year while admiring himself in the rear mirror, and whose limp form he then propped up in the passenger seat. Still, there we were in the parade with a young woman in our midst. Of course, female fans are just a part of life here at the top and they often display their fondness for the Blanks shamelessly—the tossing onstage of motel keys and undergarments, for example. We, of course, reject such crude advances, and so it was that we tried in vain to dislodge this determined fan from the float. As it happens, Miss Emily, as we've now come to know her, is a professional singer and it was this gift and the likelihood that a few minutes in our shadow might boost her career that compelled us to relax our usual standards and allow her to hum a minor harmony part.

The parade was one of the best in recent memory and the band concert that night after Colors was its equal. The musicians, once they'd witnessed bass drummer Paul Byard's hat taken off (it might have been his head had he been less responsive) by the Director's exuberant gesture to port, quickly adapted to her enthusiasm and were soon leaning as one to windward each time she came about. Subsequent cymbalist interludes and syncopations from the percussions section lent a nice dramatic effect.

Phil Crossman

Evolving

We have an answering machine, but I was reminded, when Camden National instituted voice messaging, that we need to get serious about bringing automation to the motel. "Hello, you've reached the Tidewater. Please leave a message" is not good enough anymore. I intend to emulate the bank. Even though there are always the same (charming) six ladies likely to answer the phone, and even though any of them can do any of the things required, and even though nearly everyone who calls knows that, the bank's home office feels they have added a certain level of sophistication by having installed the following voice messaging system. "Thank you for calling the Vinalhaven branch of Camden National Bank. For the purposes of quality assurance and as a means of keeping our customers entertained, your call is being broadcast over the speaker phone here in the lobby. Your call is very important to us so please don't get frustrated even though you know that the installation of this system is but one more way to make actual human interaction obsolete. Now, please listen carefully as our menu has changed. For English, push 1. For Spanish, push 2. For French Canadian, push 3. If you are from North Haven, push 4 or have someone push it for you. If you are from Matinicus, breath into the phone; we'll know who you are. If this is to inquire about the supply of animal crackers, push 5. If this is "you know who," your application for a personal loan to make bail has been rejected. If this is Phil, please come down here right away. We need to talk to you. "

Phil Crossman

Quackery

This year marked the tenth consecutive Great American Duck Mill Race. The race is dependent upon the tide, which an hour or two after slack water is surging into Carver's Pond estuary at a clip sufficient to give the ducks a good head of steam as they converge on the illusive finish line, existing only in the mind and eye of whomever has the fortitude to serve as judge.

This is the purest form of undertaking. Volunteers who will profit from the event staff the sales booth for a week or so beforehand selling tickets at five dollars each. The beneificiary this year was the Babe Ruth Baseball League, and the young men ensconced therein, except for a brief interlude when two scantily-clad and somewhat more worldly girls of about the same vintage sidled up either side of the booth and queried the boys as to their age and inclinations, aggressively netted $3,000 to be divided between the league and playground.

The ascribed purity, however, has ended. As proprietor of the Paper Store, which sits astride the Mill Stream like a 500-pound gorilla and whose command of the adjacent waterway can hardly be ignored, Carlene Michael, pretender to the board of selectmen, is always in charge of the race. I'm a good sport, and so it was that this year, in spite of having been denied — by her and by fraudulent (there, I've said it) election proceedings — my rightful place on the board, I was willing to bury the hatchet in the interest of the greater good. Accordingly, I again hung the banner, in spite of my game but underqualified assistant, who, with his hand snared in the fencing around Carlene's deck, couldn't get his end of the banner up. Likewise, I volunteered to serve again as retriever of "also ran" ducks. I cannot find the words (actually, I can't print the words) to describe my dismay when among the ducks retrieved by my devoted bowman was my own blue duck (#131), floating upside down, quite dead, with its tiny head split open and with two tiny cinder blocks attached to its little web feet.

The message was not lost on me, but I am not intimidated and will run again.

Phil Crossman

Acme Moving and Storage

Opportunities of entrepreneurship abound out here. But opportunity alone will not suffice to keep a new enterprise afloat, and so it was that the Acme Moving and Storage Company, an enterprise conceived by a summer person, it should be noted, fell short, actually about six feet.

Peter Richards, ever imaginative and enterprising and concerned that Karol and I were wasting away due to a dearth of physical activity, was responsible for Acme and he was equally responsible for its demise.

Our first assignment, a lucrative one, I might add, and one that, were we successful, might have nudged us to the top of the heap of movers and storers, was to transport an upright piano from a barn (a location that Acme had its eye on as a facility at which we might accomplish the "storage" part of our mission) a couple of miles down the road to its new home. At Peter's insistence — time wasted is money lost, he argued — we did not tie the piano down. He assured us — and he was the boss — because the three of us struggled so to get even one end of the piano off the ground, that the instrument was so heavy it could not possibly dislodge itself. That might have been the case were it not for three hot and sweaty ladies bicycling our way whose progress Peter insisted we monitor. His STOP carried such urgency that we stopped rather suddenly, and as we settled into attentive observation, the presence of a looming shadow, rolling first in one direction and then another, swept back and forth through the cab. So daunting was the realization that the shadow was that of our cargo that our attention was shifted even as the bicyclists drew abreast, as it were. Moments later, with the piano, which had rolled 360 degrees, upright on the side of the road and we erstwhile movers and storers contemplating the assortment of ivory and mahogany strewn about the area, passersby began slowing to inquire as to the time of the concert.

On the drive back home Karol asked plaintively, "What am I going to tell Gigi?" (whose piano it was). "Tell her nothing," was my advice. "If she asks how it went, just tell her fine and change the subject to George Bush." "And what do I say when she asks about the piano she heard about on the side of the North Haven Road?" "Oh," Peter offered, "just tell her we saw that on our way but we didn't stop for it. We only needed one."

Phil Crossman

~

Although he was blind, my great-grandfather, Charles Shields, loved motorcars.

Sometime around 1930, he bought an open touring car, and pressed Lauretta Chilles's father, Vic Shields, into "on-call" service to drive it.

I expect there were many times when Vic was called away from a baseball game or a pleasant dalliance with a young lady to satisfy his grandfather's wanderlust. However, his job had perks for the young chaufeur, as well.

One day, when I was seven, he invited me to ride with him out along the North Haven Road, as far as Round Pond. All I had to do was ask my great-grandmother, Aura Marcella Coombs Roberts, for permission, and away we went! I was perched on the leather front seat, next to my Uncle Vic, very full of myself, very proud to be invited.

The road was gravel, unpaved all the way, and we threw up a fine spray of grit as we flew along. Just as we drew abreast of Round Pond, Vic let out a yelp, detached the steering wheel from its post and held it over his head while he stepped on the gas. It seemed like forever that we flew along the road with no one steering, but after maybe a minute, he set the wheel back in place, and we proceeded without incident.

Later the same day, before delivering me back to my great-grandmother's home in the building most of us know as the Block, Vic took me down Around the Mountain Road beside Indian Creek, and drove with a great rumble of timbers, across the small wooden bridge that crosses the creek where Earl Hamilton now has his workshop.

There was no provision for auto traffic on the bridge — just two planks a few feet apart, lying on the bridge frame. No guardrails, nothing to keep us from plunging off the side into the swift current flowing out toward the open sea. For the second time that day, my heart was in my mouth.

"How's that?" Vic asked, as we drove up the railroad tracks toward the East Boston Road.

"Scary," I gasped, "but fun!"

"Did you have a nice ride?" my great-gram asked, as I came in for supper.

"Yes, we did!" I declared with great sincerity. "We're going again sometime."

But we never did!

by Pat Crossman

OBSERVATIONS

James Roberts moved here from England in 1792 and married Sarah Hall of Matinicus. They were married down at Robert's Harbor, and Dottie Young prepared the first Vinalhaven Baked Bean Supper for the occasion. She had her little brother Louie pick over the beans the day before but the next day she picked them over again in case he'd missed a rock or two.

In 1819 James and Sarah produced the eleventh of their fifteen kids, William, and sixty came over to the house for the christening. Dottie made fish chowder with sweet and sour cucumber pickles and buttermilk biscuits. According to a diary left behind, Dottie was unhappy with the condition of the milk and sent Louie off to the barn to coax another gallon or two from the reluctant cows. Louie came back from the milking in such a foul temper that his sisters made him chew a lemon. That's what accounts for the expression he's worn ever since.

In 1839 William's wife Eliza gave birth to James II. Dottie went to the cold cellar and emerged with parsnips, potatoes, onions, carrots, rutabagas, and a well-cured corned beef, and assembled for the occasion, and for the first time in one pot, the dish that has become the classic New England boiled dinner and whose authorship, until now, has been wrongly credited to Abigail Adams.

In 1856, the same year catsup was invented, James and Jane Shaw became the first couple married in the newly constructed Union Church. Dottie made Red Top Casserole.

The whole town, a big place by now, turned out in 1872 to see Hannibal Hamlin Roberts marry Aura Marcella Coombs. This was one of Dottie's biggest gigs yet; over a hundred folks turned out for corned hake, pork scraps, boiled potatoes, fresh pickled beets and buttermilk biscuits.

In 1898 Hannibal and Aura produced a daughter, who eventually became my great-grandmother, Rena Johnson. Gram J baked the best beans I ever tasted right up until she was in her mid-nineties. I can see her now hovering over a battle-worn old bean pot she'd retrieved from the oven with a brown and stained china saucer that served as a lid. Removing the lid, she'd poke about in the beans with an ancient wooden spoon and mumble something about how Dottie always added a little water at this critical juncture, particularly on a hot day.

Three years ago Perry and Annie Boyden's daughter Sarah brought her husband, Tom, a flatlander who claimed to cook beans, home. I told him how unlikely I thought that was, given the extraordinary beans I myself produced with Gram J's recipe, and the result was the great Boyden Barn Bean Bake-Off. Folks from all over town came. On the appointed night forty or so were seated at a long table in the Boyden barn overlooking Carver's pond. It was a special evening full of wonderful fellowship, good music and conversation, and unbelievable beans. They were all so good that no single winner could be determined, and every cook credited their beans to their grandmothers who, in turn, all claimed to have learned from Dottie and whose efforts never quite met with her unqualified approval.

Once, while walking a visiting dignitary from the motel to a Lions meeting, my guest glanced up to see Dottie peering out the kitchen awning windows at the Legion Hall where she and Frances were preparing another fine dinner for thirty or forty lucky men. The awning windows were about six feet off the floor and the wall below hid the fact that they were both standing on high benches, which would allow them to peer out and see who was coming. "Who're those ladies?" my companion asked. "Oh, they are Dottie and Frances; they cook for us," I responded. "Gorry, they're tall, ain't they?" he ventured. "Well," I acknowledged, "you certainly might say that."

Dottie has secured for herself the esteemed position she holds today as chief cook, sous chef, waitress, hostess, dishwasher, and cleaning crew for the Lions, twice monthly, and the Masons and the Commandry, once monthly. Additionally, she provides the continuing Pleasant River bean suppers and Legion suppers, monthly; the Pleasant River Chapel breakfast, weekly; fund raisers for class trips; math team spaghetti dinners, all year round as needed; dinners and luncheons for special events; breakfasts for one organization or another; refreshments for funerals, weddings, birthday and anniversary celebrants, and on and on.

Dottie is more than just a tall woman. She is an institution, an indefatigable spirit. This town can happily claim to be home to quite a number of selfless, energetic people from whose energies we benefit enormously. The difference between Dottie and the rest of these is that while many of them have been at it for years or even decades, Dottie has been at it for hundreds of years. At least it seems that way.

This Saturday at a benefit supper to help her deal with medical expenses, we will have an opportunity to repay, in a tiny way, all that she has done for us. If the invitees were only those of us who have not enjoyed her generosity, there wouldn't be many in attendance.

Phil Crossman

Eight high school students attended a Model United Nations debate. The topics ranged from women's rights and terrorism to disease control, biodiversity, and the unpredictability of North Korea.

Work on the municipal sewer and the associated drilling and blasting that continued all day, day after day, frayed a few nerves, but by and large we all accommodated one another, and the work crews all received high marks for their behavior and courtesy and the efficient way they went about their business.

Town Manager Marjorie Stratton reminded us, in her now regular "Town Manager's Corner," of our responsibilities if we were ever to get the upper hand on vandalism and misbehavior. Her column had become a comprehensive and useful account of things going on at town hall.

Town Manager's Corner

Island Justice — I quite frankly do not understand the senseless vandalism and petty crime that continually plagues Vinalhaven. These are pretty simple life skills that you learn in kindergarten and Sunday school. Respect the rights and property of others. Do unto others as you would have them do unto you. People have told me not to say anything about it because I, too, will become a victim. Or people say, if you respond, that is just what they want, public reaction. Citizens will frequently come into my office and complain about vandalism, ATV destruction, and other general nuisance crimes. I first ask, "Did you file a report?" with either Knox County or the State Trooper, whichever is on duty. More often than not the answer is no. They do not want their names involved with any report for fear of retaliation. People ask me, "What are you going to do about this?" To be quite honest there is very little I can do. People have to start taking responsibility when they witness a crime. You have to actually file a report, give your name, and be willing to testify honestly about who and what you saw. Until you are willing to do that, nothing will change. For the people that do file a report, thank you for taking that first step. So don't ask me what I can do, ask yourself what you can do.

Sewer Update — this week we will continue installing 8-inch gravity and/or 4-inch force main on Frog Hollow and Clamshell Alley and begin installing 8-inch gravity on Atlantic Avenue. We will also continue crushing at the treatment plant site, and continue drilling and blasting on Chestnut Street, East Main Street, Cottage Street, and Atlantic Avenue. We will begin setting tanks at the treatment facility.

Service Stubs — If you have questions about the location of the service stub after you see the stake placed on your property, please come into the office and fill out a project issue form for Tom Hazlett. If the location is correct, you do not need to do anything.

Thank you for your support and remember, be kind to one another.

Marjorie E. Stratton, Town Manager

Evidence of the nasty, cowardly, and, unfortunately, historic custom of cutting traps loose and otherwise sabotaging fishing gear, and an account of equally despicable behavior appeared in two separate columns.

Dear Fishermen of Vinalhaven,

I was born in my Aunt Rita's house on May 16, 1954. I graduated from Vinalhaven High School in 1972 and served my country for many years in the Marine Corps and the U.S. Army.

It is my BIRTHRIGHT to lobster fish Vinalhaven territory, regardless of what some may think. I have been attacked with malice and my equipment missing over the past few years, and have not done the same to you. Instead, I have brought your gear back to the harbor and notified you that it was recovered. Some of you people are responsible for my recent loss of traps, rope, and buoys that I have worked hard on to get ready for this year.

I call you cowards. This letter is not intended for the honorable fishermen who conduct their business admirably, it is intended for the less honorable. You know who you are, and so do I. I heard about your meeting this spring, and I guess that some of you feel you can decide my fate in this business. Well, you are wrong and in doing so you may have decided your own fate. Perhaps another meeting is now needed for those of you who challenge my birthright to fish Vinalhaven. I am prepared to get totally out of this business, sell my new boat, and get a job.

Some in this community have attacked me, and it would be a good thing if the traps I have lost are recovered and returned to me in a timely manner. From this point on I will accept nothing less than 100% support from this community for the business I conduct honorably.

Sincerely,

James O. Knowlton

Murder the Cat!

If any of you people in town have a pet you love — your cat, your dog — then you had better keep a close eye on them lest they be murdered. A few days ago "Mr. D" and "Mr. B" murdered our dearly loved family cat we've had for 14 years — deliberately, wantonly and cruelly. They shot him, over and over — 15 times to be exact — and then threw him out on the road for us to find. Then they went around town bragging about a cat they shot to death — ha ha ha — while our grandchildren were home crying their eyes out (and me, too). How despicable can anyone get — murdering innocent animals for fun!

"Mr. D" moved into this neighborhood about a month ago and there's been a lot of shooting heard going on since then. There are people who walk this road all the time — especially kids. When there's a drunken idiot (and his buddies) out there blazing away, who's to say where a stray bullet will end up? Who's going to get it next? Our dog? Our kids? Your kids? Where's the law, I wonder?

No one ever wants to complain about atrocities committed around here — to point a finger where it belongs — for fear of retribution.

Well, I have no problem with pointing MY finger at the perpetrators of this atrocity — and have proclaimed it publicly and loudly — "Mr. D" and "Mr. B" admitted killing our cat — and I'm NOT going to shut up about that. And I don't care who gets mad. They can't be any madder than I am now! Let the retribution come — you can bet I won't be a silent victim!

Those two cat murderers have gone far enough. They did a brutal, cruel thing and I'm going to make sure everybody knows it! I'm going to complain loud and long — starting with this *Wind* — in every way I can, to everyone I see until justice is done — and it will be done.

The moral of this story is you better keep an eye on your pets! You never know when those cat murderers are going to show up and use your pet for target practice — so beware!

Rusty Warren

Happily, there were also frequent reminders of folks helping one another, as the numerous occasions, some acknowledged, some not, when a fisherman with traps out found himself laid up and others tended his gear.

The Ambulance Service became the Emergency Medical Service (EMS), under the leadership of Burke Lynch, and comprised eleven certified members.

Issue after issue carried, as they had since the *Wind's* inception, birthday greetings, most of which lacked much imagination, i.e., "Lordy, Lordy, look who's forty" or "Ain't that nifty, see who's fifty," each accompanied by a grainy photo of that individual as a kid and inviting us all to guess who was featured.

The Tidewater began the yearly publication of a Vinalhaven Visitor's Guide, a useful publication for visitors to the island full of information about places and events, maps, and advertisements.

I published this announcement in an issue that came out the day after a local election but which required submission the day before the election:

OBSERVATIONS

Thanks to all of you who voted for me. I intend to work on your behalf with other members of the board of selectmen who feel the same obligation. If I did not win please disregard this notice.

I did not win.

The first EMS benefit concert, featuring local groups, and organized by Phil 'n' the Blanks, was presented in August.

Work was completed on the magnificent Washington School, now home to our town offices and related spaces and activities. An open house was held in August, and tributes to Bill Alcorn, who'd served as Clerk of the Works, flowed in from every quarter.

A revaluation of island properties was underway.

I'd been concerned about the messy accumulation of bottles and cans behind the Old Engine House and the unappealing entrance it created for folks entering the Haven's dining room. I asked the town for permission to install a redeemable collection center at the west edge of the town's Main Street parking lot, against the fence separating it from my own Tidewater property, and offered to tend it myself. The intention was to clean up the Haven entrance and to continue and maximize this fund-raising component of VES.

Work began on remodeling what had been the town office/fire hall to more fully accommodate the fire department.

The community experienced an outbreak of viral meningitis.

The PIE-funded new auditorium was named the Smith Hokanson Memorial Hall after Kilton Smith and Leonard Hokanson, two island boys who went on to lead very meaningful personal and professional lives— each was an accomplished musician — but whose hearts remained forever on and with the island.

The Community Calendar, a weekly display of everything going on or about to go on, produced by the Tidewater but under the Chamber of Commerce banner, became a regular weekly feature.

THE COMMUNITY CALENDAR

Chamber of Commerce/POB 703/863-4618

WEDNESDAY the 16th
Library Trustees Annual Mtg/6:30 p.m.
American Legion mtg/supper/6:30 p.m.
Fox Island Concerts/St. Lawrence String Quartet/7 p.m./Union Church

THURSDAY, the 17th
FOG Gallery/"The Island and its History" Photography Show/ARC
Fox Island Book Club/11 a.m./Fox Island Inn
Bean Supper/6 p.m./Union Church
Planning Commission/7 p.m./Town Office

FRIDAY, the 18th
NE Women's Center Ice Cream Social/7- 8:30 p.m./ICMC

SATURDAY, the 19th
Flea Market/9 a.m./Webster's Field
Grange Bake Sale/9 a.m./Webster's Field
Silly Reading & Story Time at the Library/10 a.m.
VLT Annual Mtg/11 a.m.

SUNDAY, the 20th
VLT Mushroom Walk/9:30 a.m./Skoog Park
Sunday Evening with the Artist/7 p.m./ARC/Chip Harkness/Dick Morehouse

MONDAY, the 21st
Overeater's Anon/6 p.m./PR Chapel
Monday Night Movies/7:30 p.m./ARC

TUESDAY, the 22nd
FOL/Emily Dickinson/A Contemporary Interpretation/10 a.m./Library

WEDNESDAY, the 23rd
Storytime at Eldercare/10 a.m.
GIS/5:30 p.m./Town Wharf

THURSDAY, the 24th
Fox Island Book Club/11 a.m./Fox Island Inn
Lions/5:30 p.m./Legion Hall-Bean Supper/6 p.m./Union Church

FRIDAY, the 25th
Turkey Hollow Benefit Concert/7 p.m./Union Church

Karen Jackson penned a very nice tribute to a grand lady when Ruth Fox, the poet who first inspired the Hunker Down Cultural Society, passed away.

My Friend Ruth

by Karen Jackson

Last week the island lost a beloved member of our community, Ruth Beebe Fox. I know that so many Vinalhaven people hold such precious memories of our own Island Poet. I am deeply grateful to the *Wind* to be allowed to share some of mine and my family's. I hope others of you will also have the opportunity to share your stories and love of Ruth.

Many people have made the natural assumption that Ruth was a mother-figure to me. While that thought is a gracious one, certainly one that I would feel as a great honor, I would like to try to explain that my relationship with Ruth encompassed so much more.

Ruth was, in words that will only fall short, the best-of-all best friend. At exactly twice my age, she subtly and lovingly offered me the wisdom of her years. I reciprocated by providing her with, not nearly so subtly, my meager gift of hindsight and remembering. Over cups of coffee so strong it removed the plaque from your teeth, we discussed marriage, child-rearing, the joys and fears of motherhood, war, peace and politics, and the damned endless chase after the elusive Muse.

As the best-of-all best friend, Ruth provided complete empathy for whichever passionate mood I would burst upon her doorstep with. If I was in a rage over some injustice, she immediately would join in to rail against the dark forces with me. If I arrived with joy in my heart she would immediately laugh her tinkling laugh, clap her hands, and shout, "Yes! Yes!" If I was sad, her sweet face fell in sadness, lower lip protruding. With Ruth you could bear your heart, your guts. She never responded with an "oh well" or "tut tut." Ruth encouraged all of us to speak truth to our emotions, better yet, to put them into words, on paper.

I will forever hold dear the years when I would take a piece of my writing to Ruth for a first reading. I would sit on the edge of my chair watching her face as she chuckled right where I had hoped for a chuckle, murmuring throughout, "Oh, my! Oh, that's lovely. Oh, what a nice line…" A visit between us was never complete without each of us asking the other, "Have you written anything lately?" Often I enjoyed her lovely voice, her lovely stature, as she read to me her latest poem, shyly asking afterwards, "What do you think?"

My family's perspective on Ruth was from a different view than most of you. Ruth was, by physical proximity, our nearest neighbor. A straight shot across the Reach, closer even, than most of my Green's Island neighbors, we watched for each other's light on those early winter evenings — ours, the yellowish glow of kerosene lamps, hers, the brazen-red beacon from the red lamp that hung over her kitchen table.

To the Green's Island children Ruth served many roles, but probably their favorite was as "Ruthless the Pirate Queen." Keith, Flora, Brady, Oakley, and Hope would dress up out of the costume box in full pirate regalia, cutlasses in their teeth, row across to the opposite shore and run up Ruth's lawn screaming "garrr and grrrr!!" and "hand over your treasures!" Ruth would stand at the door, hands clutched to her heart, and in a simpering voice disarm the young marauders with promises of ice cream and cookies. As my son Oakley says, "Ruth was never an old lady, she was always playful."

Everything about Ruth was compassion. She prescribed books the way a pharmacist dispenses medicine; "a good pick-me-up," "a thoughtful book," "a cheap, racy novel." More than a pharmacist, perhaps more like a medicine woman, a shaman, she chose authors as one would choose herbs and potions. Of her thousands of beloved books, Ruth could walk immediately to the author she was seeking and hand it over to you with genuine care and concern.

Ruth, as I had the pleasure of knowing her in her 80s, had fine-tuned to perfection the art of being truly present in each moment. She adopted orphan plants and trees and enticed them to bloom again. To her, shards of broken glass were jewels to be displayed in a sunny window. A chipped teacup was still deserving of love and admiration. She treated us humans with the same patience and consideration.

Dear Ruth, you have forever changed my view of the world. Your friendship has been a gift of the hugest proportions. You have expanded all of our hearts, and we will miss you.

The Comprehensive Planning Committee was nearing the end of its work and published a succession of summary columns in advance of presenting the draft to the town for a vote.

Natural Resources Sub-Committee of the Comprehensive Plan

The Natural Resources Committee concluded that Vinalhaven's limited supply of water, both ground and surface, is the most important issue facing our island.

BACKGROUND FROM FINDINGS AND INVENTORY OF GROUND WATER

Vinalhaven's ground water supplies are limited because they are replenished solely by rainwater and snow melt. Demand for water continues to rise. Through 2002, 431 bedrock wells had been recorded on Vinalhaven. The number of wells per year has been increasing to an average rate of over 22 a year. In addition, town records are probably on the low side. For example, in 2002 there were 10 well permits issued by the CEO and 25 wells were actually drilled by Knowlton Well Drilling alone.

SOME RECOMMENDATIONS PERTAINING TO THE GROUND WATER SUPPLY

1. Take strong measures to protect, monitor, and conserve groundwater, and educate water users.

2. Enforcement of the VH Land Use Ordinance requiring that a well permit be approved for any building that will have plumbing before the building permit can be issued.

3. Establishment of a Ground Water Research Committee, whose responsibilities will include the following: a voluntary well-monitoring program for selected areas, and a survey of existing well conditions in general. The purpose will be to create an ongoing database to give us the information we need to make wise decisions about the capacity of our aquifer and the best ways to protect our water supply.

In 2003 fifty-five million pounds of lobster were landed in Maine by 6,800 license holders, and the price was $3.74 per pound.

2004

I CONTINUED TO BE AN OCCASIONAL COLUMNIST, usually, not always, penning something amusing, now and then addressing the ongoing fictitious friction between the Paper Store and my own business. On one occasion someone had erected staging at the Paper Store and it seemed a good excuse to feed the flames.

Speaking for the board, Chairman Karol Kucinski announced last week, "There is no precedent for the appeals board to act unilaterally but neither have we ever been presented with so flagrant a violation of the ordinance. Mindful that Island Spirits may have successfully prosecuted their hostile takeover of the Paper Store and mindful further that the acquiring consortium has never been shy about their intentions to expand Island Spirits across the street, we find that the presence of ladders and a few roof brackets does not constitute good intentions. Neither do they preclude the obvious. Accordingly we find that the deck hastily constructed across the street from the Tidewater Motel may not become an extension of the eventual wine bar, is illegal, and must be removed."

In the Name of the Father and of Saving Time

If you position an Aim'nFlame so its tip is adjacent to the tip of your index finger, and the barrel is aligned along the inside of that finger, and the trigger is just beneath the ball of your thumb, and the rest of the handle is tucked up under your cuff, you can point that index finger at something, like a candle, and, by depressing the trigger with your inverted middle finger (it takes practice), you can produce a flame that appears, to those of your audience who are on the other side of the aforementioned finger, to emerge from your finger tip, and you can light that candle. The effect is pretty magical, but if you are a minister and are calling upon the Lord to light the candles on the altar, the effect is particularly profound.

It is to these extremes that Pastor Bob comfortably and regularly descends and it is these "miracles" that hold his congregation spellbound. They're also time-saving exercises: no need to find a little kid to light each candle and recite something appropriate, no need, either, to try to get damp matches to light. In the interest of saving time — precious minutes during which he might extend his sermon— Bob is thinking of other ways to save ceremony during the service. The latest invokes communion. Brace yourself. He has a super-soaker, and he has wine.

Just out for a ride the other day, having biked to the summit of Harbor Hill, I began a meteoric descent down the other side, seeking the thrust to make the long climb to Lawson's Quarry. As I flew by, I saw Mark wheeling his bike out of the garage. I was grateful, flying as I was, to have built up a significant head of steam and surmised I would not have to suffer the humiliation of having him pass me, perhaps even on the approaching uphill passage. A few moments later, as I peddled furiously, he glided by effortlessly. For one frightening moment, it seemed he might even try to engage me in a little casual conversation, an effort which, had I undertaken it, might have done me in. For a while I was a little discouraged by how quickly he disappeared over the horizon. When I passed by the Boom Quarry, though, I saw some bushes wiggling off to the left, and their movement was not in concert with the prevailing wind. I suspect that he'd mustered, but then expended, all his reserves to pass me and, once out of sight, ducked into the bushes to recover.

All of us who live in these stereotypically uptight communities of rural Maine would do well to follow the progressive forward thinkers of Vinalhaven who, recognizing both the curse of immorality and the likelihood that we'll not get rid of it, have established a red light district in that historically sleazy area of town known as the Mill Stream. Gone are the days when the pure of heart and mind quickened their pace as they made their way between the Gawker and the bank in a vain effort to elude the unapologetic and shamelessly forthcoming Madam Michael and the ne'er-do-wells who are her constant hangers-on. Now, with denial in retreat, pedestrians, women and children in particular, are free from the taunts of those who have fallen from grace. Now, by law, Madam Michael and her girls must retreat indoors when the light is green, allowing innocents to pass unmolested, their ears unassaulted and their sensitivities unoffended, and may only emerge to conduct their unsavory business during the brief intervals during which the light is red.

An Islands Coalition was formed by the Island Institute to give island communities a little more representation and heft in Augusta, and Vinalhaven was asked to provide a representative.

With a new transfer bridge (boat ramp) being constructed, the town sought input from residents about what to do with the old one and whether to install a public landing at the site.

After a difficult period in the eighties when interest in maintaining the library lagged to such an extent that one participant at a town meeting suggested it had no use, a suggestion was put forward that our beautiful Carnegie library, built in 1907, be expanded. The idea began to gain traction.

The Medical Center solicited island photographs and produced its first calendar. This became an annual fund-raising event that found intrepid and intimidating board member, Dick Littlefield, moving, six times a day, unabashedly but profitably, up and down the ferry line of vehicles waiting to board, selling calendars.

The new wastewater treatment facility, final cog in our new municipal sewer, was dedicated.

Karen Jackson undertook a big project to landscape the vast grounds around the new school and wrote an appealing "Observer" spelling out the objectives and inviting participants. The fabulous new school was dedicated May 2, and not long after Karen wrote another "Observer" describing the accomplishments that resulted from the first.

> For anyone with the gardening lust beginning to stir in their souls, this is a trying month. The earth is loosening up, birds are chirping, and you can smell spring in the breeze. Many of us are drooling over seed catalogs and just itching to have dirt under our fingernails again. Take heart! Here is a fantastic opportunity awaiting you!

> A Landscaping Committee is being formed at the Vinalhaven School to beautify all that open ground. Imagine gardening without a crow bar, rock-free soil awaiting your artistic input and green thumb.

OBSERVATIONS

The initial projects will include planting rugosa roses to outline the parking areas, creating several children's gardens in the large, circular area by the flagpole, and creating a memorial garden in the half-moon-shaped area near the student parking lot. *Anyone* with *any* energy to give this project, from an hour, to an afternoon, to a week, to a plant or shrub or pack of seeds, is invited to participate. We will need seaweed, compost, manure, rakes, shovels, watering cans, divided plants, but most of all, enthusiasm and willingness.

Any individual or group with knowledge of landscape design, interest in working with young children starting seeds, anyone wanting to donate a plant, tree, or shrub in memory of a loved one, is invited to call either Kathy, at school (4800), or Karen (9325). A planning and input meeting for the community will be announced in the near future.

As this project unfolds, please take care to drive slowly on Arcola Lane and the school driveway. Please stop driving and walking on the loose topsoil and littering on the school grounds.

210 of our children, ages 5 to 18, spend 7 or more hours, 5 days a week at our community school. May we all see it, embrace it, and cultivate it as the sacred space that it is.

Karen Jackson

[excerpt]

There have been innumerable large and small blessings that have taken place since the school landscaping project has begun. As always, with any "project" this town undertakes, the thank-yous and acknowledgements become like a pebble thrown into a pond — the ripples just keep reverberating outward and bouncing back once they meet the shore.

Thanks to the blessing of the recent rains, the gardens are flourishing nicely. The children's gardens are such fun; their radishes and lettuces are up, peas climbing, and pumpkins in hot contention for the fall harvest festival. The children come out at recess to water and whisper to their plants; their excitement is precious. (Thank you to the garden fairies who have been dropping off grass clippings.)

The memorial garden is becoming a peaceful and beautiful place to sit and ponder. A cluster of pines have been planted in memory of Orren, with black pansies and orange calendula in front, his favorite colors. Randy Knowlton's crabapple has been replaced, along with an ornamental cherry for Billie Jo, surrounded by daylilies and hostas. A dwarf spruce, in honor of Doris Chilles, has great hopes of being our official Christmas tree (when it grows up…).

The high school science students are busy researching and planting a hummingbird and butterfly garden. The sixth grade science class stunned the landscape committee with the thoroughness and sophistication of their soil studies. The fourth graders have become expert vermiculturists (ask them what that means…) with the aid of their garden guardian, Rhoda.

A small apple orchard has been planted honoring our past and present teachers, each tree separated by a cluster of high bush blueberries.

The Vinalhaven Land Trust has generously offered to replace the large hawthorn at the entrance to the school, along with four dogwood trees. The Garden Club, as well, has donated a "large tree" to the school. Many, many folks have donated trees and shrubs in honor of loved ones. Memorial dedication signs are being hand painted by Jennifer Fox.

There is one more portion to be completed and that is the replanting of the trees between the school and the Pequot Road neighborhood. We have 200 spruce and pine seedlings and dozens of periwinkles, donated by the Knox County Extension. Any help with that necessary project would be greatly appreciated.

Special thanks to the tractor cowboys: Dennis, Mark, and Peter, and to Than, Martha, and Emily for planting in the pouring rain, Pam Alley and ALL of the plant donators, Bob "Softy" Candage, and Linnell, for her endless patience and consultations.

I had visions in my head of this being a "community garden" and, as usual, it, and the community, has surpassed even my wildest dreams.

Karen Jackson

Whether to establish a shore access reserve account in the amount of $131,000 was a town meeting warrant article. The article would set aside an amount equal to a late filing fine paid the town by the Maine Coast Heritage Trust and hold that money to defend future commercial shore access if needed.

The rampant destruction of public and private property by irresponsible ATV riders resulted in appeals from all quarters, including several state agencies and the Responsible Rider Association, a state-wide organization. I penned an "Observer":

> One or two salt marshes, breeding grounds for microscopic species upon which much of the higher food chain — lobsters, for example — ultimately depends, have not yet been destroyed by ATVs. When ATVs first appeared on the scene we expected them to destroy these unsightly salt marshes and others of our critical wetlands in short order and we are more than a little disappointed to find that they have let us down. A recent survey of what remains of our fragile groundwater recharge areas, wildlife habitat, scenic vistas, and carefully nurtured private woodland reveals that a few areas remain that have not been destroyed. The ATV owners who are responsible for the instantaneous degradation of environments that have taken thousands of years to mature are invited to stop by the Town Office or the Land Trust for directions to the few remaining areas they've overlooked that they might more quickly transform the entire island into one big muck hole. Chain saws will be made available for those ATV owners who feel the need to remove obstacles to unobstructed travel, i.e., trees belonging to others.

"Observer" columns in 2004 became less and less frequent but, frustrated, along with others, with the lack of performance of the Knox County Sheriff's office I submitted one:

Trying a Triad

Effective immediately, our contract with the Ghost of Christmas Past, otherwise known as the Knox County Sheriff, will terminate. In its place will be a three-person local police force consisting of Sue Dempster, who will serve as Chief; Gigi Baas, her Deputy; and Leigh Ann Chilles, who will constitute a one-woman SWAT team. Sue brings welcome energy to the position of Chief and professes to be excited about this new challenge. When asked how her experience as a school librarian — a role she does not expect to relinquish — will help her as Chief of Police, and whether she was really tough enough for the job, Ms. Dempster replied convincingly, "I have wiped their bottoms and wiped their noses. If I need to, I'll wipe up the streets with them." Under expanded new powers afforded by the Patriot Act, Sue will, if she feels an overdue book may be a risk, be free to stop vehicles and conduct searches without a warrant or to detain and incarcerate suspects indefinitely without being charged, and to deny them access to an attorney.

Deputy Gigi, having (as we all know) once negotiated herself and fellow workers out of a hostage situation, will handle the subtleties of negotiation and is expected to be invaluable in situations where compromise (not one of the Chief's strengths) can achieve desired results.

Leigh Ann will be assigned to dispatch enemy combatants and anyone who refuses to cooperate.

The creation of this local force is the result of a recommendation from the Committee on More Effective Law (Enforcement) for You, known by the acronym COMELY.

On a happier note I could continue my practice of reviewing local stage productions.

Chicago

Karen Burns must have been a vaudevillian in another life. How else to account for her poise on stage? I've never, as an audience member, been put at ease more readily than by her at the *Chicago* Dance Recital the other night. She's a natural both as an emcee and as a dancer. And what has she done with our women, and our men, for that matter? Who'd have thought Mark Jackson, bowlegged and all, could glide around like that? Karen sat right in front of me and nearly swooned. And I thought I had those ladies pegged: Kerrie O'Donnell, a refined young professional who is great with GIS mapping and computers; Hope Jackson, a demure and quiet friend of my daughter's; Gloria Smith, a teacher, after all — I thought that meant dull; Emily Brownsword, a beguilingly shy and quiet student; and Heather White, a cello player and a fan of chamber music — how exciting could that be? Clearly I haven't been paying attention. Turns out they're all wildly extroverted seductresses, hoofers, tramps, exhibitionists, murderesses, accomplished dancers, and wonderfully entertaining. (Dylan, what can I say? You only had to stand there.) Great Show!

The draft Comprehensive Plan was submitted to the State Planning Office for review. They subsequently declared it to be superior to any they'd received.

The Vinalhaven Rowers went to the Icebreaker rowing tournament in Hull, Massachusetts and won every single race.

Vinalhaven Rowers are Victorious!

On Saturday, 11-20-04, the Vinalhaven High School Rowing Team (Chad, Hillary, Flora, Morgan, Oakley, Sam, Chris, Willard, and Nate – cameraman extraordinaire) traveled to Hull Massachusetts to compete in the 2004 Icebreaker (the Open Water Youth Rowing Championship). They did an absolutely phenomenal job — just superb. They were entered in the "first gig" category (which is as high as you can go) and competed in five races for that category. They were up against other teams from all over New England and New York. When it was all said and done, the Vinalhaven crew won every single race they were in! That's right, EVERY SINGLE RACE.

Not only did they cross the finish line first in each of their races, but they showed their usual excellent sportsmanship, as well. What an awesome team we have! We are all extremely proud of them.

We'd like to thank the parents and community members for coming down to greet us off the ferry. It was quite a welcome home! We'd also like to thank ARC Sail for letting us use their boathouse and dock all season long. You guys all make it possible! Yahoo!!

For more information on the race results and photos, please visit lifesavingmuseum.org. Look up the 2004 Icebreaker.

VES held its first annual auction. I was auctioneer, and Phil 'n' the Blanks were the entertainment. This year also saw another summer concert benefiting the EMS and fire department, featuring the Blanks and several other local music groups.

Emergency Services Benefit Concert

Do you feel you are mired in a cultural wasteland because classical music and jazz is too highbrow for you and Karaoke too low? We are here for you. Come see how much local talent we have. This is the second annual Emergency Services Benefit Concert during which we literally sing the praises of our volunteer Ambulance Service and Fire Department. Tickets are available at the Paper Store and at Port O' Call. If you don't enjoy yourself and don't think the evening was worth it we'll give you your money back.

Mezzo Soprano Debbie Stone

John Gasbarre

Phil 'n' the Blanks

The Granite Chicks

CanAreys

Off 'n' On

Smith Hokanson Auditorium, Friday, July 20 at 7 p.m.

EMT Benefit Concert

Why beat around the bush? If you attend this gala event, your name will be recorded and that list of names will be referred to when the eventual call of distress originates from your house. If you are on the list you can rely on a speedy response. If you had the bad form to have missed this special event, the EMT on duty may finish his dinner before responding, perhaps wait until the ambulance cab is sufficiently warm and comfortable before setting out on a leisurely drive to your place. Don't let the last words you hear be, "Didn't see you at the concert, did I, Elmer?"

OBSERVATIONS

Second Annual Benefit Concert

Last year's sold out benefit concert, the proceeds from which were given to our Volunteer Ambulance and Fire organizations, was a tremendous success with one glaring exception. An emergency occurred during the concert making it necessary for ambulance and fire personnel to abandon the concert and tend to business. This year's concert will be presented at the auditorium on July 20 at 7 p.m. Those of you planning emergencies are asked to have them before or after and not during the concert.

The fire station remodeling was nearly complete and accomplished primarily with the volunteer labor provided by members of the department. We were reminded of the sacrifices of those volunteers in a "Town Manager's Corner."

Town Manager's Corner

Fire Department Operating Budget — Yes, our fire department budget has increased significantly since 2003. Yes, we have hired a full-time fire chief. What I would like to talk about is the reasons why. First and foremost, we do not have the luxury of mutual aid. Let me say it again, we do not have the luxury of mutual aid. Mainland towns can call in support that will arrive in minutes. When we have a structure fire, or some other emergency, there is no one else to call. While the fire department is always looking for new fire fighters, we have 36 dedicated, trained volunteers that give their time not only responding to fire calls, but to train properly for the job. The state requires 120 hours of training to achieve Firefighter I certification. These people take time away from their families and jobs to get the required training. Last year the department volunteers received 927.5 hours of training, all on their own time. They also provided 928 additional hours to build the new addition. Nobody got paid for those hours. The fear of many small fire departments, as reported in the *Working Waterfront*, is that "small departments will be mandated out of business." The federal and state governments require documentation of fire calls, training, policies, etc. etc. All of this takes leadership. Marc acts as Emergency Management Director representing Vinalhaven. We have to join in county-wide hazard mitigation plans in order to qualify for Federal Emergency Management funds. As part of this coalition, we applied for and received a grant to provide two new radios for the fire department. Marc also applied for and received a separate FEMA grant for $13,455 to provide five new Scott air packs. He will also do the mowing for our town parks and properties. All this in between responding to emergency calls. I don't know about you, but if my house is burning, I would like to know that the people responding are dedicated, trained people with the proper leadership to get the job done and do it right. Please support your local fire department.

Thank you for your support and remember, be kind to one another.

Marjorie E. Stratton, Town Manager

The Pleasant River reclamation project got underway and eventually devolved into a frustrating fiasco that spoke volumes to bureaucratic boondoggles. Ignoring advice from knowledgeable locals, the Army Corps of Engineers replaced a small pipe that allowed a modest exchange of tidal water with an enormous culvert that resulted in significant flooding. In the months of back and forth, someone superimposed a photo of the ferry cruising in toward the periodically (every full moon) flooded North Haven Road.

Town Manager's Corner

[excerpt]

Pleasant River/Vinal Cove Project — Well this certainly has been a topic of discussion for the past few weeks. Let me begin by announcing that in recognition of the excellent work done in restoring a wetland, the Knox-Lincoln Soil and Water Conservation District Board of Supervisors has selected the town of Vinalhaven for the 2004 Wetland Restoration Award with special recognition to Vinalhaven resident Lydia Sparrow for her efforts.

The scenario of this project is analogous of my job in general. I am often asked, "How do you like your job?" or "How are you doing?" If I think about the daily grind of the constant issues and complaints, it isn't much fun. But when I think about the big picture and what the general goals of the town are for the future, it gets a little brighter. I guess what I am trying to say is that I still believe this is a worthwhile project. We just did not foresee the extent of the flooding on the North Haven Road and all the subsequent issues of increased tidal flow.

On Monday, October 18th, a survey was completed of the flooded road portion by Mary Thompson, District Conservationist for Knox and Lincoln counties, and Dan Baumert, both from the USDA Natural Resources Conservation Service. They surveyed the road profile every 25 feet and cross sections every 50 feet for a 500-foot section of the road. From this survey it was determined that the highest water level that has occurred flooded the road for a depth of 1.5 feet for approximately 350 feet. Mary Thompson is also currently working to secure funding for the raising of the road surface. At a meeting held October 18th that was attended by representatives from the Department of Transportation, it was agreed that MDOT would provide design oversight, a new culvert, if needed, and asphalt for the road.

We have certainly achieved the goal of restoring tidal flow to a marsh after many years of being blocked off. This project will not only restore this marsh area but will also help to restore approximately 70 acres of clam flats, eel grass beds, and other areas important to wildlife.

A very special thank-you to Paul Bates for helping out with traffic control and to Knox County Deputy Dennis Dorsey for assisting the town road crew. I would also like to personally thank the Public Works Department for stepping up for all this extra work. In addition to monitoring the flooding, the Public Works Department assisted in placing the concrete footings for the new culvert in order to push this project forward. The goal is to get the Round the Island Road opened as soon as possible.

I will be on vacation this week. I'm sure some will say, "How can she leave in the middle of this project?" Well, there is never a "good" week for me to be away. All the problems and issues will be there when I get back.

Thank you for your support and remember, be kind to one another!

Marjorie E. Stratton, Town Manager

Observations

Town Manager's Corner

[excerpt]

North Haven Road Reconstruction and the Pleasant River Bridge/Causeway Project Update— Where do I begin? The culvert project is essentially complete. USDA Natural Resource Conservation Service and U.S. Fish & Wildlife are still having discussions with property owners to address individual property issues. Beyond that, what do we do with the flooding issue on the North Haven Road? One proposal is to replace some large rocks on the north side of the culvert to reduce the amount of flow through the culvert. The selectmen asked me to inquire about the necessary permitting for this. The Army Corps of Engineers responded to say that we would have to submit a new plan with diagrams showing the location of the rocks and the area covered. They said we could probably get these from USDA, but I doubt if USDA would provide a new plan, as they do not support replacing the rocks without more study. I have not heard from DEP, but my understanding is that we would submit a new Permit by Rule application. Along with this, we would need a Request for Approval of Timing of Activity from the Department of Marine Resources. They responded to say that DMR would not be supportive of placing rock to restrict tidal flow, particularly given the effort recently taken to enhance tidal circulation in the pond. The Department of Transportation would like to raise the road. This had always been part of the plan and we had already submitted that project to DOT. It would have been done regardless of the flooding issue. USDA has offered to appropriate $50,000 for the road project now so we can get it done sooner rather than later. U.S. Fish & Wildlife will appropriate the necessary matching funds of $12,500. We do not have letters of commitment for the funding but we are very confident. We talked with Mills Excavation and they are ready to go. In order to proceed, we need work permits signed by abutting landowners. To date we still need four permits signed. If only one landowner doesn't sign, DOT cannot proceed. I don't understand the hesitation to sign since the work will be done one way or another. If DOT doesn't get the voluntary temporary work permits, they will proceed with formal condemnation or a taking. This procedure takes more time and DOT ends up owning the property. Representatives from DOT have said that there is a very real possibility that the road will be closed if we can't get the work done soon.

Thank you for your support, and remember, be kind to one another!

Marjorie E. Stratton, Town Manager

The Flooding Project

The focus continues to be on raising the North Haven Road and NOT on fixing the flooding. It appears that USDA, who ran the Pleasant River Restoration Project, had been planning to raise the North Haven Road even before the arched culvert was in place. (Please know that MDOT has been very, very clear to point out that their only involvement in this has been to pave, not raise, the road in 2005.) USDA and U.S. Fish & Wildlife were quick to come up with the money to try to fix how their mistakes damaged the North Haven Road. What have they offered all the landowners who have been so greatly impacted by the USDA miscalculations and errors in planning?? NOTHING, except "we, USDA, won't leave town until everyone is happy." The town manager mislead when it was stated that there were still discussions with property owners to address individual property issues.

At the only meeting held for property owners to voice concerns, one landowner aptly expressed his sentiments by saying: "I will sign the necessary permit if USDA will sign that I'm justly compensated for the damages done to my property." The response from the USDA representative was that she "would need to check with her boss." No landowner caused this flooding problem and no one wants the road to be closed, but it isn't looking too hopeful that whoever is in charge is willing to fix the problem at its source. Sadly, everyone can join the property owners for the next round of high tides and flooding from 12/10/04 on. Carlene's tide calendar is predicting a 12.3-foot tide height at 11 a.m. on 12/13/04. Unfortunately, the head state conservationist with USDA, Joyce Swartzendruber, declined to attend this important event. Winter is coming and we all will continue to be inconvenienced and damaged.

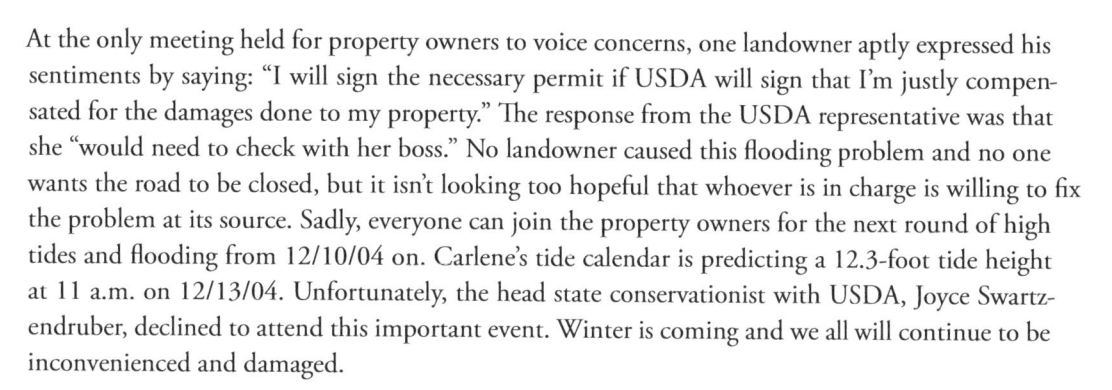

Del Webster

Island Spirits began hosting First Friday wine tastings, a popular event that soon became a tradition and has has continued to this day.

The *Wind* ended the year $7,024 to the good.

Photo by Mike Mesko

In 2004 seventy-two million pounds of lobster were landed in Maine by 6,800 license holders, and the price was $4.04 per pound.

2005

An experience I'd had at the Harbor Gawker prompted a short "Observer" and the mishap of an older local lobsterman spawned another.

Dining Tips

Some of the tables in the Harbor Gawker sit unevenly due to the undulating surface of the floor whose supports long ago sank comfortably into the mud beneath the building. The big 8-person table, #5, next to the knee wall by the piano, is one of those with a decided list. For the convenience of diners planning to enjoy a fine Gawker meal at table #5, I offer this tip to make your dining experience more enjoyable, and your meal less likely to wander off to starboard. The northeasternmost leg of table #5 must be shimmed to achieve a steady, if not level, surface from which to eat. The thickness of shim necessary exactly equals a Class II Maine Driver's License, two Camden National debit cards, and an AARP MasterCard. If you decide, as I did, to leave your shim under the table for a few days, it's best not to leave your pin number written right on the debit card, and its best not to leave a MasterCard that carries, like mine, a 19% interest rate. It's best not to do these things because Lonnie is looking to remodel.

An early morning drive by Lawson's Quarry, usually in deep fog, reveals a woman in a one-piece patiently teaching a covey of supple and pliant youngsters to swim via the Lions Red Cross Swim Program. A bevy of mothers, relieved of an hour's responsibility and required only to register intermittent support, are arranged and mutually engaged on a rocky outcrop. The lithesome and graceful form of the instructor stands in jarring contrast to the somewhat less comely bulk of Ivan (the Elder) Olson, whose marginally similar program at Sand's Cove got underway last week.

Flipper, as he is now known, has apparently undertaken to offer a course of waterfront instruction for commercial fishermen called Precision Aquatics: Rescue in a Hostile Environment, and quite a few of his fellow fishermen were in attendance for the first lesson last week. Although the program was not certified by the Red Cross and received only a lukewarm endorsement from the Association of Geriatric Olympians, none were disappointed as Ivan, with only a few feet of runway from which to launch himself, executed a flawless twisting half-pike in the tuck position to rescue an imaginary lobsterman in distress and then exhibited the grace of a much younger man as he just as speedily extricated himself from the inhospitable 50-degree waters of Sands Cove. Everyone agreed that Flipper's form was pretty good, given its advanced condition, but he is not expected to attract a bevy of young mothers at his next demonstration or at any other, not in this life.

Kevin Waters, owner of Penobscot Island Air, negotiated an arrangement allowing the exclusive use of our little airfield.

There were no "Observers" for weeks on end but now and then one would appear:

As I sat in the Vinalhaven Public Library last Wednesday evening for the July trustees meeting, I was reminded of a shockingly significant moment about seventy years ago, when I entered the building to replenish my reading supply.

I paused inside the door, that summer afternoon, and looked around me. Riches! An abundance of treasures beyond price! Fairy tales, adventures, explorations, Pompeii and the great volcano that buried its inhabitants alive, Robinson Crusoe amazed at Friday's footprints, Marmee comforting and caring for her "Little Women!"

Worlds within worlds; so much waiting to be revealed! I felt a great swell of affection for every faded cover and torn binding. Joy and gratitude for the library and all it contained filled my heart. At that moment when I felt most blest, a sudden horror seized me. Until that moment of epiphany, I had only the slightest awareness of my own mortality. Now, surrounded by books, I clearly understood; I would never live long enough to read them all! I could read night and day for the rest of my life, and still there would be words on those packed shelves that I would never see! My great-grandmother saw the change in me when I returned home. I tried to explain what I had experienced inside the precious library. No words seemed adequate to describe it. In the writer's world such a moment is known as a "come to realize." But at age eleven, I had yet to learn that.

But a cuddle with Grammy Roberts in her rocking chair, a molasses cookie, and cold milk went a long way toward restoring my equilibrium.

I now thoroughly understand that I may never see the Nile or the Ganges, the Alps or the Andes, and I, for sure, am not going to read all the books in our library!

by Patricia Crossman

Now and then, too, an interesting column would appear that might have easily been an "Observer" but was labelled otherwise.

Vinalhaven Re-Evaluation

by Karen Roberts Jackson
As appeared in the *Courier Gazette* (8/5/04)

July 31, 2004, the year's only Blue Moon, was the twentieth anniversary of our family having bought land on a small outer island off of Vinalhaven. Coincidentally, it was also the day of my "informal review" appointment with a representative of Cole Layer Trumble (CLT) Company to explain Vinalhaven's recent re-evaluation figures. What I had hoped would be a day of nostalgic reverie became a day of debate, angst, and a troubled heart. The wet, isolated, five acres of land that we had purchased for $8,000 in 1984 was suddenly worth $290,000, according to CLT.

As I sat having our numbers explained to me — the first copy I had seen of them and one I was not allowed a copy of — I couldn't help but think of a lecherous groom debating a bride price for a beautiful young girl. We were obviously speaking different languages.

Our home is a 20' by 20' owner-built home from purely "recycled" materials. What that means in simpler terms is that we scavenged, felled, milled, tore out, sanded, refinished, re-caulked, flattened nails, tied a rope to, lugged, hauled, and towed home every piece of material in her. When I say we, I am talking about my husband and our four young children. We bartered for solar panels, researched and established grey water systems and composting toilets. We worked steadily day in and day out establishing a self-sufficient life for our family. For nine of those years, we educated our children on the land, it being their true teacher.

For each of those things I mentioned to the interviewer, a light went on in his eyes. A 20' driftwood beam salvaged from the beach? "Driftwood is very popular right now," he said. Cedar shake shingles hand-split with a froe by my husband throughout one entire winter? "Ah, just like the A-mish," he said, pronouncing it with the long A. The lack of any services, and accessibility to the land for four hours either side of the tide? "What you have is privacy, and that is fetching a very high price these days," he said. I left feeling violated, and sad for my children who could one day (soon) lose their entire childhood's worth of memories and toil.

With only twenty years under our belts I realize fully that I have very little stump to stand on. My heart aches for the multi-generational true islanders who have worked throughout their lives to make their family homes, and the community itself, the paradise that it is. By virtue of living on an island, every project undertaken is a multi-faceted effort— of will, wit, common sense, sweat labor, love, and very often, the help of friends and neighbors. At least that is how it once was. Now, it seems, with the right amount of cash, anything is possible. I have been amazed to see helicopters with nets carrying loads of topsoil out to once-remote islands. I was once hired to water a stand of twenty- and thirty-foot trees, newly planted at an estate so that it wouldn't look as if it had just landed there. We drained the wells and had to hire water trucks to keep them alive.

I cannot be as eloquent as Chief Seattle in a speech that he wrote 150 years ago, so I will humbly quote him: "Even the rocks, which seem to be dumb and dead as they swelter in the sun along the silent shore, thrill with the memories of stirring events connected with the lives of my people, and the very dust upon which you now stand responds more lovingly to their footsteps than yours, because it is rich with the blood of our ancestors, and our bare feet are conscious of the sympathetic touch."

I know the only thing constant is change, but we islanders are feeling very bruised right now. There seems to be a trend in America that believes we all want to be rich. We already were rich. We had our family, our land, our homes, farms, and working waterfronts built with our own hands. We never wanted to be land barons on paper.

Island Spirits produced a weekly column that was often entertaining, and began their First Friday wine tastings, which continue to this day.

Island Spirits
863-2192

Distracted by our efforts to acquire the Paper Store, we barely escaped an aggressive move by a fellow retailer last week to execute a hostile takeover of Island Spirits.

The discovery, hidden amidst our regular weekly shipment of fine wine, of several bottles of

Thunderbird, Night Train, Boone's Farm Wild Island Berry, and a case of Ripple, suggested the aggressor might be Fishermen's Friend.

Several six-packs of Bud Light, poorly disguised as one of our real beers, and a box of Velveeta, crudely carved into a circle and standing out like a poor relation amidst our gourmet cheeses, confirmed our suspicions.

Our real Maine butter is produced by a cow that is hugged regularly and milked by hand. Roger Hufsey hugged the cow that produces Velveeta. Your call.

~

Our competition has clearly taken advantage of our winter downtime to improve their circumstances. Fisherman's Friend has been busy alphabetizing their line of beer and wine to make it easier for John to stay on top of things. Customers will now find, from left to right: Ballantine, Bud, Bud Light, Coors, Coors Light, Michelob, Michelob Light, Miller, Miller Lite, Muscatel, Old Milwaukee, Pabst, pink wine, Red Dog, red wine, Schlitz, vanilla extract, and white wine. Carver's, too, has improved their line of fine wine and beer and improved their merchandising. We think that is due in large part to Ken's role in that process, so we hired his wife so we could have a leg up.

~

It's final; the rumors were true all along but we didn't want to reveal anything that might've messed things up. Linda Bean has abandoned her project at Calderwood's Wharf and is instead buying Island Spirits (for somewhat less). Although much of our retail space is expected to be sacrificed for the lobster buying and bait business, we still expect to offer the very best wine and beer (Linda agrees: no Bud) and fresh cheeses. (Try not to slip on the herring and please don't track any of it into the motel lobby.)

~

I'm chagrined to admit it, but CEO Carlene and her stockholders have proved much more resilient than anticipated. Consequently, the hostile takeover of the Paper Store by Island Spirits has been reduced to an agreement that I can affix some advertising providing I paint her east window. That said, Island Spirits is clearly still in need of more space and other opportunities do exist. The Harbor Gawker, for example, had a moment last week when the line didn't stretch all the way to the sidewalk, an indication, perhaps, of a softening food service economy. If that's so, Island Spirits can be expected to move quickly and Gawker CEO Kathy Morton may even forego her customary post-Labor Day cruise ship debauchery in an attempt to forestall the inevitable. CEO Carlene is expected to attend this weekend's Island Spirits wine tasting and will likely be seen sharing some fine French wine with Spirits officials. Like in *The Godfather*, it's not personal; it's business.

The Last Tasting of the Summer
The Gathering Place
Sunday, 8/22 at 3:30 p.m. Featuring Fine French Wines

Pat Lundholm, this time in her capacity as a member of both the Sewer Committee and the Vinalhaven

Garden Club, oversaw landscaping of the various pump stations, an element of the original sewer plan that saw its funding reduced drastically. Pat and her husband, Ted Johanson, had, since moving here a few years earlier, and to the town's great benefit, undertaken community service on all levels.

Thank You

Several months ago Pat, a member of the Sewer Committee and the Garden Club, asked the club if it would be willing to act as general contractor in order to get the pump stations landscaped. Because the original funding was reduced by almost 25%, a way had to be found to buy the plant materials, loam, mulch, labor, and deliveries, and still get the project done as originally promised. Pat researched nursery sites for appropriate materials all over New England and negotiated discounts in several diverse locations. She worked from a landscape plan designed by Sara Stein, another member of the club. Pat coordinated all purchasing and delivery including the early delivery of 1,500 Little Blue Leaf grasses to Martha Reed's greenhouse and, with Gillian Creelman, kept them alive (the grasses had to come early both for price and availability). Pat and Ted rented a truck and went to western Massachusetts etc., to pick up the results of her research. Sara and her husband picked up a truckload en route from New Jersey. Pat then worked with the excellent help of three students from Rutgers and a local team from the Garden Club of Merry Boone, Gillian Creelman, Anne Godfrey, Philip Greven, Ted Johanson, Sue and Hugh Martin, Christa Mattson, Deborah Pixley, and Dot Webster to get the materials into the ground. Sara Stein was the soul of this project and Pat was the heart. Pat's commitment to see this through deserves the thanks of Vinalhaven.

The Vinalhaven Garden Club

The Green/Greer Island dispute, involving permitting, lack of permitting, valuation, and endless confusion and angst over a small island on the east side consumed pages and pages of the *Wind* for months on end, and the Pleasant River Boondoggle consumed only slightly fewer.

Over the years I'd been the regular back page contributor to the *Working Waterfront*, the Island Institute's monthly paper. Those 800 or so words were more often humor or satire related to island living. In 2005 the University Press of New England at Dartmouth College published a collection of those, assembled as *Away Happens*, and hosted an on-island reception celebrating the occasion.

The movie *Sternman,* later to be retitled *Islander*, was filmed and released. It was written and directed by Ian McCrudden and Tom Hildreth, the latter a long-time summer resident.

The Vinalhaven Rowers went to the Icebreaker rowing tournament in Hull, Massachusetts and again won every race.

The ninth annual Jerry Michael Roast was held at the Pleasant River Chapel.

The library addition was begun, and we were reminded that the island's first library, tucked away in the Old Engine House, consisted of three hundred volumes.

Volunteers continued to do for us what we should be doing for ourselves. This time Father Jim Clark and twenty-three youngsters from the Holy Family Life Team came to the island and painted the Old Engine House.

The *Wind* apparently had in its archives, or retrieved from VHHS, a half dozen or so historic photos which appeared now and then year after year without any particular relevance but of interest to the few who hadn't already seen them in earlier issues.

The Union Church Choir — Back row left to right: Dave Duncan, Louise Anderson, Emily Winslow, Ruth Skoog, Leola Smith, Margaret Adams, Doris Arey, ?, Harry Coombs, Front row: Greta Skoog, Jean Kelwick, Pat Skoog, Rev. Charles Mitchell, Cora Peterson, Hazel Roberts, Phyllis Borren

Photo provided by the Vinalhaven Historical Society

The *Wind* announced it would no longer be a forum for the back and forth of opposing views due to space limitations. I suspect it was proving to be more trouble than it was worth as the combatants often chose to voice their frustrations to the volunteers trying to get the paper put together. They asked that I compose an Editorial Policy:

The Wind Publishing Policy

The *Wind* is an Island News Weekly. It was begun decades ago by Rev. Ray Blaisdell, a resurrection of its predecessor, also known as the *Wind*, which was published each week here in the late 1800s. Each was intended to be a vehicle through which business owners and entrepreneurs might make themselves and their services known to others and through which islanders and visitors might know what's going on around them. While it might be of interest to some to know that a local feud is ongoing and to know the details, the *Wind* does not need the aggravation of having to deal with the aftermath of publishing such particulars. We are not a publicly owned company, not an instrument of one political faction or another, and not funded by taxpayer money. We are simply a group of volunteers happily engaged in a weekly labor of love whose sole purpose is to provide our fellow islanders with useful information. Although we do recognize the value of publishing viewpoints on issues of importance to us all and will continue to do that, we reserve completely the right to refuse to publish anything we feel will be needlessly inflammatory, objectionable, or likely to result in hurt feelings in one way or another.

The *Wind* Staff

The Key of She, a wonderful ladies a cappella group from New Jersey, made the first of several annual treks to the island to provide a lovely evening of great music for the benefit of VES.

And this:

One of our teachers, a single young lady, has had all her tires slashed. That's not unusual out here, of course. Such an approach to conflict resolution is a long and oddly honored tradition. Still, the rest of us might want to take this opportunity to let her know the subspecies is out-numbered and dwindling.

Island Spirits wanted to host a beer tasting or a tasting featuring a particular cocktail but found those to be illegal. Consequently announcements like the following brought these events to the public's attention:

Martini Tasting

As we all know, martini tastings are against the law. Therefore the purpose of the gathering on April 16 will be to discuss martinis, not to drink them. Refreshments will be served, however.

Woodrow Bunker took another spill, this one on the wharf outside Surfside, a local breakfast restaurant, prompting me to observe:

The long-running early morning competition between Ducky and Woody to get a table at Surfside came to a bloody end this week when, in his haste to be the first to receive Donna Jean's loving attention, Ducky tripped Woody, who was ahead by a length, leaving him pretty banged up on the deck. But his victory was short-lived because the object of his affections, Donna Jean, rushed to Woody's side and held him to her breast till help arrived. A disgruntled Ducky was heard to remark, "Woody will do anything for attention." Visitors to Woody's convalescence report he looks pretty much the same as always.

My mother died suddenly.

Patricia Crossman, beloved wife and companion of Bud Crossman for sixty-three years, passed away suddenly on Saturday, February 19, after having struggled with the flu and the complications of aging. She died in spite of the valiant efforts of our EMTs, the Medical Center staff, and ferry crew. Her island roots meant a great deal to her. Patricia was born here on Vinalhaven in 1923, the only surviving child of Ted Maddox and Phyllis, whose mother was Rena Johnson, whose father was Hannibal Hamlin Roberts, whose father was James, whose father was William, whose father James

Roberts landed here on Vinalhaven in 1792. Pat and Bud have four sons: Phil, Dick, Dave, and Matt, twelve grandchildren and three great-grandchildren, one of whom, Valerie Pritchard, was born within hours of her great-grandmother's death. Pat's contributions to the island she loved were many and varied. A memorial service will be held on April 23 at the Union Church, when her brand new great-granddaughter can travel more readily.

Her family asks that remembrances, when practical, be made to the Friends of Vinalhaven Public Library, on whose behalf she worked tirelessly.

The upcoming vote on the proposed Comprehensive Plan touched of a flurry of alarmist contributions, often from folks who hadn't bothered to attend any of the hundreds of meetings preceding its development but also from folks who were informed and had serious objections. The proposal was defeated, a blow to those who had worked hard for two years to compose and bring it to fruition.

The town hall originated column called "Public Notices" had by now become "Town of Vinalhaven," and the wonderful windfall festivals with music, games, pie eating, wood chopping contests, etc., begun in 2003, continued at the Sparrow Farm.

Soccer was by now a major, successful, and popular component of high school athletics.

Lucille Burgess published a book of her poems titled *As I See It,* and I described arriving in Spain for a recent sailing adventure.

The Observer

On November 19, 2005, Hurricane Delta struck the Canary Islands. A few days later repair crews still hadn't reached the Tenerife Marina where water mains and the lesser lines feeding the slips were splintered and spraying water amidst similarly shredded but very much alive and arcing power lines strewn amidst the wreckage. Characteristically oblivious, I was delivered by a taxi at dusk, and, high stepping over all the aforementioned wreckage, found *Scout,* our 42′ catamaran, clinging to the outermost berth on the outermost slip, the captain confidently sequestered in the cabin enjoying a glass of wine. He was confidant with good reason, for, having chosen this seemingly most exposed position, he was still in possession of a virtually unscathed vessel even though the slip, torn from its mooring and flung against all the inboard wreckage, was destroyed. The catamaran was bobbing in relative serenity just beyond the chaos. During the next few days the other two of our crew arrived. We made minor repairs — there was a hole just above the waterline where an aft rail had been torn off — and major repairs too. We helped restore water and power to the marina and, to the jubilant relief of fellow boaters, particularly the women, to the dockside showers. Then we provisioned ourselves with food and drink and, oddly, mood music, and cast off just ahead of Hurricane Epsilon for a sail across the Atlantic.

In 2005 sixty-nine million pounds of lobster were landed in Maine by 6,700 license holders, and the price was $4.63 per pound.

OBSERVATIONS

2006

A YOUNG COUPLE EXPRESSED THEIR APPRECIATION for help extinguishing a fire in the home they'd been renting. The home once belonged to my grandparents who in 1979 had submitted a similar note of thanks for the help they received in saving the same home when an identical fire began in precisely the same spot, just inside the east gable end window.

Maine voters, thanks perhaps to the concerted presence of the Maine Islands Coalition, voted to tax commercial waterfront land for its "current" use rather than the "highest and best" standard applied elsewhere.

A mighty effort to collect money and useful items for the victims of Hurricane Katrina was undertaken. Ultimately, over 10,000 pounds of food and supplies, an additional 10,000 pounds of rice and over $4,400 from Vinalhaven and coastal communities were trailered to New Orleans.

Caitlin Cahow, daughter of Barbara Kinder and Joe Adams, gained a spot on the 2006 U.S. Olympic Women's Ice Hockey Team, ultimately medaling that year and again in 2010. Eight years later President Obama would appoint her as a member of the U.S. Olympic Team Delegation.

Island Spirits continued to produce amusing or evocative ads:

ISLAND SPIRITS
(863-2192)

In a startling move that will surely set the island economic community on its ear, the employees of the wildly popular Island Spirits, fine beverage and specialty food emporium, have concluded a hostile takeover of the Tidewater Motel. The move left founder and CEO Phil Crossman, who arrived at work Wednesday to find his wine glass overturned— in the wine business there can be no more ominous omen — out on the street. The Island Spirits former employees (now directors) are interviewing candidates for the new position of CEO. Carlene Michael was seen emerging from the first of these. Crossman declined comment.

The women of Island Spirits completed their takeover of the Tidewater Motel last week, owner Phil Crossman having accepted the inevitable, and gone into temporary exile in Canada (he called it a vacation). Kathy Wentworth was installed as the new manager, and Carlene Michael was officially appointed financial manager. Crossman returned to find himself demoted to Chamber Lad, in which position he is expected to show up promptly for work and remain on the premises all day. Part of his new tasks will include ensuring that all the motel rooms are clean and safe, and free of hammers, saws, drills, 2 x 4s, and cinderblocks under, on, or in the beds.

Now being relieved of the task of managing the motel, the staff of Island Spirits looks forward to focusing their attention on providing you with personalized service and great suggestions for wines, cheeses, and other culinary delights.

Join us this Sunday, January 13, at the Gathering Place for a "romance wine tasting." What is a romance wine? Well, it's one that enhances an occasion already off to a pretty good start. For example: Long after the sun has succumbed to the horizon's warm caress and you have the house to yourselves, a red French Bicyclette Merlot (like the one we will offer this Sunday) is poured for you a few minutes after, in the shimmering shadows of a few carefully placed sandalwood candles, you settle luxuriantly into a tub full of hot water infused with rosewood and red mandarin essential oils and just enough bubble bath to add mystery to the moment. That would be a romantic wine.

Two for one special, this week only. Stop in; if you tell the sales clerk that you read about this special offer in the *Wind* you'll be given the chance to buy one bottle for twice its usual asking price and can then have a second bottle of the same wine for no additional charge. If you mention the magic word (oenophile) you can do the same thing with cheese.

Island Spirits
Monday, Thursday, Friday & Saturday
11- 6 p.m.

An effort was undertaken by the Chamber of Commerce to infuse the school curriculum with an island sustainability component, a subject that would address the many issues that impact our island, and its character and independence. The program would address issues like our water supply, the preservation of wetlands, economics, public space, tourism, the future of lobstering and fishing, and so forth.

My dad passed away, and a community lobster feed at the Mill Stream Cottage he and my mom built and most recently shared was held to commemorate their extraordinary life together.

> On their anniversary several years ago our folks wanted to host a community picnic. They felt such an event would be not only a celebration of the sixty wonderful years they had together but also a reflection of the love they had for this community and all who live here. At the time circumstances conspired to make that a non-event. On Monday, August 6th, following an 11:00 a.m. celebration of Bud's life at the Union Church, everyone is invited to join us for a lobster picnic at Mom and Dad's Mill Stream home. Dennis Warren and crew have graciously offered to help us pull this off. The picnic will be free (we sold off Bud's clubs to Ducky Haskell) and all are welcome.

Town Manager Marjorie Stratton wrote an interesting account of her winter hiking adventure on Mt. Katahdin.

Town Manager's Corner

Winter Hiking Trip — I guess you could say that I have developed a love/hate relationship with winter hiking. My feelings about it range from "You're nuts" to "this is awesome!" We drove up to Millinocket Friday morning from Rockland, leaving at 5:30 a.m. so we could meet the rest of the party at 8:30. We then continued up the Golden Road to the parking lot just before Abol Bridge. It was cloudy and snowing but the temperature wasn't bad. We geared up with our sleds. We all towed our gear behind on plastic sleds rigged up with rope in between PVC pipe. The PVC pipe kept the sled from moving around too much and bumping into our legs on the down slopes. Anyway, we headed up the Foss Knowlton Trail to the first pond, Foss Knowlton Pond. As we started up the trail, one of the park rangers stopped and asked us where we were headed. He told us they were in the middle of a search and rescue. Four ice climbers had gone in the day before and only two had returned. (And tell me again why I am doing this?) The cloudy weather was a little disappointing, as normally you would get views of Mt. Katahdin and the whole mountain range from this trail, but there were too many clouds and the snow was blowing, so visibility wasn't good. Crossing the lakes was neat, but the wind hit us as soon as we stepped out onto the frozen pond. I'm glad my friends had done this trip before and knew where the trail was on the other side of the pond. I never would have known where to go. I'm not sure what the name of the trail is from Foss Knowlton Pond to Lost Pond, but that is where we headed. There was no real steep elevation, just a gradual uphill climb made less enjoyable by a muscle pull early on in the day. It was also difficult to keep my hands warm. We made it to Lost Pond and it was also a windy crossing. I think the next trail is called Lost Pond Trail that we hiked over to Daicey Pond. It was strange walking across a pond that I have canoed many times. Again, there were no views because of the cloudy weather. We had rented the new six-person cabin at Daicey Pond called Nature at Peace. It is a beautiful, spacious cabin with six single beds with mattresses. My friend Gerilyn had hiked in before us to get the wood stove going, but it was still pretty cold. The hit of the evening was some Glug I had scored from a Swedish friend of mine. It is a heated alcoholic drink made with red wine and spices. Anyway, we heated it on the wood stove and it really hit the spot after a day of winter activity. Nick and I spent Saturday at the cabin playing cribbage and keeping the fire going. I didn't want to push my minor injury, so I rested for the day. We replenished the woodpile for the next group. My hiking buddy friends, Gerilyn, Sherry, and Sandy, hiked over to Katahdin Stream campground. Saturday was a better day. There were helicopters out most of the morning still searching for the lost ice climbers we had heard about the day before. Sunday was a beautiful, bright, blue-sky day, but bitterly cold. I was a little nervous about the temperature, but I put on all the clothes I had and hoped for the best. I managed to stay warm despite the cold temperatures, and the views on the way out were spectacular! I'm not sure if I will do it again, but if I do, I will invest in the expensive ice grippers or STABLicers, as the Yaktrax just don't work well. I would also look for a heated toilet seat to carry with me to the outhouse. (I know — more information than you needed.) I guess the thing I like best about these challenges is the sense of accomplishment that I did something a little out of the ordinary and a bit adventurous. I also cherish the camaraderie I share with my hiking buddies. I have hiked with the same group of women for almost ten years. It's a great feeling.

Thank you for your support and remember, be kind to one another!

Marjorie E. Stratton, Town Manager

I penned a short column on Clam Shell Alley in transition that was not well received by some (although Jeff received it well).

The Clam Shell Alley Neighborhood Association is pleased to announce its official formation. Our first meeting was held in an undisclosed residence within the narrow confines of this upscale neighborhood.

Refreshments were provided by seasonal (winter) resident Jeffrey Aronson and were followed by a business meeting. A president and vice president, treasurer and secretary were named. The identities of those four will not, for the time being, be made public. The meeting was called to order and the first order of business was to eject, not only from the Association but from the neighborhood entirely, the aforementioned Aronson who was banished in perpetuity to Granite Island and asked to take his dirty dishes with him. The second item of business was whether to hold a bake sale to raise enough money to buy out the last remaining Clam Shell Alley fisherman. The third item of business was a proposal to make Clam Shell Alley a gated community. It passed without objection.

Similar angst on the Sands Cove waterfront where my wife maintained a studio resulted in another column.

Sands Cove Neighborhood Association

Good fences make good neighbors, and good traps make good fences, and in that spirit the Sands Cove Conlict Resolution Association continues to pave the way having mutually agreed that captains whose last names begin with letters A through O will have access to the shore Monday, Wednesday, and Friday and captains whose names begin with the letters P through Z can do so on Tuesday, Thursday, and Saturday. Sternmen must be accompanied by a captain, and mouthpieces may appear during pre-dawn hours only. Artists can come and go as they please.

Dr. Rich Entel began work as our primary physician. It looked like another memorable tenure had begun.

A plan was announced to build, and ask island artists to paint, benches that would be auctioned off to raise money for the new library addition. Paul Flagg offered to build twenty outdoor benches, but then became seriously ill. Sixteen local carpenters took up the slack and a phenomenal fund-raising project was launched.

The town engaged the Maine Chiefs of Police to perform a management evaluation, the goal of which was to consider the formation of a Vinalhaven police department under the town's management. Subsequent efforts to form our own police department foundered when, after a recommendation that we maintain an ongoing law enforcement committee and thereby demonstrate support, not one person responded to an appeal to serve on that committee. The town manager voiced her frustration with being asked to do something about rampant lawlessness on the one hand and the refusal of anyone to formalize complaints or to help solve the problem on the other.

"School News" now often consumed an entire interesting page and usually spoke volumes of the vibrancy of the curriculum, teaching staff, administration, and student body.

The Maine legislature, typically passing laws and then muddying the waters of compliance by structuring exemptions, were about their usual work in the spring, exempting lobster traps from personal property tax and waterfront property used for fishing from conventional property tax assessment. Perhaps a case could be made for there being no property tax, or personal property tax, or sales tax, but imposing a universal tax and then endlessly creating exemptions seems not the way to go, although the two were popular here.

ATV riders tore through the Round Pond and Folly Pond watersheds after tearing down the signs prohibiting it, prompting real concern about the effects on those reservoirs.

OBSERVATIONS

Jeannette Lasansky published *Island Saltwater Farms: Vinalhaven Farms 1820-1960*.

High school student Holly Walker produced *Vinalhaven A to Z*, an alphabetic book of places on the island.

There were hardly any "Observer" columns during this period but toward the end of 2007 I was warming to the idea of becoming a regular.

Things I Learned at This Year's Science Fair

I always learn something interesting at the science fair. This year, while judging a wonderful experiment about balance and the inner ear, I learned two things from reading the student's notebook. First this sensible advice: "You should not look at a person experiencing motion sickness because then you'll become sick and no one will be happy." But the most thought-provoking was this illuminating observation: "Men only use the right half of their brain, but women use both halves to talk." The implication seemed to be that while men are generally half-witted, women are fully engaged but only when talking. No doubt the women will agree that the other half of men's brain is engaged in ignoring whatever it is they (the women) are saying.

Lower Pequot Motocross

The daily scooter competition between WWII vets Bert Dyer and Penny Pendleton as they race to Surfside for the attentions of certain of the wait staff there and again later for the coveted pole position in front of Carver's got a little nasty this week when Bert drew a caution flag for blowing smoke in Penny's face as they crested Net Factory Hill. Neck and neck at the time, Penny was forced to execute an evasive maneuver to avoid a nasty pile-up but still managed to pull to the curb at Harbor Wharf a length ahead of his rival. Later, having parallel parked so precisely that his four-foot scooter straddled two spaces, Bert settled in to his sidewalk chair between Port O' Call and Carver's to greet those coming and going and to offer companionship and advice to the many seeking it.

Lesser Loser

Certain signs began to appear last fall that I was getting older, so I decided to take better care of myself. I started walking two miles a day, and since then I've walked exactly the distance from here to Manhattan, 394 miles, and I've lost 18 pounds. An obsessive counter, I have calculated that, at this rate, I will completely disappear on July 3, 2019 and probably won't be taking any calls for a few weeks before then. I know this is the big year of the Loser here on the island, and many of you have lost a lot more weight than me and are looking very good. If it's of any interest, I have also calculated exactly when each of you will also disappear (I had to guess at your starting weight), which is going to be a disappointment to some of us because, as I've said, you are looking so hot.

I'll have about used up my allotted time by July 3, 2019, according to gerontologists, so my disappearance doesn't trouble me, but I do hate the thought of missing a Fourth of July by only one day, so from now on, I'm only going to walk 1.9 miles a day. That way I will still be here on the Fourth of July, 2019. I'll only weigh a pound and a half, though, so I surely won't make the next one.

2006

Sightings of a Sort

Our feeders have proved most entertaining. Among those visitors we've been able to identify are mourning doves, grackles, purple finches, various sparrows, and brown-headed cowbirds. It's hard to believe the velvety and appealing cowbirds are among the most notorious brood parasites, laying their eggs in other nests, leaving those inhabitants to hatch the eggs and raise the young. Not unlike some of us, now that I think on it.

The only species at our feeder we had to struggle to identify is, it turns out, an infrequent visitor to these parts. It's the rare red-headed, yellow-bootied, blue-jacketed trespassing woodpecker. It's a flightless bird, like a penguin or kiwi, but unlike other flightless birds this bird doesn't walk, either. It can only travel if carried from perch to perch by a similarly yellow-bootied neighbor intent on confusing our regulars. We have several neighbors, Bodine, for example.

Municipal Parking

There having been little effort to obey or enforce parking ordinances, the town cautiously announces the appointment of Sidney Smith, Crown Prince of Creed Cove, as our new Superintendent of Municipal Parking (STUMP), hereinafter referred to as the Stump Grump. The position is an honorary one, involving no stipend other than the satisfaction he and we will get from knowing that he will have full authority to bring violators to heel and to dispose of offending vehicles by rolling them down the marine railway into the harbor. He will, however, be assigned a permanent seat at Port O' Call from which he can exercise his duties.

Let's be sure to give him our support.

Tag 'em and Drag 'em, Sid!

International Business News

Rupert Murdoch's News Corporation, rebuffed in its efforts to purchase the *Wind*, instead paid $5 billion for the *Wall Street Journal*. Murdoch has not given up his hopes on entering the media market on Vinalhaven.

Stock exchanges worldwide now report that Murdoch has offered a strategic partnership to media magnate Carlene Michael of the Paper Store, whose business empire sells more *New York Times* than any single outlet in Maine. Financial gurus on the Fox Business Channel recently reported that Michael will insist that Murdoch finance her takeover of the Tidewater Motel in return for her carrying the *New York Post* and the *Wall Street Journal*. When asked for an official announcement, Michael would only say, "Perhaps I'll move into the palatial suite at the Gathering Place."

Louise Bickford was treated to a big and appreciative reception for her many years as the Union Church organist and wrote an eloquent thanks:

"Great Surprise/Well-kept Secret"

I would like to thank my family, all my relatives, Church family, and friends that came to Union

OBSERVATIONS

Church on Sunday, June 4th, to honor me for my years at the organ. Betsy and I played the Prelude, the choir processed to "Holy, Holy, Holy," then Rev. Michelle asked the people at the far back to come forward. I turned from the organ and saw my daughter Henrietta, her husband Charlie, my grandson, granddaughter, and two daughters who I assumed were on the ferry on their way back to Connecticut and Vermont. I decided the ferry didn't go. Then, I saw my stepson Harold Lee Anderson and his wife Mary from Long Island, New York, with son Michael from Boston.

My quickest thought, "What shall I feed all these people today?" Again, as I looked around I saw nieces, nephews, and their families (22 in all). Surprise is not the word for it! I wondered if I would have the "Big One" right there. After my great "shock of surprise," and I realized what was going on, I enjoyed the rest of the service so much, and wondered how I deserved so many flowers, gifts, hugs, so much love, kind thoughts and words from so many — my daughter, son, Choir, Circle, friend and pianist Betsy, Grange, neighbor Burke, school friends, and so many others.

Later, a delicious luncheon and cake was waiting. What a wonderful tribute — what a wonderful day! There were ninety-one present. I am truly blessed! I'll try to live up to some of their kind words. At the many times of losing my loved ones and wondering if I could go on, the Lord, my family, faith, Church, music, and friends have kept me going on. I wouldn't be here today without you. God bless you each one, as He has blessed me — love you all.

Louise

Islander, filmed on Vinalhaven the year before, was released and shown to us all at the Smith Hokanson Memorial Hall.

Jeff Tolman was a young fisherman and an accomplished musician. His boat was named *Rampage*, an anagram incorporating the names of his grandparents. After Jeff died suddenly, a music awards program was set up in his name and funded by Musical Rampage, a musical event held every year since at Charlotte's Field. Charlotte Goodhue had for some time made the considerable grounds of her Robert's Harbor farmstead available for this and for other worthwhile events. The Jeff Tolman Music Award provides for musical instruction, instruments, etc. Charlotte's field is also home to the annual Easter Egg Hunt and has been since 1980.

A moose was seen swimming across the Reach to Green's Island.

In 2006 seventy-five million pounds of lobster were landed in Maine by 6,600 license holders, and the price was $4.05 per pound.

2006

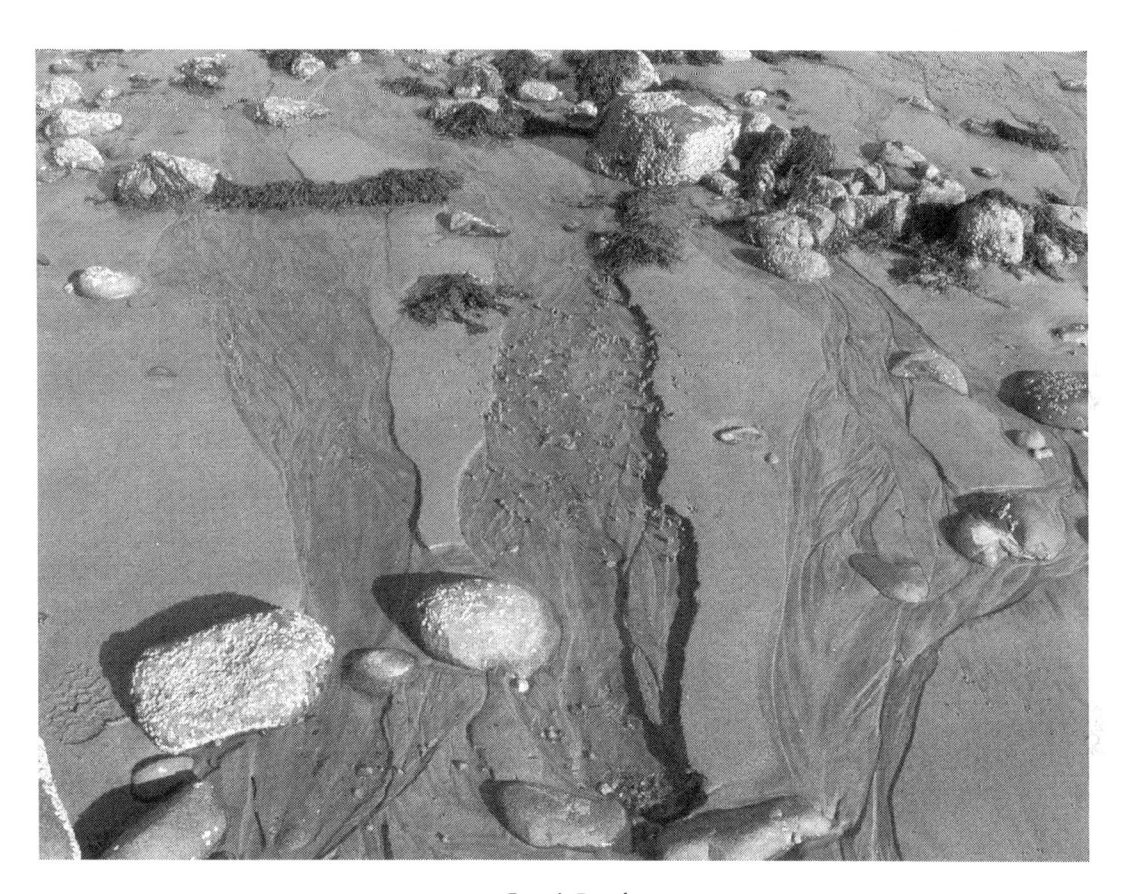

Geary's Beach

OBSERVATIONS

2007

TWO COLUMNS, "Homestead Happenings" and "Historical Society," produced by those two organizations, appeared and were very comprehensive and interesting.

A new column, "Kith & Kin," put in an appearance. It was always a surprise, each week, to discover, from among us, whose biography would be the weekly feature. It was penned by Sue Radley. This one featured Dominic Andrews, who subsequently died peacefully at four years of age.

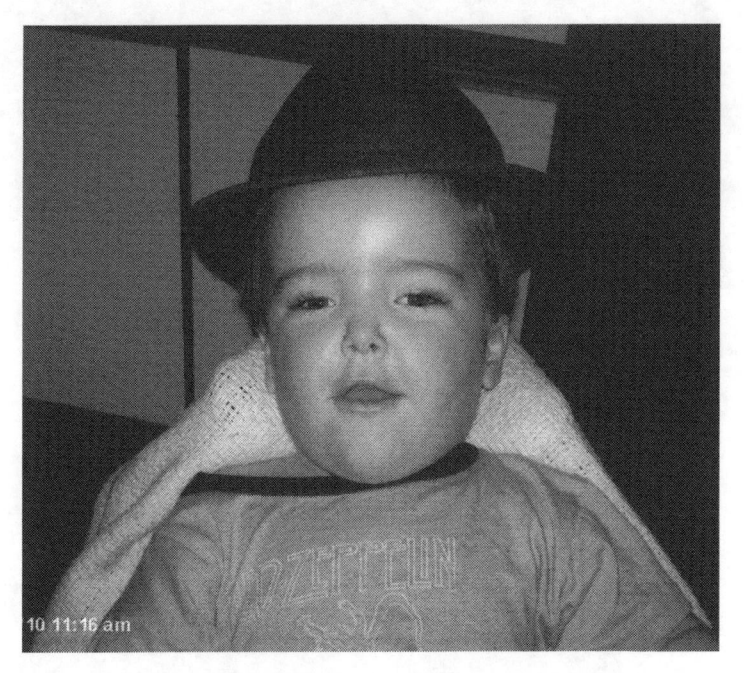

Photo credit: photo provided by the Andrews family

KITH & KIN

Dominic John Andrews

Born February 12, 2004

Most of us have never heard of Canavan Disease, but the Andrews family of Vinalhaven has learned firsthand everything there is to know. George and Stephanie's youngest son, Dominic, was diagnosed with this terminal genetic condition when he was seven months old. Canavan Disease is a devastating neurological disorder in which the brain deteriorates due to an inherited defective gene. This is the only known case in Maine. Dominic cannot perform the simplest of tasks: walk, talk, swallow food or water, or even sit up on his own. His diet consists of PediaSure and water, which is fed to him every two hours through a gastro-intestinal feeding tube. On rare occasions, birthdays for instance, Dominic gleefully licks a dab of chocolate frosting off his mom's finger.

Some of his interests are music, bright lights and loud voices, swimming at the quarry, Friday night wrestling, the Patriots, the Red Sox, and *Jeopardy!* Dominic gets very excited at the end of the day when his dad gets home and is especially fond of a visiting nurse, Lucia. A new kitten, Lily, sleeps with Dominic each night.

Tickets were recently provided by the Jason Program, and he and his mom went to Portland to watch the *American Idol* finalists perform. Dominic loved it! The Andrews family has been fortunate to have help from the Home, Hope, and Healing program of Smithield, Maine. This group finds and, if necessary, trains home health caregivers, thus providing George and Stephanie with a much-needed respite.

Older brothers Stephen and Sebastian adore Dominic and cuddle and play with him. Stephen, twelve, has learned how to run most of the equipment, prepare meds, and handle the feeding tube. Dominic visited his big brothers' classrooms to help all classmates become aware of and understand their situation. Stephanie welcomes any and all questions, so feel free to stop her, ask your questions and inquire how she and the family are doing. If you should see Dominic in his carriage, stop, look into his beautiful eyes, smile, and say hello!

On May sixth, three minutes and four seconds after two o'clock became a moment in time: 02 03 04 05 06 07.

Some folks took it upon themselves to honor the town's volunteers with a celebration which revealed that there were over eighty organizations or individuals among our volunteer community.

The town had finally given up on ever doing anything profitable with the fish plant and tore it down. Around the same time they thought it prudent to adopt a wind power facility ordinance before it became an issue locally.

The auction of the sixteen benches brought in an astonishing $45,000 to the library expansion coffers.

Nurse Practitioner Jen Desmond arrived and brought with her a selfless devotion to her adopted community and to each and every one of us.

VIVA (Vinalhaven Island Viking Adventure) SAIL got underway literally when several students sailed down the east coast of the United States and back, accompanied by Vocational Education Instructor Mark Jackson. The students, part of the Marine Technology Class, had rebuilt their thirty-foot sloop during the preceding two years in preparation for the trip. The journey was divided into "legs" of several weeks duration. At the end of each leg departing students returned home and arriving students rendezvoused to take their place.

A second moose was sighted, this time on the island.

The fourteenth annual Candidates Night was held in 2006.

The *Governor Curtis* cleaned up the ferry line of stranded vehicles on one memorable run by maneuvering the ferry and the ramp so that a few cars could drive up onto the back of Tiny Arey's otherwise empty flatbed trailer.

An ill-considered statewide school consolidation was proposed by the governor, a suggestion that would have left us and other small schools without local leadership of any kind. It didn't go far.

The new library addition was dedicated, an event that produced a related column and a relevant memory of my own.

> The Vinalhaven Public Library is fully functional once again. In the original renovated building, the new arrivals for both adult fiction and nonfiction are in the new bookcases on the left as you enter, with a beautiful LOVE statue, a gift from Robert Indiana, greeting patrons. On the opposite side

of the entrance are pamphlets, the *Wind*, and notices on the bulletin board. Be sure to also look at the outside notice board for special notices. Check-out is at the new granite counter, while books can be returned on either side of the librarians' area.

There now is a room just for adult fiction books, paperbacks, audios/CDs, and videos/DVDs. This room also has a table with an outlet strip to accommodate four wireless computer users and a couch for casual reading. The other room houses the adult nonfiction collection and reference. Two PCs for public use, the Book Search computer and a table for five with outlet plugs are available in this room. The library in these two rooms has space for at least nine laptop computer users.

The new addition houses the Friends of the Library quiet reading room with art books, other oversized books, and magazines. No computers in this room, please. Enjoy the current exhibit of former librarians, books, and art by a few island residents, and Sara Stein's carved turtles and armadillos in the display case. On the walls of the nearby hall and passageway are draft lists with names of donors and 'In-Memory-of' recipients that will be put onto permanent plaques in the fall. Please check them to be sure we have your name correct. Make corrections directly on the draft typed sheets.

The outside door to the addition enters into the Becky Bruce Teen Area that has two Macs and a table for reading, games, or wireless computer users, although teens have preferred use in this area. Juvenile reference, nonfiction, and young adult books are on shelves here. Juvenile fiction, audios/CDs, videos/DVDs and children's picture books, easy readers, and board books for toddlers are in the Sara Stein Children's Room. There is a window seat where you can sit and enjoy the wonderful stained glass panels by artist Janet Redfield that represent some of Sara Stein's art. No computers in this room, please. Rather we wish you to read a book to a child.

Many people have asked how many books they can take out at once. A family may have up to 20 items checked out at one time. In 1907 you would have been allowed to take out one book at a time with no renewal and all books had to be returned one week before the annual town meeting.

In 2007 new books can be taken out for ten days, other books for three weeks, and videos and audios are now five days, but if you keep them too long there is a fine of twenty-five cents a day for books and fifty cents a day for videos. We will be offering an amnesty week at the beginning of September.

A recent addition is our online catalog. You can browse our collection and contact us to place holds and have your book renewed. Should you not find the book you want, Inter-Library Loan Service, paid for by the Friends of the Library, is available and you can get most books within a couple of days. We have wireless Internet access available from 7 a.m. to 8 p.m., seven days a week and seating outside to use when the library is closed. The parking area is for patron use. There is no parking there from 8 p.m. until 7 a.m. and please respect our neighbors by not using their driveways to turn around in.

Just a reminder that due to a couple of accidents, dogs are no longer allowed in the library.

A Remembrance on the Occasion of the Library Addition Dedication

In 1956, at age twelve, I climbed the granite stones that are the front wall of the library and put in an appearance at the window overlooking the librarian's desk within.

With a Howdy Doody mask over my face and with my gangly young appendages spread over the window as if, perhaps, a great otherworldly praying mantis had been flung against it, I clung to the glass and waited.

I was out to frighten, on a dare, our long-suffering librarian, Alice Gould, to cause her to lose her historic composure, thereby allowing me to enshrine my name in infamy and perpetuity among my peers who had nonchalantly and uncharacteristically gathered inside, each pretending mightily an interest in the volumes of reference material before them as they, too, waited.

Wedging myself even tighter onto the window ledge and into its tiny granite-framed opening and making myself as grotesque as possible, I loosened my grip long enough to draw my fingernails malevolently across the glass.

The sound was chilling. In the long silence that followed, my younger brother, among the assembled boys, succumbed to the stress with a little gas. Mrs. Gould's head began a slow halting turn toward the boys and in an equally halting voice she queried, "What fright in yonder window rakes?"

Her eyes, unblinking, remained fixed on the boys, and theirs, blinking wildly, darted about. One's mouth hung stupidly open. He gulped and a tiny cry escaped. Suddenly, like a startled covey, the boys flew from the building — and from me, from the tenuous perch where I clung, my glasses fogged up behind my Howdy Doody mask.

Unable to loosen even a finger to remove the mask, unable to see, unable to disengage, it seemed unlikely I would have my name memorialized in quite the way I'd imagined.

I bleated a modest plea for help into the empty night before I availed myself of Mrs. Gould's gracious offer of assistance, her strong hands reaching up to give my bottom purchase.

I stood humbly before her, my mask askew but at least still concealing my identity. "Phillip," she said affectionately, "No doubt you've come to check out a book. Let's go inside and get you a library card." I removed my mask and crumpled it into a trash can as she ushered me within.

Phil Crossman

A hearing to consider an application for a ten-year Basin aquaculture lease for the purpose of growing oysters was scheduled for August of 2007.

Legislation to protect whales and other species, rules that would forbid floating ground lobster trap lines, was introduced.

Town Manager Marjorie Stratton won the 2007 Rookie of the Year Award from the Town and City Management Association.

A pipevine swallowtail butterfly was spotted on Lane's Island, reportedly the first sighted in Maine since 1907.

The ARC transformed itself into a youth center and student staffed Internet café.

In 2007 sixty-four million pounds of lobster were landed in Maine by 6,500 license holders, and the price was $4.39 per pound.

OBSERVATIONS

2008

A $74,000 GRANT PLUS $35,000 RAISED THROUGH TAXATION provided $109,000 for improvements to be made at the town wharf (former site of the fish plant).

School superintendent George Joseph, who'd so capably overseen the construction of the new school, resigned.

The Biggest Losers, an aggressive and wildly successful weight loss group, announced the particulars of their accomplishments regularly and unabashedly.

Building a Sustainable Island Community (BASIC) was a school program designed to promote environmental stewardship and advocacy.

BASIC: BUILDING A SUSTAINABLE ISLAND COMMUNITY
IDLING LESS -SAVE MORE

Why is vehicle idling such a big problem? First, with the price of fuel at $4.15 and expected to reach $5.00 by the end of the year, it is important that we remember that when we idle our vehicles, we are getting zero mpg. It is a waste of fuel and money, and is damaging to both the environment and our vehicles.

But shutting off and restarting your vehicle is hard on the engine and uses more gas than if you leave it running, right? Wrong. In fact, ten seconds of idling uses more fuel than it takes to restart your vehicle, so the general rule of thumb is that if you have to get out of the car to do something for more than ten seconds, shut it off.

In the average vehicle with a four-cylinder engine, every ten minutes of idling costs you about .03 gallons of wasted gas and more than twelve cents. If your vehicle has an eight-cylinder engine, every ten minutes of idling costs you about .09 gallons in wasted gas and more than thirty-six cents. Additionally, your four-cylinder releases about 9.5 ounces of CO^2 every ten minutes and your eight-cylinder vehicle about 28.5 ounces. These numbers may not seem like a lot, but they add up fast — especially when millions of motorists idle their vehicles needlessly.

Over the course of a year, if you idle your four-cylinder vehicle for ten minutes a day, on average, for 250 days of the year, you will have wasted a little more than $31, wasted 7.5 gallons of gas, and produced about 148 pounds of CO^2. For an eight-cylinder vehicle, multiply these figures by three.

On top of it all, idling is actually damaging to your vehicle's engine because when idling, the engine isn't running at its peak operating temperature and the fuel doesn't undergo complete combustion. This leaves fuel residues that can contaminate engine oil and damage engine parts.

So remember, idling less saves you money and gas, prevents carbon emissions, conserves energy, and is easier on your car!

For more information and the source of information, visit Hamilton County Environmental Services at www.hcdoes.org/airquality/Anti-Idling/idle.htm

The Gulf of Maine Lobster Foundation conducted a rope exchange program to help fishermen comply and cope with the Federal Whale Rule requiring that floating ground lines no longer be used. They redeemed floating line for $1.40/pound.

Our own Song of Peace Concert, featuring over forty island musicians, was held in March.

The middle and high school honor rolls were published as they had been for several years.

Vinalhaven got an indirect taste of the struggles experienced by desperate people from less privileged parts of the world who try to make a home for themselves here in America without passing through the proper channels, pathways that are often too forbidding.

Troubled Times

Many of you probably know Reyes Gilberto Mira-Echeveria. Most of us know him as Gilberto. He's been a fixture, a hard and dedicated worker, on Vinalhaven for a couple of years. He's also gotten himself into an occasional, usually trifling, mess. This time it's not so trifling. He was arrested a couple of weeks ago for assault and was taken to Knox County jail. Once there, federal immigration authorities got wind of him, and he has now been remanded to them without any chance for bail. He will remain in jail till his trial on this assault charge and then be taken to a federal detention center where he will likely languish for several months, maybe a year, till he is deported back to El Salvador, a country whose horrors of civil war he tried to escape a couple of years ago. Gilberto needs encouragement. His address is Knox County Jail, 327 Park St., Rockland 04841.

A young woman who'd fallen victim to excess and addiction but who was struggling mightily with recovery, wrote an extraordinary note of appreciation to the many members of the community who'd offered support in one form or another.

> I would like to extend my deepest gratitude and avid apologies to my family, friends, and the community. Your unconditional love and encouragement has helped tremendously with my recovery. I am truly blessed to have grown up in such a loving and caring place where people aren't quick to judge you, and where there's always somebody to lend support — even though you've really messed up. This is something that I will be forever grateful for, and hope to pass on to others in their time of need. All the cards, flowers, phone calls, and forgiveness — that in this case is undeserved — has nonetheless been heartwarming and very much appreciated. Thank you for caring so much about me.
>
> Love, respect, and prayers,
>
> Becky Guptill

Island Village Childcare (IVC) got started.

Louis Martin was made Grand Marshall of the Fourth of July parade, an honor that made his day, his year, for that matter, and a local enthusiast at that parade, performing seductively in a passing float, slipped as she lunged for an admirer (I like to think it was me).

OBSERVATIONS

CRAWLING FOR DOLLARS

The Conways have always had a good name here on Vinalhaven, and so it was sad to see one of their aging own—a woman whose character, while near the edge, had generally passed muster—crawling across the pavement, in the fading hope that she might still attract a man. The fact that it was the Fourth of July could hardly disguise the ease with which she passed herself off as a bawdy trollop, and as she tripped over her drooping skirts and descending garter in her desperate lunge toward the object of her affections, plowing her delicate chin along the asphalt in the process, observers felt sure she'd fallen for the last time. Not so. She recovered enough to continue, if not consummate, her pursuit, but as any visitor to the ferry terminal during the last week can tell, she was not her old self.

Barack Obama prompted me to reflect on his candidacy.

In 2000, during the South Carolina primary, it was alleged that John McCain had fathered a black child. I don't know how a white man does that exactly. Those making the allegation probably meant to say he'd fathered a child with a black woman. That rumor was credited with costing him the nomination. I never knew what was so troubling about the possibility that he may have done such a thing. What flaw, if true, might that have revealed — that he was adventuresome, careless, impulsive, unfaithful, an adulterer? Given the precedent set by earlier candidates and by earlier presidents, it doesn't seem likely that he'd have been denied the nomination on that basis. More likely, I'm afraid, is the notion that he had sullied his race.

Now, only eight years later, we are giving serious consideration to the candidacy of a man who is the product of a relationship just like the one that put McCain on the rocks, but in reverse.

If a white man who fathers a child with a black woman is said to have fathered a black child, does it follow that a black man (like Obama's father) who fathers a child with a white woman (like Obama's mother) has fathered a white child? If so, we are back where we started, because Obama, thus once a white child, is now just another white man, and he's fathered not one but two black children and is quite unapologetic about it.

How far we've come.

A certain peacock that had taken up residence near the landfill and was partial to the headlights of parked vehicles prompted me still further.

WARNING

I am a mature male peacock. My territory is the little bluff and environs on the Round the Island Road just east of the airstrip. It's not much but it's enough for me and for my little brood of appreciative and attentive female companions. Until last week they have been content with me. They are not, however, the brightest girls and have succumbed to the attentions of a purple Ford Taurus. You know who you are. Earlier this week you got a taste of my territorial sensitivities. Don't make me get my tail feathers up.

Zone C Lobster Hatchery asked for volunteers to take out divers from the Department of Marine Resources (DMR) to check on those juveniles released.

The Emergency Services Benefit Challenge replaced the Duathalon and Family Fun Run.

A proposal to spend $6,000 to buy an intoxilizer was defeated fifteen to fourteen at a poorly attended town meeting. The equipment would have allowed the arresting officer to determine blood alcohol levels and would have eliminated the need for medical service personnel, already stretched, to determine, with a blood test, whether a driver was under the influence. A subsequent effort to purchase the equipment through donations proved successful but enormously and bafflingly contentious.

Whether to build a transfer bridge at the north end of the island was again considered. Such an arrangement would allow ferries coming and going from North Haven, but less than full, to pick up overflow traffic from Vinalhaven.

A new line-up procedure was adopted at the Rockland ferry terminal providing that no car could be used to hold a place in line unless that substitute had a notice in the windshield identifying both the vehicle expected to take its place and its intended departure time.

Ducky and Addison are two authentic natives:

Ours is Not to Question Why

On a walk in the Basin woods I suddenly found my companion crouched next to a huge old birch tree. She was mumbling "eighteen." I asked her what she was doing and she pointed to an old carving in the majestic big birch beside which she hunkered down. Carved in the bark was:

DUCK
&
ADD
1971

If this makes sense to you, you're probably not from Away.

A "Superintendent's Column" appeared.

John Drury produced a comprehensive play-by-play column describing soccer games.

[excerpt]

The field was dry, just a couple of slippery muddy spots in the goalmouth. The Vikings were: Nathan Hopkins in goal, Sam Rosen – Sweeper, Ethan Watt – Stopper, outside backs – Virgil Cray and Ladd Olson, Midfield – Tyler Chilles, Corey James, Willie Drury and John Morton, Andrew Guptill and Stephen Osgood – Wingers, Keith Drury – Striker, with Ryan Jones, Bobby Beckman and Joey Reidy. Not available, Ansel Andrews, Corbin Osgood, and Brian Stanley. Greenville had knocked us out of the tournament the last two years and had beaten us 2-1 twice this fall. The game started cautiously, there were no good shots generated until the sixth minute when Andrew ran on to a through ball in the box near the end line, took one touch before passing it by the goalie to the right foot of Stephen making a run at the far post who first touched it in. There were good chances for both teams later in the first half, none scored. Nathan had an outstanding game; diving to his left he extended to get one hand on a low, hard shot at the corner and recovered quickly to block what looked like a sure goal for the wing who tried to finish the rebound. The Greenville keeper dove to his left to save a fine shot by Corey from 18 yards. Corey got an eye scratched and had to sit for much of the middle of the game, so Keith dropped back to fill center midfield. Greenville worked hard to get even but Ethan was giant; with great timing he won many balls near the edge of the box. Sam used his speed and good positioning to contain their quick striker again and again on one-on-one situations. Ladd and Virgil both played very well. The three freshman midfielders covered the field well and worked the ball forward. Our attackers built some good chances but could not find a second goal. The second half ended scoreless, the final was Vinalhaven1 Greenville 0. The team travels to play #2 Rangeley Tuesday in the western Maine Semi-final.

Elaine and I were invited to a neighbor's to play croquet.

Cutthroat Croquet

A few women play lacrosse and soccer, some wrestle, but generally these rough and tumble games are the domain of men and last week's Leo Lane Croquet Invitational was no exception, as evidenced by the crippling ankle injury suffered by erstwhile but ill-advised competitor Carlene Michael. While the hosts tried to temper the inherent aggression of world-class croquet with an endless stream of great finger food and good wine, and to rein in hostilities with light conversation and jurisprudence, the game evolved, as everyone knew it would, into a match of endurance, strength, and brute force. Carlene will doubtless stick to duck racing next year.

Our frustration when comparing the range of bird life at our own house with that experienced by others, particularly those illuminated in Kirk Gentalen's Vinalhaven Sightings blog, prompted a column.

Birds of a Feather

We have installed an inviting tree branch in place of the umbrella on our patio table and beneath it placed a heaping plate of birdseed and eye catching snacks.

We hung a log of sunflower seeds sandwiched in honey and goop in a nearby tree for woodpeckers.

We scattered seeds on the ground for mourning doves and pigeons and hung a thing-a-ma-jig on the side of the shed for hummingbirds.

We stapled several tree branches to the house next to the kitchen window and stuck a smaller feeder on the glass with a suction cup.

Now we stand, expectant and hand wringing, at the sink, only inches from the feeder, hidden within, we're quite sure, by the tree branches without. Like hopeful new shop-keepers we wait pathetically for traffic.

We're on Kirk Gentalen's mailing list, so why have they forsaken us?

A Men's Book Club was formed.

The Vinalhaven Rowers won the Northeast Regional Open Water Youth Rowing Championships at Hull, Massachusetts for the fourth year in the last five.

Senior profiles became a regular feature, one appearing each week, with an accompanying photo, till the entire class had been featured.

Phil 'n' the Blanks was having trouble with its tenor:

Needed:

A real tenor. Must have a stable love life and be, thus, reliable. Other desirable qualities include an element of modesty and a diminished ego. The slightest presence of either would be welcome. The need for him to be fully grown cannot be overstated, as the rest of group must be able to communicate with him without continually bending over. Finally, he must be able to distinguish between a Jeep and reliable transportation, and the size of his mouth should be in reasonable proportion with the rest of his body. Agents need not apply.

Phil 'n' the Blanks

In 2008 seventy million pounds of lobster were landed in Maine by 6,300 license holders, and the price was $3.51 per pound.

2009

THE SECOND INSTALLMENT OF THE *BREAKING WIND* WAS PUT TOGETHER in anticipation of the Fourth of July celebrations when it was intended to be sold and the profits given to the *Wind*.

Noah Thompson died in his crib just after enjoying his first Christmas. Words failed us all.

Twenty volunteers from Meals on Wheels delivered over twelve hundred hot meals over the winter to over forty elderly island residents.

The ARC began offering a broader range of programs, to adults as well as to kids. A March offering was "Small Business Marketing and Image Building."

The Maine Department of Agriculture proposed to conduct an environmental assessment on a suggested wind farm site on the North Haven Road on behalf of Fox Island Wind, LLC (FIW) and then things moved very quickly.

The "Biggest Loser Update," "Homestead Happenings," and "Superintendent's Column" continued to be a big presence in the *Wind*.

Biggest Loser Update

Sorry there was no update last week. There were a few people gone on vacations. Our biggest loser for that week was Angela "Bone Crusher" Hopkins losing 6.5 pounds. If anyone has seen her husband, Jim, walking around in a sling then you probably know how she lost all that weight. This week's weigh-in was won by the Belching Beauties. We also had a biggest weight loss tie this week with "The Chief" and "Bouncer" dropping 5 pounds each. Way to go, you losers!! Hopefully we can get back on track this week when everyone can be here. By the way, the bank special of a frosting covered brownie for every deposit is no longer in effect. One announcement for you losers: eat healthy and be ready for a surprise dinner visit from Coach Lynn and myself. Keep pushing yourselves!

Homestead Happenings

Lots of things are happening at the Homestead these days. First of all, we would like to welcome Jennie to our Homestead family. Jennie joined us on Sunday and we are all very pleased. Jennie has been a frequent visitor over the years. She came every Tuesday to visit Margaret Webster and has continued to come to all of our activities. Welcome, Jennie. Jan and Barb both went out for rides on one of those nice sunny days we had. Remember them? I think there were two. They gave us hope that spring is really just around the corner. It didn't look or feel much like spring on Spa Day. But that didn't dampen our spirits. The ladies were treated to facials, massages, manicures, strawberry daiquiris (virgin, of course), and bingo. Everyone enjoyed themselves so much that we decided to do it again next month. I must tell you, though, I'm still not a girlie girl. Matthew commented on his way through the living room that this is a happening place, and that's what we strive for. If you would like to join us for any of our activities please give us a call at 863-9980. Don't forget about Tai Chi every Wednesday. Kirk Gentalen will be presenting another one of his informative and entertaining bird talks sometime in March. We will let you know the date. A reminder about our auction coming up in July, if you have any "quality items," please save them or bring them up to the barn. We still have a few children's chairs left to be painted. If you would like to help please give me a call and I will get them out of storage for you.

This has been an incredibly long, snowy, and slippery winter. Be a good neighbor, and call or visit our shut-ins regularly. It helps to make a long and lonely winter much shorter. Stay warm and safe, and I hope we'll see you at the Homestead soon.

Superintendent's Column

The stimulus package recently passed by Congress, and signed by the President is starting to trickle down to Vinalhaven, apparently. You may recall that the Maine Department of Education "curtailed" 27 million dollars due as state subsidy to school districts last fall for the current school year '08-09. The state has cut district subsidies before, but always in the next year, never in the same year. That translated to a $10,039.78 cut for Vinalhaven. So, I found $10,039.78 in this year's budget which we would not be spending: varsity cheering stipend, high school drama supplies, reduction in custodial hours, savings in fuel and electricity over what we had budgeted. Now, it appears that the 27-million-dollar "curtailment" will be lifted with the arrival of Maine's stimulus money. Thus, we will get our 10 grand back for this year. That's great, but I have been reading that Maine is due to get between 260 and 300 million dollars for education under the stimulus package. I'm wondering where that money will be going. Of course, it couldn't be as simple as dividing the money up on a per pupil basis! So, I'm glad we have gotten our 10 grand back, but I wonder if it is just a tease and I wonder what will really happen to the big money which has been targeted for education and tax relief in Maine. Stay tuned…

Mark Hurvitt, Superintendent

In September I became the regular "Observer" and have presented a column nearly every week since. Generally, but not always, I fill the assigned 2 ¼" page length column by employing different font sizes and hyphens to accomplish that precisely. The Big Bush Bailout got me worked up on this occasion.

Stimulated (Again)

Stop griping.

Big business is what makes life possible for the rest of you. Big business has big executives who make big decisions and deserve the big bucks. The Tidewater is big business (everything's relative). That makes me a big executive. When things started to look a little scary last year, right after I installed the six-foot plasma TVs and sonic vibrator beds, I asked for and got a big chunk of the Bush bailout money, and I gave it to myself as a bonus for running my business into the ground.

I asked for more money from Obama. Obama gave me more money, but sent Treasury Secretary Geithner to ask that I consider limiting executive bonuses in '09. Is he joking? This is big business and I am a big executive. I don't think so. I told Geithner to give me the money and be grateful I've accepted his offer.

Observations

> I agree with AIG's Edward Liddy who, responding to a similarly unreasonable suggestion from Geithner, said, "We cannot retain the best and brightest to lead AIG (those being the same folks who bankrupted AIG in the first place), if their compensation is subject to continued adjustment by the U.S. Treasury."
>
> You at the bottom of the ladder should ante up your April 15 pittance and be grateful that your contributions are making life at the top affordable.

Later that month, I was stalled at the head of the ramp waiting to board the early morning ferry and found myself gazing between the passenger cabins at Doug Hall working from his pea pod across the harbor.

> Looking aft down through the alley on the ferry, just before departure, the view is framed first by the nearby sides of each cabin and then beyond, across the mouth of the harbor, by the western end of Lane's and the eastern end of Potato Island. Each shore slopes downward toward the other, as if they were holding hands underwater. There, the bow and most of the hull of a really sweet pea pod is just visible beneath a thin, undulating ribbon of fog, a ribbon so narrow and so closely described that, while the port oarlock and the blade of its oar are visible, the lobsterman's fist around the handle is not. Emerging above the fog, though, his head and torso, clad in orange foul weather gear, seem to work independently of the disjointed oar below, which, along with its unseen starboard companion, moves the double ender gently forward. Then he boats his oars to gaff a buoy, taking it aboard and laying it in the bottom before reeling in, hand over hand, the slack warp. It's not far to the bottom; a few fathom are pulled in before the warp becomes taut and the trap breaks the surface. Hauling it over the side, he carefully removes its occupants one at a time, appearing to exchange a word or two with each, a starfish, some crabs, a couple of shorts, and a counter.

One of the most interesting contributions to the *Wind* came from Van Conway who was born and raised here but had been living on the mainland for a long time — too long. He missed Vinalhaven and was working on a memoir called *Growing Up in Paradise*. He excerpted "A Stroll Downstreet" for several successive issues of the *Wind*.

Nostalgia

by Van Conway

Foreword: For the past couple of years, I have been working on putting my life experiences to paper and after reading Pat Crossman and Woodrow Bunker's "Observer" articles, I have decided to share some of my memories with the People of God's Gift to the Universe — Vinalhaven. I was born on October 25, 1938 in what was called "the Block," which sat between Carl William's Garage and Ed White's house on Water Street.

For those of you who remember life on the island in the forties and fifties, enjoy. For those of you who never knew or don't remember, I should point out that I have taken many liberties in use of remarks regarding certain location and persona, but by no means intend to belittle or tarnish these places or people I so dearly love. I hope you get an idea of what it was like to stroll from Injun Hill to Plato's Wharf in those bygone days. I have titled my memoirs Growing Up In Paradise, *and what follows are excerpts from that narrative.*

Let us take a nostalgic stroll down street in the '50s and see what made up the island in those days.

As we begin our walk at Injun Hill and head west, our first stop is at the Kelwick Farm, a short dirt road that leads past Leon and Doris Arey's neatly cared for home into a meadow among the trees. As we approach, we notice the family (Bruce, Bobby, Jean, and Betsy, to name only four of the children) working in the hayfield. Mother has a lunch set up on a flat wagon bed and Dad and Jean are on the mower while the boys and Betsy are busily raking the hay into rows.

We then continue on our trek down past Ira MacDonald's home where we see his new white 1949 Chevrolet (Slope-back) he just purchased from Peaslee's Garage (the first new car ever sold from a "showroom," as I recall). Next, we came upon George Geary unloading Vinal's Dairy Products into his garage. He had just recently moved, to a semi-retirement state, from his dairy farm at Poole's Hill to this, Jimmy Calderwood's old house. Lucille was helping him, her flaming red hair shining in the early sunlight. We are now walking in School Lane past Mr. Bradstreet's (Herb and Marge Conway's) home to the Lincoln School building, which housed 3rd, 4th, 5th, and 6th grades downstairs and 7th through 12th upstairs. The Stars and Stripes were flying in the slight breeze and "Cubie" Winslow was sweeping the front steps off as we rounded the flagpole and headed for Fronie's Store at the end of the lane. My companions had an ice cream cone, but I decided to wait until we got to Mont's Store so I could get a Nissen's Cream Roll. As we leave Fronie's, we see Wendell and Leola Smith chatting in the back with Ivan and Isabel Calderwood; we wave and continue on our way and move on down to Mont's. As we leave Mont's Store, we see Lucille Burgess come out to meet Gene who has just arrived from the post office to have lunch. They say hello to Andy and Carrie Bennett next door. Andy was the lighthouse keeper on Heron Neck and had recently moved in here. We then pass "Nubby" Lane pulling into his drive, headed back to his blacksmith shop behind his home. Ann, Susan, and Kenny Webster come running out to say hello as we pass their place and we see Gwendolyn Greene standing near her petunia patch talking to her neighbor across the street, "Pung" Young. She is the principal at the high school and he is president of the school board, so we know she is receiving her marching orders. We now head on down the Hill past Stony Lonesome and are fascinated at the majestic sight of Mike Lander's stately elms and exquisitely manicured hedgerow ahead of us. To our left, we see Chuck Berndtson and his VHS baseball team working on the ball field, spreading sawdust on the infield so it will dry in time for this afternoon's game with Thomaston. I see Van Guilford, "Hinky" Davis, Brother Clarence, Jack Carlson, Ed Dyer, Wyman Philbrook, and others "toning up their muscles" with rakes, mowers, and shovels. At the top of the hill, we wave to Phyllis Ross and her sister Virginia as they pull into their drive to unload groceries.

PART II

Just then, we heard a wee cry of a new baby upstairs at Mamie Sukeforth's Maternity Home. Isn't it ironic that she brings them into the world and just across the street, Joe Headley takes them out as an undertaker? Next to Joe's home, the Union Church Ladies Circle are getting ready for tonight's Circle Supper. The menu consists of baked yellow-eye and pea beans with pork, cole slaw, Parker House rolls, homemade brown bread (including Carrie Burn's), steamed hot dogs, and various beet and sour pickles. To drink, they serve steaming hot coffee, tea, milk, and water. We cross the street and peer into the vestry below and see the ladies quilting over near the big furnace, and a couple members of the Lions Club are gathering songbooks for their meeting following the Circle Supper tonight. We look down at the tables directly below us, and our mouths water as we view the heavily laden tables of homemade cakes. Among them are the cream pies: coconut, banana, chocolate, squash (my personal favorite), and pumpkin, apple, peach, lemon, cherry, and blueberry. Numerous cakes, including Vera Johnson's double chocolate with double chocolate icing, real whipped cream cake, and angel food, to name a few. Our tongues are hanging out, so we quickly head for Main Street — and food — passing the War Memorial and the huge American flag gently moving in the slight breeze.

Across the street Faye Coburn is chatting on the front steps of the library with Harold Vinal (Vinalhaven's Poet Laureate) and Alice Lawry Gould, author and the Vinalhaven correspondent for the *Maine Coast Fisherman*. She and Harold are next-door neighbors down Round the Mountain and I mowed their lawns for several years. A couple summer people were looking over the Galamander and sipping a cold drink from the fountain as we continued on our way. As we walk down the Net Factory Hill, we are greeted by "Cousin Kiltie" Smith, home on vacation from the Boston Symphony/Pops Organization. Carl and Dick "Weakeyes" Williams and Jim Roberts are talking out front with State Representative Ted Maddox. Ted lives in the cottage on the pond nearby. As we near the bottom of the hill, Malcolm Whittington turns into the garage parking lot in the "freight truck." We start down Main Street; we see Bob Lloyd moving some new bicycles out front of his rental business next to the poolroom. Even though it is lunchtime, several boys (and a couple of girls) are playing tennis ball in front of Ed White's house, while Bud Crossman unloads his carpentry supplies into his storage shed under the stairs up to the apartments where he and Pat live with their two "little" children, Phil and Dickie. We see Everett and Ida Libby watching these events from their huge front yard. Everett is a state representative now, but will become known as "The Father of the Maine State Ferry Service" in the coming years.

Meanwhile, as we continue along, someone is coming out of Will and Hanna's bakery with some fresh home-cooked pastries. I slip into the drugstore and order a vanilla frappe and a straight vanilla for my companions. Ed serves them up in a flash, and then I move down to the end of the counter and hold a half-dollar around the corner for Ed to see. He goes to the drawer below the big mirror and then deftly hands me my "merchandise" — now I'm ready for tonight.

We say hello to Henry Anderson, Lester Pendleton, and Ray Tibbetts (three of the Legendary Lawmen of island lore) who were just "hanging around." When we get out on the sidewalk, we see "Cubie" and Emily Winslow entering the stairway up to their apartment and Laura Handley, who is drawing a "curlicue" cone for a customer. We then pass by L.R. Smith Co., where Tim Lane is putting down the awning and his dad is fitting a new pair of shoes for a young boy inside the store. Through the upstairs open window, we hear "Number, please" and feel secure knowing that Muriel Chilles or Mae Davis are keeping our connections with the rest of the world top notch. We say hello to Al Townsend, our Head Selectman, and Harold Wiggens, the School Superintendent, as they come out of the town offices upstairs. Al is ecstatic of how many fine grocery and provision businesses we have here on the island — pointing out the Vinalhaven Grocery, E.G. Carver and Sons, E.C. MacIntosh, and down a little further, the A&P Market (I worked for Albert and Lucille Carver, Andy and Francis Gilchrist, and Don Peacock during 1951 until 1957). We move along now and see that Brother Harry has painted a new Bon-Ami sign on Carver's window, "Fresh Native Ice Cubes and Haddock 4 Sale."

PART III

Across the street, Keith Carver stops to light his pipe while loading a new gas range onto his truck and "Ducky" Haskell joins Rob Arey on the front stoop of the Vinalhaven Grocery to get some air. Ducky looks like a penguin in his white apron. MacIntosh also has a Bon-Ami ad on the window: Fresh Tongues and Cheeks, and Tripe. Andy also has a big display in the window advertising the upcoming *Pirates of Penzance* production on Friday, Saturday, and Sunday at the Memorial Hall. I slip in and buy fifty cents worth of "whack-off" New York Cheddar cheese to munch on.

Just as I step out the door, the fire whistle begins to wail and I have just enough time to get out of Andy's way as he bolts across the street to open the station for the onslaught of volunteers who will miraculously appear on the scene. I follow him into the station and quickly grab the phone and get Muriel, who, just as quickly, gives me the location of the emergency. I then help open the doors while Andy jumps into the primary pumper and starts the engine. Within five minutes, the station house is empty and I can hear the sirens wailing in the distance as they negotiate the route to the call — it is amazing how deftly the firefighters respond to an emergency situation in this small town. It is just as amazing to know that they are "alone" in their efforts as the nearest aide is over an hour away. What makes it more astonishing is that in all these years, except for the forest fire up near Long Cove, the collateral damage during any of the conflagrations has been minimal, considering the sites of these fires. The "old burnt store" on the corner of Clam Shell Alley, the Masonic Hall, Dr. Earle's office, and Mary Wentworth's "Ships Wheel," naming those on Main Street only. (Having been associated with several fire companies throughout my life, I feel qualified to state that I have never seen such professionalism and dedication anywhere.)

As I rejoin my fellow travelers, they are enjoying the smell of the fried clams coming from the Plants' small restaurant. Just then, Dr. Earle pulls into the empty parking spot from his 50-mph approach, and as he disembarks from his '49 blue Chevy coupe, he acknowledges our welcoming gestures, and we ask him to recite "The Highwayman" for us, but he is rushing to get back up to Mamie's, as Dottie Hanson is having another child. Just about the time we reached Vinal's News Stand, Fire Chief Dick "Shadow" Healey pulls up and heads into the station and we can hear the throaty sound of the fire trucks returning. The alarm was for Ray Webster's field, as he was burning some empty oil cans and debris from his garage.

We "window shopped" Charlie Bowman's Paper Store. Sid Winslow's book *Fish Scales and Stone Chips* was the main display, with Harold Vinal's *Voices* also occupying a prestigious location. These books had all been autographed by the authors and were selling like hotcakes. Just then, Charlie came out and got into his '30s black 4-door Chevy, popped the clutch, and roared off. Martha Lou Robinson's sister Ann was sweeping the front of Herb Carver's Spa, so we asked her if they still had some orange-pineapple ice cream. She said yes, so we said we would be back later. She said Herb was developing and printing some new Vinalhaven postcards which would be on display later on today.

The post office was closed for lunch and Viv Drew was just coming out the door as we approached. We asked him what shows besides *The Pirates of Penzance* were scheduled, and he said that he had booked *Sky King* and a couple of other cowboy shows, and headed off for his lunch. Bill Clayter was busy serving a crowd of lunch customers inside the C&C Restaurant. Ken Hatch had just completed the mural in the dining room and it had become quite the place to dine. While my friends enjoyed the aroma, I ran around the corner and down the alley to the old Carriage House. As I passed the loading dock of the A&P, I saw a couple of guys at the "Cocktail Corner"— it was early for the "social hour," but time was not a priority for these boys. When I came out of the restrooms, I waved at Kim Smith feeding boxes into the trash fire on the rocks behind the I.W. Fiield store, then I went back up the alley and joined my compadres who were talking to Don Peacock and Scott Littlefield in front of the A&P and I thoroughly savored the fresh Eight O'Clock, Red Circle, and Bokar coffee being ground inside. Across the street (now the Public Landing/parking lot/festival ground) someone pointed out the flood tide level marker on Floyd Robinson's stack of slab lumber.

PART IV

The old *Sophia* was unloading coal at the dock and across Tea Dock we spotted Cap'n Robinson and his son Ralph scrubbing the *Eva R* and preparing for an excursion over the weekend. Also we notice Carroll and Harland Gregory getting ready to launch a new boat when the tide gets high. The big doors of his shop are open but we cannot make out the name on the stern. Meanwhile, John Morton, "Busky" Ames, Ralph Clayter, and Harvey Tolman and his sons are building new lobster traps and repairing the old. Looking further out toward the harbor, we see Al Guptill with "Dike" and Billy getting the scallop drags cleaned and repaired. So much activity in such a small area shows the prosperous endeavors of this small isle.

Continuing on our way, we say hello to Ida Libby and Charlie Webster as they come out of the Vinalhaven Light & Power Office. They are followed by Pete Peterson, owner and president of the company, who is headed towards his West Main Street hilltop home.

Alex Christie came out and got into his taxi parked at the curb. He said something, but by the time he finished, he was out of earshot. The 5 & 10-cent store was busy with several small tykes making purchases. Mrs. Barton waved as we passed by. When we reached the bench in front of the bowling alley, we sat down to take a breather. Bruce Grindle turned and waved as he joined Joe Kitteridge for the walk (marched in 4/4 time) to their homes up past the Islander, on the pond. We overheard Marie Clarke telling one of her beauty shop customers about the little dolls she had in her window, her French accented English fitting her small, animated personality so well. We heard the water cascading through the mill run beside us, and the laughter of some young people bowling a string inside the Cascade Bowling Alley. (I had set pins for the League Bowling, learning all the tricks of the trade from Donny Martin. Some sound advice he shared was to be ever alert when "Wymie" Guilford was on the line, as the pins flew when he let loose.) I recalled that the Pirates were rolling against the Ganders tonight. Across the street "Allie" Cobb was finishing sweeping the GEM heater out and was preparing to go home for lunch.

This was the third day of the week-long run of *Deep Waters* and this afternoon's matinee would be packed once again. What a thrill to see the actors on the silver screen after seeing them every day in real life as the filming of this Twentieth-Century Fox movie, directed by Henry King, was ongoing. Some of the well-known cinema stars spent several weeks on the island. Among these were Dana Andrews, Cesar Romero, Dean Stockwell, Jean Peters, Mae Marsh, Anne Revere, and Ed Begley, Sr. The more familiar names were Johnny Bickford (Stockwell's stand-in), Clarence Conway (paper boy with a speaking part), several ladies, all members of the Creed's Square Tea Party (Water Street, Atlantic Avenue, and Leo's Lane Junction. Jean Peters "home" was the Max Conway house and Clarence tossed her a newspaper from his bike as she came down the drive), who were Jean Peter's neighbors in the movie. There were many, many islanders who appeared in the film as extras.

We crossed "the Bridge," and we all chuckled when someone asked if I had ever seen the "natural gas bursts" that take place over the rail here some evenings. I was about to respond when John and Etta Morton came out of Hebo's Store, now their net making building (now the Paper Store) and nearly collided with us. The tide was rushing in beneath us and Carrol Burns, on vacation from his job in the Athletic Department in the giant Jordan Marsh Company in Boston, was reeling in a twenty-pound pollock to go along with the several he had already landed. He said to me, "Hello, little man," as we passed. (This was a title he had given me many years before when I mowed his mother's yard and helped him dig clams for bait during his summer visits. I had spent two weeks at his brother-in-law's dairy/strawberry farm in Northwood, New Hampshire when I was fourteen and learned how to milk cows, pick strawberries, and gather real cream for whipping for some great eating. I also had the unforgettable experience of taking his products to the Haverhill, Massachusetts Farmer's Market). I passed the time of day with Carroll and we started on our way once again.

PART V

"Link" Sanborn came out of the bank and started for his car, only to be stopped by a fleet-footed Ada Creed from her taxi stand across the street. He was saying, "…but Ada, I have to get on home because Laura is preparing the pheasant I got this morning before opening, and she will throw them out if I am late, so…" Ada acquiesced and off he went. John Stordahl was pumping gas while Roy Arey checked under the hood at Roy's Garage, also across the street. We stopped and shared a few somber moments at the Honor Roll — I was proud to read my two brothers' names; Stanley and Herb both served in WWII and Herb's fiancée, Marge, had a brother, Edward Smith, killed when shot down over the Pacific (I recall the phone call to my mother and dad, and I had the honor to have seen the photograph honoring Edward aboard the U.S.S. *Yorktown*, moored in Charleston, South Carolina, now a museum). Vinalhaven sacrificed heavily during that war, and this tribute to those who served and died is yet another remarkable facet of the social structure of this chunk of granite in the Penobscot Bay.

We cross Harbor Hill to help Clyde and Edith Poole carry some tables and linens into a building and stop to glance at the photographs and memorabilia of the wars standing and hanging inside. This is the Woodcock Cassie Coombs Post 18 of the American Legion, Department of Maine. As we passed Bob Johnson's Boat Shop, I can't help remembering my freshman year in high school when marine science teacher Guy Johnson obtained the sunken *Eleanor* and our class jack-hammered the concrete from under the deck in an effort to rehab and, eventually, sail her — a task that never got completed.

Across the street we saw several of Fred Jones's employees as they sat on the piazza of the Central Hotel (where the fire station/town offices sit now). We all crossed over to admire Neil Sutlife's Soap Box Derby Racer in the window of his dad, Morgie Sutlife's, Photo Studio. Neil and his mom, Dot, came outside to say hello before we continued on our way. We noticed that Pete Peterson had nearly reached the top of the many stairs up to his beautifully kept shingled home.

The others all looked at me and laughed when, off in the distance, we heard "Harr-eeee…come home to dinner!" My mom Eleanor's voice scaled the distance across the cove. They asked if that embarrassed me and I told them then, and reiterate today, this was as much a part of Vinalhaven as the standpipe, noon whistle (fire and B&Ms), and the Union Church bell. At night: Heron Neck foghorn, the frogs at the trolley, and the humming of the power house generators. These were sounds we all heard, all the time. Somewhere from the boatyard across the street we heard Harold Chandler call Harry and Roy Coombs to tell them "Eleanor just called the kids, must be time to go eat."

As we walked on, Roy and Harry came out of the front of the boat shop, and headed across the road to the path up to their homes. We all held our noses as we passed the old house where Fred Jones raised his hens next to the boat shop, and as we passed by we noticed all the slack-salted codfish lying on the screen dryer racks at Grime's Fish Wharf. I told my traveling companions about the time when they were bringing in tuna and my Uncle "Staffy" Smith had sat me astraddle one of the huge tuna and took my picture. I had worked there for a few months as a kid, assembling wooden boxes used to ship their fish product. We said hello to Fred and "Spider" Grimes as they headed for lunch. And turned down the hill into Jimmy Calderwood's Marine Supply and the wharf where several men were sitting around on trawl kegs watching Sofia Pallazola and my dad, Max, repairing a large hole in the drag net from the *Dora and Peter*, which laid alongside the dock. Captain Ira Tupper was in the wheelhouse making some adjustments to his sonar gear and cussing to Clarence Bennett in the *Dorothy M.*, which lay alongside, about how much more Fyler's was paying for groundfish in Rockland, and that he would be selling there next trip. That perked me up, as I had accompanied them across the bay a few times when they did that. We would get aboard around three o'clock a.m., and I would crawl into one of the bunks while Dad prepared fried lobster, scrambled eggs, home fries, and toast for breakfast on the trip across. On several occasions, I had followed brother Clarence in the task of "lumping" fish at the Vinalhaven Fisheries across the harbor. That was, indeed, a job I was only too happy to retire from.

Conclusion

Dad broke away long enough to buy us all a cold Moxie or ice cream bar inside and then we headed across the lot to the B&M plant where the ladies were packing codfish cakes. We all tried a sample from the bin at the end of the conveyor and stepped outside just as the steam whistle emitted a blast, and as it subsided, we heard the fire whistle sound the noon hour.

As we walked down in to the Port District parking lot, we see Verne Mossman in his Dodge Power Wagon with the wooden and canvas box on back. He would be back later today when the boat arrives to transfer the U.S. Mail up to the post office. We slipped on down on the dock to say hello to my Uncle Hud Conway who was watching the unloading of "Hakey" Nelson's catch-of-the-day. Uncle Hud was the administrator/bookkeeper at B&M and also owned the GEM heater. We then proceeded around the front of the Port District office/warehouse and headed past the power plant where "Sparky" Warren was sitting on the bench outside, eating his lunch from his lunch bucket. Inside, we could hear the giant Fairbanks-Morse turbine diesel engines humming away. We spoke and sauntered on past Mr. Elwell as he worked on an engine in his shop (across from where the Burger-Ped now stands), and headed down into Plato's Wharf parking area. We watched them loading ice into the crusher as the *Dorothy M.* pulled in under the chute to receive her load of ice. We then walked the dock alongside the sales building and looked down on the "car" where we saw "Goose" Arey unloading lobsters from Ted MacDonald's always clean and neat boat and placed the lobsters into the "car" where they would stay until crating and shipping to the mainland on the *Althea & Bick* in a week or so. Ted looked up and waved to me and asked how my folks were. He and his wife, Josephine, and daughters, Olga and Edith, were very good family friends. I said Dad was getting nets ready to go out to the Grand Banks, and Mom was feeding Harry, as usual. When we entered the building, Henry Anderson was just walking in and asked us how far we had walked. We told him that we guessed a mile as that was all the state had paved. He laughed and said that someday the state would spend some money on this island's transportation needs. (This turned out to be a fairly accurate assessment, however, the roads didn't get that much attention, but the ferry sure did.) When we were walking up the hill from Plato's, we all agreed that it sure didn't feel like a mile and we felt we had just begun, which adds to the saying, "time (and distance) passes quickly when you're having fun." Deciding that we were hungry, we walked around to Van Guilford's lunch stand. As we were eating our lobster rolls, we discussed another trek from Injun Hill when we celebrated our 50th Alumni get-together in 2007.

This concludes my rendition of "What Life Was Like" in a short span of time in the 1940 and 1950 era. I purposely wrote this in fictional prose including misspelled and misused words as well as taking grammatical license in its presentation. I surely hope those of you who take the time to read this don't feel as if you have wasted that time. I know in my heart that most of you will look at it in the way it was presented because people who "Grow Up In Paradise" are a species all to themselves. Thank you for your time. (VC)

I'd begun regular reviews of school plays by now and the productions were exceptionally good and kept getting better and better.

The high-spirited cast of *Pippin* wowed the audience with its exuberance. Great performances were turned in by everyone, and their own enjoyment was infectious. The choreography was amazing, the costumes wonderful, the makeup and the hair! The lighting was perfect and never missed a cue. As the Leading Player, Dana Marie played and commanded the entire stage with confidence. She regarded her fellow performers with a perfect bemusement but even more effectively seemed to view herself and all of us in attendance with the same wry regard. John Morton is a terrific dancer, has a really nice voice and, as Pippin, was convincingly put upon and unabashedly seductive. There wasn't a female heart anywhere that wasn't fluttering with fantasy when he removed his shirt. We've come to expect great things from Kate Hamilton and she came through again, reining in Pippin, a reluctant lover, and employing precious asides to great effect. Trey Warren, imperious, disdainful, dismissive, employing all those wonderful qualities we expect from a detached monarch, was utterly convincing. Karen Krager as the scheming Fastrada, employed her coy facade and sweet singing voice to great effect. Francis Warren was a perfect foil as the arrogant and conceited Lewis. Katilynn Willis was wonderful as Berthe, Pippin's grandmother, distracted at first then convincing him to lighten up a little and live. Frank Morton is plainly bursting to do something bigger and more demanding and pulled off his character effortlessly. The troupe of players carried the production along seamlessly with all sorts of unrelenting stage business, all of which contributed mightily, but none of which distracted from other things going on at the same time. Finally, though, dripping irony is the vehicle within which this production moves along so well. Dramatic irony, situational irony, every cast member, the leads, the players, all employed it effortlessly, relentlessly, to their own great entertainment and to ours. Thank you, Meridith Richards, for a terriic job!

Whether to add fluoride to our water supply became a big and contentious issue.

Construction of the windmills began in April.

Nebo Lodge opened on North Haven, broadening our dinner options and making dining out and the evening boat ride required to come and go a little adventure.

Methicillin-resistant Staphylococcus aureus (MRSA), a dangerous skin infection, began making the rounds, particularly of lobstermen.

Steve Small introduced an interesting column of "Recollections." Unfortunately, it only ran three weeks.

Recollections
by Steve "Hardy" Small

The year was 1964. I was nine years old, living on an island off the coast of Maine called Vinalhaven. Most people were fishermen, including my father. He was captain of a boat, the *Hippo-Campus*. We chased herring boats, but we didn't carry herring; we just carried the scales from these small fish. This was done a lot at night. My first trip was overnight to a place called Hatchet Cove in Friendship. Wouldn't you know it — I got homesick. It was pitch dark out, I didn't know where I was, and I really wanted to be home in my bed. My father must have realized because he said, "Steve, what do you think of this?" I said, "I want to go home!" He replied, "Jesus, boy, it's a beautiful night, and the fish are here. This is what puts food on the table and pays the bills." I was nine years old; I didn't care about the bills. Finally he talked me into staying by giving me his knife to have. Such was my first trip! But after a couple more trips I was hooked.

Part II

About the same time I was working on the *Hippo-Campus*, a lot of guys were setting tub trawls for mostly hake, and doing fairly well at it. They would have people on shore bait the trawls, which usually consisted of a ground line with 800 to 1,000 hooks attached to them with gangions. They would go out at night and set the trawls and haul them the next day, more often than not for a boatload of fish. The price was around six cents a pound. Then there was hand-lining that my dad and I did. A hand-line was a line with six to ten hooks on it called Norwegian jigs. Mine only had four on it, lest I get hauled overboard. These were later replaced by automatic jigging machines after hand-lining kinda petered out. The old man took a sardine carrier (not the first) called the *Double Eagle*. He ran it for North Lubec Canning Company in Rockland. He taught me how to navigate by compass and clock. There wasn't much for electronics back then. By then I was hooked. I would be able to captain a boat myself before long.

PART III

> Here on the island in the '60s and '70s, there were small boats rigged for dragging. Guys like Hartland Small, Phil Bennett, "Honka" Holmquist, Veli "Goat" Holmstrom, Richard Elliot (mainland), Harmond Alexander (down east) and a lot of tub trawlers from about anywhere that came here to sell their catch. The fish plant was run by Clyde Bickford, who I worked for at one time. He would box fish and ship them out. He also had racks (flakes) that he would put fillets on to dry in the sun and they would be brought in every night. This was slack-salted fish, which was very good. I know because kids, including me, used to ride by the flakes every so often on our bikes and grab some (fish and taters for supper!) This was all manual labor. The men put the fish out to dry, but it was the women who filleted the fish. Ruth Gray, Mary Ewell, Evelyn Thompson, Norma Wallace, Thelma Ames, Hildred Hutchinson, Frank (Honey) Small, and Everett Jeffers to name a few. I'm getting off track — dragging is what I was thinking of.

A second Site Specific art project was organized and was even more successful than the first, held in 2002.

FIW began producing a regular column updating progress of the windmill project. By midsummer the logistics of getting components, particularly the enormous windmill blades, up the North Haven Road from a barge at the waterfront was an exercise that required a great deal of patience on our behalf and on behalf of the workers trying to make that happen. It went remarkably smoothly.

> We're pretty much all impressed with this wind power project, impressed with its timely completion and with the thoughtful folks responsible for its planning and execution and who had the good sense to award the contract to Cianbro. The other day, with things winding down, a Cianbro employee delivered to the Eldercare redemption center all the empty drink containers that had accumulated at the job site during these last several months. It's a tiny measure of their comprehensive planning. They've kept us well-informed of progress and of likely disruptions to our lives and as a result nearly every conceivable obstacle seems to have been anticipated and overcome, and an enormous project has been completed with hardly a ripple. Although they've been here for the entire summer and now into the fall, I've not seen nor heard of a single unpleasant incident. Neither have I heard any of their employees speak ill of Cianbro management, and the reverse is true, a novelty in today's labor relations climate. I've watched them work; not many moments are wasted. I'm always apprehensive housing work crews at the motel, particularly during the summer when others are in residence. More often the two don't mix — for all the obvious reasons — but these guys were a pleasure. Organized labor could take a cue.

My regular "Observers" were sometimes relative to what was going on in town but often not. Jim Boone is an indefatigable seasonal resident, as is his wife Merry. They had taken on the formidable task— every morning they were, and are, here among us— of picking up all the downtown litter that has accumulated the night before. This, even if they are only here for an overnight during the winter! Jim also coordinates most of the VLT's summer programs and manages to now and then find time for a boat ride. I went on one.

> Jim Boone treated me to a boat ride last week, a circumnavigation of memories. Sands Cove: trying to eat more lobsters than Joe Nelson; Green's Island: a gift of a crow's nest into which had been woven a ribbon from their daughter's hair; the Reach: a ghost story at Ted n' Tweedy's that left me

traumatized for years; City Point: the end of a romance; Dyers Island: the first house I built (which lead to a sail across the Atlantic in a catamaran); the Basin: a moonlit paddle with a hot dish (food) to dinner up at the former Johnson & Young lobster pound; Long Cove: accidentally knocking my father overboard in winter; Leadbetter's Narrows: a treasure hunt through the woods with the Rhinelander children; the Thorofare: sitting in Muriel Lewis's boathouse when Joel Wooster fired off a shotgun to start a North Haven dinghy race he thought had delayed long enough, Senator Leverett Saltonstall giving my dad a can of bent nails he hoped could be reused; Perry's Creek: catching smelt but losing another girl; Barley Hill: our wedding night spent in a van looking out at Saddleback and Isle au Haut; Lane's Island: my first kiss of any real consequence. Thanks for the ride. There is no litter between Main Street and Jim and Merry Boone's house. Thanks for that, too.

Ollie Handley, the last of a famous foursome of octogenarian golfers, passed away.

> The Old Duffers are gone: Woody, Ducky, Bud, and now Ollie. When God was wondering what to do with them he thought up golf, and it was one of His best ideas. One year with an open January and a little warm spell in February, the foursome, each over seventy-five years of age, golfed North Haven at least once in every month of the year, quite an accomplishment, given the latitude of the course and the longitude of the participants. They argued endlessly, criticized style and technique, talked while others of them were teeing off, and accused one another of breaching golf etiquette. They took merciless advantage. Bud was at the top of his game when his foot wasn't bothering him; Woody was at the top of his game when his back wasn't bothering him; Ducky was at the top of his game when his leg wasn't bothering him. Ollie was at the top of his game when he was bothering everyone else. They loved it, though, loved the game, loved the give-and-take, and loved the insensitivities, the indelicacies. I like to think the other three are now criticizing Ollie's approach shot.

Phil 'n' the Blanks finally made the cover of the *Wind*, and the sixth annual a cappella On the Rocks concert was performed in August.

A fall evening became ARTS Night. It may have been the first and has continued. Rachel Noyes created a magical hand-drawn map of Main Street for the occasion. The map was eventually incorporated into the Vinalhaven Visitors Guide and has been in each issue since.

Ketch Secor is the founder and lead vocalist for the very popular Old Crow Medicine Show, and summers here on Vinalhaven. I helped arrange for them to perform a summer concert here in town and on North Haven, and then, hours before the concert was to begin, I was medi-vacked to a mainland hospital because of a scary episode of atrial fibrillation.

I'd rather be scary on Halloween.

> Last Saturday night was scary. The wind had been blowing hard, and as darkness fell it blew harder, the full moon obscured by sinister forms. Fear and foreboding lurked in every quarter. As a trick-or-treater, it was hard to stay focused on the threat one posed when so much more evil clearly lurked at every turn. The kids returned to their homes earlier than usual; it was too scary.
>
> Later, around one o'clock a.m., an island couple was fast asleep in the cozy second floor bedroom of the big house they occupied by themselves when suddenly she was up on one elbow and shaking

him urgently. "Something's coming up the stairs," she whispered, sobbing. She clung to him, her nails digging into his arm, but let go with desperate reluctance when he dutifully swung his legs out of bed. He grabbed his robe and headed for the door, flicking the hall light switch as he went, but, though he could see a streetlight through the window, the hall remained dark. He flipped the bedroom light switch, but there was only more darkness. Paralyzed with fear, she despaired as she realized that, in fact, they were not alone, that something had turned off the power to the house and was now advancing up the stairs toward her husband, who stood waiting in the doorway, brave and resolute but groggy and disoriented. She pulled the covers over her head, sobbing hysterically.

I hiked the new, short, and undemanding VLT Basin Trail and was blown away by the magical environment. It made for a column that, at first glance, alarmed VLT members.

> The Land Trust has been going through the motions* recently. In particular, the new Basin Preserve Trail goes through four readily identifiable motions and one of them, the larger, an enterprise that nearly matured into a real quarry, has been reclaimed by nature in stunning fashion. A carpet of moss covers the quarry floor and steep walls, closing the wound created by hopeful prospectors. It's easy to imagine the noise, the clamor, the anticipation, a hundred years ago, of a harvest that might prove their salvation. It's even easier to imagine, a hundred years later, a twilight production of *A Midsummer's Night Dream* with a woodland cast of faerys, gnomes, elves, and sprites, perhaps a small dragon.
>
> Enjoy this walk. If necessary, as it was yesterday morning, pick your way around the trash left at the head of the trail and then retrieve it on your way out. As mind boggling as such disregard is, an entirely different and more pleasant boggling can be had a little farther down the trail when you reach this fragile amphitheater. Stay on the trail; resist the temptation to intrude. The carpet won't stand it. Neither will the dragon.
>
> *motion: an individually undertaken, often exploratory, usually modest, stone quarry

As work on the wind farm neared completion I was moved to settle in nearby for a couple of hours and watch the choreography of some final assembly.

> Several guys climbed 180 feet inside two coupled sections of the wind tower and emerged, their tiny hard hats barely visible, on a shelf just beneath the rim. The final eighty-foot section lay nearby. A small boom lifted its base a few feet to keep it from banging on the ground as a huge Manitowoc 2250 crane began to raise it with two straps attached at its other end. With the section airborne, the smaller crane detached itself and moved away and the big one continued to lift the column up slowly toward the tiny hard hats. A little top heavy, at sixty-six tons, and with the enormous weight dangling from its rigging, the crane seemed impossibly vertical. Still, the column rose up gently. The tiny men beneath the hard hats had a walkie-talkie. So did the crane operator, who must have been a seamstress in a previous life, so precisely did he thread his way to the top. The Manitowoc is over 300 feet tall; the column is 90 feet tall, and the combined weight is over 100 tons. Still, the tiny men — the bottom of the air-borne column even with and just over their heads — were now air traffic controllers, asking for inches, a few left, a few right, one or two up or down, until the column was bolted down to the section below and the Manitowoc withdrew. Now the tower is also impossibly vertical. What if someone leans against it?

OBSERVATIONS

Carver's Pond is alive with wildlife, particularly birds. They and other goings-on in the pond are always worthy of observation.

> I live out here in the Atlantic Ocean with another oddity, a great blue heron, one who takes his breakfast most mornings behind the Paper Store, perched above the eddy formed by a calm embrace of the two Mill Stream currents. Some early mornings I stand near the bridge or up on the deck across the street and watch him. He has enormous eyebrows, like Leonid Brezhnev. Sometimes he composes them to appear so coy I think there must be a girl heron nearby, or perhaps I am not unlike one myself. At other times his countenance is one of benign complacency, as if he's just eaten one of my motel guests, a tourist. More often, though, he has a droll expression and a long suffering regard for my interest in him. I suppose I'd feel the same if every time I sat down to enjoy a meal someone appeared at the window with binoculars.

I had an impulsive moment and decided to walk all the way around Vinalhaven and, of course, then felt compelled to account for why that seemed like such a great idea — which, as it turned out, it was.

> Is there any way to enjoy being obsessive other than to do so compulsively? I think not, and that's why undertaking a walk around every inch of the island, below the high tide mark, appealed to me. Of course, the real attraction lay in the notion of starting at one spot, walking a while, going home, coming back a few days later to the exact same spot where I left off, walking some more, going home, coming back, and so forth. Imagine my surprise when, very quickly, I discovered the walk offered even greater satisfaction, greater even than the mindless appeal of putting one foot in front of another endlessly, forever. Although I've been here all my life, I've seen more interesting things and places on this hike, looking at the island from outside in rather than from the inside out, than I'd have thought possible. OK, I can hear some of you obsessing over my contention that I've lived here all my life when you know perfectly well I didn't come here till I was four years old. Close enough, I say courageously. Besides, I wasn't really living till I came here. Is that enough homage?

> I began my walk on October 6 at the Dyer Island Bridge and in 19 outings have gone around that island, around Granite Island, in and out of the Basin, Long Cove, and Crockett River and am nearly at the Thorofare, about 15% of the total, I think. On day 16 Elaine convinced me to start a blog describing the adventure. I needed some coaching, but it's up and running at: islandcircumambulation.blogspot.com. Even if I hadn't been compulsing obsessively, I couldn't resist undertaking an exercise called circumambulation.

The ARC, still up on Skin Hill, had become "the place" to be. The Internet café was often busy and when it wasn't it provided a cup of coffee and a quiet space for reflection or composition.

> Thirty years ago or so Perry and Annie Boyden headed up a group to buy a house that had come on the market. At the time it was hard to find a space where groups could readily meet or where organized activity could take place. Space at the old school or gym was not available after hours or in the summer, and church was not always a suitable place. The Arts and Recreation Center was born, and now there was space for movies, games for kids, arts, crafts — all sorts of things. Perhaps most importantly, it provided kids an alternative to having nothing to do and no good place to do it. Within a year a grass fire got out of control and burned off the back of the building. A timber frame theater addition, designed by Dick Morehouse (gratis) and already under consideration, was

built. Now community theater had a suitable venue. There was more room for space-consuming games, for public meetings, auctions, dances, concerts: the possibilities were endless. Over the years, particularly after the new school was built and a big comfortable auditorium became available, the need for the alternatives offered by the ARC became a little less pressing. Today, though, under the indefatigable leadership of Tristan Jackson and Gabe McPhail, with help from an inspired and far-sighted board and with financial assistance from the Island Institute and from donations from supportive community members, the ARC has been reborn as an Internet café and, staffed mostly by kids, as an instructive vehicle for learning the intricacies of running a small business, particularly a service-oriented small business. The theater addition, now the Vinalhaven Youth Zone, morphs now and then from a center for one kind of activity (skateboard half-pipe) to another (basketball or ping pong) as demand and interests shift, continues to host auctions, art shows, and concerts and, last month, a wildly successful community Thanksgiving Dinner. Open now from seven a.m., the ARCafe attracts ever growing numbers to its cozy community living room to enjoy delicious (and unfailingly wholesome) pastries and very good coffee (or tea) and continues to serve as a living laboratory for the great high school students who work there and who make it such an appealing place.

November 11 was Veterans Day, an occasion which, in my mind, doesn't get the attention it deserves.

Here on Vinalhaven we gathered on Veterans Day to acknowledge the contributions of some of those in attendance, some not in attendance, and many more who had given all and who will never again be in attendance. We flew our flags at half-mast, our little ones and the magnificent colors that preside over the monument. Other towns do the same, and some have even more vivid reminders of sacrifice. In one town in particular a fellow who did his own bang-up job in Vietnam has left his employment a few years short of retirement, as has his wife, to care for their son who has been returned to them, pieced together and alive but incapable of feeding himself, speaking, turning over in bed, or changing his diapers, all as a result of his encounter with a roadside bomb. He requires care all day, all night, 168 hours a week. The government graciously provides, but for only 80 of those hours. The parents, no longer contemplating the retirement they'd imagined, provide for the remaining 88 hours themselves or by paying for an outside service to help. They've mortgaged their home and cashed in retirement funds. They can avoid bankruptcy if their son dies soon, but if he lives they can only avoid it if the government meets its true obligation — unlikely. Some of us take better care of our own than others.

The windmills went on-line and suddenly there was cause for concern. Those living nearby were bothered, some very badly, by the noise and other sensory extremes.

It's difficult to acknowledge, after these long months during which we endorsed it, but an ill wind is threatening our wind project. We have all been expecting significantly less noise from the turbines than we hear now. It's easy for most of us to dismiss concerns about noise because we don't live in the windmills' shadow, but several of our neighbors do, and their distress is real. As many of us hasten to learn more and study the experiences of turbine installations elsewhere, it quickly becomes clear that this is a complicated problem. It involves not only noise, but waves of low frequency sound that move through air and earth as something felt rather than heard and about which there is evidence suggesting sustained exposure can be unhealthy. Fox Islands Wind will need to make every effort to find ways to mitigate these effects on the properties nearby, and some farther away, that are adversely affected. Fortunately, we own these windmills. They are not the property of some giant corporation that couldn't care less about this level of impact. Fox Islands Wind and the other folks who have brought this stunning achievement this far have committed themselves to making this project compatible with the lives of those in the area. We should be mindful of the plight of these, our island neighbors, and encourage and support Fox Islands Wind as they work to do all that is necessary to minimize the negative effects of the turbines on their lives and property.

Our wonderful rowers were rabid and began to make a name for themselves, particularly at the Hull Icebreaker Competition in Boston Harbor.

Heroes are welcomed, as they should be, whenever a returning ferry deposits our basketball or soccer contenders back home at our doorsteps. It's quite a display of support. Last week there was another show, smaller though, when our rowing team returned, again victorious, from the Hull Icebreaker Competition in Boston Harbor. It was a challenging event, testing navigation, coordination, and strength against six big high schools; some were twenty-five times our size. Our team beat them all handily. In another event they rowed against eight veteran teams in a one-mile power row and came in first again. This year's rowers feature a few holdovers from last year's championship team including Karen Krager, a returning member who is this year's rookie cox and who slipped into the hot seat as if she was born there. Judging the subtle distinctions between the strength at one oar and another, discerning the need for more here or less there to keep a true heading or to make a turn, she guided her six rowers to victory. In the stroke position, Sarina Wentworth, and behind her, Ginger Swears, set a relentless pace. Together, Francis Warren and Max Morton, in the "engine room," supplied plenty of power amidships, and in the bow, providing vital stability and added strength, were Josey Doughty and Fiona Warren. Where else might one find a cohesive team of superbly coordinated rowers than on an island in the Atlantic?

Christmas every year brings back some terrific memories and some great stories. This year was no exception. I've been asked to retell these two often.

When I was a kid, a youngster, who shall go unnamed because today he is a sensitive older man, wandered away from home, crawled into the nativity by the galamander, and snuggled up with baby Jesus. The boy was well bundled up with a coat, hat, and mittens and had a Superman badge pinned to his jacket. In his pocket he had a very poorly constructed sandwich he'd put together surreptitiously at home, and he carried two blankets and a pillow. He'd been told the familiar story repeatedly as he passed by day after day, walking with his mom or being pulled on a sled by his dad. The whole business — Jesus there in the freezing cold with his poor parents unable to provide for him as well as they might had things been going better and had the government not typically passed some knee-jerk legislation compelling their appearance away from home — had resonated to a greater degree than anyone imagined. With Mary on one side and a sheep on the other, he and the Son of God covered themselves with the blankets and, resting their heads together on the pillow, settled in for a long winter's nap. Of course, our hero hadn't been gone long before his folks realized it and, when a quick search turned up nothing, the fire department was called. Chief Dick Healey responded with several firemen in tow, fanned out around the neighborhood, and quickly discovered the missing child who would abandon his post only after being assured that these grownups would pay more attention to the Savior's comfort than did Marge Peterson, Grant Duell, and Berthe

Slaughter, whom he'd watched unload and assemble the installation a few days earlier, then quickly abandon the poor child to the elements. It has not gone unnoticed today, by the same older but no less concerned individual, that loyal disciples Charlie and Grace Mullen, who have been faithfully helping Jesus fulfill the Christmas promise every December for over forty years, don't keep him that well bundled up either.

On Christmas Eve in 1952 Santa came to the church to separate the worthy from the unworthy. This was scary stuff. Standing before the judgment seat of Christ was not as scary as sitting *in* the judgment seat of he who knew whether we'd been bad or good, for goodness sake. This was the eighth annual visit from Santa in my own young life, and that was eight more times than I had even seen Christ, let alone sat in his lap. We sat next to Billy Sweets and his mom. With no apparent dad, Billy had long claimed he was the product of an immaculate conception. What that meant was a mystery to us but we always nodded soberly as if we understood. Across the aisle Pearly Nelson caught my eye and flashed from his jacket pocket a little glass ball in which reposed a female figure whose skirt, when the globe was inverted and snowlakes descended, blew up a little.

At 5:30 we were stilled by the sound of approaching sleigh bells. In a shiny red suit, boots and mittens, he was pretty much what we'd expect as someone who knew everything we did, were doing, or had done and from whom we could hide nothing. He strode down the aisle and when he got to Pearly and patted him on the head I was sure he would ask, "Son, have you been bad this year? Do you not have a little female figure in your pocket whose skirt is billowing about provocatively?" He didn't, though, and the first kid to come down and sit in his lap was Lillian "Treetop" Roberts, a girl whose appeal to me and my buddies was undeniable if not identifiable but who was still way ahead of her time. "Lillian, have you been good this year?" "Depends on who you ask," she responded coyly. I was called about halfway through the evening and headed warily down the aisle. Santa reached down and scooped me up.

"So, Phil, have you been a good little boy this year?"

"I guess so."

"What about telling the truth? Have you told the truth this year?"

"I guess so."

"Are you sure?"

"I guess so."

"Are you really sure? Is there anything you'd like to tell Santa?"

"Well, yeah. You smell just like my Grandpa Maddox."

In 2009 eighty-one million pounds of lobster were landed in Maine by 6,100 license holders, and the price was $2.93 per pound.

OBSERVATIONS

2010

THE FIRST ANNUAL NEW YEAR'S DAY POLAR ICE DIP, hosted by the library, attracted seven stalwarts and raised $600.

Walt Smith began composing a memoir about growing up on Vinalhaven and submitted several successive, lengthy, and interesting essays.

Tommy Cod
by Walt Smith

Several fellows had already gone to Whitinsville, Massachusetts and were employed at the Whitin Machine Works where they manufactured textile machinery. Textile machinery was needed in Europe, as the war was heating up. They needed machinery to make cloth for uniforms. Allan Middleton and I wanted to give it a try, too, but we needed money! It was early November 1936. The country was in a deep depression, and Vinalhaven was no exception; not many ways to earn enough money to make the trip. Someone told Allan that tommy cod were coming into Perry's Crick and Indian Ladder on the high tides to spawn, and that John Morton (caretaker at the closed fish plant) would buy them for five cents a pound.

We found some discarded nets, old but hopefully good, and long enough to dam both brooks at high tide. The nets were about ten to twelve feet wide, wide enough to bury the bottom in the mud and hold down with rocks. We ran the net across the bottom and up the bank on each side of both brooks. We tied ropes at the top of each end, and at high tide one of us was on each side of the brook. We could then pull the top up from the bottom and tie it to a tree. Then we waited for low tide, put the fish in burlap bags, and reset the net for the next tide. Then we carried the bags of fish on a stretcher up the hill and loaded them in the car. Most sets, we would have to salt the fish to prevent freezing. I remember one set, we had a good catch, but lost every fish because the net caught on a rock and ripped a hole in it. A lot of work, and nothing to show for it!

We did not have much spare time because we tended two tides a day for four or five weeks, and each tide took an average of seven to eight hours. Each day's tide was about an hour later than the day before. We slept odd hours. It was a relief when it was over. I'm not sure of the actual amount we made after expenses, but we had enough to make the trip.

Allan went before I did. I waited until after Christmas, January 7, 1937, to be exact. My '29 Chevy was already on the mainland from a previous trip that Kim Smith and I took up to Canada, but that is another story. I took three other guys: Bill Wahlman, Ed White, and another, I can't remember who. It was much different to drive to Massachusetts in those days. On the weekend, especially, sometimes it took a half hour to an hour to drive through towns such as Freeport. There were others, too, with three or four traffic lights, and only two lanes all the way. Holiday weekends were nearly impossible. The cars were unlike what we have become used to; there was no A/C, no automatic, underpowered and uncomfortable.

We got to Whitinsville and we all got jobs. Bill and I were put on the night shift. Allan worked days so we didn't see much of each other. However, early in the summer he looked me up to tell me he and a friend were going to Canada to join the Royal Air Force. He wanted to learn to fly. I suggested he try his own military first, maybe there was a way to learn to fly and stay in the U.S.A. That was the last time I ever saw Allan. A long time later, at least a year, probably longer, I received a framed photo of Allan in his U.S. uniform. I believe he must have been among the first to go when we got into the war in '41. I heard that he had been shot down in North Africa. That is where the early U.S. action took place.

I was laid off later in the fall. In the meantime, I had met Martha. Her sister's husband, who was in the fruit and vegetable business, offered me a job. He bought a second truck, and I built up a second route. I continued on this job, Martha and I were married, and we had a son.

During those times, everything revolved around the war. The war was paramount to everything else. Almost every conversation contained "when the war is over." Future plans always had "after it's over." I don't recall anyone ever saying, "We can't win the war." We knew we could, we just didn't know when. It seemed everyone in the country was of one mind. We'll do whatever necessary. The war required workers in the defense plants, so in 1942 we moved to West Hartford in Connecticut to work at Pratt & Whitney, a defense plant that made machine tools. I never did return to Vinalhaven to live, but we spent every vacation with my parents, Madeline and Langtry (Staffy) Smith. My son, Kenneth, spent several summers with his grandparents when he was young.

I got a call from an elderly native who lived elsewhere and needed to vent.

Eleanor Robinson, aged ninety-two, called to complain that her husband's name wasn't among those listed in the *Wind* two weeks ago along with Hollis and Honey Knowlton, Arnold Sturks, and others. Furthermore, she was still miffed at the three of them for tormenting her when they were in school together, and related a story about one day in Ethel Doughty's class. It seems Hollis was passing her notes during class promising not to let her get on the bus, a contraption built by Cris Holbrook and drawn by a team of horses, after school got out that day. Eleanor was being bullied and was already in fragile shape when Mrs. Doughty caught her passing a note back to Hollis during class. Mrs. Doughty picked up the big yardstick she kept on her desk for just such a purpose and came up the aisle. She asked Eleanor to stick out her hand and when she did Mrs. Doughty brought the stick down across her knuckles three times. Eleanor was determined not to cry and didn't. Mrs. Doughty then went to Hollis and stuck out her own hand as she had with Eleanor requiring Hollis to put his own in hers, but when she brought down the stick Hollis pulled out his hand and she struck her own palm. Eleanor says she was a little upset. She also wanted me to know that her husband's grandfather lived in Snippershins but she couldn't remember why it was called that.

The "Town Managers Corner" continued to be entertaining as well.

Town Manager's Corner

I submitted a picture of myself to the *Wind* Editor this week with the caption, Vinalhaven Manager Forced to Walk Plank. I thought it might be good for a laugh. We originally wanted to send it to my sister in Arizona to show her what winter is really like. She thinks it's cold when it hits 60°. The

OBSERVATIONS

wooden plank is necessary because of the "glacier" that builds up under the steps on the hill at the lighthouse and eventually on the deck. It's not really bad this year. The first winter I was here, in 2002-2003, it covered the bottom four or five steps and had to be chipped away daily to keep it from blocking the door leading to the house. There is another exit out the basement, but certainly not a good alternative.

Browns Head Lighthouse can be a challenging place to live. As I have heard over the years, "it is the best and the worst place to live." I moved to Vinalhaven in June of 2002 for the town manager job that officially started July 1st. My furniture and most of my belongings did not arrive until later on in July. The first weekend of my arrival there happened to be an open house at the lighthouse. It was a little awkward, but everyone was friendly, and when they saw my sleeping bag on the floor offered up beds and cots and places to stay. I assured them I would be fine.

My first days at the lighthouse were anything but peaceful. There was no water and no heat. No one had thought to prepare the house for my arrival. The foghorn was sounding day and night without any apparent reason as the sun was shining and the nights were clear and bright. I cried, wondering what the heck I had gotten myself into on this island.

For several years before coming to Vinalhaven, I led hikes into Baxter State Park and Acadia National Park and had learned to expect the unexpected, mostly in terms of weather and personal injury or comfort. Because of those experiences, I was confident that I could conquer these problems. The water got turned on, the heat came on, and a call to the Coast Guard in Southwest Harbor eventually corrected the malfunctioning foghorn.

Oh yes, the foghorn. People kept saying I would get used to it, but I still resort to earplugs on those nights when it is sounding. On a foggy day or night it sounds every ten seconds. And then there is the wind that comes out of the north and literally shakes the house. Add in the bell buoy and it is a wonderful symphony of sounds!

In the middle of winter with all of this and a frozen pipe or two it is indeed a challenging place to live. Did I mention the short hike up to the garage every morning over more ice and snow? Oh well, I won't go into that.

But then there are the gorgeous moonlit nights and the clear starry nights. And those sunsets! The colors are stunningly beautiful. Sometimes when I leave in the morning I stop at the top of the hill and turn around just to take it all in. Despite the challenges, it is a very special place, one of the most beautiful on the island. And that's the truth.

Thank you for your support and remember, be kind to one another!

Marjorie E. Stratton, Town Manager

Someone asked how many live out here. I had an answer.

Yesterday there were 1301 people living in Vinalhaven. 637 were male and — some of you will have figured this out — 664 were females. 235 were dependent children. 201 were retired. 176 are lobstering, as captains, either part-time or full-time. A tiny handful of these are hiding out, never seen in town.

My walk around Vinalhaven had turned into a big adventure, one I was enjoying enormously.

During my walk around the island, an exercise now in its second year and which I hope to complete at the end of 2011, I've come across structures, new homes and the like, about which I'd been unaware. Yesterday, heading north around Calderwood Neck at sunset, I stumbled on an old shack, sagging under the weight of years, right at the water's edge. Wrapped in the arms of several foreboding old spruce trees, the approach from the shore was nearly obliterated by rugosa roses. A vine I couldn't identify crawled up the walls and over the three small waterfront windows. I negotiated a passage of least resistance through the thorns and huge spiders that had clearly had the place to themselves for a while to peer in at the nearest of these. Cobwebs covered the inside of the glass, and at first I couldn't see anything within except shadows, minimalist apparitions afforded by the modest light that penetrated the thick blanket of obstruction. After a while I was able to make out a form in the corner. It moved a little, forward and back, rocking. Suddenly she — I could see now it was an old woman — looked up and at me. She never blinked, and in a moment a smirk crossed her lips. From the stillness a whimper could be heard from elsewhere inside, out of view, but it was getting dark so I left.

The noise produced by the windmills continued to be a huge issue and it evoked compelling contributions from all quarters. Clearly this was going to consume us for some time to come.

Beyond Noise

No two of us are exactly alike. We all process auditory stimulations differently. If an audible vibration, such as the roar of a jet engine, annoys us we call it noise, whereas the vibration heard from reeds, strings, or lips we refer to as sound.

Since the replacement of the failing Vinalhaven Light and Power Company plant by a submerged "umbilical cord" cable to the mainland, Vinalhaven has been nearly as quiet as prior to the Civil War, except for noise from automobiles, diesel engines, rock hammers, stone crushers, chainsaws, and skidders. From the 1850s to the Depression the Fox Islands thrived as vibrant, active — and noisy — communities. Places cannot be exporters of sheep, wood, granite, and fish without creating noise. Audible vibrations are the sounds of life, work, and prosperity. Presently, with the old power plant gone, *A Cruising Guide to the Maine Coast* writes that Carver's Harbor is quiet, yet it still remains a working, often noisy harbor.

The level of the noise from the power plant that operated from 1914 to 1975 is difficult to remember precisely. Being brought up with it I didn't really hear it. We only started to listen for the power plant when the "power hour" began and individual home generators phased in to help provide the comfort of electricity. When Mr. Hopewell from across the harbor complained about the power plant and the purr from the gasoline-fueled straight-piped breathing eight-cylindered Buick-, Cadillac-, and Oldsmobile-driven lobster boats, I said, "What noise?" In earlier days from up on Mountain Street I easily heard those glowing red hot, exhaling straight-piped six-cylinder Chevys and flathead Chryslers. We certainly didn't have to go to the harbor in the afternoon to know that the five-boat Dyer fleet was safely back with each boat revving up their 160 horses for a little racing fun.

OBSERVATIONS

From the 1850s to the 1930s, din from the island's many quarries overwhelmed any sounds made by small engines, luffing sails, or pastoral activities. On Vinalhaven, noise (or was it sound?) of many active men yielding hammers, drills, steam engines, and explosives muted sounds from the prosperous fisheries and related factories. According to Vinalhaven historian Sidney Winslow, the industrial period from 1860 to 1920 was a "happier time" for the island: "Times were good, wages were good…Vinalhaven's populace was well fed…[A] great many of the townsfolk were born to the musical click of busy hammers and the puffing and groaning of [quarry] machinery…Many and many a night was the neighborhood lulled to sleep by the incessant puffing of the steam pump and awakened in the morning by the shriek of the 7 o'clock whistle that called the men to work… The quarry's busy clatter came to be synonymous with the sunrise. We paid little attention to the heavy blasts that were set off just a short distance from our dooryard, even though the air was often filled with sticks and stones because of them…" (See *Fish Scales and Stone Chips*, 1952). If Sidney Winslow were alive today he might say Maine and its laws should do less to lead us down the road of being a gated state for vacationers and retirees but do more to create an environment for productive, decent-paying jobs. Our educated young people would not have to leave the islands or the state for meaningful employment.

Today the noise of progress and sustainability and our step forward in the battle for life on these islands and this planet happens at the site of the former Swenson Quarry (formerly Maltzman Quarry, Bodwell and Webster Quarry, Carver and Grafam Quarry, and Amaziah Mills farm). If this is to be our islands' energy producing site, would we prefer oil, coal, or nuclear power over wind? Imagine the noise level created in this area from all the stonecutting required to keep three derricks busy in the quarry and two at their wharf on the shore. Following Maltzman a quieter period ensued until the early 1960s when the John Swenson Granite Co. introduced a technique of freeing granite from the earth with high temperature flames fueled by kerosene and compressed air. Islanders on both North Haven and Vinalhaven thought of it as a jet port with continuous jet departures. Although the Long Cove, Seal Cove, and Mill River neighbors were certainly blasted, Jake and his crew were well received by most folks. They provided local employment, paid their taxes, and brought new money to the island. The Vinalhaven Garden Club members loved visiting the quarry to gather burnt granite dust for their gardens. Even though the noise level was not quite like that experienced by Sid Winslow, islanders felt excited to see Vinalhaven granite being shipped again.

I empathize with people living near the Fox Islands Wind turbines who are adapting to the changes in their neighborhood. The Norton and Mills families of this same neighborhood experienced change as well with the arrival of the early granite cutting operations. Seth Norton, who farmed the thirty acres west of Gulley Brook, may have walked the short distance down the road and worked as a blacksmith for Bodwell and Webster.

All of us believe we are entitled to the benefits of our infrastructure, which is often associated with noise or some other notable feature. Many of our daily activities on the island require acceptance of change and in some cases, increased noise. Some of us tell time by the drone of the ferry; some listen to the changing tune of departing and arriving lobster boats. Others put up with the smell, smoke, and noise at our dump and transfer station. Since the road repaving, neighbors of East and West Main Street listen to faster — and thereby often noisier — traffic. Some neighbors of the shooting range wonder when the shooting will stop. How does the quality of life near the wind turbines compare with that of life and property values near our dump, shooting range, airport, sewer plant, busy harbor, gravel pits, school playground, or Main Street?

One billion people, one-sixth of the earth's population, face risk from sea level rise driving them from the land they love and need by the results of our desire for a life style of ease and comfort. (Many of these people live on islands like us.) Let's help keep the fossil fuel in the ground and lower our carbon dioxide output. Let's stop the burning of coal, which deposits ammonia, carbon, mercury, nitrogen, and sulfur on Maine whenever it rains. Let's listen less to our politicians and listen more to our scientists. My science teacher says the wind turbine blades are 50% efficient, and 1.5 megawatts equate to 2,010 horsepower of energy. Therefore the three FIW turbines harvest 6,000 horsepower of the 12,000 horsepower of available wind energy passing by the three 240-foot diameter blade swept areas. Wow! Our electric rates will be lowered and stabilized with free non-polluting energy. Fox Islands Wind Project is only the beginning for taking local responsibility to get us off oil and coal. Our local natural resources of tides, sun, and wind, and our educated youth could allow us to become the Samso Island* of Maine. Let's go, Fox Islands. Perhaps one golden opportunity missed was that Fox Islands Wind, LLC did not build six turbines in 2009. Up and down the Midcoast, mainland folks look out to sea and admire what North Haven and Vinalhaven have done. Instead of "drill, baby, drill," let's choose "SPIN, BABY, SPIN!!!"

by Del Webster

*Samso Island in Denmark has become famous for producing all of its own energy, a transition it made within only ten years.

A Community Works to Resolve a Community Issue

The Fox Islands Wind Power Project in Vinalhaven is already, in many ways, a great success. The brainchild of a few visionary island residents almost a decade ago, the project was developed by the community, for the benefit of the community. And these benefits have proven to be real: after the turbines came on-line in November, electricity prices on the islands fell to their lowest levels in many years, and the project will stabilize these rates for decades.

The year-round communities of the Fox Islands (Vinalhaven and North Haven) are fragile, their survival threatened by high bait prices, high fuel prices, and electricity prices that are three times the national average. The wind project provides relief from at least one of these burdens for the 1800 residents who spend the winter connected to the mainland only by the Penobscot Bay ferry and the submarine cable.

The project was built to meet rigorous environmental and land use standards established by state and municipal law, including a sound standard that establishes a maximum of 45 decibels at night and 55 decibels during the day. Maine has some of the most sophisticated noise standards in the United States, and its rules have served Maine and its population well for more than twenty years.

Some households who live near the wind project have expressed the feeling that the sound of the

OBSERVATIONS

wind generators is bothersome. A few have been very vocal in expressing this concern. Many of those who live closest to the turbines remain supporters of the project, as are the vast majority of all island residents. However, the sound issue, first raised when the turbines were turned on in November, has been a concern for Fox Islands Wind, and the locally-elected board of the Fox Islands Electric Cooperative, which operate the turbines and distribute the electricity on behalf of the community.

FIW and the Co-op have listened to the neighbors, and acted swiftly to measure and try to understand the nature of the sound, and the bother that it causes. They began collecting sound levels, as well as asking neighbors to keep track of their experience of the sounds, within days of when the turbines were commissioned. Several equipment adjustments have already been made, in cooperation with the turbine manufacturer, to reduce the sound of the turbines. The results of these measures are still being assessed.

The community has also reacted. Many island residents who do not live near the turbines have been going up to the site, visiting those who do, and assessing the sound situation for themselves. Thus, many island residents are able to form their own opinions about the nature of the sound, and the sort of impact that it is having on island life.

As part of the ongoing attempts to understand the nature and impact of the sound situation, and to inform the community about it, the Co-op has initiated an unprecedented experiment. Beginning on Monday, the turbines will be slowed down during the night, reducing the output and the sound — by different amounts on different nights — from the turbines. Simultaneously, the neighbors will be asked to record their subjective assessment of the sound from the turbines.

At the end of one month, the results of this experiment will be collected and presented to the community. Costs (in terms of higher electricity prices resulting from reduced power output) will be assessed, and benefits (reduced sound for neighbors) weighed. Ultimately, the community will be asked to weigh in and decide how to resolve this issue. We look forward to a solution that is in the entire community's best interest.

Fox Island Electric Cooperative, Inc.

Suitable material for a column can be found almost anywhere, particularly if there are no writing assignments involved. Chance encounters like this one worked pretty well. So did the expressions on the little faces of kids encountering me, a stranger, at the wheel of the bus.

It was a terrific moment. Most of us only encounter toddlers as part of a team, in a stroller perhaps or elsewhere with a parent. On this day several of them happened, by chance, to find themselves near the checkout at Carver's, some just coming in with attending adults, others getting ready to leave. Suddenly the air, till then occupied by the mundane chatter, or worse, the awkward quiet, of adults, was full of gleeful babble as the kids all recognized one another from Island Village Child Care:

A couple of girls who ride their dad's shoulders all over town and from that lofty perch regard their island kingdom, graciously bestowing greetings on their many devoted subjects.

Another who, though being pulled along by her mother, is clearly in command of the wagon she navigates along Main Street and who is equally solicitous of the attentive passersby.

2010

A boy who trots along with his mom but no longer holds her hand, a young man's courage and self-reliance beginning to assert themselves.

Another boy who, though an underclassman, is clearly a person of consequence, one who, given his dad's propensity, can probably distinguish a delicious *Inonotus obliquus* from a toadstool.

And a girl, who, with older parents, busy people but no longer youngsters, has adopted a *laissez faire* attitude toward raising capable adults who can take care themselves.

What do some school kids look forward to more than anything else? A substitute bus driver. He doesn't know who most of them are, where they live, or who they are related to, so it's great fun to see whether the old guy can be convinced a kid is someone other than who he really is and should be dropped off somewhere where he'll have more fun than if taken home.

Others, first-graders in particular, are terrified, because clearly this old man is not capable of returning them home; they will never again see their own room or the reliable folks who tuck them in each night. Bad enough that these kids, for long weeks after school began, worried about whether they'd get to school safely and, more importantly, whether they'd ever see home again. Having ridden with the same driver for a few months, they had begun to relax, and now this. Rather than the small assurance of John's familiar, albeit stoic, presence, there sits instead an old man, certainly too old to be driving anything, let alone a bus. They glance down hopelessly at the notes in their fists, notes indicating all sort of legitimate alternatives to being dropped of at home such as, "Carrie is going to her Grammie's" or "Jake goes home with Brandy" or "Don't let LeRoy get off the bus with Sam — he bites!" and they despair for they know these notes mean nothing to him. In fact, he seems to have already dozed off.

The Vinalhaven Lions Club conducted their thirteenth annual Diabetes and Healthy Heart Screening Clinic. This generous effort makes the test, normally $50-$100, available to all for only five dollars.

People have begun to give me mementos, reminders of work my father and grandfather did here during the late half of last century. My dad acknowledged every project he completed, tucking his signature and the relevant data in some inconspicuous place. I was given a piece of Formica recently, for example, testifying to his having remodeled the parsonage in 1971. A friend stopped by to present me with a pay stub from earnings from when he'd worked for my dad long ago and to complain playfully about his wages in 1961.

Today Paul Chilles stopped to ask if I was putting on any help but before I could answer he qualified that facetious inquiry by demanding that, if I was hiring, I do better by him than my father had done back in 1961, whereupon he presented me with a pay stub from April of that year reflecting his $1.40 hourly rate from Crossman & Maddox. I hastened to point out that my own rate — I was 16 at the time — was 65 cents and he was being treated twice as well as I was. Paul was gracious enough not to carry the comparison further still, perhaps telling me why that disparity was reasonable.

That week he worked 49 hours, none of which was considered overtime, and from his $68.60 had been withheld $5.50 income tax withholding and $2.06 in "Old Age Benefit." Back then there was no compunction about calling things as they were. Today, of course, it's Social Security.

> Still, old age is what it was for and, given how grateful I am for it now, I can only imagine how much it must mean to Paul.

Robert Shetterly, an artist and activist famous for his "People Who Tell the Truth" portrait series, visited the school to work with students.

Tara Elliott was another in a succession of talented drama teachers. Actually they seemed to be getting more and more capable. I happily reviewed the middle school's *Humpty Dumpty is Missing!*

> Today this space is inadequate. Having nearly forgotten about it I was reminded of the middle school's performance of *Humpty Dumpty is Missing!* For as long as I can remember theater has played a big role in this community. Some, not many, productions have been memorably so-so; many more have been terrific; a handful—like this one—were exceptional. The mastery of rapid fire dialogue in this great spoof was unrelenting as was the timely delivery of endless wry asides, the dubious obliques, the feigned sincerity, the flamboyance, the affronts, the affectations, the nonchalance, the duplicity, the askance, the flawless memorization of lines and delivery, the costumes, the set, the mischief, the lighting, certainly the direction and encouragement, the relentless stage presence, the incredulity, the distress, the imagination, the arrogance, the apprehension, etc. there was not a dull moment, not one. So many kids turned in really exceptional performances that I literally do not have space to mention them all. Some, though, displayed a remarkable mastery of subtleties and I've got all I can do to resist calling attention to their exceptional performances, but I know better than to praise some middle schoolers and not others, and in this case it's easy to avoid because the cast was universally wonderful. It seems clear that Tara Elliott has a rapport with these kids. I hope that's true. What's next?

In the prevailing spirit of conflict resolution that is manifest in a tiny minority, some misfits settled a score.

> It's not comforting to know one has enemies but if it's undeniable it's helpful to know who they are. There are unmistakable signs. A person steps right up and says, "I do not like you," for example, or punches you in the nose. A person once said after reading something I had written, "I hate you, but, by Christ, you're funny." I didn't like hearing that I was so disliked but I did get a kick from her honesty, the same honesty that may result in being punched in the nose. All those folks, those who indulge such transparency, have evolved as was intended, maturing and becoming forthcoming.

> A lesser species, immature, dishonest, and cowardly, given something to stew about, will sneak about in the dark and, if convinced they cannot be seen by anyone, that they will not have to confront anyone face-to-face, will indulge that most pitiful form of retribution: tire slashing. Imagine witnessing something like that. Imagine watching someone sneak up on a defenseless vehicle, skulking about, perhaps crawling through the mud, trying to keep hidden, and stabbing the tire or, as was the case on New Year's Eve, four tires belonging to someone, a native son who is everything the slasher was not: capable, hardworking, dependable, honest. Happy New Year! God said, "Pity the tire slashers for they have a very limited range of expression." Well, he would have said it if chariots hadn't been all the rage.

I was watching some youngsters smoking and remembered my own troubled smoke-filled past. Fewer seemed to indulge than did in the past; still it was sad to see any succumb.

2010

Sometime during my freshman year, or maybe it was the eighth grade, I was enticed to smoke a Pall Mall in that little area halfway up the lane leading to the school from the East Boston Road.

A couple of years later a friend and I were setting up pins in Viv Drew's bowling alley (now the Harbor Gawker). We got a nickel a string, enough to keep us at the pool table, in trouble, and in cigarettes. Camels were twenty-seven cents a pack, filters were thirty, but Viv would sell singles to us for two cents apiece. I set up pins all evening. During one string Victor Ames rolled a ball so hard the flying pins nearly took my head off. There were several who bowled like that. Later that night we were still at the bowling alley but had had a couple of contraband Haffenrefers and were behaving badly. Viv asked us to leave. We hung around outside. Before long one of the bowlers came out and told us to move along home. I asked him what he was going to do about it if we didn't. He was very obliging. He is still here but he's older and has a hard time getting around. He walks with a cane. If I could be sure he wasn't trying to trick me I might try to trip him. Thirty-two years, thousands of dollars, and countless efforts later I finally quit smoking by renting a houseboat on the Erie Canal with three others who didn't smoke, and staying on board for a week.

Exercise, especially in the off-season, increasingly consumed some of us and, as the years went by, opportunities to shed pounds and get fit grew.

Richie Carlson, Biggest Losers CEO, no longer able to keep up with Lynn James, his second in command, had the good sense this year to recruit Sue L'Africain to take up some of his slack. Lynn, who once said, "A woman who wants to be a man's equal lacks ambition," has a comrade in Sue, a firm believer that "pain is just weakness leaving the body." Sue has cheerfully stepped up to the plate, driving "Sweat Equity," her team of middle-aged stalwarts, mercilessly to the brink.

Richie calls his teams of spring fanatics the Biggest Losers. In fact it is we, the Losers' beleaguered home companions, who are suffering. The struggling disciples drag themselves home four times a week and whine at us about how horrible, unfair, and sadistic Richie and crew are and how their attempts to circumvent the rigors of exercise with idle chatter are mercilessly thwarted; how, no sooner have they mastered the intricacies of milking the less strenuous elements of one regimen or another, they are compelled to learn new and even more demanding exercises, agonizing routines that presume too much. And we, waiting at home at the scales with heating pads, Tiger Balm, and sympathy (never enough) share the pain.

Tellingly, as soon as Sue got on the ferry for a little R&R this week, several members of "Sweat Equity" were having cheese Danish and singing "Ding Dong, the Wicked Witch is gone." The scales will tell the tale.

A sturgeon swam into Carver's Pond!

The off-season activities of some of our seasonal residents and the spirit of volunteerism that had similarly moved several of our young folks to venture abroad doing good work seemed an appropriate topic.

Amid the chaos around the world are individual efforts to improve things on a fundamental level, and some of that selfless effort comes from our own folks, year-round and seasonal. The Holy Apostles Soup Kitchen in New York City, for example, is run by a summer resident. Several of our young people, after finishing school, have embarked on remarkable adventures, determined to improve conditions for folks elsewhere. The El Salvador Project was begun by Hope Jackson and Ben Dorr in 2005, focused on providing a high school education for the seven children of a single family for whom an education would have otherwise been out of the question. Now, five years later, all those kids are either in high school or have graduated and are in college preparing to return and make a real difference themselves. Hope is now in Senegal as a midwife and advocate for women whose prospects, particularly during childbirth, have historically been very grim. The African Birth Collective is a project of the $10 Club (thetendollarclub.org), which proposes to "Save the World, $10 at a Time." Hope financed the trip herself, and the $10 Club, with 340 $10 contributions, provided her with sutures and other supplies. This week she began delivering healthier babies to healthier moms who, in many cases might not have lived or had…*Hope*.

Living here comes with all the benefits and challenges of living in a small town, where not much escapes attention.

Recently a friend sat down in an island restaurant. The waitress took her order but returned with a different selection saying, "The chef says given your condition yours was not a good choice."

An acquaintance recently recounted his mainland birth back in the mid-1900s. His mother and another lady were in labor at the same time and Dr. Earle hadn't been comfortable tending both simultaneously so he sent them to the mainland hospital. Much later the boy had remarked on the coincidence of his birth and that of his fellow islander. "Well, it was no surprise to me, I can tell you," replied his mother. "You were both conceived on the same night." No one needs to remind us we live in a small town.

An electric thermal storage program got underway whereby mechanical units that draw power from the grid when the windmills are producing more electricity than the town is consuming and stores it in the form of auxiliary heat, were made available to consumers.

I have a hard time paying attention unless something really interesting is going on. I was at a meeting at the library but just outside the window was something more interesting: a tree.

I came home from a meeting the other day, a meeting at the library. I told Elaine that during the meeting my attention had wandered a little. She said, "Yes, I know. I was there."

I'd been looking at the little plaque acknowledging my mother's contributions to the library but had also been looking at the trees outside the window. The one nearest was Bodine's chestnut. Chestnuts are uniformly unruly, particularly during their stark, undressed winter, but this one is positively foreboding. If a tree can be said to have something to say this one says, "Make my day." Its feral branches appear unable to agree on anything, to coexist not by choice but like tethered lunatics who only have an apocalyptic purpose in common. Its lower branches are carnivorous, reaching for a careless pedestrian or maybe a stray dog or cat, perhaps a child. The upper ones rake the skies maniacally. Nearby but across the road is an ethereal hardwood, ambivalent and fanciful, like the blonde in a blonde joke, flighty, the kind of tree whose simple optimism can rise above anything, even in such proximity and contrast with the angry chestnut. If it could sing it might be singing "I Feel Pretty," like Natalie Wood from West Side Story. Nearby is a cedar, cerebral and long-suffering, contemplative, capable of thoughtful reflection. Its composure drives the other trees nuts.

2010

Elaine and I went to England to visit our daughter Sarah and her husband, Chad, who was finishing up his education at University of Bath, west of London. In the process we visited a couple of fascinating castles and got quite a surprise, one that left me quite satisfied with my choice of a spouse.

Contrary to what we may have heard, England is not just another island. It's much bigger, for example, and whereas we are casual regarding our *r*'s, these islanders employ them eagerly while treating *h* with a particular economy. They once had a great penchant for attaching adjective modifiers to a King's first name that effectively quantified that monarch's accomplishments.

During our visit last week we chose, from the many alternatives that presented themselves, the ruins of an old castle to visit. Corfe Castle, in Dorset, was only an hour or two from our lodgings in Bath. The castle was once presided over by King Edgar the Peaceable who'd succeeded Edmund the Magnificent. King Edgar was succeeded by Edward the Charitable and had it only ended I'd have very little to write about. As it turns out, though, a dear member of my family is directly descended from the hapless monarch who, when his half-brother Edward was assassinated by his mother, ascended the throne at Corfe Castle and became King of England at the age of ten.

Until we arrived at the site we had no idea we'd randomly selected the very castle once occupied by Elaine's great, etc., grandfather. Faced with invading hordes of Vikings determined to overthrow the Anglo Saxons, the ten-year-old was in a bind. Although the consequences were predictable, King Aethelred the Unready — we call him Gramps — reigned off and on until 1016.

The Wells Cathedral was begun in 1180 and rises above everything else in the town of Wells in Somerset, England. Our own Union Church, which celebrates its 150th birthday this summer, could fit inside the Wells Cathedral about 50 times. A cat lives there. In the morning, when it opens to the public, the cat saunters 400 feet or so down to the cathedral from Vicar's Hall, the oldest building on the oldest residential street in England, Vicars Close, constructed in the 1300s. Every day the cat heads for the gift shop where it graciously receives visitors from all over the world. Around midday it tires of being the center of attention and heads down the nave to choir practice. Lying down between a steam radiator and a young harpist and basking, harpist and cat, in a shaft of sunlight pouring in from the silver stained windows in the clerestory (thanks, Bill), it surveys the assembled musicians. Fanned out are the violins, a cello and upright bass; clarinets and, one each: a bassoon, an oboe and a lute; drums, a bass, snares, cymbals and timpani; trumpets, trombones, and a tuba. Behind them are 48 choristers: eighteen girls, eighteen boys, and twelve men, and next to the harpist, on the other side of the cat, on a platform, stands a rhapsodic soprano whose magnificent interlude during Evensong makes everyone's hair stand on end, except the cat's. It glances up contemptuously. Clearly it's heard better.

An effort to hang a flag on nearly every electric pole in town and to display the names of donors and honored veterans was underway about the same time a veteran of World War II, a friend, passed way.

Les Williams passed away a few days ago. That Les Williams was eighty-seven years old and looked about sixty-five was not the most remarkable thing about him. Neither was his having lived life to the absolute fullest since a heart attack ten years ago that left him with only a tiny bit of heart left. Nor was it his determination to serve his country in WWII when he flew hundreds of combat missions from a dozen different aircraft carriers in the Pacific. It wasn't the fact that he returned to serve his country, flying more combat missions during the Korean War and again during the Cold War, when he undertook sorties about which a great deal remains classified. Neither was the fact that, a few days before his passing, he was there at the Nashua Air Traffic Control Center, still at work, having never retired, at eighty-seven years of age, doing what he'd loved doing for nearly sixty years. The most remarkable thing about Les, in my estimation, was his extraordinary modesty. For nearly thirty years Les and Diane have returned to Vinalhaven, his birthplace, brightening the lives of a lot of us, holding court at the Tidewater and enjoying to the fullest the company of his many close friends, particularly Abbott and Bobbie and their family. He enjoyed hearing all about what was going on here in our lives much more than he enjoyed talking about his own great accomplishments. We should all do as much with as little heart.

The increasingly energetic efforts of the many women involved in the various exercise programs in town prompted me to take up a modest exertion of my own.

Some men I know are getting older. They make noises, noises that speak of discomfort and of effort, when, for example, they get up and off the couch. They spend more time on the couch, too, and nod off quickly and easily, sometimes in mid-thought, even during a lecture, perhaps a domestic lecture concerned with things that need doing. They make these same noises — actually it's a different noise but expresses the same great struggle — when they bend over to put on their shoes or bend over to do anything, for that matter. Some have solved the shoe problem by having acquired a three-foot shoehorn that hangs by the door so that a change from boots to slippers and back again is effortless. Many are up before the sun, doing pitiful little exercises and curling pathetic little eight or ten-pound weights in the cold but forgiving darkness, darkness that allows them to engage in this desperate activity without having to watch themselves doing it, darkness that keeps the prying island world at bay, as well. These kinds of efforts, any effort really, prompt other noises as well, unpleasant noises. Sit-ups are particularly productive. These older men have a lot of loose skin flapping around, too, behind their biceps, where their triceps used to be, and little tummies whose determination to remain conspicuous is easily the equal of any effort to do otherwise. They get up more during the night, too, and often (not always), to their credit, can still remember why when they get to the bathroom. And they walk and walk, trying to forestall the inevitable. I see them when out for a leisurely stroll myself, having been helped on with my sneakers.

Leaving Surfside after having breakfast almost every Saturday morning, I'd come face-to-face with Phyllis Peterson's extraordinarily beautiful apple tree. It and a copper beech that had been taken down recently were among the most beautiful trees in town.

The copper beech tree that was taken down a couple of years ago just beyond the Norton's Point Road was a majestic and magnificent thing. Up on the east shore of Calderwood Point, anchored in a rocky slope with hardly any soil and looking out toward Stonington is a huge old oak tree, equally impressive, ancient and simply stoic, for longer than any of us has lived, in the face of relentless nor'easters. The apple tree in Phyllis Peterson's front yard, however, is easily their equal and this year it's outdone itself. Dwarfed by either of those giants I've described, its tensile trunk extends a voluptuous abundance graciously and gracefully toward admiring passersby and does so effortlessly, at a seemingly impossible fifteen degrees or so. Some years ago, I think there was a prop, a stick or something, under the thick trunk, an offer of assistance, but it's gone, cast aside disdainfully by the tree, it needing no help. Each year it offers its thick vibrant tresses in a different style, like a starlet with a new 'do. This year though, buns, particularly side buns, are enjoying resurgence and, not to be upstaged, the apple is displaying blossoms only port and starboard like Mary Pickford or *Star Wars*' Princess Leia. I don't know what Phyllis feeds that tree or what she says to it but the effect is sumptuous.

Each year we've customarily enjoyed the harvest from halibut season. Increasingly the season has been shorter and shorter. In 2010 it was very short and, as usual, the few guys who were fishing for them were taking orders. We have always loaded up the freezer.

By this time I was about mid-way in my walk around the island. I rounded a point on the southeast shore of Mill River and my heart sank. The Carrying Place Bridge had been "repaired."

Vinalhaven has seven granite bridges — eight if one counts the causeway at Old Harbor — the same number of bridges as Manhattan. All of our bridges — Carrying Place, Dyer Island, Barton Island, Lane's Island, Mill Stream, Mill Creek, and the Boondoggle — are carefully constructed from Vinalhaven granite. So are at least some of those — the Manhattan, Henry Hudson, Williamsburg, George Washington, Queensboro, Triborough, Brooklyn, and Broadway — in Manhattan, although, I think, not so artfully. Each of our bridges, particularly the smaller ones, those that have not been beefed up with steel and similar augmentation, is a thing of real beauty. Looking up or down stream at any of them is a treat, one most of us, simply traveling to and fro over them, don't get a chance to enjoy. One of these historic landmarks, the Carrying Place, has recently undergone "reinforcement," mandated by the DOT, which found that the old chinks had fallen out leaving it weakened. The reinforcement was completed by a mainland engineering company, an undertaking that could surely have been completed more creatively. The result has been the complete obliteration of its stone exterior by the application of what appears to be a fiber concrete coating. We have six bridges left; three are of a type similar to the Carrying Place. I hope they can get by without reinforcement.

A few days later I was just northwest of the bridge watching the wasted efforts of a pair of osprey.

Sunday morning at dawn the tide was on its way out, nearly low. Overhead, two ospreys circled the trickle of water still draining from Mill River out toward the Thorofare, a female and a male, paired for life, likely. Gliding back and forth looking for movement below in what was certainly not more than a foot of water, they didn't expend much energy. They stopped, though, several times a minute, four usually, turned backs to the wind, adjusted the attitudes of their bodies and the pitch of their wings and flapped repeatedly in such a way that the combination compensated perfectly for the wind speed and direction, and rendered them stationary in midair for a few seconds that they might survey the possibilities hundreds of feet below. It was the equivalent of me looking from my bedroom window and trying to decide whether that speck on the roof of the Star of Hope was a piece of sandwich and whether worth the effort to retrieve. I watched them while I walked around the point. They never ceased but never found a target. If they had, though, I know from having seen before, they'd have executed the most magnificent maneuver, folding their wings against their bodies and hurtling downward, extending their wings at precisely the instant required to snatch a fish from the shallows and change their trajectory from down to up.

OBSERVATIONS

I tried to launch a new column, called "Louie Lives Here," featuring the priceless remembrances of Louie Martin, a contemporary who wanted and still wants very much to share his memories with the rest of us. Louis is an institution, no two ways about it. He and I grew up together. He's a proud and vital member of the Vinalhaven Lions Club, the Moses Webster Masonic Lodge, and we feel the same about him.

Louis Martin and regalia
Photo provided by the Vinalhaven Lions Club

2010

LOUIE LIVES HERE

Louie Martin knows more about the people who live and have lived here than anyone. I asked if he'd like to record some of what he remembers. "Folks have been pesterin' me to do that," he said.

When we were in school together we each tried to be the funniest kid in class. One day when we were in the 5th or 6th grade, a frustrated teacher broke a yardstick over his head. Louie looked up and said, "There's no use knocking; nobody's home." He was funnier than I was on that day, anyway, but he was wrong in his assessment. There certainly was somebody home and there still is. Louie's words:

"I was born in Jimmy Oscar's Barbershop on December 15, 1940. It was just a barbershop, not a maternity home like Muckle's old place was, but that's where I was born. It was on the ground floor of the house on the corner heading down into Frog Hollow, the one where Delma and Burt Carter used to live; that's where I was born. I've lived here all my life and want to talk about the neighborhoods and the people who lived in them." An excerpt:

SKIN HILL

"George MacDonald and his wife Eva lived up there, above where our house was. George used to smoke his corncob and put us kids up to mischief. One time, when Eva was having a tea party, he talked us into painting the outhouse seat green. Soon one of the ladies had to go and—you guessed it. Eva was some wound up. She gave George a wicked thrashing and chased us over the hill."

THE BUTLER DID IT

Tara Elliott gave us another wonderful production. *The Butler Did It* tapped the exceptional talents of a singular bunch of kids.

> Director Tara Elliott reminds us in the program *The Butler Did It* to remember to laugh, as if we could do otherwise. She and the cast, an appealing bunch who've been taking liberties with one another their whole lives, treated this farce the same way. It was a stroke of comedic genius to stuff Frank Morton and Joey Reidy into a single outfit and call them the hapless Louie Fan. Their choreographed fingertips alone could have carried the evening. Pleasant Garner, superb as Miss Maple, was never out of character or at a loss for words. Karen Krager was perfectly cast as the sketchy, snuffly, and deceptive housemaid, and so was Alex Slivinsky, as the nervously attentive and rightfully suspicious secretary, fingertips drumming anxiously on her hatbox. The mystery writers all worked very well together. Tyler Chilles was deceptively fragile; John Morton, lecherous and shamelessly full of himself; Francis Warren, very good as detective extraordinaire Peter Flimsey; Izza Drury, superbly snooty and imperious; Trey Warren, fey and dramatic; and Blake Reidy, staggeringly seductive as Charity Haze. The climactics worked nicely and Charity's huge assault on the convict maid was astonishing. This space is again inadequate, no room for proper tribute to technical accomplishments: costume, set, lighting, makeup, sound, props, everything. Another great production from Tara Elliott.

The controversy "revolving" around noise from the wind turbines continued unabated. FIW published columns expressing concern and outlining plans for addressing the problem. Neighbors and allies alleged to have been misled and had by now retained an attorney and were petitioning the DEP to take corrective action. For weeks every issue of the *Wind* carried a full-page article from one quarter or another.

The legislature was debating a bill, ill-considered according to many, encouraging offshore wind turbines.

Body conditioning for women began at Aerofit under the guidance of Sue L'Africain, and a very trim bunch began to take shape.

In May there was a brief flurry of controversy over the cost of maintaining a volunteer fire department and ambulance service.

> Many years ago when I was on the board of selectmen, a proposal was made to create and fund an ambulance service. The suggestion generated heated debate, most of it having to do with costs and the likelihood that such a service would result in higher taxes. Some argued that the creation of such a service was a step toward making historically volunteer positions, such as that of fire chief, permanent and, once accomplished, irreversible, even if one day an appointee proved unworthy. The prediction that we'd eventually make the role of fire chief a full-time position funded by our taxes was fulfilled, but the concerns about whether we'd benefit have certainly been unfounded. The fire department and the ambulance service cost us money, but so do lots of other things. The question of whether we get a tangible return on our investment should decide the question of whether the investment is worthwhile. The return on having invested in an ambulance service and a full-time fire chief is lives saved and our security as a community strengthened. As the time to consider funding for these services draws nearer we might want to think about those investments and returns and contrast them with the kinds of returns we're getting elsewhere, repairs to the Carrying Place Bridge, for example.

Baseball season had begun, and, like most of us, I was anxious to see whether the Red Sox would get off to a good start. I got distracted, though.

> I was always a Red Sox fan as a kid. Frank Malzone, Jimmy Pearsall, Ted Williams: these guys and their heroics were topics of conversation in our family for years. I remained a fan until the '94–'95 players strike. The injury I felt at having the entire postseason cancelled and the selfishness I perceived in that travesty took the winds of enthusiasm out of my sails and I never watched again until three years ago when, inexplicably, my wife Elaine took a vigorous interest in the Red Sox. Since then we have hardly missed a game.

> The only interruption in her otherwise unrelenting support for the team revolves around spitting. The players and managers are like camels, minus the dromedary's pinpoint accuracy. We enjoyed watching Daniel Nava in his first appearance at bat. Although not spitting at all, he hit the first pitch he'd ever seen in the big leagues for a grand slam home run. Now, he's been playing for nearly a month and, in the interest of team spirit, he's begun to spit. At first it just dribbled down his chin, typical of a rookie, but now most of his expulsions are big league projectiles, falling within the broad arc of acceptability that defines that soggy area around home plate. The other day, when Pedroia singled in the bottom of the ninth, Nava, with the winning run, slid into home on his face, the skids having been greased, so to speak, by his own saliva and that of his peers. Nice.

2010

We were all very unhappy to learn that Tara Elliott was leaving. *Nobody Sleeps* was terrific.

I broke into a place once. I wasn't caught but if I had been I'd not have liked it to have been by the cast of *Nobody Sleeps*. My ego wouldn't have survived it. It's hard not being taken seriously; I know firsthand, but even I have not experienced the level of frustration undergone by Fiona Warren as the beleaguered burglar in this — sadly, one of the last — of Tara Elliott's dramatic productions. Poor Spike, a heretofore self-respecting burglar, is driven to inadequacy by a family of females whose disregard for the danger he poses is maddening and insurmountable. The three sisters, Daisy, Ada, and Glory, portrayed just about perfectly by Bethany Candage, Hannah Noyes, and Jessie Creelman, are entirely dismissive of the threat Spike presents and short circuit his every effort to persuade them he is otherwise. Rather, they subject his ever more hopeless determination to go about his business to endless, if playful, ridicule. In the process they share with the audience some great asides; a couple were priceless. He stubbornly resists and clings admirably but desperately to his macho image but is finally undone when the provocative Mrs. Busby, the mom, in the person of Ellie Reidy, arrives on the scene and subjects him to a withering assessment of style and technique and reduces him to a poor imitation of what he imagines himself to be.

I try to write at least one piece each year about being an island native (or not) or where one falls in that vast schism between the two.

Today's population is 1274. One or two, depending on how one views an ill-considered mainland fling back in the early 1900s, are Thoroughbred Natives, those being folks for whom there is no recorded evidence of their ever having left the island and for whom there is no evidence their ancestors did, either. Forty-seven are Super Natives, that is, they were born here and so were their parents and grandparents. One hundred and twelve are Prime Natives, parents and themselves having been born here; three hundred and eight are Normal Natives, having been born here themselves but being the first in their family to have made such a prudent move. Eighty-nine are Apprentice Natives, having been born in a mainland hospital but brought back quickly to avoid contamination. Six hundred and six are Wanna-Be's, having come here from Away and then done everything they could do to endear themselves to the rest of us, often, if not always, contributing far more to the health and well-being of the community than might otherwise be expected and more than most of us. Seventy-one are Opportunist Natives, having moved here from Away to marry an islander with no more noble goal than the understandable desire to improve their own circumstances. Thirty-nine are Never Natives, having moved here from Away with no intention of staying long and not much caring what the rest of us think about it.

I was a little hasty last week when characterizing various of us as one species of native or another. I've been taken to task for having overlooked all manner of variation. One fellow, till now unconcerned about his roots and with good reason — his parents were both born on the island and so were both sets of grandparents — has been anguishing since the column appeared because he was born in a mainland hospital and didn't return here till he was two days old. He hastened to point out that every effort was made to get him home the same day but the weather forced cancellation of the ferry and, furthermore, his mother, without much thought about how this would impact him later in life, opted for a second day of rest, exposing him to further contamination, the results of which can be seen in certain of his mannerisms. Still, given his ancestry, he does deserve special consideration and must be somewhere between a Super Native and an Apprentice. If he hadn't spent that second day lounging in purgatory it would be an easier call. Another example is of a summer girl born here during July (the 4th, I think) but hustled away before Labor Day. Although she returns each summer her situation is one of limbo. Much has to do with the enthusiasm with which she was taken away just before there'd have been no one left for her to play with but natives.

I'd ridden my bike during a couple of the preceding EMS Benefit Challenge races. Each time I prudently teamed up with a young runner who'd make us both look good. This year was no exception.

This year, as in years past, I cleverly teamed up with a teenager in the EMS Benefit Challenge. Kelsey McDougle has been coming to Vinalhaven since she was an infant and I have been surreptitiously watching her develop into the fine athlete I knew would be required to carry me and my bike respectably to the finish line. She did not disappoint me. As a consequence I appear to the casual observer of results to have done well in the race. In fact, I'd have done even better had I not had a couple of harrowing encounters in those remote regions of the race where supervision is nonexistent. The first was with a young woman who, pedaling effortlessly by me as I began my ascent of our version of Heartbreak Hill (actually there seems to be more than one of those nowadays), reached over as she glided by and, suggesting I'd do better if I encountered less resistance, flipped my shift lever from high to low while I was pumping hard standing up. The time required for me to recover from that jarring transition cost me precious seconds, and when a fellow went by flashing the sharp end of an open Leatherman very close to my tire I was still rattled. That I finished the race at all is no thanks to Paul Bates who, at his post where the Round the Island Road encounters the North Haven Road, carelessly ignored my plea for oxygen and ordered me to move on. Still, I did finish ahead of some summer residents who missed the boat.

Bert Dyer was an old timer, certainly an institution for as long as I can remember. By 2010 he was beginning to wind down. He was in residence at VES, could no longer drive, and had been reduced to riding a motorized scooter into town for breakfast and to fulfill his numerous social obligations.

It's not true that Bert Dyer came over on the Maylower, but he was crewing on a herring trawler that was close behind and would have beat them here if he hadn't had to climb into the dory every now and then to tend a sein. When I was a kid Bert was already over 300 years old and it was pretty clear that a lot of water (not all water) had gone under the bridge. In ten years this remarkable island artifact will be 400 years old, but this week he's celebrating his 390th, and on Sunday there'll be an open house for him at the Homestead from 2-4 p.m. In his advancing years, after overcoming daunting obstacles and after having dealt with more than his share of loss, Bert has settled comfortably into the role of island greeter. Manning his duty station outside Carver's every day, proudly displaying his ribbons, he meets, greets, informs, flirts, and cheers us all. He has taken it upon himself to reacquaint us all with real music, a trove of which he keeps up forward, in the basket of his motorized scooter. He awakens the half-mile of neighborhood between the Homestead and Surfside each morning with stuff like the "Hawaiian Wedding Song" or "Crazy Arms," and slows traffic compelled to navigate through the cloud of cigarette smoke surrounding his scooter during its inexorable advance toward the village. It's reasonable to think we're the only town with such a fixture.

2010

A visiting fire chief and I found ourselves chatting at the motel just as our own chief and two of his predecessors appeared nearby. The contrast between them and the visitor was striking.

> A few years ago the fire chief of Denver, Colorado stayed at the motel. He wore his dress uniform and shoulder boards. He was telling me about his own department, about the discipline he maintained, the spit and polish. Unfamiliar with a volunteer department, he was quizzing me about ours when Mark strode out of the Paper Store. "That's our fire chief right there," I said, "the one in cranberry sweatpants." At that moment Tiny stepped out of his pulp truck looking like he'd been romancing a wood chipper with an oil leak. "That's his predecessor," I pointed out. Before the visiting chief had a chance to comment Cy emerged from the cellar of Carver's covered with cobwebs. I couldn't resist and told him Cy'd been chief before Tiny.
>
> For as long as I can remember we all rush to the door when the whistle or sirens sound. We who live in town can determine first whether the event is on our side of the bridge or the other. That narrows the choices by about half. By the time the rescue vehicles have been dispatched we know which part of town they're headed for and, before long, who's involved. Next Friday the grateful among us will enjoy the seventh annual Emergency Services Benefit Concert at SHMH, and this year, with a new fire hall and ambulance on the horizon, the need to show our appreciation is great. Tickets for this fun event are available here and there on Main Street.

The annual Fourth of July Great American Duck Race, a very popular fund-raising tradition begun by Carlene and Jerry Michael of the Paper Store, takes place right at the Mill Stream bridge at an appointed — according to the incoming tide — time. For years I'd playfully accused the organizers of shenanigans.

> I took a couple of kids last week, as I always do around the Fourth, out to do some duck plucking at the Great American Duck Race, now in its eighteenth year. At each event these kids and I pursue the elusive banner of wholesome activity amidst the inescapable stain of corruption and malfeasance. Veteran duckers will recall, back in the early nineties, when a duck — it was mine, in fact, a duck I'd worked hard to train and to invest with the noble spirit of competition — was hacked and drowned at the finish line by an evil duck plucker who, inexplicably, still paddles his wretched mischief around the finish line, compromising the race's noble goals and confounding the efforts of worthy competitors. This year was no different. It was obvious to us all, particularly the disenchanted children in my canoe, *Points of Preeminence*, that the winning ducks were being obscured from view and held under water by the same evil duck plucker whose business, year after year, is to disrupt the apparent course of events in favor of whomever has greased his palm. Thus it was that a duck, out of shape, obviously ill-equipped, apparently under the influence, and not wearing a lifejacket — a duck belonging to a judge at the race, no less — was declared the winner. How do you sleep nights, Pam?

I had a great relationship with Sofia from the moment she arrived as an infant. Her gleeful response to my appearance anywhere was a real treat for me and for all who witnessed it.

> It's not true, what people are saying about Sofia and me. Just because, when her parents try to distract her attention, she makes such a fuss from her car seat they have to stop so the two of us can have a few moments together, does not mean she will never develop an interest in anyone else. Just

because her dad had to remove her from Baccalaureate Service so the continually broadcast affections to me in a front row from her in the back would not interrupt the proceedings does not mean she never thinks of anyone else. Just because, when in Carver's, she heard that I was outside but was unreasonably denied the opportunity to leave the store to be with me for a few minutes and so dissolved in hysterics does not mean she will never have a healthy relationship with someone her own age. All Sofia is trying to accomplish — and this has escaped the attention of many critical observers, although certainly not her folks or anyone else in close proximity to our moments together — is to see to it I not forget the name of her dog, Marcel. The endearments she seems to be imparting are, in fact, only that one utterance — Marcel. She is clearly concerned that when I eventually become acquainted with Marcel I will not have forgotten the dog's name — Marcel. Perhaps now we'll move on to another topic, the cat perhaps, whose name escapes me.

Often I've seen a duck and her brood of new chicks waddle up the boat ramp from the harbor intent on gaining access to the pond and unwilling to wait for the tide to turn. They customarily cross Main Street to the sidewalk on the bridge between the Harbor Gawker and the Paper Store. Mom issues some sort of admonishments and instructions, then jumps in the isolated and quiet little eddy next to the Gawker. From there she quacks her encouragement to the chicks above, and, usually after a few moments during which they screw up their courage, they jump in too, and gather closely around her, whereupon she waddles them over the rocks under the Gawker and on into the pond. One memorable day an uncharacteristically cautious mother led her chicks instead to Port O' Call knowing, I suppose, that Bob would be accommodating. He let them into the store, past the brain trust gathered around the stove, on through the racks of merchandise, and out the back into the pond.

On this day years later, however, an inexperienced duck nearly lost her brood and would have had it not been for certain heroics.

It takes a village to raise a child but it only takes one Jackson to raise — or at least play a role in raising — a brood of ducks. The three in question are the only survivors of at least three broods comprising over twenty eggs hatched out near the Mill Stream Cottage and the Paper Store earlier this summer. They've been entertaining passersby for several weeks as they fed ravenously and without cessation under mother's watchful eye in the waters between the former Adair Studio and the Paper Store. Mother, however, was a first timer and one error in judgment almost cost her and us these remaining three. She summoned them from one side of the Mill Stream to the other when the current was running out and hard. The three were washed under the bridge and toward the three cisterns that once held the turbines that once powered the polishing mill. Had they not paddled hard for the west wall and found there a few little pieces of weed to cling to, they'd have been washed into those cisterns and drowned, as the water within churns circularly, tumultuously, and at great speed for hours. Enter Dylan, who, in his effort to save the trio, crashed through a rail at the Tidewater and fell into the fray along with his little charges. Undeterred, fighting to keep from being swept into the cisterns himself, he rescued the three and returned them to their mother who scolded them as if it was not her own fault.

In August the Union Church, built in 1860, observed its one hundred and fiftieth anniversary and appropriate celebrations were held.

Ricki Soaring Dove Brownsword, who was as nearly an institution as a seasonal resident can get, and who had been one of Milton Berle's regular dancers in the forties, decided to forego her regular summer visits to Vinalhaven in favor of Florida and Vermont. We all would miss her and we all have.

> Ricki Soaring Dove has given herself and us the elfish luxury of beginning to leave and will be missed. She's chosen a typically generous way of saying good-bye, returning gifts she's accumulated over the years to those or to families of those who gave them to her in the first place, or donating memorabilia and treasures to worthy causes such as Eldercare that they might be redeemed to their benefit. Pretty much everyone can expect to be hugged before the end of September. Many of us have anticipated Ricky's arrival each year for all sorts of reasons. We look forward to her unmistakable and purposeful stride and to answering puzzled queries of the unfamiliar who ask, "Why does she walk like that?" And to answering, "That's what happens to former Milton Berle dancers; they walk like that for the rest of their lives." And to that wonderful shoulder massage that creeps up on us when we are otherwise engaged but apparently looking haggard. And to the "real" massage enjoyed year after year, first up in the A-frame on the Reach, then down at the Magic Kingdom at Charlotte's, her finishing stones settling themselves here and there on a relaxed body to cap an hour of blissful refreshment. We should all take our leave in advance and as graciously.

Summer resident Pete Jaques bravely (and for one issue) took on the mantle of "Observer" himself as he contemplated his return to the "real world."

The Guest Observer

Lately there has been an epidemic of back trouble on Vinalhaven. Just yesterday another fifteen workdays were lost in America, a decline in productivity that only amplifies the costs of the Great Recession. These are perilous times for this nation, and it hurts to know that this island is a significant contributor. No, there have been no night medevac helicopter lights from Vinalhaven International Airport. The Medical Center has never been called. Rather there has been a spreading stain of dereliction of duty. It starts with conspiratorial whispered meetings beginning on Sunday mornings or over Sunday lunches on decks everywhere, at houses down those mysterious dirt roads, at the Tidewater, and on kayaks, Grady-Whites, and Herreshoffs. The long weekend or the vacation on Vinalhaven claims another victim of cool sea breezes, spruce and granite, simplicity and community. "I don't want to go back." The whispers grow more animated. "You think?" "Hey, that would be great! We'll get you on the 4:30 on Monday." Then the lie on the voicemail, always too early for anyone to answer in the office. "I won't be in today. Having a little back trouble. Need to rest. Travel will only make it worse. I'll be in Tuesday morning." No phone number left, and the cell phone is, of course, out of range. An extra beer, another afternoon at the quarry or VLT trail or on the water or that deck, another supper in fresh air, with a morning just like it ahead before that Monday 4:30 boat. Good for the soul. Good for the back. America will get through it.

Pete Jaques

The lengthy articles regarding the pros and cons of the windmills finally prompted the *Wind* to decline to publish them, citing the space consumed and related costs.

OBSERVATIONS

Familiarity breeds…well…more familiarity, and the degree to which we are all, consciously or otherwise, intimately acquainted with each other is fascinating.

> Most of us who've lived here all our lives, or even a few years, have become so familiar with and to one another that we can each be identified by the way we walk. Certainly that's a mark of a small town. A certain fellow, a native who left to work elsewhere and has now retired, spends more time here at home now, usually in his island truck, but has recently taken to walking a little. I don't think I'd seen him walking since we were in school together but when I spotted his silhouetted stride a quarter mile distant he might just as well have been heading down East Main Street to school in 1958. The same little hitch, one shoulder a little higher than the other, head cocked to one side just a degree or two, he could only be himself. A town of both determined walkers and others who only get out of the truck to go to the store, the moving silhouette of each is so distinctive as to be unmistakable. Some have perfect posture and that alone distinguishes them from the pack; others favor an old injury and some of us can remember when that accident happened. One lady, two actually, walk with a flaunting bounce, quite confident. A certain summer resident employs such an aggressive walk that she seems determined to inflict damage. Sometimes the level of energy speaks to things that are going on in an individual life, things that, because we are a small town, we all know about.

The unreliability of predicting the weather and of the likely success or failure of that effort, in particular as it related to Hurricane Earl, prompted me to vent about it.

> When we were small we spoke of what we'd be when we grew up. We might have chosen weatherman. Where else might we have found such security unrelated to performance? Regardless of whether they are right more often than wrong, or wrong more often than right, or about 50/50, they continue to hold on to their secure and often lucrative jobs. The unrelentingly terrifying prediction of Hurricane Earl's destructive advance up the coast was a good example. As each day passed and the promised devastation in first one area then another foundered in the modest swells, forecasters gamely kept alerts at the highest level. As the storm passed the Carolinas an A.P. weatherman, bravely standing on the Outer Banks — in his foul weather gear but with no hat so his hair, wafting to starboard, could speak to the storm's fury — told of the tops of young trees bending in the wind and of sea grasses being laid horizontal. I was reminded of a Bangor forecaster who, a few years ago, having ventured a few feet from the station's door and standing on the deck bundled up in so much gear we could only surmise he was from away and his mother had dressed him, spoke anxiously of the tremendous forces gathering about him while in the background could be seen half a dozen Maine kids who, while they did have on long pants, were hatless and mittenless and engaged in a terrific snow fight.

The state's decision to authorize casinos and gambling to help balance the budget, instead of actually addressing the deficit, upset a lot of us.

> For a state that's been touted and a people who've been hailed as folks who take care of themselves, we sure have jumped at chances to pass those responsibilities off on others. Addressing the budget deficit a few years ago the legislature, instead of taking responsibility for having overspent, opted to increase the sales tax — on meals and lodging only — to 7 percent. While quietly acknowledging we'd overspent, the not-so-subtle solution was that we let folks from away pay for our mistakes. A few years later, when we still hadn't taken control of our budget and the deficit again loomed large,

the promise of big tax revenue led us to allow gambling to get a foothold in the state. Then, avoiding responsibility having proved easier than accepting it, an increase from 7 to 10 percent sales tax on food and lodging was suggested. A concerted effort by those who felt we should take responsibility for ourselves led to the proposal's defeat but only barely. Now, gambling having secured a foothold at Hollywood Slots, promises of more big tax revenue lead us to consider the next in what will be an inevitable and relentless onslaught of gambling initiatives. The Oxford Casino will allow us to continue to balance our own budget woes and responsibilities on the backs of others, those from away or our own folks, whose circumstances often drive them to gambling.

It was time to say goodbye to Tara Elliott and she made it easy and difficult at the same time. *Check, Please* was splendid theater, dinner theater actually, great fun to watch and participate in and a sad reminder of her impending departure. Fortunately for us, but unknown at the time, an equally capable replacement was in the wings.

For a while I agonized trying to write legitimate reviews of local productions; it's almost impossible without ruffling feathers. Recent productions, Tara Elliott's primarily, have made it easier because there've been no bad performances, not even mediocre. *Check, Please* was no exception. It was just the best kind of dinner theater and a beautiful parting gift from Tara. As usual there were some extraordinary performances. Displays, for example, of amazing self-absorption courtesy of Jami Wood and thunderous understatement from Josh Nagle, exhausting endurance from Katie Hamilton, or the over-the-top poetic license from Alex Day, or the practical and long-suffering forbearance of Hannah Noyes. Linnell Mather was possessed of clinical obstructionism, Jess McGreevy of startling disregard, Bill Chilles of numbing incredulity, and Meg Lyons of being unwaveringly one-dimensional and fatuous. Rachel Noyes, shameless, imaginative, has just been away too long and should not leave us hanging again. Elijah Bineau was a hilarious adolescent set loose too early and Perry Boyden a crumbling antiquity out too late. Francis Warren was nicely pompous and condescending, Fiona justifiably angry; Richie was outrageous at every turn (surprise) but then so was Jamie Thomas. Frank Morton was having way too good a time being a rock star and Ethan Hall was insufferably determined. Everyone else was great, too; many of us playing the straight man or foil so our dates could shine, and each did dutifully. Certainly near the top was Tara herself as the troubled half of a blind date—scary.

An equally energetic and talented drama teacher arrived in the person of Jessie Grant. The Vinalhaven Players had done *Guys and Dolls* in 1999. She began work on a revival immediately.

My daughter and her husband returned from a year in England and came to dinner. They displayed an album of photos taken during their adventure and the last one of these was an odd thing; I thought it was a photo of the cosmos, taken at night perhaps with lots of starry things in it. It was a sonogram, as it turns out, their way of announcing she was pregnant with our grandchild.

The town received a grant from the state to expand our airfield. We asked a representative of the DOT to come attend a public meeting to discuss the project and were told there was no money in the grant for travel. The town offered to put her up but we were told state employees could not accept gifts. We held a public meeting anyway and resolved to continue operating the airfield as it always had been without regard for state mandates.

Having authored the *Wind's* Editorial Policy not long before, I found myself subject to it. The news story

OBSERVATIONS

about a preacher in Florida who'd announced his intention to publicly burn a Quran — and the amount of attention it received — had struck me as sufficiently silly to write about but, alas, my submission was regarded as inflammatory.

> Last week the *Wind* rejected a piece of satire I submitted relating to the likely Quran burning we'd heard so much about. After it was rejected I showed the column to a few folks, including some religious leaders among us, and each allowed that while they found it amusing it was probably a good idea not to publish it, that everyone's sensitivities were not so well shielded. Over the years controversy has now and then raised its head in our little island community, and self-serving, inflammatory, or abusive submissions have presented themselves for inclusion in the *Wind*. The staff, dedicated volunteers whose only real interest was to see that this useful weekly made its way out into the community, were, on those occasions, faced with the agonizing responsibility of deciding whether to publish. If they didn't, they were accused of censorship, and if they did, of insensitivity. Eventually they adopted an editorial policy setting forth parameters for submissions — a policy I wrote myself — so I'm hard-pressed to complain of having fallen victim to it.

And the offending column:

> It was revealed this week that the Community of Christ plans to burn copies of Mary Baker Eddy's *Science and Health* and the Union Church will shred copies of *The Hymnal*, official song book of the Church of Jesus Christ of Latter Day Saints. Our Lady of Peace will suffer several copies of the Baptist's liturgy to be immersed in holy water until mushy while the Church of Jesus Christ has impaled copies of *Hymns for the Family of God* on a stake in the town parking lot. The Christian Scientists are subjecting a likeness of the Burning Bush Tapestry to fire, while two Whirling Dervishes on Calderwood Neck will trample the Bible into eternal dust. Our only Muslim (we know who you are and where you live) will stone a Protestant effigy into submission or until he has exhausted himself. The Jews have declared Latter Day Saints to be "other than" chosen and will desecrate *The Book of Mormon* on the altar, and Glenn Beck is looking for a summer place on Vinalhaven.

Our very popular doctor, Rich Entel, was leaving his practice here at the Medical Center. Everything surrounding his departure was a mystery to most of us. Jen Desmond, who we'd come to call "Dr. Jen," penned a lovely tribute to him.

> Over four years ago my Medical Center pager went off for the first time. It was a stormy September night, and after I spoke with the patient I wondered what I had gotten myself into. I had come from working at an inner city homeless shelter in Boston, where hospitals and specialists were just around every corner. I called Rich Entel, and within ten minutes we were both at the Medical Center, evaluating the patient. I learned the important things quickly: how the wind direction makes all the difference when you need to transport a patient, Burke's phone number, what the world looks like at four a.m., when the fishing boats leave Dyer's Island. I also learned how important it is to have a good teacher, and I certainly found this in Dr. Entel. When I think back to how many times I called him over the past four years I am overwhelmed and very grateful. Not once did he express frustration and was always there when I needed him. Thank you, Dr. Entel, for sharing your love and practice of island medicine with me.
>
> Jen

High school student Chrissy Martin was raising money to finance her trip to Ghana where she intended to work in an orphanage, another in a long line of island kids who've had that kind of worthwhile adventure.

The Vinalhaven Water District was one hundred years old, and completed installation of ultraviolet disinfection at Folly Pond, our auxiliary water source, and of a mixing system to produce a uniform water temperature in the reservoir, as well.

Jeff Aronson, an agreeable foil who also happens to be the Phil 'n' the Blanks tenor, passed his last EMS examinations. He's been an invaluable member of the team ever since.

> Jeff Aronson has passed the last of his EMS exams and is now qualified to participate in rescue missions, subject to certain reasonable restrictions. This has been an uphill road for Jeff, but when looking up is the only way to navigate, uphill is the only road there is. In the face of Jeff's determined efforts to join the Vinalhaven EMTs, the state reluctantly waived certain of its customary requirements. Until now, for example, an applicant must have been able to demonstrably show he (or she) is an adult. Jeff has received a limited license, and henceforth those of us who suffer injuries below the knee are likely to receive the same quick attention that had heretofore been more likely to come to those whose injuries were in the higher elevations. Jeff is now one of the guys (and gals). A stool has been placed next to the ambulance driver's door in the event Jeff is the first respondent driver. If someone else shows up first they can just push the booster seat aside and jump in. This is a win-win situation. At the scene the regular team members, some of whom have a little trouble bending over, are spared the effort because injuries below the knee will be, if he shows up and can get through the crowd, Jeff's responsibility. It's good for Jeff because he can now get regular recognition beyond his marginal role in Phil 'n' the Blanks.

Every now and then something would move me to compose something a little more esoteric than my customary take on things. One early morning, parked at the waterfront, I suddenly felt I was being watched. On another, a particularly stunning snowfall held my attention.

> A little before five a.m. one day last week I drove down to the parking/loading area recently created for fishermen. It was the day after the biggest and scariest of the most recently forecast big and scary storms, and there was quite a sea. I sat there for a while. No boats were moving and all were looking directly at me as if I were a stranger, someone to be wary of, which, I suppose — well, I guess it depends on who one asks. In the modest light of a quarter moon the boat nearest me was the only one clearly visible. A little residual breeze made it roll a little from side to side. Never taking its eyes of me, it seemed to be contemplating my next move, first from one vantage, then the other. A rhythmic swell that crept astern through the little gut between Lane's and Potato Island caused it to simultaneously bob up and down as if nodding in acquiescence or acknowledgement, letting me know, perhaps, that I could stay there as long as I behaved myself. Lights from a residence across the harbor broadcast a path across the water directly at me, alerting those that hadn't noticed of my presence, and a light from down near Clam Shell Alley did the same thing. Each cast me in a different light. An engine started up to my left and a boat, having picked up its crew and bait, left the float there and headed out, coming slowly abreast of the wharf and myself as if to suggest I'd lingered long enough.

OBSERVATIONS

As an adjective, "breathtaking" is overused, but it works to describe the beauty of last weekend's whiteout. Such a perfect combination of sustained snow fall, conducive temperatures, the right amount and direction of wind, and the absence of too much moisture combined to leave nature free to work its magic from one end of the island to the other. Our nooks and crannies, wetlands, hills and hollows, the rock passage at Tip Toe, open fields or spans of open water, stands of mature spruce — they all worked to modify the trajectory and force of snowfall in different ways, and the diverse results were astonishing. On big spruces it often left huge dollops from top to bottom but not always. In some places on the east side the top branches are bare and unencumbered but those on the bottom three-quarters are sagging under the weight of precarious piles. Narrow drives like the plowed path to Zeke Point, overhung with big alders and small birch, each bent from one side of the road to the other, are enchanting and otherworldly snow passages. Maple concentrations on Fox Rocks expose much less surface than spruce, and what snow they manage to harvest perches delicately wherever there is a branch on a trunk or a fork on a branch and, here and there, amidst only whiteness, twenty or thirty crows will not sit still for a photograph.

Carlene Michael, my favorite and most appreciative and tolerant foil, is a good neighbor, a quality I intended to milk for all it was worth which, as it happens, is a great deal.

A few months ago I purposely left an outside door to the cottage open. Sure enough, a neighbor I'd been cultivating called to report the door being ajar. She was concerned, she said, that critters might get in or that I'd lose valuable heat. After a few days I left a different cottage door open and in no time got another call. A week or two later I did it again, but this time when she called I didn't answer and let her leave a message. I didn't return her call but watched the cottage, which I can see from my kitchen window. Sure enough, before long she left her own place, went over to the cottage, and closed the door. In doing so she had to go inside to see that the door latched properly, and once inside and having secured that door she walked across the living room and exited through the back door. I'd anticipated this and had intentionally left the floor unswept. Sure enough, I got a call alerting me to the floor's untidy condition. I didn't return that call either but watched again from my window. As expected she headed out in a few minutes with a broom and cleaned up the floor. Her training is coming along nicely. Next week I plan to leave a door open at the motel and a bed unmade.

I seem to have nothing unfavorable to say about the dramatic productions that emerge from the school's drama department.

"What a piece of work is a man," said Shakespeare, who must have foreseen that six of our young men, each undeniably a piece of work, would have engaged themselves and us in a frenzied submersion in all of his thirty-eight or so plays. *The Complete Works of William Shakespeare: Abridged* was presented on four successive days by a cast of six: Alex Day, Joey Reidy, and Francis Warren one night, Trey Warren, John and Frank Morton the next. Each cast was terrific and each was completely different. They flawlessly mastered all that dialogue — exhausting! Francis Warren, as Cleopatra, Juliet, and all the Bard's other females, was frightening. Trey, in the same role, was alarmingly beguiling. Each was hilarious and each tortured the myriad costume changes perfectly. All brought their considerable talents to this production. I compared it with a clip from the original Reduced Shakespeare Company and found Jessie Grant's production easily equal. She had big shoes to fill but clearly her feet are the same size as Tara's. We're going to lose two of these seniors this year but I noticed the front rows were full of enthusiastic underclassmen. I hope they take encouragement and spend their remaining high school years enjoying themselves equally, "…they have entrances and exits and one man in his time plays many parts." That is true with these guys and has been for a while.

The ARC planned a move to Main Street, and, given its nonprofit status and the degree to which other retailers might find that an issue, they invited comment.

The *Wind*, having benefitted from the efforts of volunteer consultant Ken Reiss, who developed a formula for advertising costs based on column inches, was solvent and would be thereafter.

A year hence I would be asked to be the commencement speaker at graduation. I built that address around observations made this one night in December.

I sat with a contemporary (there are still a few left) Saturday to watch and take part in the PIE Christmas program. We spoke now and then, during those portions of the program that partnered, literally, the young men and women of high school with much younger counterparts, about the older kids' overwhelmingly positive attitude and their enthusiasm for involving themselves so completely in programs that paired them with very small children. The youngsters were so enjoying the pairings. We joked about how much luck this drama teacher would have had (or not had) trying to entice us to do such a thing when we were in high school, about how much more trouble we and our acquaintances would have been than these kids were. Gradually, though, it dawned on each of us that Jessie Grant may have overwhelmed even us, may have overcome even our monumental indifference. She's very good. Of course, back then we did not have a drama teacher, more's the pity. Who knows? Maybe we had the same potential and might otherwise have been as appealing as these kids are. We're appealing now, of course, but back then we were less so. These kids are an engaging, energetic, entertaining, and positive presence in our lives, and not only on stage. When a cluster of them comes down the Net Factory Hill and turns the corner, the energy along Main Street picks up noticeably as they pass. Maybe Jessie is as lucky to have this bunch to work with as we and they are to have Jessie. Whichever is the case, it works. A particular adjective comes to mind whenever I see this crop of high school students. I hope it won't frighten them. If anyone had used it to describe me (not likely) when I was in my teens I'd have been mortified. I, however, was ill-equipped to handle such accolades. These guys seem to suffer no such insecurities. It's a credit to them, their parents, this school and faculty and, certainly, this year, to Jessie Grant that this adjective seems appropriate. They're kind of wholesome.

Barbie Dyer began a short-lived but moving column called "In Loving Memory."

In Loving Memory
Of William Vallee, Fay Dyer and Ethelyn Gertrude Dyer
by Barbara Dyer

It was autumn. The year was 1930. William's father, John, was a quarryman who died suddenly from influenza. He was only forty-eight years old, leaving behind a wife and fourteen children.

William was five and didn't really understand. He felt everyone's grief, including his own. He wanted to say something, but didn't. In fact, he couldn't. The trauma caused William to become mute for well over a year, and his speech would forever be labored and slow.

William's mother, Emma, couldn't support the family. There was no income. The town of Vinalhaven provided them with enough money to return to their hometown in Norton, Massachusetts. They left Vinalhaven with great reluctance and unspeakable sorrow. In the spring of 1932, William and his family returned to Vinalhaven to attend the funeral of his infant niece. He was seven years old when he sat in the parlor viewing the little white casket covered with red roses.

Part II

My father was Fay Dyer. He was born on Jan. 3, 1910. I don't know much about his young life except that he didn't finish high school, he nearly died from brucellosis in his mid-thirties, and he was born with a congenital heart defect.

My father was kind, gentle, and soft spoken. He was rarely seen in public, except for the times he rowed us to town to get groceries or to sell lobsters from the few traps we had in the "Crik."

Our house was filled with love. My parents played instruments: my mother, the piano, my father, a harmonica. They also recited poetry; my father's favorite poem was "The First Snowfall," written by James Russell Lowell. I knew at an early age there was much sentiment and symbolism connected to this poem for him.

At Christmastime my father was always a bit sad and preoccupied…many people can relate to that!

Another childhood observation involved a tiny box with the name Ethelyn written on it. Inside the box was a tiny gold ring on which the raised word BABY was written. I perceived that this was one of the most sacred items in our house, yet it was shrouded in mystery.

Part III

There is something to be said about growing up on a small island. Generations of the same families are born here, live here, die here. Histories of people and families unfold day after day, month after month, year after year. As a community we know each other's lives intimately, feeling great joy in each other's accomplishments, great sorrow in their losses. We rarely forget times, events, and people from our past. If someone has been part of this community, even for a brief period of time, they leave a lifetime imprint. It seems someone always remembers them, even if they have touched this community in the smallest way, or moved as a young adult to pursue life elsewhere. On a warm August day, someone came into my life in a most profound way. The chain of events that were to unfold allowed a dying man to fulfill a lifelong dream and to come full circle with his life.

Part IV

On that August day, a co-worker told me that a man and a woman were looking for me. They had inquired at the ferry terminal about my father, Fay Dyer, and when they found he had passed away, asked if there was anyone in town who might remember him. Someone at the ferry terminal told them that I was Fay Dyer's daughter. Had these visitors come to the island between 1973 and 1988, I would not have been here to greet them. I lived off-island during those years. Had they come here on a Tuesday, Friday, or Sunday, I would not have been at my place of employment, as those were my days off. Fate?

But as it were, we did meet. Since I had yet another hour to work before I was free for lunch, we merely exchanged formalities and names, agreeing to meet outside the store at noon. I wondered through the next hour who these people were. I knew they had known my father and I was always pleased to meet someone from his past.

Part V

While waiting for my lunch break, Mr. Vallee and his companion went to the Village Deli for a bite to eat. Chance/fate cast them into a group of older community members who often met for their noontime meal. Many remembered his family, where they had lived, and the circumstances that had led to their departure from the island so many years before. Mr. Vallee couldn't believe his good fortune and the kindness of these strangers, who welcomed him and his companion into their circle.

When my lunch break finally arrived, I went outside and sat with them on the curb. The man's name was William Vallee, and his partner's name was Lena Levesque. She did most of the talking at first. She didn't mince any words. They both had terminal cancer, and she added that for years Mr. Vallee had wanted to return to the island to pay his respects and say good-bye to his father and niece who were buried here. Time was no longer on his side.

Part VI

Mr. Vallee's sister, Estelle, was my father's first wife. Together they had had a daughter, Ethelyn, who was born on Christmas Eve, 1930. Sadly, she died the following spring and Mr. Vallee's memory of the red rose-covered casket was that of my half-sister, who had lived and died twenty-five years before I was born. As for the sacred baby ring, it had belonged to Ethelyn. Her name, though worn, is still on the lid of the tiny box which holds the delicate ring. Finally, an answer to so many childhood questions.

I knew now more than before how imperative it was for Mr. Vallee to find the site of his childhood home, and the graves of his father and niece. This was not an easy task, but again, fate was on our side.

Our first visit was to the Vinalhaven Historical Society museum, where Mr. Vallee could see firsthand tools, types of stone quarried, and images of Vinalhaven's granite industry in which his father had worked so very long ago. The helpful people at the museum also found birth, death, and burial information pertaining to Mr. Vallee's family. We knew both father and niece had been buried at Cummings Cemetery, but there were no markers to be found. Someone mentioned that Bob Tolman had "maps" of each cemetery on the island, and that perhaps he could help us. Luckily, Bob was home, and sure enough, the records existed!

PART VII

Bob Tolman said the burial site of Mr. Valllee's father and little niece was on the southern side of Cummings Cemetery. Ironically, it faces a small quarry. It was a very somber drive to the cemetery. Once there we went directly to the site. At this point in the story, words truly elude me. There are no words that can adequately capture the witnessing of a man's lifelong dream. Nearly seventy years of love, loss, anguish, and hope were released as we stood there. As tears streamed down Mr. Vallee's face, I, too, was overtaken with many emotions: gratitude and awe, sadness and relief, joy and humility. The moment was spiritual and cleansing, and I wanted it to last forever. Perhaps this is why I felt so compelled to tell this story. It seemed beyond what we human beings could orchestrate. Fate? Divine intervention? Perhaps both. Indeed, his life had come full circle. We had only a few more hours to share together before the strangers — now friends — had to leave the island to return to their home. We visited his old homestead, now just a shell of a granite basement, on Pogus Point. Mr. Vallee recalled several stories which had been imprinted in his five-year-old mind; he took pictures of the field he once played in and told of the fun times he remembered here on the island. We did hear from him one time a few months after he returned to Massachusetts — then no more. I pray that he died a happier man, with peace in his heart, and that he is once again with whom he loved.

It was December and I succumbed to my usual inclination to write about Christmases past.

I was resisting going to bed on December 24, 1948. I said I needed a drink and was permitted to help myself from the icebox. My dad had harvested a new block from the icehouse at Round Pond and it dripped on my hand. I was four years old and too worked up to sleep. Santa Claus was coming, and notwithstanding we had no chimney in our apartment (over what is now the Sand Bar but was then my mother's gift shop), I'd had assurances he would find his way in. Reluctantly, I went back to bed. My little brother, only two and oblivious, much like he is today, was asleep. My mother came in to try and settle me down. Suddenly I heard sleigh bells coming in over Ed White's roof. I closed my eyes, knowing I couldn't be awake when he came. It was a long night. A few Christmases later in the Kittredge house up on the flat, my brother and I were each wide awake and stalling. We needed to go to the bathroom — an outhouse in the backyard. A younger brother was asleep in the top dresser drawer in my folks' room. Eventually Mom persuaded us to close our eyes. As we did we heard the bells from over Goose Arey's roof. Later, renting the Robinson house on Clam Shell Alley, the three of us listened for the expected bells and heard them coming down from Armbrust Hill over Carl Williams's. In '54, Christmas in Harold Vinal's house on Lane's Island, I heard the bells sail in from seaward over Freddy Jones's Rockaway Inn. Down at the Bucket the bells came in over Kitty Hopkins's roof one year, Alfred Hall's the next and, another year, from above the field at Ruth Ann's. The youngest brother, the fourth, asleep in the drawer, was unimpressed, much like today. Christmases in the Moses Webster house, the first we'd owned, were different. Each of the four brothers had his own bedroom and the sound of sleigh bells could be heard from here and there on our own huge roof. Dad never heard them. He was always elsewhere.

A local fellow was ill. He'd been a year or two ahead of me in high school, and I was reminded of a time when he was quite a ladies' man.

I pull up behind a truck and, of habit, concentrate on the silhouette at the wheel. His head has a distinct relationship to his shoulders, just enough so that, coupled with the angle of his cap together with the degree to which his torso leans to the left leaving his right shoulder a little higher, his profile is his own. One of his ears, the one on his high shoulder, is also a little…different, bigger maybe. Anyway, this combination of things leaves me to conclude that this is Ronnie Warren. He, in turn, has now recognized me and, having made that tiny adjustment which allows him to see me in his mirror, presents his face for confirmation. He gives his little wave, the one familiar to us all, as certain as dental records, the right forefinger and thumb lift from the wheel and do a little clockwise rotation of about sixty degrees. I return my own peculiar acknowledgement, all five fingers splayed out and up for a moment. I feel a certain satisfaction for having enjoyed a moment of intimacy not experienced by travelers elsewhere.

I remember, back in '59, when as a sophomore I had, for the first time, a girlfriend, here for the summer. I took her to a record hop and before we'd been there even ten minutes Ronnie had stolen her away from me. He was so smooth on his feet. Girls lined up to dance with him. He'd twirl them around like it was nothing, jitterbug like he was all hinges.

The Open Bible Baptist Church had by now established itself as essentially a third island congregation. They'd begun services at the residence of Bill and Joy Mills and were on their way to completing construction of a suitable house of worship on the same Coombs Neck property.

In 2010 ninety-six million pounds of lobster were landed in Maine by 5,900 license holders, and the price was $3.31 per pound.

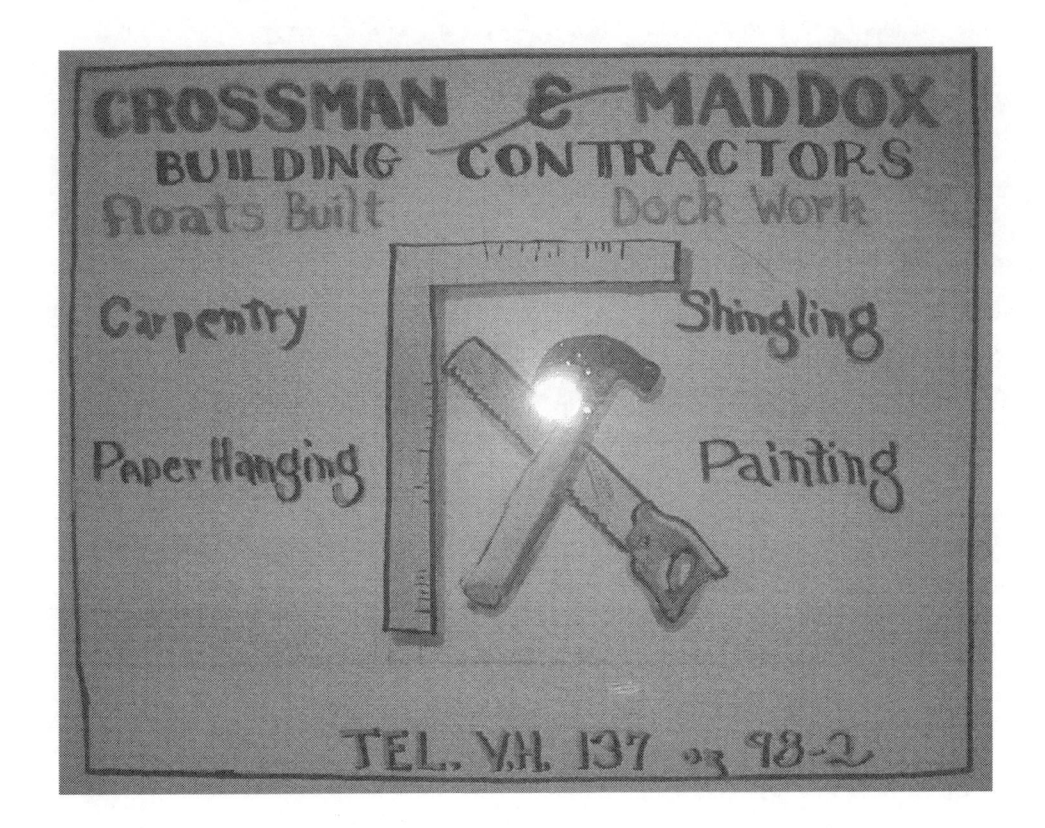

2011

CROSSMAN & MADDOX
BUILDING CONTRACTORS
Floats Built — Dock Work
Carpentry — Shingling
Paper Hanging — Painting
TEL., V.H. 137 or 98-2

2011

FOR SEVERAL YEARS I'D RECEIVED A COFFEE CAKE FOR CHRISTMAS, always left on the motel counter for me to find. It came with instructions.

> I got a coffee cake from Betsy again this year. For years she has sent a coffee cake to me with a card admonishing me to share it with my employees, and reminding me that they are a great bunch and I should be very proud of and happy with them. Paul made his usual surreptitious delivery, leaving it somewhere he knew I would find it. In fact, though, someone else found it and delivered it, in an equally surreptitious manner, to my house. I read Betsy's note, took appropriate notice of my faithful employees, and then, time at that moment being of the essence, I made a delicious cup of Island Spirits coffee, lopped off a good chunk, and enjoyed again, the first time since last January, a piece of Betsy's legendary coffee cake. I put the rest in the fridge, in the back, behind a big turkey. That night I volunteered to do the dishes, and when Elaine settled in at her study I cut off another hunk and snacked privately on it while I worked. I put the rest in the freezer, under some other stuff, recalling how good it was last year, frozen. The next day, mid-morning, Elaine at her studio, I came home and enjoyed another piece. I tucked the rest away in the freezer. I kept this up for a week. On Christmas Eve Elaine sat reviewing the cards we'd received and came across the note from Betsy. "Did you get a coffee cake and did you share it with the girls?" And my reply would have been the end of it had Betsy not asked Carol.

A friend began remodeling her new house and found evidence of my father having done work there nearly sixty years earlier.

> Dad and my grandfather, Ted, formed Crossman & Maddox in 1948. Their sign (preceding page) hangs today at the motel. Nearly every job he did, large or small, was acknowledged by a note tucked away somewhere that included his name and the date and a couple of words describing the work done. Since his passing, several folks, having undertaken remodeling jobs of one kind or another, have brought me tokens he'd tucked away in a place that would only be discovered in the event of a dismantling. I have a piece of Formica from the parsonage that attests to his having installed a new kitchen there, for example. He was a perfectionist, particularly when it came to paper hanging. He had a self-storing pasting table and a zinc trim plate, long cutting shears, pasting brushes, and a seam roller, each hung in its place along the back edge of the table. He also had a plumb bob, and began each project by striking a plumb line on the wall of each room being papered. Some folks, my wife for one, have come to recognize that plumb line, and thus it was that when a friend took possession of her newly purchased house on Clam Shell Alley and Elaine helped her strip paper they uncovered the familiar plumb line and then the predictable note "Papered by Bud Crossman 1953 and again in 1986." The note will be framed, as is, in perpetuity.

I was getting more and more forgetful. It was problematic each summer to try and renew acquaintances and at the same time seem interested in doing so while it was clear I couldn't remember who anyone was. I devised a solution, kind of.

OBSERVATIONS

This is an easy time of year for me, easier than summer, anyway. Nearly everyone I meet lives here year-round and so I am spared the embarrassment I feel so frequently during the summer of not knowing who I'm talking to, an unpleasant experience if one is an innkeeper, and one that often leads those with whom I am in conversation to think I may also not know what I'm talking about. I recall less and less, too, with each passing year. I keep a notebook in my pocket. (I can't seem to get my mind — or my fingers — wrapped around a Palm Pilot or whatever this year's incarnation is.) On the inside cover of my notebook is written in large bold letters, "WHO'S THAT BEHIND ME?" When I am in the company of my wife or an employee or friend and come upon someone whose name I can't remember, I turn my back to that person for a moment, flip open the notebook and display the message to my companion who then, if time affords, scribbles the individual's name (I have also proffered a pen) or, if time doesn't permit, speaks the name softly or, on those occasions when even that would be awkward, mouths the name. It works for me and has for so long that Elaine and those who know me best comply agreeably and the whole system works pretty well. Of course, those summer visitors who read this will now know the truth, but we are all declining in unison so it probably doesn't matter.

A friend who summers some here but writes for her hometown Marblehead newspaper wrote a piece about the Red Mill theater which my folks owned and ran before turning it into the Tidewater Motel. In the fifties I sold popcorn and took tickets in the lobby. The projection booth is now my office. One of the movies that had played there was *Attack of the Fifty Ft. Woman*, a concept I found frightening then but which sounds kind of exciting now. It reminded me of other frightening apparitions.

Fraffie Welch published a nice piece in her hometown newspaper last week in which she spoke kindly about the Red Mill theater. When I was a kid I sold popcorn and took tickets in the area presently occupied by the motel lobby. The elevated area where Island Spirits used to be was the projection booth, elevated so Dunc could aim the projector over the heads of the theater goers. My job, after selling popcorn and taking tickets, was to sit in the back and be alert for the big meltdown, an occasional but dreaded event that left our customers hooting in derision and bellowing good-naturedly about getting their money back. The big meltdown occurred whenever Dunc dozed off on his stool. That he might do so was understandable, particularly if it was the second or third time he'd shown the flick, and that after having worked all day. When that happened, when he dozed off, the critical transition that was supposed to take place between the end of one reel and the beginning of the next did not happen. Instead, the last image remained on the screen and was hideously consumed from the inside out. That was funny now and then, like when Gary Cooper was doing a slow burn as Man of the West, but when Allison Hayes, the gorgeous star of *Attack of the Fifty Ft. Woman*, bent to squish her philandering husband and instead melted away as if consumed by acid, it was just too much.

Someone left copies of *Vogue*, *Vanity Fair*, and *Allure* at the motel. I'd never looked at them before and now I'm sorry I did. There were probably some articles hidden in there somewhere among the photos of angry-looking women in bizarre costumes arranged in positions that must be the fashion equivalent of extreme sports. Most wore really grim expressions and make-up that made Gene Simmons look like Caspar Milquetoast. Each had gone to extraordinary lengths to call attention to themselves and some certainly deserved to be admired. It's best, though, to look at their footwear first and then admire them on the way up because the demeanor of each is a window to a world of trouble. I've been having bad dreams about these women. One in particular revisits. She has bright red patent leather shoes. Only the tips touch the ground. From there her feet angle vertically upward, elevated by ten-inch heels. She has white sheer hosiery and azure leggings, the leftmost of which extends nearly to her ankle while the other barely covers the top of her stocking. These are held up by red suspenders, not unlike my own, over a torn tee shirt. Her electric pink curls hang down over yellow-tinted heart-shaped sunglasses and completely obscure her face except for her "make my day" invitation to the blues.

A fellow caretaker got his truck stuck trying to plow out the A.W. Smith Road, but I helped.

Plowing is guy stuff. We are the Get 'er Done Guys, going the extra mile that others might travel safely, and we don't get nearly enough press or credit. An example: A fellow Get'erdoner undertook to plow out the mile-long A.W. Smith Road a few weeks back after our first big snowfall. He'd only gone a few hundred feet when he encountered an uphill icy place with a drop off to leeward. After wasting a few minutes in thoughtful deliberation he chose every Get'erdoner's first choice: "Give it to 'er!" an exclamatory usually preceded by "Ye Haw!" Later, having exhausted himself but having failed to extricate his truck, and with nothing to show for it but a broken hand winch and a bad attitude, he headed back to town on foot, fetched his other truck, drove back, and tried again to tow himself out, and although he broke another winch in the process, he did manage to get truck #1 back on the road. Now, though, he understood his adversary, the tricky places in the road, and steeling himself, whispered bravely if with less assurance, "Give it to 'er!" and, it must be acknowledged, advanced a few more feet than he had the first time before again landing in the downhill bushes. Learning of all this later, I, older and less inclined to behave impulsively, headed on up to finish what he'd started. I resisted saying "Give it to 'er" 'til I got to the top of the hill but by that point had been cautious for way too long and finally succumbed, seeing level ground and no further obstacles, I "gave it to 'er." Later, a friend, a fellow Get'erdoner, and I drove seven miles to Zeke's Point, spent four hours resuscitating a comfortably hibernating and reluctant backhoe and driving it back to my truck to perform the required extrication. Last week it snowed again, and this time it really piled up, wet and heavy. The Get 'er Done Guys were not dissuaded, but that's another story, not unlike this one. Suffice to say, we again went the extra mile.

It was tournament time again, Vinalhaven vs. Richmond, and we were trying to have a Blanks rehearsal while the game was on TV.

It was silly to think we could have a productive Phil 'n' the Blanks rehearsal while the game against Richmond was streaming live in the next room and with the volume up. The game was way too distracting, too exciting, and certainly too anxiety producing. By the end of the first half it was obvious we were never going to strike that harmonious chord at the end of page three. Every time we got close the Vikings hit another three-pointer or executed a spectacular save or snagged an impossible rebound or dribbled through an impenetrable-looking defense or stole the ball from someone who looked like he'd never let it go or glided gracefully by a press that seemed to have no way out. Finally we gave up and focused on the game. It was probably more excitement than guys our age should experience often. Pretty much everyone knows what an extraordinary bunch of guys make up this team, how much depth there is and how well coached they are, but there may be someone out there who hasn't stayed in touch and they should know what they missed in not seeing this breathtaking game. It couldn't have been better. Well, who am I kidding? Of course it could have been better. Bobby's three-pointer might have cozied up a little better with the basket. That said, though, while that was as much adventure as I think is good for me I expect we'll see a great deal more next year.

I hiked around Perry Creek one spring morning, long after every trace of winter was gone elsewhere, and found a tiny cave of ice.

In the spring of 2011 the last vestige of winter to melt away was a piece of ice tucked under a rock overhang in a shaded area on the Perry Creek Preserve at the end of the Indian Ladder/Fox Rocks Trail. It was on the south shore of the creek just to the left of a small tributary of Indian Ladder Brook. The ice was hidden by the rock but further shaded by a lush colony of interrupted ferns *(Osmunda claytoniana)* that had put down roots in a rich layer of leaf litter. During the winter the ice had been a little glacier, about a yard wide and maybe six inches thick, and it drooped over the ledge extending icicles toward the ground as if feeling its way in the dark. Behind the ice, in a fairly roomy recess there has, for all of last year and until recently, lived a star-nosed mole *(Condylura ristata)*. It was quite comfortable during the winter (in a state of partial hibernation known as torpor) for long stretches but ventured out now and then to stuff itself full of spiders and other things that thought they'd tucked themselves safely away for the winter. The ice in this little nook is still substantial today and will probably be the last place on the island to be ice-free again this year. The mole, however, was caught and consumed by an osprey *(Pandion haliaetus)* last weekend. Sad, because it enjoyed living next to a thing called an interrupted fern.

I read an article by Eva Murray of Matinicus (where my great-great-great-great-great-great-great-grandfather Hall was killed by Indians in 1757) about homemade donuts and was intrigued.

I didn't know lard was still an available commodity. After reading a column on donut making by Eva Murray and taking note of her observation that in these delicate health-conscience times rendered pig fat might be hard to swallow, I stopped in at Carver's Market and inquired, "I don't suppose you've got any lard?" "Course we got lard," replied the clerk scornfully. "Ain't you never had a decent donut?" Eva's column appeared in mid-March, a vulnerable time for me, a time when my winter inspirations have now and then proved problematic, a time when, if left unattended, I find myself gravitating toward places long ago established as boundaries. As I grow older, in fact, I've submitted reluctantly to regular monitoring from my wife and family. I'd rather that humiliation was less evident but that's another story. So, when Elaine came home, she regarded the several blocks of lard with skepticism and subjected my plans to a withering nutritional assessment. Mustering my diminished self-assurance and prepared to suggest, if that's what it would take to silence her, that her Vermont roots had perhaps not left her with quite the sophisticated palette I'd acquired here on this island, I framed the question that had earlier been so succinctly put to me and asked, "Ain't you never had a decent doughnut?"

The due date was approaching. Elaine and I were excited about becoming grandparents.

I'm practicing to be a grandfather. My grandchild and her parents are going to be living right next door for the next year so it's necessary that I be prepared to be grandfatherly all the time, not just now and then when we or they, like, come to visit. Forgive me if now and then I use "like" as a conjunctive adverb. I figure if I'm going to be the grandfather of a twenty-first century child I should become, like, more contemporary. My relationship with my grandchild will not be occasional. They will be living only a short distance from our house. It's nine feet, ten inches, give or take a fraction, to their bathroom window, which is where I expect to take delivery of the child most often. That makes sense because it will quickly become apparent to my daughter and her husband that handing the child through the window means I won't come in at the door and then linger, offering parenting suggestions. I might, after taking the baby in my arms, opt, weather permitting, to hover outside the window and offer the same sage counsel, but whichever of them has given me the child has only to offer an excuse and shut the window, much easier than trying to push me out the door. If he is fussy I will walk her (I'm experimenting with pronouns) around the first floor of our house (seventy-eight steps) singing "Up a Lazy River" and "You Made Me Love You" quietly in his ear just like I did with my daughter. I've been practicing with the cat, who prefers "Lazy River." If she's not being fussy, though, I will play with him on a rug I've installed for that purpose in my office. I've some toys — a dollhouse and a toolbox — and am ready.

The EMS team requested the town purchase a new ambulance, a request that had been made a year earlier, but which hadn't even made it to the warrant.

It was tax time, a ritual that has grown way too cumbersome and way too easily manipulated.

The IRS and the tax code is the best and worst example of what happens to well-intended legislation. A few amendments are introduced, each requiring oversight by additional staffers, each providing exceptions or exclusions, and each of those requiring additional oversight by still more staffers, and each born of a strategic effort, often involving benefits for legislators who are willing to help out, on behalf of whatever industry or special interest will benefit from the exception or exclusion. This happens and has happened every time Congress is in session, and now, decades after the enabling legislation was introduced, the IRS employs about 100,000 people and has a budget of over thirteen billion dollars. They have produced a tax code over fifteen thousand pages long, containing over five million words, and have produced laws that require each of us to, one way or another, be familiar and comply with every word. Accordingly, an industry of accountants and tax lawyers has grown to protect us as, each year, thousands of pages of exceptions and exclusions are added until, now, we march obediently to the post office each April to make a contribution, often a wildly disproportionate contribution, to fund ill-considered legislation here at home, or adventurism in parts of the world where our efforts are of dubious worth.

The bandstand was getting some long overdue and loving attention from a devoted bunch of local guys.

The bandstand is re-emerging from years of neglect and worse thanks to a concerted effort by island strongman Bill Chilles. While he's been criticized in the past for despotic tactics to induce others to do his bidding, including blackmail, threats, physical violence and, even worse, a good talking-to, there is something to be said for the results now and then and this is one of those times. Cowed by his bullying, as is so often the case, an assortment of islanders — carpenters, laborers, and one old man — converged on the derelict bandstand last week, in spite of blizzard conditions, to wrap the old monument in tarps, providing a space for them to begin work. Not surprisingly, others, too, fearful of the consequences should they not cooperate, dutifully turned up with coffee, snacks, even hot lunches. The bandstand, a revered community fixture, idle and abandoned for too long, looks like it will again be ready for summer, for band concerts and for impromptu entertainment of all sorts. Presumably it will, as always, continue to be an appealing hangout, but maybe nowadays, with a more engaged and involved bunch of young people among us, and of course ever mindful of the likely consequences of desecration, it will be treated a little more thoughtfully for the foreseeable future.

The granddaughter of a close friend died after a prolonged battle. Then the most remarkable thing happened.

Jackson is a five-year-old Waldorf school student. Waldorf schools teach the existence of a comprehensive but understandable spiritual world closely integrated with our day-to-day physical experience.

Jackson's friend, a determined five-year-old girl from a nearby Waldorf school, had spent the last three of the five years she'd been given fighting an even more determined brain cancer. On the last day of her life she snuggled into bed with her parents, told them she loved them, and, later that night, passed peacefully away.

A few very sad days later the little girl was laid to rest. Jackson was in attendance with his mom. After the service he asked her why the girl's folks were so sad. "Because their little girl has died," his mom replied. "But she's OK," he explained, "She's crossed over the Rainbow Bridge and has become a boy, a boy waiting for a family." "How will the new family find this boy?" pressed his mom. "They just will," he replied with complete assurance. Puzzled, she kept his revelation to herself.

A few days later the little girl's dad dreamed they were presented with the opportunity to adopt a baby boy. Puzzled, still grief-stricken, and reluctant to share such an audacity with his wife, he kept it to himself.

The next day the little girl's mom was at the grave, where she'd been every day since her daughter's death. A friend appeared and came to her side. "I don't know why I'm telling you this so soon after having lost Phoebe," she said, "but a friend is a surrogate mother for a couple no longer able to go through with the adoption. She's having a boy."

Puzzled, mom did not keep it to herself. She came home and told dad, whereupon he told her about his dream. Mom called her close friend, Jackson's mom, whereupon she learned of the boy's prediction.

Last week Phoebe's brother, Skip and Carol's new grandson, came into the world and was welcomed home.

Bert Dyer passed away in May, disappointing me, and others, who thought he'd live forever.

I confess I am surprised to find Bert Dyer has passed on. I'd grown accustomed over the years to thinking he'd be with us forever. I think he thought so himself and treated dying not as a likelihood but as an opportunity to take center stage and rehearse for it over and over like a kid in high school who is continually held back, always rehearsing the grand march but never graduating. Of course his rehearsals were all public performances, as was his entire life. I remember as a kid coming across Bert in the midst of one or another of those rehearsals and thinking then that his end was at hand. That was fifty or sixty years ago. As time went by and the rehearsals went on I regarded that outcome less and less seriously and came to believe he was capable of anything. Certainly miracles were a piece of cake and resurrection was routine. To have overcome the adversities life dealt him and those he chose to take on was remarkable, but to have overcome them as often as he did was miraculous. I hope some other old veteran can be found to take up the banner and spend the last few years of his or her life driving a motorized wheelchair, flag flying, to town, emerging from a cloud of cigarette smoke at the bottom of Net Factory Hill with the "Hawaiian Love Song" blaring from a cassette player fastened to the handlebars. Every community needs a standard bearer, and no standard ever looked better than one emerging from a cloud of smoke. He cut the ribbon for our grand opening at Island Spirits a year ago this month. I'd intended to invite him to our reopening tomorrow. I may yet.

John Wulp, an old friend and one of the most interesting and extraordinary people I've ever known, came by to watch the Tony Awards.

I was alone on Sunday night and an old man came over. Once he was famous everywhere. Now he's famous here. He'd won a Tony for having produced *Dracula* on Broadway in 1978. The next year he'd been given the LA Drama Critics Circle Award. He won an Obie for having produced *Red Eye of Love* off-Broadway, a production he's been trying to revive in recent years. He was the founder and, for several years, the director of Playwrights Horizons School of Theater at NYU. Before that he served as a U.S. Marine. In 2001 he produced *Islands* on North Haven and took it and the island cast to NYC for a well-received production at the Victory Theater.

He doesn't have TV reception at home. On this night he came to watch the Tony Awards. He knew everyone and was enthralled throughout but also pining to be there with them. He's also a very well-known painter. Yesterday I found him alongside the road photographing a purple iris. I stopped, and he complained that the iris was very wet, given the rain, and its leaves were drooping making it impossible for him to get just the right photograph. He'd intended to take the photo home and paint the image. I told him I'd speak to the authorities and see if I couldn't get something done about the excessively wet iris. He seemed relieved.

The Harbor Gawker reopened around the first of May, an event we all look forward to and anticipate hungrily. On this occasion, however, we who were inside were not the only ones who got what they ordered.

If you have a weak stomach or a penchant for ducklings I suggest you forego "The Observer" this week.

We waited eagerly, as did many others, for the Gawker to open again this year. We were not alone, however.

Unbeknownst to us and to the dozen mallards gathered in the lee afforded by the juncture of the dining room and the extension of the old bowling alley, our national symbol circled overhead. He, a mature male, was, like us (not the mature part), eagerly considering his options. Elaine chose the corn chowder, I, the shrimp basket, and the eagle chose an adorable but unsuspecting mature female duck that was preening shamelessly for some attendant suitors. We were sitting in the corner. Elaine always sits next to the monitor when it's cold and I sat at the adjacent window. There were five other diners in the room, all engaged in conversation, but I — she and I having nothing more to discuss — was looking out at the ducks (they were adorable) just a few feet from the window. The eagle dropped like a meteor from the sky, wings straight up, talons extended, and the eruption of death (it could not have been otherwise) of brown and white and of wings exploding in an instant recovery five feet wide was so sudden and unexpected I couldn't find words (no, really!). By the time I'd leapt to my feet and called it to the attention of the others he was airborne with his "duck to go" (adorable little dead webbed feet dangling beneath him). He landed on the stone wall in front of Jane Duell's. There, in plain view, right next to Jane's house and oblivious to its storm door banging open and closed in the wind, he disemboweled, then enjoyed his still adorable (for the first few seconds) dinner.

Incidentally, I couldn't help noticing, as did the eagle and others, that the food at the Gawker is just as good, although Lonnie is lounging at Windward Gardens, and that leads us to wonder who's really in charge and how long it has been thus.

A new ferry line number system, the one we use now, was adopted and worked well.

It pains me to admit the government, on any level, is right about anything. That said, however, although we have for sixty years routinely gone to war for no good reason, often simply to profit others, although we go to extraordinary lengths to deny basic freedoms and our own precious liberties to folks we think are undeserving, and although we avoid the cost of employing one additional person at the Vinalhaven post office by sending our local mail off on the ferry, then by truck to Portland where it is sorted, trucked back to Rockland and sent back to us on the ferry, and although we pay more people to plow perfectly good crops back into the ground (or to grow nothing) than we do to provide needed health care to wounded veterans, and although we have dozens of generously characterized intelligence agencies operating with such independence and proprietary angst they refuse to share information and so the 9/11 disaster— about which several had foreknowledge — was, perhaps, not avoided, and although the state of Maine employs an individual whose job it is to count the bottles of wine in a retail store to be sure it has enough, and although I can leave a bag at the terminal but only if I don't ask if I can leave a bag at the terminal… although these things are true and troubling, the new ferry line number system is working perfectly.

Watching the work on the Old Engine House, an observer asked me to describe the long gone and much missed Memorial Hall.

I am rhythmically challenged. When, in the Memorial Hall, I took my first step in the Grand March in June of 1962 my mother, who was not similarly handicapped, moved with grace and precision around the hall appearing to have her arm looped through my own. In fact, she held me in a steel grip ensuring that I turned each corner in a timely fashion and appeared, if not graceful, then at least compliant. Earlier, during the ascension of seniors to the stage, I was paired with a girl who did not share my mother's interest in seeing that I put one foot in front of the other. She was entirely composed, regally resigned to but advisedly dismissive of me, beautiful in a gown that had been carefully tailored at home to accentuate her many beguiling features and who found in "Pomp and Circumstance" a perfectly obvious and accommodating rhythm. I lunged along, now and then next to her, more often simply in the vicinity. Although the long ordeal presented many opportunities for her to nourish our partnership she instead ignored her awkward and distracting companion and moved elegantly and in step, eventually settling gracefully in her assigned seat amidst the happy folds of her gown. A few minutes later I arrived, stumbled toward the chair I thought was mine and, unsuccessful in dislodging the fellow who was already there, moved down the line till I found a vacant lot. I recall she'd taken sixty-eight steps.

Jessie Grant, Tara Elliott's replacement as drama teacher, had been at work for a few months. We needn't have worried about whether she could fill Tara's shoes.

> Thank goodness English has an abundance of adjectives. Last week's production of *Guys and Dolls* was amazing. Blake Reidy turned in an astonishing performance as Adelaide. She sang beautifully, worked the stage masterfully, employed her perfect asides deftly, and was never out of character. Trey Warren, stressed with trying to reconcile his love for her with his obligation to make craps happen, was her equal. They were an entirely beleaguered and believable couple. Willie Drury was charmingly urbane and dangerous. Arvide was tender and caring. The tinhorns were magnificent and harmonic. John Morton made the stage seem confining. The gangsters were an entirely credible bunch, as was the Mission Band. Karen Krager did a terrific job as a beguiling and tortured Sister Sarah, and Sarina Alley, as a skeptical and pious superior. Alex Day (Lt. Brannigan) and Frank Morton as Benny Southstreet, were, as always and like everyone else in this production, perfectly larger than life. The impeccable set and costumes lent real credibility. The show was full of little strokes of genius and insight, throwing Henry and Elijah in with the gangsters, for example. The Hot Box Girls were real babes: harmonious, in step, and outrageous. The choreography throughout was very impressive, and the whole production — an enormous achievement — was a joy to watch. I'm tempted to call Jessie Grant a miracle worker, but, in fact, as she acknowledges often, these are a magnificent bunch of young people: talented, energetic, enthusiastic, and enormously appealing. This has been a fun theatrical year and these kids and this director have been a real gift to our community. The notion that so many of our young people could again be so absorbed by such an exercise and enjoy themselves so completely was, also again, a revelation to the kids in the audience on Sunday who now want to grow up to be just like them. We're all looking forward to it.

Every now and then I have an unusual night at the Tidewater, probably not the kind of thing they experience at the Hampton Inn.

> I had a bad day. It began with an incident unrelated to the motel. I won't bother you with the details. The day started at four thirty a.m. and by ten p.m., when things were really bad, this time at the motel, I was really irritable. The problem required that I remain there until two a.m., by which time I expected a guest with whom I had an issue to return. As I waited in my truck, growing more and more miserable, I heard a big noise in the town parking lot, followed by a string of expletives delivered in a slurred baritone, and then the unmistakable crash of a municipal trash can being dealt a death blow. Having seen it before, I knew what the parking lot would look like if the gulls got to the spilled contents before I did, so, still waiting for my errant guest to return, I walked over to see what I could do. The fellow who'd delivered the oratory and kicked over the can was standing next to it and he challenged me to continue approaching. I did, explaining that I only wanted to stand the can up and put the stuff back in it. He warned me that would be contrary to his own aims and dared me to continue. I did, mindful of his objections. Suddenly I heard a car stop at the motel and realized it was the fellow I was waiting for. I dropped what I was doing and ran back across the lot with my nemesis screaming that by running I had made the right choice.

My first wife, Janet, didn't like it here and once we'd broken up and she returned home to Connecticut she never came back again — until our grandson was born. Now, of course, she's a regular — who can blame her—and she brings her very helpful electrician boyfriend with her, and I'm very glad she does.

> What goes around comes around and often in the oddest ways. So it is that my first wife's boyfriend comes up here from Connecticut with Janet now and then, and while he's here he either finishes up the projects I have left incomplete or takes on the things I should have done had I taken the time. These he brings to my attention and then takes care of them himself when it becomes apparent — and it always is — that I'm not going to get to it. He's a master electrician, mechanically inclined, doesn't mind getting dirty or seem to think any job is beneath him (and he's a short guy), and is inclined to help others who, like me, so obviously need it. Recently he's taken a keen interest in helping with my redeemable activities, getting the bottles and cans to Eldercare for the Sunday brigade. He's a little pushy, however, standing out by the collection center earlier than I might otherwise get to it, tapping his feet in obvious impatience and now and then stalking across the motel parking lot in my direction as a means of urging me on. When I finally show up he's chafing, "I been wai-in," he barks good-naturedly out of the corner of his mouth. He says "wai-in" instead of "waiting" like he says "New Bri-in" instead of "New Britain," which is the way people from New Britain talk. It gives them a tough facade like guys from South Boston, but he's not so tough. He is helpful, though, and I look forward to seeing him again.

The agonizing search for someone to take Dr. Entel's place was ongoing. Most of us were very confused about why he left, whether he left voluntarily, and about the prospects of finding someone with whom we would be quite as content as we'd found ourselves with him.

Lyme disease became a real threat, and comprehensive instructions for dealing with deer ticks were provided by ICMS.

An interesting debate raged over the proposed school budget and the amount needed to be maintained in the school's fund balance.

Town Manager's Corner

> First let me say that I have a great deal of respect for anyone that serves in an elected position and I believe the SAD #8 School Board does a great job. I work for the Board of Selectmen and they asked me to write this article, which is similar to a letter I addressed to the individual members of the school board. Selectperson Penny Lazaro abstained from any decision about this article, as she is an employee of the School District. We have no argument with the expense side of the school budget. We trust that the school board, as elected officials, will develop this side of the budget to the best of their abilities for what is in the best interest of the town and its students. Our difference of opinion lies on the revenue side of the budget related to use of fund balance. Our opinion is that SAD #8 has an excessive amount of fund balance and to ask the Town of Vinalhaven to raise tax dollars when there are funds available to appropriate from fund balance is unreasonable and an unnecessary burden on taxpayers. The total school budget this year is $3,565,763 and the town assessment is $2,417,451, which is $85,540 more than the previous year. Mr. Collins is right, this amount in and of itself will not increase your tax bill to a large degree, but it will certainly add to, not reduce, your tax bill.

Our understanding is that the school board has a policy as part of their strategic plan to maintain 30% of the operating budget in an unreserved fund balance. If you consider the operating budget is the total school budget, less debt service, their goal for 2010-2011 would be $738,463.74 ($3,415,706.56 - $954,160.76 x 30%). We disagree fundamentally with this policy.

As quoted by Stephen J. Gauthier in *An Elected Official's Guide to Fund Balance*, "the 'right amount' of unreserved fund balance is a question open to some debate, particularly in the general fund. Bond raters and others often use 'rules of thumb' to measure the adequacy of unreserved fund balance in the general fund. For example, 5 percent of annual operating expenditures is a commonly cited minimum amount. Others argue that unreserved fund balance should equal no less than one month's operating expenditures (i.e., 8.3 percent). Care must be taken, however, to avoid applying such rules of thumb mechanically. A variety of factors must be taken into account when evaluating the adequacy of fund balance in the general fund." He goes on to say, "Another important factor is the timing of cash inflows and outflows. Governments whose cash flows are less predictable may need relatively higher levels of unreserved fund balance to maintain liquidity than those with highly predictable cash inflows and outflows."

The school cash inflows are very predictable in that the Town of Vinalhaven writes a check to the school each month. They know they will receive that check. Let's make an analogy to the fishermen. They know that their income is variable by the seasons and whether or not the lobsters are running. They also know that because their income is not predictable, they have to put some of their income aside for the lean months. So the fishermen are comparable to the town, in a way. They have to keep more in reserve so that they can continue to pay the bills when there is little or no cash coming in. The school is like a trust fund person, someone that receives a check each month without fail. While they may have a little bit in savings, they don't have to worry about so many variables like the fishermen. They don't need as much in reserves. Do you see what I mean?

The question that always comes up is how much unreserved fund balance does the Town of Vinalhaven have? The town has $1,084,013 as of June 30, 2010. My philosophy is to keep enough fund balance so the town does not have to borrow money in anticipation of receiving tax revenue, which is due May 1 and November 1. For instance, on March 31, 2011 we had $430,944.14 available in cash. With one more school payment of $194,325.82 due on April 20th and other monthly bills, we will just about squeak by without borrowing money to pay our bills before tax revenue starts to come in May 1. Many towns and cities borrow money in anticipation of tax revenue. My philosophy avoids unnecessary borrowing, earns some interest income, and keeps the bills paid, including the school bill. Read the fishermen and trust fund person analogy again in the paragraph above.

Even if the school has a policy of maintaining a certain percentage of their operating budget in an unreserved fund balance (and I am not saying that is a bad idea), my argument is with the amount. My opinion is that 30% is excessive. The Maine Town and City Management Association recently did a survey on their list serve about this very subject. And remember, my opinion is that a town or city needs a lot more fund balance than a school district. The maximum goal any of the towns that responded was 15%. Many use the "rule of thumb" mentioned above at 8.3%. The minimum average was 8.7%. The maximum average was 12%. I'm not sure how the school came up with 30%, but it is high by anyone's standards.

OBSERVATIONS

The Superintendent, Lew Collins, reported in a memo titled BUDGET HIGHLIGHTS 2011-12 SCHOOL YEAR, Updated 4/4/11, that if the school "uses all of the $200,000 dedicated to this year's budget, our reserve could dip to below $250,000 by the 2012-13 school year." My answer to that is "so, what?" 8.3% of your operating budget is $204,308, which is a healthy fund balance by anyone's standards. My previous career was that of an Audit Manager for Horton, McFarland & Veysey, CPAs in Ellsworth, Maine. I have prepared financial statements for dozens of school departments, SADs, CSDs, and School Unions. I have never seen a fund balance that high for one school.

Mr. Collins goes on to say in the memo, "that is not a healthy situation given the age of our building, unanticipated special education costs, further reductions in state and federal funding, and other needs that always seem to crop up in school and municipal operations." Let's take these one at a time. He mentions the age of the building and needed repairs. At the close of fiscal year ending June 30, 2010, there was a balance of $163,446 in the Schools Capital Repair and Improvement Fund. This amount is over and above the general fund unreserved fund balance of $700,534. So the school already has $163,446 set aside for capital repairs. This was reported in their audit report dated June 30, 2010.

The audit report also lists a School Construction Reserve for Capital Projects with a balance of $87,312, a Technology Reserve of $15,000, and a Minor Capital Project-Sprinkler System Reserve of $6,845. So the School District already has extra funds set aside for this purpose.

For Special Education, the memo infers that we need the big fund balance because of "unanticipated special education costs." Well it seems to me that in this small community we know when a child with special needs will be entering the school and probably have three or four years to plan. I suppose there is an outside chance that someone could move to the island with special needs children and in that case it would be unanticipated, but the chances are fairly slim that would happen.

As to state and federal funding, we don't get much anyway. The total Special Education Allocation in the 2010-2011 budget was $60,766. Other than the Debt Service and school lunch subsidy, we don't get much of anything for operating costs anyway, so what is there to lose?

Yes, there are always things that "crop up," as you say, but a fund balance of 8.3% would be more than enough to get us by, in my opinion.

At the end of all the budget meetings, town meetings, and referendum votes, the tax bills are mailed from the Vinalhaven Town Office. It is me and my staff that stand on the other side of the counter when people come in to complain about their tax bills. It is the Board of Selectmen that are "blamed," if you will, for the tax rate, not the School Board. In my opinion and that of the Board of Selectmen, the School District can easily appropriate another $85,000 from fund balance and still have enough to get through a rainy day.

You are welcome to investigate the facts and form your own opinion and we encourage you to do that. It is the opinion of the Board of Selectmen and me that the School District could easily use more of their existing fund balance instead of asking the taxpayers for additional money.

I have attended the School District Budget meetings as Town Manager for several years now and typically the only people that attend are school employees, some town officials and a few residents. The school budget is 45% of your budget. Let me repeat that: the school budget is 45% of your total budget, and very few people bother to show up to vote on this part of the budget. Yes, it is confusing. The School District Warrant Articles are so complex that they have an attorney draft them. The first half of the warrant articles authorizes expenditures and the second half raise funds for the proposed school budget. We disagree with the amount in Article 14, which asks for "additional local funds" totaling $469,998.87. A written ballot is required. It is our opinion that this amount should be reduced by at least $85,540.

This is our opinion, and again, we urge you to investigate the facts, ask your own questions, and form your own opinion. We also want to repeat that we have a tremendous amount of respect for the School District Board of Directors. Our argument is not with the expenditure side of the budget. We respectfully disagree with the fund balance policy.

Thank you for your support and remember, be kind to one another!

Marjorie E. Stratton, Town Manager

Pat Lundholm wrote a gracious note declining to serve as Selectperson.

Thank you to those of you who wrote in my name for the position of Selectman. I truly appreciate your expression of support. It helps to mitigate the negative feelings expressed during one of the past elections. Unfortunately, I feel that I must decline to accept the position of Selectman at this time and in this manner.

Since coming to Vinalhaven, I have strived to be of use to the community. To that end, I am currently enrolled in an advanced course in emergency medical service. The class and clinical work involved requires three or four days and nights per week away from the island for a period of approximately five months. Because of this and the study required, as well as my other obligations to the ambulance service, I haven't kept up with the issues facing the town, and didn't even know that there was only one candidate for the two positions of Selectman until I looked at my absentee ballot. Before accepting a position with any organization I should understand the issues or problems facing that organization.

In addition, I feel that accepting the position after garnering only 28 votes would be a little like sneaking in, especially after the rather upsetting signs displayed when I was voted out of office. I realize that there was a sizable portion of Vinalhaven voters who did not agree with my stand on several issues.

However, I still wish to be useful to my community. If the time comes when I am up-to-date on the issues facing the town, see that there is a need, and have the time to serve effectively, I will take out nomination papers and appear on the ballot so that the whole town can decide whether I should have the job.

Sincerely, Pat Lundholm

I was asked to be the Commencement Speaker at graduation. I was honored and reminded of circumstances that existed when I'd graduated in 1962. The *Wind* subsequently published the speech.

OBSERVATIONS

You and I and many of the others gathered here have a great deal in common. We each finished high school in Vinalhaven and we each have the rest of our lives ahead of us. I hope you're looking forward to the rest of yours as much as I'm looking forward to the rest of mine.

Nearly fifty years ago I stood, symbolically, where you are today. I say symbolically because this auditorium was not here. This school wasn't here. None of the teachers were here. Neither was the superintendent. Your parents weren't here or, if they were, they were of little significance. A certain energy wasn't here either because you weren't here. I wish you had been. With you it would have been different; it would have been better.

A few months ago I described you as wholesome in an "Observer" column. I said at the time that I'd chosen that term only after weighing the consequences. For years, beginning around the time I was in school, the town adopted a defensive posture toward many of its young people, and with good reason. We were troublesome; not all of us, by any means, but enough to have an impact. Our aim was mischief, to begin with, but that morphed, for a few of us, into more serious trouble and as time went by the bar kept getting raised, or perhaps lowered is a better term, so that in the eighties and nineties it wasn't enough for some to begin a high school career just burning a little rubber. Of course, trouble here kind of pales when compared with trouble here and there around the world, but it was real enough for people who were trying to make a home for themselves, and if anyone had called me and my buddies wholesome we'd have gone to great lengths to prove otherwise.

On this last Memorial Day we heard "The Star Spangled Banner" played in the bandstand for the first time in many years. We hadn't heard it for a while because another generation of those same youngsters had nearly destroyed it, and the folks who'd tried to stay ahead of their destruction over the years had given up. I know. I was one of those who gave up.

This year, though, a team of volunteers invested a great deal of their valuable time to rebuild the bandstand and to make it possible for us to use and be proud of this historic artifact. Ultimately, that expenditure of time and money was an investment in you. The people who put the bandstand back together did it because you and your underclassmen and the students who've attended this great new school over the last several years have inspired the rest of us. All of you — an enormously diverse and interesting bunch — have breathed new life into our community, positive and full of promise. We are among the beneficiaries and as such are inspired to do more ourselves. It's fun having you among us and it's been a long time since that observation was made so freely. Because of you and the infectious and wholesome spirit you bring to everything you do the rest of us are reinvested with optimism for the future of Vinalhaven and an eagerness to share in your lives and in the good fortune you all deserve so completely.

Suddenly here among us are young people unafraid to make eye contact, kids who exchange pleasantries and engage us in conversation. A few years ago one of our own offered a prayer at a baccalaureate service and he included in that prayer the hope that the kids graduating that year would acknowledge the adults in this community who made it possible for them to get through school: who baked the brownies, bought the raffle tickets, bought the brownies, and otherwise supported them. He wasn't asking for a round of applause, only that we be acknowledged, be spoken to. We didn't want much more than to say "Hi" and to find a responsive kid saying "Hi" in return. But it was kind of a badge of honor to dis the adult community, to disparage them. You are a breath of fresh air.

2011

Today we are happily riding the wave of passion and excitement that has carried you down over the Net Factory Hill in a rambunctious knot or into the auditorium to express your unqualified enthusiasm for the achievements of a fellow student or to the other parts of the world to better understand the true breadth of our humanity or onto the stage for an unbridled performance or into an outrageous demonstration of acrobatics in the town parking lot or into a ball game or impromptu concert on Main Street or simply carried you for the last dozen years to this special day.

I believe it's customary to end a commencement address with some sage advice. Mine is twofold. First, continue to set the bar high for yourselves and for those youngsters who, full of admiration for each of you, are so very plainly following in your footsteps. Set it high for us, too. We, the adults, need to be reminded of our own potential. Second, try not to use "like" as a conjunctive adverb. "Like" is a quantifier and qualifier. It diminishes what you have to say, makes it seem you are unsure of yourself, that you may not know what you are talking about or that you lack conviction, are on the fence or wishy-washy. At some point down the road you are going to be presented with an opportunity to voice your affection for someone. When that time comes tell him or her "I love you" not "I, like, love you." "Like" will dampen the moment and leave your intended wondering how much less than love it is you are trying to imply. And while I won't be remotely surprised if one of you has this opportunity, it will not do to one day hear you respond to the Chief Justice, "I, like, solemnly swear that I will, like, faithfully execute the office of President of the United States." I, for one, would be, like, bummed to hear that. Totally.

"Doing the bottles" was revealing. I really could tell when certain seasonal residents had arrived because I was so familiar with their choice of libation. The bottles revealed other things as well, many of which I kept to myself.

Gathering the bottles and cans is one way to stay in touch with my community. Having done this for so long I can now tell when certain people have arrived on island just by observing the containers that suddenly appear. I can tell, too, when they've left. Annual events, parties at summer places, parties at fish houses or at the homes of islanders, are all signaled by the appearance the next day of returnables, each cumulative arrival a clear indication of whose party was when. I was encouraged this year by a clear sign of evolution at work when the bags of returnables from a certain fish house bash included, beyond the predictable crushed Bud Light cans, a few containers that had once contained real beer. I've come, too, to associate the sudden appearance of certain containers with events in town. For example, when Roscoe McFadden returns home again after an ill-advised dalliance, a Grey Goose bottle with lipstick around the neck appears within a few days. I can't figure out the significance but it's predictable. Lots of empty Smuttynose bottles signal the beginning of tidying up in anticipation of Rusty's wife returning from a frequent road trip. Every mid-July a case of 2010 Cotes de Provence shows up and every September 11 someone deposits two bottles of David Bruce joined by a ribbon.

If I have nothing else to do I reflect on my own island history, and it nearly always results in an amusing story.

Until recently I'd been becoming more and more comfortable, a little less anguished and guilt-ridden as, with each passing day, one after another of the folks who knew me when I was a kid became more and more forgetful or passed away, taking their testimony with them. Then, not long ago, referring to my volunteer work for Eldercare, someone asked an acquaintance, a person who'd only moved to the island a short time ago and who'd only known me for that long, "Why does he do bottles?" and my acquaintance replied without hesitation. "I've always assumed it's remorse." It was a little startling to realize I was so transparent or my past such common knowledge. On the other hand there are a few old-timers who slow down as they pass me sorting bottles and cans and suggest that my sentence of community service must, by now, have been fulilled. Others, Geez for example, suggest just the opposite, that my debt to society can't possibly have been retired so soon. Although a few forgiving folks who should be forgetful by now but who are not, like Sidney Smith, never pass an opportunity to remind me of my transgressions, they do so playfully and now regard me as benign, a label that would have really irritated me fifty years ago but with which I am growing more comfortable.

The Maine Farmland Trust had allied itself with the ARC and was presenting a food film series in advance of further educating us all on the possibilities and benefits of home grown food.

A couple of the ticket agents at the ferry service went sky diving and could talk of little else, certainly nothing having to do with travel on the ferry. The fact that one of them was in a neck brace, the result of an unrelated mishap, did nothing to diminish their enthusiasm, nor did they seem inclined to offer an explanation.

Jeannie and Ellen went skydiving a few days ago, and after listening to them recount their experience I think the Maine State Ferry Service should pay for it and make it mandatory that they and all ferry service employees do the same thing, maybe at the beginning of each summer season. It would put them all in the right frame of mind. Ellen and Jeannie are effusive about the adventure, and they have carried that warm glow and excitement in to work every day since. It becomes a part of their interaction with the public. Never mind that all you want is to buy a ticket and get to the mainland. They'd rather talk about being sandwiched together at fifteen thousand feet with a nice young man with his own rip cord. Never mind that you need to get back to your car before the line person arrives. They want to talk about singing "Nearer My God to Thee" in three-part harmony while pretending it was God they were singing about. Never mind that you are at the head of a long line of impatient travelers. They are recounting the horror of seeing how quickly free fall transforms their triceps and that little wiggly thing under their chins into so much loose skin flapping in the wind. Never mind the boat leaves in five minutes. They have held hands and who knows what else with a young man in free fall and they were not afraid. Perhaps the same can be said of him.

The other day I headed down to the ferry just before six thirty, line number prominently displayed in my windshield, and joined others similarly compliant. I went into the terminal to fetch my ticket and found the ticket agent, her neck in a brace and her left arm apparently in a cast, eagerly encouraging me to take advantage of a special being offered that day by a skydiving company. The offer provided for instruction and a free dive for 150 dollars, much less than the hundreds usually charged. It was hard to resist, particularly when being pitched by such an eager, albeit bandaged and medicated, enthusiast. I begged off, however, and hastened back to my vehicle. A few minutes later the lineman prepared to begin the loading process, an exercise which, on this day, coincided with a swarming of blackflies. The swarm drove him to distraction and his frantic waves to dispel the offending critters were interpreted by the many of us in line as a signal to board and thus it was that seven vehicles moved out of the regular line and out of the reserved line and advanced toward him simultaneously. Undeterred and composed, the lineman dispatched one after another of the offending bugs with one hand while directing our reformation with the other, a remarkable, if not entirely graceful, bit of choreography.

Dr. Jen became a lobsterwoman and authored a very nice note extending her thanks to many among her large circle of friends.

> As most of you know I am now the proud owner of five new lobster traps and buoys and a non-commercial lobster fishing license. Without all the help and support I've gotten it would not have been possible, but here I am hauling my traps and loving it. Thanks to the entire Warren and Lazaro families for all your kindness. Without the assistance of Laura, Geno, Stubby, Sonny, and Bobby Warren I may have not have passed my test (do you know the difference between ferrous metal hog rings and stainless steel hog rings and why that matters? I do now!!). Thanks also to Ruth Ames for the beautiful hand-knit bait bags and to the entire Ames family for their offers of help and advice — especially to Sonny Ames for filling me in on the important superstitions to be aware of. I'm very careful when choosing my fishing wardrobe.
>
> Thank you Brian and Albert Osgood for delivering my outboard motor; being out on the water has truly been an escape that I treasure!
>
> Thanks to Chris Weller for helping to install the pulley line on my maiden voyage. I suspect Geno had a lot to do with preparing my boat and everything else, and, as usual, I'm humbled by his kindness. Kevin has become quite a sternman and is ready to expand his cooking talents to include all things lobster.
>
> Thanks to the ladies of the town office for walking me through the boat registration process, and to Sue and Hugh for the wonderful outdoor lobster cooker.
>
> Finally, and most importantly, thank you to Sonny Warren — for the traps, the gear, and the patient teaching. From sharing his fishing and gardening expertise to keeping me fully supplied with kindling wood all winter long to ensure I would be warm and not combing the woods for flammable sticks, he has made me feel like a part of his wonderful family and I couldn't be more grateful. The kind of love I've received from Sonny and everyone mentioned above is something I will never forget. It has been a difficult year and this is just what l needed. See you on the water!

Several years earlier I'd delivered a life-size portrait done by John Wulp to the Lincoln Center in New York City. It was of a very imposing woman in a red dress. She was Elżbieta Czyżewska. The name meant nothing to me, but in July an extraordinary production came to the New Era Gallery's adjunct Windy Way Barn. It lasted about forty-five minutes and was enthralling.

> I was smitten by the woman in the painting, not because she was beguiling but because she had such presence, such an attitude. I had no idea who she was. Last week the painting, having been retrieved for the occasion, along with three other compelling portraits and a dazzling apple blossom panorama, was hanging in Windy Way Barn. On Sunday a play, *Elżbieta Erased*, was read by John Guare, its author, and Omar Sangare. I assume, since I'd never heard of Omar, that I must lead an isolated existence. He could communicate more with a flick of one eyebrow than most, including

me, could manage in an evening of oration.

The play, forty-five minutes of dialogue, beyond reminding us of post-WWII Polish history, illuminated the edgy life of Elżbieta Czyżewska. The elements of her life were not so much different from any of ours — love, abandonment, adventure, addiction, achievement, betrayal, ecstasy, despair, fame, humiliation, all that stuff — but were much more grandiose. The play was a great tribute to her but also to John Wulp, who painted her portrait (and the others) and so inspired the production. The Windy Way Barn exhibit will remain up for a couple more weeks.

For years between postmasters, Sharon Philbrook had been an unflappable postal worker, holding the operation together under conditions that now and then get a little overwhelming. She deserved a tribute.

The U.S. Postal Service is contemplating the closure of over six hundred post offices around the nation. Vinalhaven's will not be one of them. A postal inspector was sent out recently to evaluate the service and performance of our own staff. He reported back to his superiors that the island post office was performing well, filling a real need, and ought to remain open. He further observed that while rural post offices around the country are routinely staffed at a ratio of one employee for every thousand inhabitants, Vinalhaven seemed to be doing perfectly well with one woman taking care of thirteen hundred or so island residents. Summarizing, he noted that while the island's population is rumored to increase by a handful during the summer, and while that increase might require her to move a little faster for a couple of months, he didn't see any reason she couldn't handle it. She is, he reported, pleasant and energetic, hard to discourage and "probably has several good years left in her." The report went on to remind the reader that, while other post offices are up and running by eight a.m., the mail often comes to this island outpost by ferry so there really isn't much to do, just tidy up and stuff, till eight thirty or nine. Once it arrives she only has to distribute it among a couple of hundred boxes, shuffle the rest off to the rural route carrier, and now and then respond to the needs of someone wanting a stamp. So capable and efficient was this one employee that the inspector, who'd read earlier reports, asked "What was this guy Bo doing all those years?"

His conclusion was that post offices generally are overstaffed and Vinalhaven, even with only one woman, is no exception. Vinalhaven, he noted, having once had a postmistress and several employees, has winnowed down sensibly to one whole woman working capably in a stress-free environment, but we could still do better, just part of a woman perhaps.

My walk around the island was well on its way and afforded a perspective I'd never enjoyed before, that of looking from the outside in rather than from the inside out.

My circumambulation continues, but with other obligations it's getting more and more difficult to get out so my progress has slowed. I'd hoped to finish up my walk at the end of this year, but it looks more like 2012 now. I began in October, 2009, stepping down into the flats at the Dyers Island Bridge and since then have enjoyed myself enormously. My most recent landfall was last week when I came ashore near the Poor Farm after having taken several walks to get around Penobscot Island. Every corner I've turned has revealed something new to me, something I'd never seen because I've spent all my sixty-some years within the island looking out and never the other way around. Every other corner, though, brings some distant memory to the surface. I can usually see up through the woods to a remembered spot attached to a particular event, or a house comes into view that my dad and I worked on together or that I built myself. Last year I passed by a place where I spent time with a guy who later succumbed to addiction, a person I should have taken some time with. Rounding a bend on Seal Cove I found myself at a spot where Louis Martin and I misbehaved half a century ago. From the shore on Calderwood Neck I glimpsed an oak tree, still very majestic after all these years, under which I squirmed around an encounter with a girl. At Perry Creek I examined the underpinnings of Saltonstall's boathouse. My dad and I had shimmed the piers a little when I helped him shingle the roof. I came ashore and walked up Murch's Brook to the spot where some other guys and I shared a bottle of Muscatel and cast an occasional net in the water for smelt. On that night I learned that a girl I'd been terrified to approach had told a friend of the cousin of one of the guys I was with that she wished I'd call her. I did, and later that year we parked at the end of a dirt road leading down to where I came ashore last week and talked about the rest of our lives.

The bandstand repair and restoration was achieved as promised before the Fourth of July.

In 1895 the W-14 Club had a secret meeting. They were, after all, a secret organization, so secret that almost nothing is known about them. We do know — because a fragment of the minutes of that 1895 meeting recently surfaced — they voted to build a sacred bandstand. They did and installed it at the lower end of the block sidewalk next to the fountain. Later it was moved to its present site. It has come as a complete surprise to discover the club has continued to meet regularly since then and continues to meet and to worship at the bandstand. During these meetings they exchange secret handshakes and recite their mantra, "Never refuse a Chilles," a motto that has sustained them for over a century. Today's membership, including Alan Lazaro, Jake Thompson, Pat Shane, Mont Conway, Elder Paul Chilles, Brooke Conway, Tom Andrews, Bruce Young, Danny Martin, Dylan Hunsinger, Brother John, and the Grand Wizard, Bill Chilles, has completed a terrific restoration of their sacred symbol.

FIW had retained a group of engineers whose job was to "feather" the leading edges of the wind turbine blades in an effort to reduce noise. Meanwhile, the folks who were suffering most from the noise and making some noise about it suffered further from our handful of neanderthals who only knew one way to express an opposing opinion.

In Rwanda and in the Ivory Coast they settle their differences quite plainly. Team One goes through a village painting a tribe affiliation on the doors of those with whom they disagree. Team Two comes along behind them and kills all the people in those houses. If both teams had access to Facebook, they'd probably save themselves the time of painting all those doors. Team One could just post the names and Team Two or whoever else had worked themselves into a friended frenzy would take it from there. In those circumstances, when the smoke clears, there is only one side of an issue left standing. Problem solved. Here, though, we're different — more civilized, one might say. If we have a disagreement with someone, a difference of opinion about an issue, the windmills perhaps, we still employ Facebook but we don't dispatch Team Two. Instead, while not quite dispatching them, we allow — even encourage — a few who haven't really made either team to run amuck as they post on Facebook their own jaundiced concept of conflict resolution. There are 1,294 individuals out here, including those few proponents of retribution under cover of darkness. There'll be 1,295 in a few more weeks, 1,295 opinions about how things should be done, about whether things are as they seem, about whether those who disagree with us are just being obstinate because they enjoy being contrary (unlikely) or are, in fact, of a different opinion because their experience is not the same as ours. If, instead of posting threats and detailing cowardly retribution on Facebook, we were to actually confront one another face-to-face, we might, if nothing else, at least better understand our differences. Certainly, though, the solution, even if one thinks the result may be that someone is driven out of town, cannot be found in harassment or worse.

Fox Islands Wind Blade Work

Work continues on the wind turbine blades. A team from Aeroconcept, the German company contracted by GE, arrived on the island on July 22 and began work at the site on July 25. The team is not replacing the turbine blades, rather it is installing small serrations or "teeth" on the final third of each blade in an effort to test whether or not they reduce the amount of noise coming from the project.

During the first week of work, the team installed a special platform that will allow technicians to easily access each blade and began applying the serrations to the first blade. It is expected that the work on each turbine will take approximately ten days to complete, continuing through August. Additional information on the beta test of these new serrations will be posted as it becomes available at www.foxislandswind.com.

An auction of handcrafted and decorated birdhouses was planned to raise money for PIE, a project not unlike the one involving benches a few years earlier.

Outward Bound was a wilderness experience and survival school begun decades ago in Wales, and until a few years ago, operating on Hurricane Island. This year the Hurricane Island Foundation took up residency.

What is Happening on Hurricane Island? Lots!

After Outward Bound made the decision to leave Hurricane Island in 2005, the incredible infrastructure and tremendous potential of the island, with its rich history and resources, was left dormant. Last year, a group of former Outward Bound leaders and island residents founded the Hurricane Island Foundation and signed a 40-year lease with the owners of the island. The island, with its unique history and ecology, is well positioned to teach us about the coastal environment and economic sustainability — while providing much needed science, math, and outdoor training for students and teachers.

Under the direction of executive director John Dietter, former North Haven Community School science and math teacher, the Hurricane Island Foundation is bringing life back to the island. "With a mission of enhancing research-based scientific learning and outdoor leadership, the new organization will focus on a variety of programs for students, teachers, and professionals — from the islands, from Maine, and from around the country.

Three core initiatives will be piloted on Hurricane Island in the late summer and fall of 2011: the Center for Science and Leadership, which will run research-based programs for students and teachers; the Field Research Station, which will host scientists conducting field research; and the Wilderness and Rural Medicine Institute, which will train basic and advanced medical practitioners who work in remote environments.

In June, Vinalhaven High School students visited Hurricane to study sustainability as it relates to Maine island communities. The curriculum delivered by Hurricane Island staff and Vinalhaven teachers took an interdisciplinary approach, challenging students to think critically and problem solve as they tried to puzzle out why the town of Hurricane Island disappeared in 1914. After participating in a similar program on Hurricane in June, North Haven Community School ninth-grader Natalie Carrier relected: "Doing field research on Hurricane Island was amazing. It was so much better than just reading about those ideas in a book or hearing a lecture. I can't wait to go back!" The Hurricane Island staff looks forward to working with Vinalhaven and North Haven students again in the fall.

We encourage you to visit Hurricane and see for yourself what we're up to: come ashore, picnic, and walk around the island. Talk with us about how you can be involved. Hurricane Island staff and board welcome questions, comments and participation from our island neighbors. For more information, visit www.hurricaneisland.net or call the office at (207) 867-6050. Talk with Executive Director John Dietter, Island Manager Sam Hallowell, Administrative Assistant Amy Peterson, or board member Cecily Pingree and get the most up-to-date information.

The annual EMS Benefit Concert was about to be presented. I was always challenged when trying to construct an inviting column. Sometimes a column, like this one, rubbed a few folks, the caregivers in fact, the wrong way.

> WANTED: Folks with nothing else to do. Join an interesting bunch of guys and gals who sit around all day playing board games and chatting while waiting for the occasional phone call summoning them to an accident or mishap. Wouldn't you look better in a snappy Vinalhaven EMS shirt and riding shotgun in a flashy new ambulance (or a less flashy older one when they're called to more than one rescue at a time) or maybe even driving? Think of it! You— riding in the ambulance with the siren blaring and folks making way for you, folks who once upon a time never paid you any mind. And the adventure — dashing off into the wilderness to rescue injured hikers or leaping gleefully out of bed in the middle of the night to save lives. Traffic accidents, fires, bar brawls, all kinds of excitement. And applause, thank-yous in the *Wind* every week. Accolades! People stop you on the street to admire your vest or give you hugs. And every summer, every August, a different team, a group of famous entertainers, also committed but with far less energy, gets together and puts on a benefit concert to raise money for you and for your organization. That brings me to the point. Next week, on Saturday, August 13 you should all— ALL — come to the annual (like tenth or something) EMS Benefit concert at the Smith Hokanson Auditorium. If only the folks they've rescued showed up the place would be full.

Historic Downstreet, Inc. was formed in anticipation of a particular historic landmark expected to go on the block, and directed their energies toward acquiring it. It was not auctioned and our efforts were redirected toward other downtown artifacts.

One of Penobscot Island Air's pilots, Don Campbell, died in a plane accident on Matinicus. The islands all responded generously to a fund established for his daughter.

Observations

Penobscot Island Air

Elizabeth R. Campbell Fund

A fund has been established for Elizabeth (Beth) Campbell, the 19-year-old daughter of our pilot Don Campbell. Don was tragically killed in a plane accident on Matinicus last week. The fund has been set up at the Rockland branch of Camden National Bank (contact person: Donalene Denapoli). Donations, in the form of checks, should be made out to Elizabeth R. Campbell. Donations can be dropped of at Penobscot Island Air or mailed to: Kevin Waters (Campbell Fund) 211 Westbrook Street, South Thomaston, Maine 04858. If you have any questions, please call Terry Waters, 594-5828. Thank you.

When I was a kid the air taxi, Arthur Harjula's J3 Cub, landed regularly at Harv Ames's farm up on Calderwood Neck. It came in from over Stimpson's Island or banked right after flying down the Thorofare. In either event, if one were parked by the barn at the top of the hill awaiting an arrival, the landing, plane careening upward for a touchdown, looked like a mighty shaky proposition. I remember being on board for one of those landings and how quickly the ground came up at us, before the pilot adjusted the plane's attitude, our level approach contrasting disconcertingly with the sharply sloping earth just ahead. In the service I watched with amazement as pilots, roaring in with jet fighters or fluttering in drunkenly in propeller driven Spads, focused their attention on a single arresting cable on our often wildly bucking carrier deck, intent on bringing a sortie to an abrupt conclusion. It's not a big deal, I'm told by those who've flown those planes, once you get the hang of it. Still, the efforts undertaken by our Penobscot Island Air, who stepped into the void created when we were abandoned by Atlantic Aviation, have been extraordinary. They've wafted in from the darkness time after time to target a little line of headlights and save a life, and that they have lost one of their own in service to us is particularly sad.

Like Christmas and sometimes Thanksgiving, Halloween nearly always spawns an irrepressible remembrance.

Years ago on Halloween, I answered the door dressed as Dracula to find a hunched over and grotesque little fellow holding his gnarled left fist out toward me while clutching a chain in the right. At the other end of the chain, attached to a big spiked collar around his neck, was an even more hunched over and, if possible, even more appalling creature on all fours. Neither spoke at first, but after a few minutes, when it had become obvious I was suspicious of whether they were really kids, the monster grunted a command and jerked on the chain whereupon the degenerate little critter came bounding up the stairs and bit me on the ankle. When I jumped back into the house it turned tail and bounded across the street, across Jane's lawn, and disappeared into the blackness with its master not far behind.

Later that night, after having spent the night terrorizing the trick-or-treaters that were supposed to be terrorizing me, I heard the young mother of one of them addressing some companions in a loud and complaining voice. She had her hands on her hips to give herself a little extra heft and was really heated up. She said, "I'll tell you one thing: if he comes around my kids scaring 'em with that Dracula outfit, I'll show him a thing or two." I approached her from behind, my majestic black cape with its white linen lining spread wide, and, as the mothers she was addressing watched in amused horror, wrapped it around her in an embrace of death and bit her on the neck. She wet herself and, really, if you're Dracula, that's as good as it gets, the equivalent of, like, an award.

Dr. Jen was presented with a Clinical Excellence Award by the Maine Primary Care Association.

> The Board of Trustees of ICMS would like to invite you to a Reception on Friday, November 11th at 5:30 p.m. at the Haven to honor Jen Desmond for her Nurse Practitioner Clinical Excellence Award presented by the Maine Primary Care Association (MPCA). Open to all community health center nurse practitioners practicing at a MPCA member organization, the Nurse Practitioner Excellence Award is presented to the clinician who exemplifies the best of primary care medicine, reaches high standards of quality care, adopts and advances innovation as part of the primary care team, and promotes greater access to health care. Kristina King, our new Nurse Practitioner, will also be there for you to meet. Please contact Dinah Moyer at dinah.moyer@icmsvinalhaven.org or 207-863-4109 with any questions.

The Pleasant River Grange appealed, as it had annually for years, for contributions to its Vinalhaven Fuel Fund, which often spells the difference between life and a very uncomfortable existence for some islanders who are up against it.

> The Vinalhaven Fuel Fund is special: it helps people you very well may know, who volunteer at Eldercare, sing in the choirs, perform on stage, mow your lawn, cook and bake for bake sales, may be your friend, your neighbor.
>
> This year the fuel situation looks grim, with cutbacks on LIHEAP and the higher cost of fuel, which is higher on the island, anyway. Here is something to reflect upon:
>
> Hypothermia is a dangerously low body temperature. An elderly or very young person need not be exposed to extreme cold to suffer hypothermia; it can happen in a mildly cool environment (60 degrees). Symptoms are: drowsiness, weakness, cold skin, followed by stupor, coma, and death.
>
> Please think of your friends and neighbors and be generous again. Every penny you contribute is used for assistance and is tax deductible. I thank everyone who has helped in the past; we were able to help sixty-plus households last winter.
>
> Please make your check payable to: Pleasant River Grange, # 492, marked Fuel Fund in the memo and send it to me.
>
> Sincerely,
>
> Nans M. Case

The Vinalhaven Energy Club, started in 2010 by Karol Kucinski and a half dozen others, was deeply involved in home energy conservation. As of 2014 they'd built and installed over five hundred very inexpensive, but effective, storm windows in public buildings and individual homes.

Several mainland overnights to see musicians we used to think were amazing were disappointing.

> I often arrange a little sojourn involving entertainment. My last four were dismal. The first was to see

OBSERVATIONS

Taj Mahal at Stone Mountain. His emphasis on sexual energy came across as a level of lechery that left us all looking around for teenage girls who might need protection. Next was Dave Bromberg at the Strand. He responded to a fan who shouted out a request by calling him an obscene name and telling him to mind his own business. Last summer we went to the Strand again to see Maria Muldaur. It was exhausting watching her try to match the energy and vocal acrobatics of her youth. When she did "Midnight at the Oasis" it sounded as if she was calling the camel to bed. Certainly, if there'd been one nearby, it would have responded. Last week we went to Portland to see Leon Redbone at Longfellow Square. He was an old man who seemed to have forgotten the words to songs he'd made famous, who spent the half hour we endured grasping in the air like a phantom in some sort of comic substitute for performing, who growled unintelligibly, who asked continually that the few numbers he cobbled together be sing-alongs, and who otherwise distracted from those welcome interludes when his accompanying pianist was left to carry the day. Our daughters have agreed to arrange our future outings.

We all braced ourselves in the fall for the end of the world, as foretold by Harold Camping. It didn't happen, which meant some of us had wasted a great deal of effort for nothing.

I'm a little disappointed about having woken up Saturday morning to find the world had not ended as predicted by Pastor Harold Camping. I'd sent him some money and the deed to the motel so he could spread the word to as many as possible in advance of the predicted end date of October 21. I'd also spent some time atoning for the sins I could remember, for those I'd fabricated or think I may have fabricated, and for those which others have accused me of and which I have long denied but about which I am no longer sure. I gave away stuff that might have been seen as evidence of less than absolute faith, things like my favorite bumper stickers, "When the Rapture Comes We'll Have the Earth to Ourselves" and "Jesus is Coming — Look Busy!" I showered and shaved and put on my nice blue shirt, the one that Elaine says is my color (I think Jesus would agree), and I had a list in my pocket of the people in town whose indiscretions and misdeeds may have gone unnoticed by the Lord. I was not being vindictive, but do admit to a modest satisfaction at the prospect of waving down to them as I am called aloft. So it was I found myself un-risen on Saturday morning but not inconsolable. Since Camping's prediction, I'd been a little miffed that my brother Dick's birthday had been chosen for the rapture, and not my own.

A renewed effort to update our Comprehensive Plan was launched with the hiring of Island Institute Fellow Andy Dorr.

COMPREHENSIVE PLAN 2011-2012

HISTORY

Early Spring 2011 the Vinalhaven Board of Selectmen and Chamber of Commerce formed a partnership with the Island Institute to hire a "Fellow," an individual who would live on Vinalhaven for 1-2 years with a primary focus of updating the island's current Comprehensive Plan. An official town vote in June 2011 approved the necessary funding, and by early September Andrew "Andy" Dorr joined our community as an Island Institute Fellow. While we interviewed many excellent candidates for this position, it was very clear to us that Andy possessed all of the attributes, skills, and talent that we need to assist us in successfully updating the Comprehensive Plan. Welcome, Andy!

Our Fellow

Andy is very enthusiastic about working in our island community. In addition to his work and research in regards to updating our current Comprehensive Plan, he is actively participating in many local organizations and events. If you would like to learn more about Andy and his interests, please check out his blog at: www.vinalhavenfellow.blogspot.com.

Andy is the official organizer and researcher of all the information that will need to be gathered over the course of the next year, and he has jumped into this process with dedication and enthusiasm. Will he alone be shaping the Comprehensive Plan or making decisions about our island's future? No, as that is up to all of us who live here, and we need your input as this process unfolds. Feel free to contact Marjorie Stratton, town manager, if you would like to become involved in this process. You also can contact Andy at adorr@islandinstitute.org.

Here are six reasons why it makes sense to have an updated Comprehensive Plan*:

- Protect working waterfronts and community farms
- Develop a discussion among neighbors
- Sustain rural living and vibrant village centers
- Preserve a healthy landscape and walkable communities
- Balance economic prosperity with quality of life
- Develop a basis for sound decisions in town management

WHY DOES IT MAKE SENSE FOR VINALHAVEN TO HAVE AN UPDATED COMPREHENSIVE PLAN?

Vinalhaven's current plan is over twenty years old. Many changes have occurred in our community since 1988 and therefore most of what exists in the current plan is not useful or applicable to our needs today. Additionally, state and federal grant programs often require a current Comprehensive Plan be in place in order for monies to be awarded, and without an updated plan Vinalhaven is losing out on many funding opportunities.

Planning is a lot of work and involves tough choices, but we all know that good planning makes good communities. Rather than be spectators of change, we can be the architects and engineers of the future of Vinalhaven. We welcome your involvement and invite you to join us in this process.

For future updates on the progress being made in regards to our Comprehensive Plan, please visit the Town of Vinalhaven's website at: www.townofvinalhaven.org and click on the "Comprehensive Plan" link.

*Reference: www.maine.gov/spo/landuse/docs/

There was suddenly a lot of talk about the lack of support for the school and faculty, and I felt compelled to relate my own impression and the impression of others.

Last week I overheard a member of the faculty, considering the opposition to the proposed school budget, lament the fact that no one cares about the school anymore. By this time the results of the

OBSERVATIONS

town's third vote will be clear but I certainly hope, regardless of the outcome, that such sentiments don't prevail among the faculty or administration and certainly not among the student population. It's unfortunate that hardly anyone shows up at a school budget meeting (I wasn't there, either). The few who do are generally supportive of the budget, so it certainly must be frustrating, after it passes in that forum, to see the proposal defeated in one town ballot after another. It shouldn't be interpreted as a lack of support or enthusiasm for the school, however. I've heard reasonable people suggest that we may have overreached when, projecting such optimistic growth in student population, we built such a grand facility. Others have observed that some extravagance, excessively high ceilings, for example, may have been a tribute nearer to passion than to reason and now we spend too much on fuel. I've listened to well-reasoned arguments on each side regarding the need for such a large reserve account or capital improvements fund, but I have never heard anyone ever speak ill of the quality of teaching that goes on there, the passion and commitment of those doing the work, and certainly not of the quality of education.

I reviewed *Aladdin* and, a few days later, corrected an oversight.

There are several problems inherent in reviewing Jessie Grant's productions. For example, I don't know who everyone is. And then there's my limited supply of adjectives. She gets the most amazing magic from her performers and certainly *Aladdin* was among the best of these. I was stunned throughout, and so were those around me. Caleb Beckman was as poised and dazzling as Joel Grey ever was. MJ blew us away as the Genie. His timing, subtleties, and acrobatics seemed impossibly mature. With him and Frank — who was also terrific as Aladdin— and their mom in residence one wonders if dad might be a little overwhelmed in that household. Lily Warren was a supremely petulant Jasmine. Her revulsion at the prospect of marrying Jafar was withering. I hope, when the time comes, she doesn't bring that rejection to bear in real life. The incidental characters were not incidental at all. Guards, Gods, Vendors, and the quartet all made the production seamless. Frances Eder parroted a parrot perfectly and did so in a costume she was clearly happy with. Joe Hopkins, as Jafar, was a really nasty Vizier, and Mitchell Hopkins was a nicely anguished Sultan. The costumes were magnificent, and the set was ingenious, perfect for this production. All the singing, both the soloists and the company, was first rate. Putting mikes on some of the performers was a good idea, given their young voices, but most of them projected like pros, were easy to hear and to understand. The choreography and razzle-dazzle looked like the results of years of training. All in all I certainly hope Jessie stays with us and continues to expose us all to the great depth of expression these kids are all so obviously capable of.

This seems like a good time to acknowledge Rhoda Boughton's selfless contribution over the years. Most, if not all, the wonderful sets we've seen in recent decades have borne the mark of her accomplished and creative eye.

Several folks have asked me to explain the procedure that results in these weekly "Observer" columns so I'll describe it here and use last week's as an example. I so enjoyed the *Aladdin* production that I scribbled down notes, often abbreviated, in the dark during the performance, reminders to myself to be sure and not overlook a certain contribution which, were I to rely on memory would, without question, have escaped me before the curtain came down. So it was then, that when I sat down to compose a column, I retrieved the program on which I'd scratched my observations and tried to decipher what I found there. With Elaine's help (she has a better success rate than I do), I could make out most of them and was able to patch together my impression of the performance and compose a column. Last night I was cleaning off my desk and came upon the graffiti-worn program. My eyes fell on a word neither Elaine nor I had been able to interpret. It looked like "Nickel" and at the time that's all either of us could make of it. Suddenly an unlikely thing happened — I remembered. "Nickel" was in fact a very badly rendered "Michelle" and was intended to remind me not to forget a critical cog in the success of that performance. Michelle Arey's passion for teaching music and her skill in getting that accomplished have produced a vastly increased interest in music throughout school. We have a band again, one we can be proud of, students who look forward to music instruction, in some cases using free time for extra instruction, and kids — even little kids — at ease and singing in perfect harmony (as if they were Blanks). Unison is now the exception instead of the fall-back. This big team, the folks who make these productions the successes they are, the folks who do costumes, hair, makeup, set, props, stage management, lighting, choreography, programs, and music are a real treasure. I'm looking forward to *Annie Get Your Gun*. So that's how I put these together.

Al Barker, who'd headed up the Parade of Lights initiative, was quite happy with the results, and Barbie Dyer and I were each reminded of Christmases past.

I recently made some interior structural changes and Elaine can now sit in the kitchen by the fire and, through the dining room, have an unobstructed view of the big comfortable chair in my office beyond. Now and then I'm in that chair and she understandably relishes those occasions. Sometimes our eyes meet and we consider one another from a distance. Then I fall asleep.

Twenty years ago Gram J sat in her rocker in the same spot. The office served then as her bedroom. She was one hundred years old, the matriarch of five generations of Crossmans living here on the island, and had moved up the street from the apartment in the block where she'd managed for herself until she was ninety-nine. Early on she'd known hard times: heartache, hunger, want and need. Need, in particular, resonated with her, and it was the needs of others, of her family members in particular, which concerned her. Needs were to be met, and the needs of others were her and our responsibility.

Excess, on the other hand, was also a concern. Unless it was obvious, she was always interested in knowing whether a gift given or received was a gift needed. Until her hearing failed badly, her questions regarding those needs were subtly delivered, but as she advanced into her nineties those inquiries grew louder, the natural consequence of hearing loss and the inescapable sense that if one speaks more loudly the response may be more clearly understood. The abundance of gifts flowing out from under the tree on Christmas morning probably troubled her; certainly she was astounded. As we gathered for coffee and sticky buns before descending on the living room, she would now and then inquire about the surplus of gifts and then, after she'd been settled in a comfortable chair near the tree, would remind us of the disparity of privilege in the world by occasionally asking of the person next to her, as a gift was opened by another of us, "Does she need that?"

Christmas Miracles

by Barbie Dyer

When I was four years old and living down Around the Mountain, I saw Santa and his reindeer fly over my house toward Indian Creek. I remember the night was still and a sliver of moon shone on the shoreline; the ice shimmered. It was a bitterly cold night, but I was warm all over. If you believe, anything is possible.

It has been over fifty years since that magical night. In the years that followed nothing has come close to the wonder I felt at that Christmas Eve spectacle.

Each year since, I have waited and watched for another Christmas miracle. I always look to the heavens as December approaches, thinking perhaps this will be the year when a bright star will appear in the east, or perhaps once again I will catch a glimpse of Santa.

One recent evening, long into the nighttime, and unable to sleep, I realized there is always a miracle found at Christmas — especially this year. I'm still alive, Joey is improving, Nate and Hardy are healing, and blessings flow in every direction in this loving community. Merry Christmas!

In 2011 one hundred and five million pounds of lobster were landed in Maine by 6,000 license holders, and the price was $3.19 per pound.

2012

THE PRIMARIES WERE DISCOURAGING.

I know many of you are curious about why I haven't tossed my hat into the Republican primary ring. For one thing, I don't want to be quizzed on nationwide TV about my indiscretions. Beyond that, though, I'm having trouble maintaining my customary Republican enthusiasm, which is not to say I'm excited by the alternative. Our government is letting us down, and the brink that's arrived in so many places elsewhere in the world seems near at hand here. Extremists in either party have rendered Congress nearly impotent. Given the disparity between those Americans who are comfortable and those who are desperately not, many in Congress seem nonetheless content to do nothing except regard every day that passes without revolt as a good day and hope for another to follow. Nearly impotent, but they do manage to do something. They pass legislation like the kind that fertilized the collapse of financial institutions and then bailed them out at our expense, and they routinely profit personally from privileged foreknowledge by cashing in, through insider trading, or by buying and selling commodities they know will be affected by the very legislation they themselves have introduced. Perhaps I wouldn't be able to resist either if I were in Congress, but if the law weren't written in such a way that those members are exempt from prosecution when indulging themselves at our expense, then they could focus on the task at hand.

The *Wind* had begun publishing biographies of war veterans. I chose a veteran I was particularly fond of.

Sergeant Bud Crossman landed in Normandy in mid-June, 1944. He was in charge of a Long Tom, the largest mobile gun in the Allied arsenal. After receiving coordinates from advance reconnaissance forces, he and his five-man crew lobbed eighty-pound explosives as far as seventeen miles as they advanced toward Germany. He learned of the birth of his first son while in England awaiting deployment, and during a trip there a few years ago he visited the house where he'd been bivouacked and found Phil's initials and date of birth there where he'd carved them in a rafter sixty years earlier. Near the end of the war, while still in Germany, he was reunited with his older brother, Mike, who'd been in the Battle of the Bulge. In 1994 he squeezed into his uniform and marched in the parade celebrating the fiftieth anniversary of D-Day. Otherwise, he didn't talk much about or celebrate the war, focusing instead on that which made him much happier: his wife, Pat, and his four sons.

I decided to retire from "Doing the Bottles."

HELP!!!

After many years of tireless effort, Phil Crossman is retiring from collecting returnables in the parking lot and taking them to the Ivan Calderwood Homestead for sorting. This is where YOU come in. We need people to be willing to take one day a week (or if there are enough of you, every two weeks) to do this for us. If you'll only be available at certain times of the year, we can still use you. This is a very important fund-raising effort for Eldercare Services and helps support Meals on Wheels, Medic Alert phones, Transportation for Elders, and the Homestead. Please consider helping us in this endeavor.

OBSERVATIONS

I was prompted, by the occasion of conspicuous anniversaries involving two brothers, to compose a tribute.

> For as long as I can remember there have been Conways. When I was a kid, Max and Eleanor lived just down the drive from my great-grandmother, and each paid a great deal of attention to me. Eleanor made a fuss over me and my little brother, and Max teased us playfully (but then, who wouldn't tease Dick?). Max worked for my dad for a while. Much later, in her eighties, Eleanor asked for a ride on my motorcycle. She climbed on back, and I drove her downtown. When I was about twelve years old my mother suggested I start earning my own money, that I present myself at the (old) ferry terminal with a sign around my neck offering to carry folk's luggage for fifty cents. Herb suggested I'd found my calling and that this was probably as good as it was going to get for me. Right after I got out of the service Harry Conway, stocking shelves at Brad Carver's store, blessed me with the funniest observation I've ever heard but which will not appear here. Twenty or thirty years ago I stumbled on a small house fire just as the whistle blew. The cause was a clothes dryer and the ball of lint at the back was still on fire. I unplugged it and carried it toward the door. Clarence, having responded to the call, met me there and made it quite clear that I had no business carrying around flaming dryers if I was not a fireman. Last week there was a big celebration of over 120 years of devotion as our two senior Conways celebrated their long-lasting marriages. I had an infectious cold and didn't attend because for as long as I can remember there have been Conways, to our great benefit, and I didn't want to be responsible for their extinction.

Henceforth, pretty regularly, I could be relied upon to write a little something about my grandson.

> My grandson is even cuter now than he was a month ago when he was even cuter than he was a month before that, and, not surprisingly, the ladies are beginning to take notice. Olivia Philbrook is a good example, although by no means the only one. Olivia is already walking about, albeit while holding onto things to keep her balance. Although, at ten months or so, she is nearly twice as old as Finn she is not shy about bucking the common trend and pursuing a younger man. Finn is advancing toward mobility and maturity at his own considered pace and so has just consented to assuming a sitting position at the end of the couch. We refer to this as his contemplative mode within which he leans back and surveys his surroundings and those in attendance expansively. The other day he was at a party, as was Olivia, and it seemed plain that she'd been waiting for this moment. She went to great pains to impress him with some of her moves. As Finn sat contemplatively, she moved gracefully around the room from chair to table to chair, stopping long enough at each juncture to gaze beguilingly over her shoulder at him to be sure she held his attention. She needn't have concerned herself. He's talked of nothing else.

That really annoying commercial that stars the guy climbing off the tractor and heading home with a knowing smile on his face accompanied by the conquering strains of "The William Tell Overture" or something similarly and singularly overwhelming worried me.

> At a birthday party a few days ago, it was needlessly observed by one of those in attendance that we were a gathering of some of the oldest people in town. What a downer! How can that be? As I reflected on some of the conversations I'd taken part in that night I came reluctantly to the realization that most of them illuminated that sobering truth. There were other parties around town, probably at that very moment where those gathered were a generation, two generations, even three generations

younger than some of us in attendance, and that the topics of conversation at those gatherings were probably not living wills, exercise regimens, organ donations, aches and pains, and male enhancement remedies. While talk of how to construct a will that will leave our descendants fairly provided for, or what sort of exercise we can still engage in, or the good feeling we will get just before we die knowing that, because we've bequeathed one worn organ or another, someone else might live may be dull, the latter — the male enhancement thing — is just plain worrisome. The ads accompany every one of the infrequent ballgames I watch on TV, and I watch fewer and fewer precisely because they are so troublesome. It's not the promised results that frighten me; those are kind of exciting. It's the side effects, the likelihood that at any moment we may find someone experiencing those tangential symptoms loose and unrestrained among us. The side effects described and cautioned against include blindness, loss of memory, upset stomach, a false sense of increased energy, and a certain alarmingly sustained condition. I am troubled at the prospect of encountering someone under the influence of bath salts, of course, but having a man loose among us who is experiencing the promised results but who is having trouble finding closure, as it were, has perhaps forgotten who he's enamored of, has an upset tummy, is full of energy and is blind is equally alarming.

Fred Granger got a notion he'd build a tower. I believe he will.

Fred's Tower

Posing naked for the cover of *Away Happens* (and anyone else who asks) is not Fred's only fixation. He's also obsessed with stone, and for as long as he's been a presence here in our community Fred has had a dream to build a stone tower. And not just a pile of rocks, either. Fred's dream is of a tower fourteen feet in diameter and thirty feet high. He figures it will take ten years to build. That dream has been a constant in his life. First he asked to build it on Armbrust Hill, which would have been magnificent. Perched up there where our great grandparents kept watch for enemy subs, visible from miles out to sea. But, as it turned out, Betty Roberts, when she bequeathed the Hill to the town, stipulated that it be free of structures. If she could see what Fred had in mind she'd probably feel differently, but her extraordinary gift carried that restriction and that's all there is to it. Fred then went to the American Legion and asked to build it on Smith Point (Grimes Park) and dedicate it to our own island veterans, but after one thing or another, the path of the municipal sewer discharge pipe for example, that fell through. Now Fred has secured permission to build it on land now belonging to Dana Peterson and has already begun work. This is really an epic undertaking, one he again proposes be a monument to our fallen warriors.

Another young local woman published an extraordinary thank-you for community support during a struggle with substance abuse.

Happy Holidays and a Happy New Year, Vinalhaven!

The past couple of months have been a whirlwind for me— life-changing. I am truly blessed to have supporting family and friends in my life. Without them I would not be becoming the person I am today.

I have THANK-YOUS that need to be addressed. On January 14, 2012, Jennifer Desmond came to my rescue and helped me make the right decision. Thank you to the ferry crew for getting me safely to the other side. Thank you to Jim Hopkins and Jeff Aronson for riding with me in the ambulance and for getting me to Pen Bay. Thank you to Stephanie Mills for loving Hunter enough to make her a permanent part of her family…and thank you Bob and Lois Candage for all your love and support.

All my life I've always wondered what I would say if the opportunity ever arose to put a THANK-YOU in the *Wind*— everyone always saying how grateful they were to our community. So knowing it's been said about a billion times, I am truly thankful for being part of such a wonderful, strong, supportive, loving community. It truly touched my heart to hear all the supportive and encouraging words. Being separated from the island has been a big challenge for me— an emotional rollercoaster with many twists, turns, and even a few loops, but I have met a lot of amazing people in AA who have helped me understand the how, what, and who when continuing questions of day-to-day sobriety come to me. My aunt has played the BIGGEST role in my recovery, teaching me everyday lessons of life.

I want to set the record straight for any rumors that are still floating around. I am not ashamed. I was taken over in January for becoming seriously depressed. Alcohol, even in my youngster days, has always been a problem for me. I hid it well, and for many of you, I didn't. After my surgery last February, my stomach became the size of an egg. The doctors told me I would feel the effects of alcohol sooner. Boy, did I ever! I was told to avoid it completely because it was just empty calories. But did I follow that advice? Of course I didn't!! Me?? Give up my best friend?? Never!!

My closest friends had always been aware of my drinking habits but became concerned when I didn't want to interact with other people any more. I would rather be home, isolated with my six-pack.

I survived detox, where I finally admitted to myself that I was an alcoholic. I am now waiting for my bed at Crossroads for Women on a scholarship. While waiting, I am going to mental health counseling and to a substance abuse counselor. To whomever this concerns, I just wanted to let you all know that I am getting the help that I need and turning my life around. Thank you, Taylor and Alex, for being there that night; I don't know where I'd be right now if it wasn't for you two. Thank you to my Co-op family for always having my back. Thank you to everyone that came to visit me in detox and to my mom for respecting my wishes, I love you.

All my love, Kirsten Barton

The *Wind* published a poem I had written years earlier when Owen Webster's name was added to the Vietnam War Memorial, and another of the veterans' bios featured our own legendary Dr. Earle.

>The Outer Bell
>(A Ferry's random perspective over the years)
>
>A cocky young man from away that one of our girls
>has brought home
>strikes a jaunty pose on the bow and, shielding her from the headwind,
>pretends at an ease he doesn't really feel.
>I waltz them by the Outer Bell.

2012

One of our old women, widowed an eternity ago
and leaving behind a simple aging son
has ventured into oblivion.
She's tucked away in the ambulance, beneath the pilot house
where she'll be less frightened,
as I ease her by the Bell toward terminal convalescence.

One of our families has packed its numbers
and generations into a van
laid catercorner on the bow.
I bring them close to port of the Bell
and one of them tosses an English muffin
to the gull perched there.

A young man has emerged from a minimally responsive state
Not the land most of us emerge from —
eventually,
but the other kind, from whence emergence is miraculous. He's just below
with his folks. There's not a breath so the Bell is quiet
but the town will not be.

Three of our boys, newly graduated, assume their
macho station on the stern.
Newly enlisted and off to kick some Viet Cong butt,
they sail by the similarly teetering Bell
and roar about approaching oriental women sideways.

Our curmudgeon rambles down the ramp coming home.
He's got a first grandchild.
A puppy sticks its nose out of his vest.
I rock the Bell to cue the puppy to piss itself,
still in his vest.

Another of our young men watches the Bell emerge from
the spotty low fog.
The sun struggles to lift his apprehension.
I'd lived half a lifetime when first he passed the
Bell a newborn,
And now chemotherapy is an hour away.

Today we're hunkered down — vulnerable,
appointments cancelled, weddings unattended.
lights missed, no mail.
Today I can't do anything for anyone
but the Bell weathers what we cannot.

Laid toward horizontal, it bobs back endlessly, mindlessly,
attracting my attention
but I'm not coming.

Our latest minister's on board, leaving instead of dying in office.
This one did well.
He gave God a good name.
He wore at our resistance.
The Bell nods respectfully.

My heart nearly feels the anguish that must fill a
car below.
After years of immunity the world has seen its slight and given us a War
Mother.
Gazing at the Bell, her mind is elsewhere.
Tomorrow his name will be added to the interminable
litany of the Vietnam Memorial.

It's unnatural but the fog demands I not try to see
where I'm going.
Through it I bring happiness and heartache.
Winds defy my passage
and against them I carry sustenance and affliction.
Wisdom and foolishness ride with me
But by the Outer Bell I bring life with the regularity
of a heartbeat.

Dr. Earle Enlists

Dr. Ralph P. Earle of Vinalhaven, who enlisted August 1 in the Medical Corps, with the rating of 1st Lieutenant, left Sunday for his home in Philadelphia before going to Morrison Field, West Palm Beach, Florida. His many friends in Vinalhaven are wishing him success in his new activities and looking forward to his return. Dr. Earle graduated from Hahnemann Medical College in June, the youngest man ever to graduate from there. His pre-medical work was done at the University of Pennsylvania, where he completed the four years' course in two years. He was permitted to do this because of his high scholastic standing at Friends Central School where he spent the last six years of his pre-college work. Dr. Earle interned at Hahnemann Hospital at Worcester, Massachusetts. From the earliest years of his study he counted on practicing among his friends on the island of Vinalhaven, which he always referred to as the "Enchanted Isle." His dream came true in 1937, and for five years he has faithfully served the people of this island, making no distinction between rich or poor; all were to him human beings to be healed. He was much interested in the young people of Vinalhaven and through his efforts a Community Hall and a Credit Union were established. (From the *Courier Gazette* Sept. 6, 1942)

Jessie Grant proved that *Aladdin* was no fluke. *Annie Get Your Gun* was even better.

No matter how small I make the font I won't be able to do justice to every one—on and off the stage—who made *Annie Get Your Gun* such a success. I'll begin at the top, though. Bill Chilles and Caroline Augusto have always been among our most enjoyable entertainers. We've come to expect great things and were not disappointed. Bill just sings beautifully. He could be a Blank if he were more agreeable. I can't imagine there was much left of Rachel Noyes after this consuming production. She was the consummate shameless bimbo, and the amount of energy that part consumed left me exhausted. Francis Warren is a big guy, which is a good thing. Chief Sitting Bull couldn't stow that much irony in a svelte frame. Ellie and Trey were adorable and beguiling as the unabashedly smitten young couple. Sarah Crossman, well, what can I say — I am resisting taking any responsibility, determined to let her stand on her own laurels. The two Indian maidens, Alex and Blake, were perfect, beautiful and mischievous. Finally, and it hurts me to acknowledge it, Jeff Aronson was also very good and never out of character. On the other hand, when was he ever? This was such an entertaining production, and there was so much going on behind the scenes that contributed to its success. The costumes, in particular, were perfectly extravagant, and what more could so many women and girls ask for than the opportunity to continually change their outfits. The set was simple but elegant and, as always, largely Bill's and Rhoda's creation. The music was great, as was lighting and sound and all the other elements that help make a production like this a success. Jessie Grant continues to amaze and bring to this community so much pleasure. Finally, where would any of these shows be without Theo Brown? He's accompanying Charlie on drums, then cymbals, then a horn, then sound effects. He's everywhere and does everything.

Cork 'n' Crow, a fun little tapas bar, opened at Island Spirits, a joint undertaking of mine and my accommodating landlords, Sue and Josef L'Africain. It was great fun and lost less money than either of my other restaurant efforts. I thought that was encouraging, but I was in the minority. On February 10 we intended to host a martini tasting but on the appointed day, Martini Master Geno Lazaro found himself incapacitated.

Martini Tasting

Do you enjoy a good martini? Even though, because at some desolate period in your youth, someone refused you a dill pickle and so you now find it necessary to diminish your martini and have become an olive-chomping barbarian, and even though you may bastardize yours with chocolate or nectar, even though you may be a fruity-cocktail-sipping heathen who shields yourself from propriety with a little umbrella perched on the side of your glass, even though you may labor under the misconception that a martini can be made with vodka, even though you may sully yours with sweet vermouth and even though you may not have read DeVoto's *The Hour*, you are nonetheless invited to join Martini Master Geno Lazaro and other disciples at the Gathering Place on Friday, February 10 during the sacred and velvet hours between 5 and 7 p.m. Bring your own or enjoy ours. Modest contributions to defray costs are welcome.

A memorable Valentine's Day came to mind at the appointed time.

A few years back on Valentine's Day, my daughter came home in the afternoon, having attended the Mid Coast Health Association's annual pre-puberty (referred to by the attendees as Pre-Pooh) class in our school gym. The actual puberty class would take place a couple of years later. The speaker had addressed the assembled eight- and nine-year-old boys and girls and was clinically democratic in sharing freely with both groups information that in another time, mine for example, might not have been imparted till later and which certainly would have been somewhat more targeted. The weighty nature of the material, intimate details of which were interjected dispassionately into the lives of these young girls and young boys, each of whom had heretofore been quite speculative and free-form as they considered one another, was sobering, and left my daughter unusually thoughtful and quiet. She lingered with mom long enough to satisfy herself, through some circumspect questioning, that everything she'd heard was true, then retreated to her room to think about whether to bring her dad, the often uninformed and more often unenlightened, up to speed. Ever charitable and optimistic, she decided I was worth saving, and when I came home later in the day, she asked if we could talk. Our eight years together had left her with a quite firmly held opinion that, while I was a loving dad, I was largely unaware on many levels, and this business of things biological or sexual was likely one of those deficient areas. She apparently felt my role in her own creation had been incidental, perhaps even accidental, but would, without question, have been improved had I attended Pre-Pooh Class. Fortunately for me, I had her, and she had happily concluded that it was not too late for me to enjoy a measure of contentment in the time I had left. I'm a better man as a result.

Tuesday morning is the deadline for submitting things to the *Wind*. Now and then Tuesday morning creeps up on me without my having noticed and I find myself with nothing to write about. Often the government provides an out. This week in February was certainly no exception.

Every now and then, infrequently, I have to think hard about what to put in this column. Not this week. The Army Corps of Engineers came to town. Last time they were here we got the Boondoggle Bridge. This time they came to do a hydrographic survey of the harbor, an exercise they undertake now and then to see if the water depths or bottom contours are changing. In command of a 33' Sea Ark, a boat made in Arkansas (where we all go to buy a boat), they were to undertake a back and forth sweep of the harbor, moving along at about one knot. The boat had twin 200-hp Yamahas which most observers felt would get them around the harbor in safety. It would also, of course, have carried them across the bay easily enough and in short order. For that matter, with that kind of power, they might have come all the way from Arkansas even if they had to forge their own waterway. Instead, though, they came by ferry, towing the boat with a big pickup. I asked about this and got a memorable answer, honestly and unashamedly delivered by the lead man (there were three and each had to have his own room). It seems that not long ago an employee of the Corps caused his boat, a similar craft, to sink in open water while on official business. The man was rescued but the boat was not and so the Corps did what any sensible organization whose business had primarily to do with open water would have done. They forbade any further open water navigation and instead restricted all their 400-hp Sea Arks to protected coves and other sheltered areas. They completed their work in three days, but then space couldn't be found for them to return on the ferry, so they all came back the next week to return their warship at a time when there was less traffic. It's hard to argue with that sort of decision-making, though, when the desired results have been so plainly achieved. The Corps has suffered no subsequent losses in open water.

Is the United States broken? The disparity between those who are comfortable and those who are desperate, including many here in Maine, languishes as the gap widens. Congress, however, is content to regard every day that passes without revolt as a good day and hope for another to follow. Unsustainability, so plain down at the level where the desperate among us feel the results with bitter clarity, appears not be clear at all to lawmakers. When we, the unsophisticated, voice concerns about our national debt, we are cautioned that economics on that level is different from what we deal with in our mundane lives and quite beyond our pedestrian understanding. Baloney!

Our multi-trillion debt, growing by billions every day, is a terminal condition that will soon overwhelm us just as surely as it has those Mainers who have gone under because debt exceeded income. America is broken because, on one hand, higher taxes, which can only be assessed on those who have it to give, need to be half of the solution. On the other hand, spending cuts need to be the other half of the solution and they can only be made in areas where cuts will not spell despair. Unhappily, compromise, like representation nowadays, is dead on arrival. Money drives everything. Legislation is the product of paid persuasion or privileged foreknowledge and is crafted by folks, in and out of Congress, who are not beholden to us but who are personally invested in the outcome. Money ensures an earmark from which sponsors will profit or drives insider trading or is just pocketed as a bribe. Wealth for these few exists now in such vast quantities that those surrounded by it are insulated from the lives of the rest of us who, squeezed hard, coughed it up. I was advised by someone who read this beforehand, if I didn't like it here I should go elsewhere. How shortsighted. Where else could I rant so freely?

A geology class from Brown University was now and then brought to the island and stayed at the Tidewater and they always seemed to enjoy themselves. This year they were nearly all girls and most — eighteen or so — slept in sleeping bags in the Gathering Place. Their instructor delivered a little lecture and I attended.

My mother was born here. My grandmother was born here. My great-grandmother was born here. My great-great-grandmother was born here, and so were my other greats all the way back to my grandfather who moved here from England over two hundred years ago. But 680 million years before my first ancestor put in an appearance, other things were moving, too. Antarctica, for example, which had been kind of a nomadic landmass, had taken up residence nearby, just on the far side of Isle au Haut. For that matter, Siberia was tucked in comfortably under California's wing and the Belgian Congo was just above Newfoundland. This was a long time ago, even farther back than, like, Addison Ames can remember. I learned all this from a geology group from Brown University that was visiting last week. Eventually, unimaginable subterranean turmoil squeezed this continent so hard that one big stretch of land, having nowhere else to go, erupted to create the Appalachian Mountains and the Green Mountains of Vermont. Siberia was pushed up to attach itself to Russia, the Congo across a great rift to Africa, and the Antarctic was dispatched to its present location. This explains not only why it's always colder on the East side, but also why there are no longer penguins on Isle au Haut (or short ones for that matter).

Historic Downstreet, Inc. agreed to take on restoration of the Old Engine House, an important artifact built in 1888 to house our first fire company and to which the town had recently acquired clear title. From mid-2012 onward until we finished on the Fourth of July the following year, the Old Engine House was either the subject of my "Observer" column or was a column of its own, the intent being to keep the project in the public eye of those on whom we were dependent for contributions.

OBSERVATIONS

In anticipation of a new steam fire engine, the Old Fire Hall was built in 1888 on land donated by Reuben Carver. The suggestion that the town fork out $3,200, about $100,000 in today's money, had been hard for some to swallow, not only the cost, but because our men lacked the experience of running such a machine. Still, communal memory of the sprawling Granite Hotel having recently burned to the ground persuaded even the doubters that the island had to take this big step. Just a few days before the shiny contraption arrived the final nail was driven and the Fire House stood ready for its new occupant. The new engine was christened the Reuben Carver in honor of its benefactor. For years Old Reuben and the Fire Hall served the town well and the fledgling fire department proved more than capable. Today the Vinalhaven Fire Department is comfortably installed in a new fire house, but the forlorn Old Fire Hall, still housing Old Reuben, is badly in need of loving care. Historic Downstreet, Inc., a nonprofit organization formed here in Vinalhaven a year ago and now with 122 members, has agreed to work with the town and Historical Society to accomplish the restoration of this important historic artifact. Look for continuing updates in the *Wind* and for information on how to join this effort.

Marty Stein, one of our members and the person responsible for designing the library addition and the New Era Gallery building, has agreed to take on restoration of the Old Engine House. Marty has been provided with historic photos and other specifics of the building and will prepare plans and drawings based on last week's building inspection. Clarence Conway has joined our committee as a representative of the Fire Company, and a representative from the Historical Society will soon round out our committee at nine members, an optimum number and one that represents a cross section of the community and, in particular, the two other organizations most concerned with this exciting project. Historic Downstreet, Inc. represents over a hundred year-round and seasonal residents concerned with preserving what's left of our old downtown area. If you are not already a member but share our interests we invite you to join us. Although we are not presently soliciting contributions of time and money for the Old Engine House project, folks are stepping forward with both and we are grateful for that support. Historic Downstreet, Inc., POB 209, 04863.

Phil Crossman, Josef and Sue L'Africain, Ken White, Kris Davidson, Bill Alcorn, Christa Mattson, Clarence Conway

---

Finn and I had taken to strolling down Carver Street to visit an old friend with Lou Gehrig's disease. They both got quite a kick out of the visits.

My grandson, Finn, is eight months old, and every few days I take him on a little walk down to Carver's Pond for a visit with Marion and Brud Carver and with Brud's caregivers. Finn loves these visits because as soon as he shows up, Lainie or Jamie or Julie or Stephanie, or whoever is on duty, gathers him up to her bosom and makes a great fuss over him. He plays it for all he's worth, clearly relishing the ease with which these grown ladies can be reduced to infantile gurgling or noisemaking. Brud, sitting at the kitchen table where he's been surveying Carver's Pond, his domain for as long as I can remember, waits patiently. Eventually Finn loses interest in the hugs, kisses (that will change), and baby talk and turns his attention to Marion and Brud. He's had enough cuddling. Pointing and reaching, he makes it clear he wants to engage with them. I sit him on the kitchen table across

> from Brud and they begin what has become their customary exchange. Brud hoots and whistles his repertoire of animal noises and bird calls and Finn, mesmerized, hoots and babbles in return. Every now and then Marion points to her husband and says, "Finn, that's Brud; can you say Brud?" Finn gives her a long-suffering glance that says unmistakably, "You told me that already."
>
> We've been leaning on Finn recently, urging him to speak his first word—"Mommy," "Daddy," "Grammy," "Grandpa," maybe "Ron Paul"— so imagine our surprise when, returning with me from a walk, he responded unexpectedly to a little baby talk from his mother. I brought him into the house and began taking off his coat and hat. His mom knelt down and gave him a little tickle under the chin and asked, "Where've you been, big boy?" "Brud Carver," he responded matter-of-factly. While those weren't what we expected would be his first words and while he neglected to correctly employ the possessive tense, we were nonetheless quite impressed.

Memorial Day usually puts me in a bad frame of mind. This year was no exception, but I decided to publish this column well in advance of that occasion so as not to unduly distress those to whom waving the flag meant more than it did to me.

> We are wasting lives, throwing them and the hopes and dreams of those who loved them away like trash. When my dad left for the war, the country had a sense of purpose. When he came back, that purpose was even stronger. There'd been no question about why we'd gone to war or of whether we'd achieved victory. The questions began soon enough, though, first with the Korean War, certainly with the Vietnam debacle and the really dumb police actions that followed, and now, in the longest war of our history, there's nothing but questions. Lives are not lost for cause; they are wasted, expended like so much ammunition.
>
> In 1944, the appearance of two crisp military men at the door, hats in hand, purpose unmistakable, was devastating. Grief, adorned but unadulterated, had arrived. Although they, with the toughest of assignments, were sworn to convey otherwise, anguish that passeth all understanding had come to settle in for the long haul, had come to substitute itself for the companionship that would otherwise have been a loved and loving human being. They dressed their condolences in the flag of patriotism, reminding the survivors that death had come in defense of our people and our flag and, in small measure, it had. In larger measure it hadn't really, but it at least came in defense of people somewhere and did have a clear purpose. Today the same scenario plays out when the shiny Department of Defense car pulls up, but the well-rehearsed condolences don't ring with that tiny consolation that once accompanied them. Instead, they fall like dead weights. If truth were told they'd say, "I'm sorry to inform you that your son has been killed in action. Not for any particular reason, but the President nonetheless asks that you accept the condolences of a grateful nation."

The Vinalhaven Alumni Association was expected to host its ninety-sixth annual Alumni Banquet. It would have been the fiftieth anniversary of my graduation from high school. Alas, the Alumni Association had run out of steam. Fewer people were offering to help and the burden of putting this rather demanding occasion together fell on the shoulders of just a few people. They called it off.

> A friend who is working on the *Exile* this year said she discovered evidence that I had graduated fifty years ago this June. That was distressing and I'm sure she was mistaken, but I was even more

troubled to find that she passed up the opportunity to say something like, "Judging from your youthful appearance, I don't see how that can possibly be true." Although I do acknowledge the numbers of my remaining classmates are dwindling and some of those who remain are beginning to look different, I cannot get my mind wrapped around fifty — or anything close to fifty — years having passed since I was born, let alone since I graduated. I couldn't comprehend it when she mistakenly suggested such a thing and I still can't. I don't understand how the passage of that much time can go unnoticed. I've seen other lives run their course and expire but never seriously thought mine would be among them. It's always been problematic for me to think about the past, particularly my past, in any context, because I just have a hard time thinking of any part of my life, especially the rest of it, as gone, as a memory. Some part of my brain (most of it) clings to the notion that I, unlike (nearly) everyone else, will enjoy eternity. I hang on to that conviction, even though I have been told by those whose opinions I value that those of you who are put off by the prospect of my never leaving needn't concern yourselves. Still, in spite of that counsel, I have not even reconciled myself to aging, let alone death. If a basket ever appears with my name on it in the Paper Store I'm sure it will only say "pending."

Singin' in the Rain was a dazzling show, another Jessie Grant production.

I want to go back fifty years and I want Jessie Grant to go with me. For that matter I'd like to have anyone who had anything to do with *Singin' in the Rain* to go back with me. I want to go back to high school and have a good time, to enjoy myself, to have something besides basketball to get excited about, to be unabashed about being excited, to know most of my peers feel the same way and will respond enthusiastically if I ask them to go tap dancing.

During last weekend's performance I kept trying to take notes about this kid's or that kid's performance or about the set or costumes or music but I didn't produce a single legible observation except an oft-repeated "wow" that spoke not only to individual performances but more often to the undisguised and relentless enthusiasm that drove this performance. I shudder to think what would have happened fifty years ago if someone had suggested I and my peers should even go on stage, never mind tap dance together. Nine or ten years ago the school included a K-12 drama program in the school's curriculum and Partners in Island Education undertook raising money so the Smith Hokanson Auditorium and expanded library could be a part of the new school then under construction. Since then we've seen smaller versions of, for example, Trey, the Reidy girls, Francis, Alex, Izza, and others on stage, enjoyed productions like *Alice in Wonderland* and *The Wizard of Oz*, and have had the satisfaction of watching these folks develop into confident young adults, their infectious enthusiasm having grown exponentially. A native about my age told me recently he, too, wished he'd had the opportunities theater has provided these kids for developing confidence, maturity, comfort with one's own self, and a willingness to employ wild abandon to such effect. Thanks to PIE and the theatrical pioneers who have driven our island's community theater to this extraordinary level.

It was spring and the Class of 2029 and their mothers took the opportunity of a nice day to have a picnic on Lane's Island.

The Class of 2029 got together at Lane's Island last weekend for another of their regular confabs. The group has stayed in regular contact since the first two of them put in an appearance about a year ago. For a while and with each new arrival the topic of conversation was the degree of difficulty each underwent in getting here in the first place. These were the "exit strategy" talks, a topic they each had in common and one which, because they'd had so little control, consumed them for the first few months after the last arrival. As their numbers grew and the miraculous novelty of those individual experiences ebbed, they turned to the need to regain the control they'd lost during birth. Toward this end they shared freely their own accomplishments and the degree to which those achievements allowed them greater opportunity to maneuver their parents. That the behavior of the adults in their lives could be so readily modified by the simplest little things did not escape this astute bunch for long. Smiling and laughing responsively, they all agreed, had produced great results early on: mobility was a real crowd-pleaser, and the boys in particular were impressed with the effects of peeing while being changed. Quickly dispensing with the difficult topic that had consumed their parents, grandparents, and generations before them, they pronounced themselves to be natives and went on to elect class officers.

Ever gracious, the Gentlemen's Book Club invited the Ladies' Book Group to our June meeting. We would do so again in 2013 and, as long as they behave themselves and try to pay attention, we intend to continue that egalitarian gesture.

The Gentlemen's Book Group has consented to a suggestion from one of our liberal members that we invite the Ladies' Book Club to join us at an upcoming meeting and toward that end has invited Phil Conkling, author of *Islands in Time*, to join us on June 6 at Ted's Den of Inequity which, for this special occasion, will become the Den of Egalitarianism. *Islands* was chosen because, while interesting and well-written, it's not over their heads, concerns itself with things colloquial rather than the broader subjects the men customarily consume, and has lots of nice pictures. While some voiced concerns that the ladies might find our customarily structured assembly intimidating — decorum, Robert's Rules, and such — the more magnanimous among us agreed to temper our regimen somewhat so the ladies will feel at home. We are braced to allow freewheeling discussion. Our usual menu, faithfully relating to the subject of whatever book we have chosen — most often animals that can be eaten — will undergo a similar accommodation. *Islands in Time* suggests a less virile *carte du jour,* and our customary habit of alternating each bite with a bracing beverage will likewise succumb to moderation: prepare to be satisied with a modest glass or two (half-full) of wine with dinner, no spitting, and cigars confined to the patio.

As was prophesied, the members of the Ladies' Discussion Group, in having undertaken to learn to read at a secret gathering a few years ago at the Palace of Marthradite, did bring and continue to bring dishonor upon themselves. This opprobrium will be compounded next month when they allow themselves to convene in decadent splendor at the sacred domain of the Sultanate of Leo's Lane where, by their compelling presence, they will understandably compel men to deliver forth drinks and goodies to them which they will likely enjoy, probably uncovered, with undisguised gusto. Further, they will cause men, the humble but flawed servants of God, whose hearts and minds would otherwise surely be directed to the Almighty, to gaze upon them with relish and other condiments. Let it be known, therefore, that a fatwa is declared upon them, and the faithful are free, encouraged even, to heap ridicule upon them, and to require them to retreat to their homes, their men, and

OBSERVATIONS

their other God-given responsibilities, and the faithful must further forgive the noble but otherwise susceptible men for having unadvisedly tended out on them, and they are to seek penance for having strayed, as they surely will, from pure thoughts and to give themselves over to the undistracted study of stuff like Scripture and the *Islands of Time* that is their usual fare.

A delegation of photography and poetry students from DePauw University visited the island and, after a week or so, presented a program of their achievements: photographic and written compositions of Vinalhaven.

A contemporary, a woman, had some dated advice to offer. It reminded me of my trip south a few years earlier when I misjudged my capacity for wowing the girls and for much else, as well.

> Not long ago a friend learned that her teenaged granddaughter was going to the Caribbean and offered helpfully, "You know, I still have a pair of thongs. You take them with you." "You know, Gram," responded the girl, "I think thongs meant something different when you were a kid; I think they were flip-flops, but if you're really offering me your, like, underwear, I think I'll pass." I thought of that today while lying here on the sand in Florida. There are plenty of thongs, both kinds, passing by, and, although I am splayed out here on my towel, long and lean and white (me, not the towel), I am attracting remarkably little attention from any of them. I allowed Elaine to rub sunblock on my back — even though sunblock is for sissies — before arranging myself appealingly on my tummy and promising to eventually apply it myself to my front. After she went inside for something I rolled over onto my back and stretched out, without the promised sunscreen, for the benefit of passersby who might otherwise have been put off by my varicose veins, which are not so evident from the front. Before long the effort of sucking in my tummy each time I detected a little thong (sorry) of likely admirers coming my way tired me, and I apparently fell asleep. Much later, Elaine having lost herself elsewhere in a book (or perhaps just sitting nearby amused), a thoughtful passerby woke me gently to suggest I might want to change positions, not only because the many noises I'd been making were alarming others but because the consensus among my sunbathing neighbors was that I was nearly done.

In keeping with our efforts to keep the Old Engine House and its ongoing restoration in the public eye, I wrote about the history of the building.

> Vinalhaven's first fire company was formed in 1870 shortly after the purchase of an "old hand tub," named the Lion. More men stepped forward than the company could accommodate so a second fire company was formed. They purchased their own hand engine, the Ellsworth. There was much rivalry between the two and competitions were common. The Ellsworth usually prevailed but neither could really meet Vinalhaven's needs. In 1872, E.P. Walker, a founder of the Bodwell Granite Company, obtained a ten-inch stroke Jeffers hand engine, dubbed the E.P. Walker, from a Brooklyn, New York fire company as partial payment for granite supplied for the Brooklyn Bridge. The E.P. Walker was used in Vinalhaven for many years but was eventually sold, leaving the town without firefighting equipment for ten years. In 1886 the Granite Hotel burned to the ground. The old Ellsworth failed to be of any use in fighting the blaze. The decision was made to purchase a steam engine for $3,200 from the Silsby Manufacturing Company, of Seneca, New York. Just days before her arrival, an engine house was completed on Main Street, the land having been donated by Capt. Reuben Carver. For decades Old Reuben and other firefighting equipment of

that era have languished in storage. Join us as the town undertakes the salvation of the Old Engine House and its creation as display area for the town's firefighting equipment and history.

The Engine House Committee

ICMS was awarded its second Federally Qualified Health Center grant, a five-year award that would cover about one-sixth of the medical center's operating costs.

I'd again seen too many alarming issues of *Vogue* and the like.

> I've been having more nightmares about frightening women recently. They've been triggered by the images in the fashion section of the *New York Times* and in magazines like *Vogue*. The nightmares take several forms. In one, several of these angry women, the ones who wear the scary "make my day" expressions, are attracted to me, and I'm compelled to do their bidding. It's a terrifying dream, one that leaves me in a cold sweat of unfulfilled expectations. In another, one in particular, the same paralyzing vision appears again and again. She's wearing a piece of purple fabric that's been fashioned to leave the left leg entirely bare, but the right completely enclosed in a single skirt of its own that envelops the entire appendage all the way to the ground. The fabric that might otherwise have accommodated the left leg appears to have manifest itself in a baggy explosion from around the left side of her mid-section, and emerging from that baggy and functionless accumulation is a bird's beak, yellow and gaping. She has a huge orange hat on, one with long pointed quills sticking out of it in all directions. There's been some sort of catastrophe — humans, except for us, wiped out — and it has fallen to her and me to ensure the continuation of the species. I am fearful and sad, and her expression does not say, "Come to Me, My Melancholy Baby."

A friend owns a spectacular piece of property up on Coomb's Neck. It overlooks the Eastern Bay and Isle au Haut. I recalled how, the year before, Elaine and I had parked here precisely to watch the rising full moon of perigee-syzygy.

> The moon always goes to Isle au Haut first. Although it's never the other way around it's no less dramatic when it gets here. In March of last year, during the phenomenon known as perigee-syzygy, we parked on the hill at Lamont's to gaze out at that favored island and wait for the supermoon. Only 222,000 miles away and closer to the earth than at any time since 1993, the moon was forecast to rise at a specific time, but, of course, that meant over the horizon— Isle au Haut's horizon. It wouldn't appear to us till Isle au Haut had enjoyed some time alone with it. About five minutes after the predicted moment a radiance backlit that island's forested profile and created an ever brightening crescent above that island's modest Mount Champlain (540') and a crescendo of anticipation as it got brighter and brighter until finally, after five minutes or so, it peaked over the island and, after another five minutes, was fully aloft and moving our way. There was a smattering of appreciative applause from others who'd gathered unnoticed till then. Last week was nearly as dramatic. The moon was in super mode again, only a few miles farther away than in March and, again, we parked on Coombs Hill and waited. It was worth the wait, but the few miles farther away made a difference. There was no corresponding crescent of light. Isle au Haut remained dark, enjoying its few minutes alone with the moon but giving no indication that it was doing so and then suddenly, where we'd been gazing for some time at only three distinct lights in that island's little downtown area there suddenly appeared more, but up in the trees to the south. For a minute they looked like two or three

individual lights because the appearance of the top edge of the moon was interrupted by treetops. It wasn't till its upper arc had cleared the trees that we finally recognized it as the moon. Then it was clear sailing and another five minutes or so to clear the island and head our way.

Spring was here, time to revisit the Red Sox for as long as they can hold my interest. My cat helped.

> My cat finally digs the Red Sox. For years, eighteen years, in fact, she ignored them, pointedly left the room whenever a game was being broadcast. Now and then, when they were playing the Yankees, she'd make it a point to come in and glare at the TV or scowl at the radio, and invariably she'd cough up a hairball whenever Alex Rodriguez was up. Now she never misses a game. Historically she has found cat-like places, soft and cozy, in which to preen and be feline. Now tottering and arthritic, she views herself as an aging athlete, like Derek Jeter. Her favorite perch is a rickety and unstable old rocker (like Derek Jeter). She takes some comfort, I think, in knowing she can jump up onto such a thing and still stay upright, and it is from this unstable platform that she flings herself whenever she sees me settle in to watch a few innings. It's an entertaining prelude to the game. Seeing her dismount, not unlike watching someone jump from an untethered punt, is even more fun than watching her get up there in the first place. Once she recovers her composure she climbs up on the arm of the couch to enjoy the game. She clearly has favorites, turning her back on Kevin Youkilis when he's at bat (I don't think she likes his form) but loving him at third, and she's crazy about Dustin Pedroia. Regardless of whether he's in the field or at bat, if the camera is on him she is enthralled; he can do no wrong. At eighteen, she's getting up there. Her last few years have been largely lackluster, albeit there have been little bursts of activity or at least interest in activity. This week, though, when the Sox swept the Yankees on their own turf, she was euphoric. Last night, when they recovered from a 5-0 deficit to beat Baltimore she hopped around the den and, forgetting that she needs all four to stay upright, balled her paw into a fist and pumped it up and down over and over till she finally fell over and crashed into the coffee table. She was unfazed.

Finn is always a good topic for a column. One day in the fall his parents decided to take a big chance and leave him with us overnight.

> My grandson, Finn, is nearly a year old and for a while was exhibiting a disquieting inclination toward decidedly liberal positions on a number of topics. To my great relief, however, at dinner with Karol and Gigi the other night, he took issue with them both when KK began his predictable rant about Ronald Reagan. Finn stood his ground with each of them, not always easy because, while their arguments customarily have little particular merit, they are nonetheless relentless and leave little if any room (or air) for dissent. These dinners, long on logistics but historically short on strategy, are— excellent cuisine notwithstanding— nothing more than equally predictable political ambushes and, when a presumed neophyte can be found, merciless. To find my young grandson so capable of deflecting in some instances, debunking in others, the vacuous assertions about President Reagan's tenure is particularly gratifying. Later he regaled me with a blow-by-blow account of the debate and it was perfectly clear to me, as I know it must have been to them, they had chosen the wrong young person upon whom to spring one of their left-wing assaults. For one thing, he learned in one night what it took me years to realize, i.e., that it is nearly impossible for KK to maintain pace while chewing and how effective a reasonable parry and seriously furrowed brow can be.

2012

Last week we babysat overnight for the first time. Finn's parents went off-island for the night and, after much consternation and chewing of nails, I'm sure, left him with us. He came with instructions. The Finn Manifesto was a little more than four pages long and arrived several days in advance and with the admonition that we should read it again and again, talk of nothing else, really, until we knew its contents inside and out. An advance team arrived the day before we were to take possession (I think it was a U-Haul but wasn't really paying attention) with a high chair, bottle, sippy cup, lunchbox (in case he chose to go on a hike, or to work or school), snack food, changing table, diapers, liners, lotion, toothbrush, laundry bag, port-a-crib, dinosaur pj's, bedding, snuggle sheep, bathtub and tub toys, toothbrush, other toys, and street clothes. Our attention was then called to the role each of these played and to the advisability of consulting the Manifesto if we had other questions. On the big day, Finn was delivered to our house by Sabrena, his oft-sought caregiver, who reported that he had napped for seventy-three minutes. The Manifesto had alerted us to this report and set forth the formula for seeing that he got just the right amount of sleep each day. Accordingly, he having napped thirteen minutes longer than ideal, we were to put him to bed that night at 7:43. Finn played piano all afternoon (he's working on "Clare de Lune"), didn't wet himself as called for in the Manifesto, then joined us for chicken, pea, and gorgonzola risotto, accompanied me to the shower, went to bed, slept all night, and got up the next morning singing "Up a Lazy River." What's the big deal?

The Sidewalk Committee, of which I was a member, was charged with getting a sidewalk built from the downtown area to the ferry terminal and was running into all sorts of opposition.

The town's Sidewalk Committee has seized upon a novel way to fund construction of a safe and attractive pedestrian walkway from the ferry to the downtown area. The sidewalk will comprise several hundred five- or six-foot sections of concrete or granite, and we propose to offer the area under each of those slabs for the internment of individuals who contribute substantially to the project. For a significant donation one might choose from several options. For example, a generous donor might choose to (eventually) rest comfortably right there in a vault or an urn beneath the slab of his choice upon which will be an engraved plaque commemorating that person's life and accomplishments. Alternatively, one might choose to have a loved one interred, perhaps someone who, when alive, was found to be underfoot and so will have chosen to perpetuate that memory by keeping him or her forever thus. A thoughtful donor might even commission a slab and plaque in the name of someone they found troublesome in life, if for no other reason than to have the satisfaction of composing a suitable eulogy for the plaque and knowing his or her memory would be trod upon in perpetuity. A spiteful donor could walk their dog in the vicinity of a particular plaque, perhaps lingering, having trained the animal to conduct some of its business on the spot. The committee is confident of and enthusiastic about the entertainment value of walking over those hundreds of reminders of those gone on before, of the stories and merriment likely to ensue, and are hopeful that those resting thereunder in relative peace will have found it worthwhile.

A new exercise regimen had put in an appearance. It would soon be overtaken by Zumba, but for now it was all the rage.

OBSERVATIONS

> Some of the women in town are growing older and there have been a number of disquieting and unapologetic observances in recent weeks commemorating those troubling developments as if they were of no consequence and without a thought for the youthful men left, as it were, in their wake. Dance parties, food fests, some drinking, and, if not wild abandon, certainly very little temperance, all seeming to celebrate instead of rightfully mourn what would seem, were it not for appearances that certainly imply otherwise, lamentable decline. But appearances cannot be denied and were it not for one raucous affair after another calling unabashed (not that there were no bashes) attention to what ought to be a worrisome turn of events we would've never known nor even thought about the difference. At one of these events, for example, the ladies gave a respectable nod to Jai Ho, a dance requiring no small degree of coordination and energy and one that left their male companions relegated to the shadows where they might pretend there was something more interesting going on. I personally am a great Jai Ho fan and have decided to make a vigorous six-minute routine part of my early morning regimen. I don't suggest anyone join me. I need a lot of room and would rather not be slowed down by an apprentice.

A group of volunteers from VES built a collection facility to replace the more haphazard system that had been in place when I was "doing the bottles." It included several shallow shelves, each designated for a particular kind of container.

> I was in Japan in the early sixties and had occasion to spend a night or two in an exceedingly imaginative and economical lodging establishment. It was, essentially, what might today be characterized as a container vessel, albeit on dry land. The thing had hundreds of little berths on any of several floors. Each berth was about eight feet long by three or four feet wide and about four feet high. They were stacked one upon another three or four high, the upper ones accessed by a little ship's ladder, each serving six or eight berths, three or four on either side of the ladder. Each berth had a light, a radio with earphones, and a little storage cabinet on the inboard bulkhead. It was very similar to my bunk on the aircraft carrier to which I was assigned at the time but — typical of anything Japanese and contrasting with my own shipboard berth — much cleaner. I'm reminded of it, in a disquieting way, as I watch the evolving redemption center being built by Pat and Del directly beneath my own Tidewater Motel sign. It seems to invite the economy-minded visitor to climb into my own version of slide-aboard.

The great winter moth infestation began, as did quick lessons in tree banding to prevent the critters from ascending to the upper branches where they would destroy the leaves.

A trick announcement in the *Wind* fooled me into believing Torry was turning over the Haven to Bill and Dennis, prompting a startled response.

> Last week's notice that Torry was stepping down in favor of Dennis and Bill, who'd be taking over, was as scary an announcement as I think I've ever heard. The notion that the kind of perfection we've grown comfortable with and (clearly) complacent about would suffer the precipitous depreciation sure to result from such a transition was, to say the least, as sobering as it was frightening. Like so many others I took it seriously and actually stopped in to offer my tremulous gratitude and appreciation to Torry for having served us so extraordinarily well for so long. Nearly in tears at the thought of such big clumsy feet trying to fill those precise and particular shoes, the degree to which the same

analogy would surely translate to the quality of food and service we could expect loomed large and unappetizing. I tried not to imagine myself at dinner later this summer, squirming in anticipation and drowning my apprehension in Jack Daniels while I waited for whatever fright might emerge from the kitchen with those two at the helm. When Torry, having recognized my panic, told me it was all a joke, my relief at knowing she would remain in charge and those two would remain closeted in the pantry dispensing libations was palpable. Every now and then I publish something inappropriate, but not scary stuff. Scary stuff should not be allowed.

I'd had my own wine shop for nearly a decade by now and so hosted wine tastings regularly even though I knew next to nothing about wine. Still, I had folks who knew what they were doing actually pour and talk about the chosen wine.

> I was surprised to be invited to a wine tasting. I guess folks think because I own a wine store I must know something about it. Not much. I know I like Old Vine Red, find the color of rosé off-putting, and I like the labels on a couple of whites. Beyond that, I'm kind of out to lunch and rely on my staff to stay on top of things. I'm sure it was because of my association with Elaine that I got to go to the wine tasting. She got invited and I kind of "go with" her, like a scarf or like Kleenex. It wasn't long ago that I couldn't tolerate wine, but then a short-lived and modest affluence descended on me, and as I prospered I felt I needed wine. The awareness came on very naturally, like feeling, at around thirteen, that I needed a girlfriend, and later at seventeen, that I needed one quite desperately. Suddenly, I liked wine, all kinds of wine, and I began to buy it by the box. I began to feel more confident about having folks over, cosmopolitan folks. Right away I'd offer them a glass of wine and go right to the refrigerator and fill a glass from the little tap on the box. Often my guests would comment about the wine, "Mmmm…interesting," or something else lacking enthusiasm, and I could tell that theirs was not an unqualified endorsement, so I'd answer with something like, "Perhaps it hasn't had a chance to breathe; it's such a short walk from the fridge."

Restoration of the Old Engine House got underway.

> The Board of Selectmen has approved the Engine House Committee's plan for restoring that old treasure to its former elegance. These plans have been developed over time with the invaluable help of longtime resident Marty Stein. Having designed the library addition, he's again offered his assistance as we move forward with this exciting project. Having overseen the Washington School reclamation, Bill Alcorn has generously offered to serve as Clerk of the Works. A priority will certainly be fund-raising and, as approval has come in midsummer and coincides with so much else that is going on, we will forego, for this year, a formal fund-raising event and, instead, rely on the generosity of the many supporters of this project to come forward and contribute what they can.

> Meanwhile we are preparing to have the building's contents removed to safe keeping and will soon invite bids for Stage I, the removal of appendages, mechanicals, and the chimney, and exposure of certain framing members that we might better understand their condition. Ever since Historic Downstreet, Inc. was formed over a year ago, attracting over 125 supporters, we have been eager to direct our attention toward a popular reclamation. Clearly this is such an effort. The Engine House is an important part of our town's history, one of the few remaining components of what was once an architectural wonderland. Deductible contributions toward this great project may be made to our

OBSERVATIONS

501(c)(3), Historic Downstreet, Inc., POB 209, 04863 and, appearances to the contrary, nowhere else. A similar appeal elsewhere may happily lead to needed repairs but has nothing to do with Historic Downstreet, Inc. or the Engine House.

The Vinalhaven Engine House Restoration Committee
August 2012
Help us save the Engine House!

Earlier this year the town appointed a nine-member Vinalhaven Engine House Committee and charged them with the restoration of the Old Engine House.

Built in 1888 to house Old Reuben and other of the town's firefighting equipment, the Engine House is a simple but classically elegant building and one of the very few remaining components of our historic downtown.

Accordingly, having enlisted the generous assistance of Historic Preservation Architect Marty Stein, who gave us the library addition, we recently submitted a plan for transforming the deteriorating Engine House into a showpiece for housing the town's antique firefighting equipment. Those magnificent pieces of hand-drawn hose carts and ladder trucks are presently languishing, unseen, in the Historical Society's basement. They deserve to see the light of day and to be seen and appreciated by us all.

The board has given our plan their blessing and appropriated $20,000 to get things going. We are in the process of drafting detailed plans for specific components of the work needed and will soon begin soliciting bids for those components. We have set a target of $250,000 for completion of the project, and, while we expect the town to appropriate further funds as it moves forward, we are asking for contributions from all those who care about preserving what is left of our architectural heritage. Given the lateness of the hour we will forego hosting a formal fundraiser this summer, conident we can find the needed support from among our year-round and seasonal community.

Bill Alcorn, who oversaw the restoration of the Washington School, has generously offered to serve as Clerk of the Works for this project, as well, and we fully expect, with your generous help, to present the finished product to you all by Labor Day of 2013.

Tax deductible contributions to either the Town of Vinalhaven (POB 815) or to Historic Downstreet, Inc. (POB 209), earmarked for this project, will be gratefully accepted.

Sincerely,

Phil Crossman, chair	Ken White
Josef L'Africain, vice chair	Bill Alcorn
Sue L'Africain, secretary	Valerie Morton
Marjorie Stratton, treasurer	Marty Stein
Roy Heisler	

2012

On Monday, the 3rd of September, 1928 Helen began kindergarten on the second floor of the Engine House under the direction of teacher Marion Lyford. Kids from all over the island gathered that year to attend kindergarten at the Engine House before disbursing to their homes the following year to begin elementary school in their respective neighborhood schools. A classmate of Helen's was Olga MacDonald (Carleton). Olga, for example, after attending kindergarten with Helen Asiala Litwak and thirty other kids from all over the island, began her elementary education the next year at the Granite Island Primary School. Many of these kids didn't reassemble again till they entered Lincoln High eight years later. In 1934 twelve-year-old Helen walked alone around the Sands into town carrying her pajamas, a pillow, and a blanket. She climbed the stairs to the Engine House, changed into her pajamas, walked across the street to Dr. Shield's office (upstairs over the ARC and Five Elements Gallery) and had her tonsils removed. She's never forgotten the trauma of that day and she hasn't forgotten her fond memories of the Engine House, either, and hopes to hear that it's been restored. Toward that end she has joined the many donors who have responded to our fund-raising efforts recently with donations of from $25 to $2,000.

Singer Marcia Ball appeared at a concert to benefit PIE.

Zumba classes began, and instructor Amy Lear attracted a faithful and energetic following.

The ARC took on a broader role, affiliating itself more fully with the school and offering all sorts of classes.

Six Writers Read, an interesting program hosted by the New Era Gallery, during which six writers each read for ten minutes from one of their own compositions, was presented in the Windy Way Barn. I was one of them.

Lobstermen began talking about a work stoppage.

> The Commissioner of Marine Resources has followed through with his warning that an organized work stoppage among lobstermen may be illegal. He paid the island a surprise visit last week disguised as a tourist and with two subordinates in tow disguised as tourist's assistants. They strolled casually along the waterfront pretending to be nothing more than curious people from away but intent on gathering evidence of a conspiracy to violate anti-trust laws. Overhearing a lobsterman on his radio referring to being "fetched up" and suspecting it was code for "tie up," they clambered over the gunnel to inquire what that might mean and were told by the captain that while he was referring to a romantic interlude, the term pretty well described the situation the three would soon find themselves in if they didn't clamber ashore quickly. They did, but, undeterred, wandered casually but purposefully into a knot of land-bound lobstermen gathered near Greet's Eats discussing the price of lobster and the universal disinterest in going to haul. Stepping out of their roles as tourists, the three now quietly changed into new sou'westers and hip boots they'd brought for just this eventuality that they might more readily insinuate themselves into the group. They assumed the same nonchalance that possessed the group, and, gradually, that they not be suspect, joined in talk about weather and the price of going vs. not going. When one guy talked about this being a good time to go on the bank, the commissioner said, "Don't you mean 'to the bank?'" Later he attributed that ill-informed remark to having given them away.

OBSERVATIONS

The state of Maine issued new rules and regulations, ridiculous parameters within which we who sell beverages were expected to conduct ourselves to remain compliant.

> Now and then something happens that affects our lives here and I feel compelled to bring these seismic developments to your attention. This week has provided a couple of examples. The Department of Quality Assurance and Regulations, a division of the state's Department of Agriculture, Conservation and Forestry, issued new rules that have brought redemption centers such as Eldercare and retail shops like mine scrambling eagerly to their collective feet in terror-stricken obedience. The new rules call for we who sell beverages or otherwise facilitate the collection of empty beverage containers to package said containers only in plastic bags and only in those that measure thirty-six inches by sixty inches, have a minimum thickness of 1.2 thousandths of an inch, and a flat bottom. The department will enforce this new rule beginning on January 1, 2013, which is why I'm shaking in my boots. No doubt they will, by then, have trained a cadre of plastic bag police (the PBP) who will be dispersed all over the state and who will be conducting surprise raids on shops like mine in a determined effort to bring transgressors (I promise to be one) to justice. The department also calls our attention to the need to forego collecting a five-cent deposit if the beverage in question is apple cider or blueberry juice that was produced and bottled here in Maine and does not contain any other ingredients except preservatives. I, for one, sleep better every time a new regulation — usually something to further stifle free enterprise — is handed down from Augusta or Washington. A second issuance comes from the Maine Revenue Services in the form of a one-time program offering each of us the opportunity to report and pay sales tax on all taxable purchases made online or from another state during any three-year period between 2006 and 2011. This is a chance for us all to report purchases about which the state knows nothing and about which we will have most certainly forgotten and then pay sales tax the state doesn't know it was due.

Two smallish dogs had been enjoying the run of the landfill and environs for some time. Everyone knew about it but me and knew which nearby home owner was derelict in not keeping them confined. I was eager to help.

> I found two small dogs in the road, tails wagging in anticipation of my stopping to play. As soon as I opened the door to investigate they jumped in, one around the pedals and my feet, then into the passenger seat, the other in my lap. Each gave me a token lick and then looked forward expectantly. As I pondered what to do — they wore no tags — they glanced repeatedly at me as if to say, "Uh, dude, we're, like, ready." I remembered George was the Animal Control Officer and headed for his place. I found a big cage placed at the head of the drive as if planned and I determined to put my two charges in it before going to find him. A hundred feet ahead was a sizable corral, formed by a loosely erected electric fence, and home to a handful of sheep. Nearby were two fat and clearly domesticated guinea fowl. I opened the door and headed for the cage, assuming they were trotting obediently behind. The dogs, as if they'd been tag-teaming guinea fowl all their lives, bolted for the birds, which, in a hysterical and overfed frenzy, managed an elevated beachhead just in time. Undeterred, the dogs flew over and through the electric fence, scattering the sheep, which tore down the fence and dragged it off in all directions. This all happened before I was able to gather my wits — something that takes longer nowadays, anyway — but not my momentum. My lunge ended in an arrested landing, greased by sheep droppings. Had not the dogs come over to see if I was OK, they'd be roaming free still.

I underwent an MRI and, as is often the case, nothing went according to plan.

I recently underwent an MRI to determine what is causing pain in my upper arm. I was cautioned again and again by the technicians that it would be a claustrophobic experience likely to last quite some time and it would be accompanied by periodic, disquieting, and sustained banging, and if I thought I might panic or be frightened I should let them know now. I assured them I would be OK, but they insisted I hold a little panic button in the event I felt otherwise once ensconced, and then stuffed me into a little cylinder as if packing a sausage. It did last a long time, nearly half an hour, and every now and then one of them would bellow reassurances through the headphones I'd been equipped with and ask if I was doing OK. Each time they did that they interrupted a dream because I fall asleep when laid on my back, regardless of the circumstances, and dream immediately. I make quite a bit of noise, I'm told, when asleep and dreaming, often issuing a revealing exclamation, and after several of these concerned interruptions a technician asked loudly and with some irritation, "Hey, who's in there with you, and what are you doing?"

This is chapter two of the saga that began with my being entombed in the MRI machine. The film revealed a torn bicep tendon, one of the two that attach the bicep to the shoulder. The young doctor who reviewed the damage suggested I had three options. I could wait it out and live with the severe limitations imposed by the tear until it ruptured, a dramatic event that would relieve me of the pain and limited movement but which would result in the recoiled and defunct tendon residing in perpetuity in an unsightly ball of flesh near my elbow. Alternatively, he could go right in and snip it free right away, thus eliminating the prolonged discomfort and affording immediate relief but resulting in the same unbecoming ball of flesh. Either approach, he observed casually, would produce the same unappealing result, something that might trouble a man likely to flaunt himself, but he couldn't imagine, at my age, that was me. Finally, he could try a "cut 'n' paste" procedure and try to reattach the tendon to my shoulder. The procedure is about 80% successful, but he observed, again cheerfully, hardly worth it given my advanced years, even going so far as to suggest that I should probably find things to concern myself with other than how I looked or the likelihood that anyone watching me flex my biceps would find it appealing. I swung at him but was pulled up short of a delivery by the pain of stressing my torn bicep. He smirked confidently.

Elaine and I returned from a nice little vacation at Baxter State Park, one of our favorite haunts. We'd had an interesting experience there that I couldn't resist embellishing.

Those of you who have spent time at Baxter State Park are familiar with the "Leave No Trace" philosophy of Baxter's visionary gift to us and the many living things with whom we share it, and will appreciate the shock we all felt when, mid-morning, long after we and the other Daicey Pond campers had enjoyed our bacon, eggs, and coffee while watching the rising sun illuminate Mt. Katahdin's south slope, a nearby gas generator coughed to life. The unmistakable sound and response of a starter cord being yanked and the jarring frustration expressed when the machine failed to start on the first pull brought us and the occupants of the other cabins around the pond to our feet, and the ranger from his cottage headquarters, with far more urgency than should be felt in such an idyllic place. The offending cabin was close enough for us to overhear the resulting exchange between the incredulous ranger and the occupants. It seemed they'd grown frustrated with the unsatisfactory performance of the little camp toaster most of us lug around, the one that props up four slices of bread, too far from the heat to do anything but extract every scrap of moisture from the bread. These folks, however, were sufficiently resourceful to have seized unapologetically on the solution for producing not only very agreeable toast but also a dark and satisfying espresso.

The debates, particularly the Presidential and Vice Presidential debates, were about to begin, and I was looking forward to them, as I always do, but having the contenders described by the host as fellows who had "dedicated their lives to public service" was too much for me.

Is anyone else struck by the absurdity of hearing a politician claim to have or hearing one introduced as having *dedicated his life to public service?* Before the Vice Presidential debate Ms. Raddatz told us she was honored to moderate the debate between these two men who have *dedicated their lives to public service.* I'm sure she was honored, and it may be that they and others who claim that distinction are noble and hardworking and have the interests of their constituents foremost in their hearts, but it can hardly be said they have *dedicated their lives to public service.* They are dedicated to making money, just like most of us, and they do it pretty well. Biden makes $230,000, Ryan $170,000. People who work for the Peace Corps *dedicate their lives to public service* for $6,000 a year. Doctors Without Borders dedicate theirs for $16,000; volunteers at Amnesty International don't get anything, although they are allowed ten dollars per day for travel and six dollars for lunch. Our recently retired EMS Director *dedicated years of his life to public service.* Volunteers in this town and in thousands of others dedicate their lives or portions of those lives to public service, but one never hears them claim, "I have dedicated my life to public service." Many politicians, as if to paint their lives in terms of endless sacrifice for the rest of us, have the audacity to say it shamelessly and often.

I finished my historic walk around Vinalhaven and wrapped it up in a column in October.

On October 6, 2009 I stepped off the Dyer Island Bridge and, for the next three years, a few hours at a time at low tide, began walking, first around Dyer and Barton Islands, then around the Basin, in and out of Long Cove, around Hall Island, through Leadbetter Narrows, up into Crockett Cove, by Tip Toe, round Crockett Point and Browns Head∗ and along the Thorofare, up Perry's Creek to Indian Ladder, around Smith Point and into Seal Cove, into Mill Creek to the head of Stepping Stone Brook, round Holt Point, in and around Dyer Pond, down Mill River to the Carrying Place Bridge and then headed up around Calderwood Neck, into Mill Pond, round Jennings Island, in and out of the Swimming Pool and around Zeke's Point and Birch Point, around Birch Island, down Carver Cove to Polly Cove, up around Thayer Point to Salt Works Cove, into Winter Harbor, past Starboard Rock and into the Privilege, back to the Bridge, way down into Vinal Cove∗ and under the Boondoggle Bridge to the Trotting Park, back out of the Cove and along the south shore of Winter Harbor, around Penobscot Island and Burnt Island and into Smith, then Philbrook Coves, out to Bluff Head∗, round Coombs Neck, Brown and Stoddard Islands, into Smith Harbor and past Barley Hill, around Calderwood Point, in and out of Cherry Tree/Fish House Coves to Geary's Beach, around Arey Neck, by Booth Quarry and the old dump, into Roberts Harbor, around Pogus Point, under the bridge and into Indian Creek, back out and Round the Mountain, around Lane's Island, into Carver's Harbor, under the bridge, in and around Carver's Pond, back under the bridge and

∗fell overboard

along the waterfront to Sands Cove, around Norton Point, and along the Reach, in to Old Harbor and its Pond, around City Point and back to the Bridge. (280 miles)

I do what I'm supposed to do on Thanksgiving. I think about my own good fortune and it's a good thing I do. I'd be impossible otherwise. One of the things I was grateful for was that I was not a juvenile lobster in Noah Oppenheimer's care.

Another Thanksgiving gone by, another pointed opportunity to consider my own circumstances in the context of other people and other places. If I don't take the time to do that I am not likely to acknowledge my own good fortune. On the other hand, there are so many and so frequent reminders of what others endure I'd be hard-pressed to do otherwise. This is a sublimely peaceful place. I can't remember the last time a bomb went off. I wander from my own neighborhood to others with very little regard for whether I'll be robbed or beaten or killed for having said something one group may have considered blasphemous. We can hardly tell one faction from another, for that matter. Our children wander similarly freely, yet to be swept up in some hideous dragnet and made to kill others. There are no drive-by shootings. Our women, when they can be persuaded to be charitable, treat the rest of us as equals. No one is required to so completely cover themselves that their identity is a mystery to the rest of us. I am as free to speak my mind and practice my own religion, or lack of it, as anyone else. By not conforming, I am not going to subject myself to public flogging. While some of us may feel a little more worthy than others we have not instituted a caste system and required their numbers to remain mired for eternity. A little indiscretion will not cost us an arm or a leg. We do not need to ship ourselves to the mainland in the bowels of an overcrowded cattle boat to seek employment in a garment fire trap just so we can put enough food on the table to barely sustain ourselves. Neither are we forced to choose between absolute allegiance to a mad tyrant or suffering our neighborhoods and playgrounds to relentless firebombing.

Hopelessness and despair, while not entirely absent, are at least not the prevailing sentiment. I'm grateful for living here and wish I weren't reminded so continually of my own good fortune.

Today I learned that Noah Oppenheimer, a graduate student at the University of Maine, studies lobster cannibalism. He presented his findings on NPR as if lobster cannibalism was his major. Can that be? It seems he tethered a juvenile lobster to the bottom in about thirty feet of water of Boothbay Harbor and, with an underwater camera, gleefully filmed the poor thing being devoured by an adult predator. As if that weren't enough, he did it again and managed to film another being torn asunder by two competing adult lobsters that fought over the grazing rights. He presents this to us as if it were a meaningful discovery, as if any of us would find it surprising to discover that sort of behavior in Boothbay Harbor. So they eat their young! It's Boothbay Harbor, that's hardly news! What does he expect? If he had tried the same experiment in the waters around Vinalhaven (down at this end, not up in the Thorofare and, admittedly, not out toward Matinicus) he'd have found concerned adults stopping by to nibble away at the tether, freeing the little thing to go about living its life, then reporting young Mr. Oppenheimer to the Department of Marine Resources.

In 2012 one hundred and twenty-seven million pounds of lobster were landed in Maine by 6,000 license holders, and the price was $2.69 per pound.

OBSERVATIONS

2013

Jack Waterbury

2013

Vinalhaven Land Trust began a fund-raising campaign to purchase Big Tip Toe mountain, a spectacularly scenic overlook on the Fox Islands Thorofare.

An old friend who shall remain nameless—but whose picture appears on the preceding page—whose comfort during this severe winter troubled some of us, proved more resilient than we'd imagined.

> An old sailor, an old friend to many of us, in fact, has abandoned us for warmer climes. It wasn't his choice. Several of his younger buddies convinced him that, in his eighties, hauling wood in from a snow pile every two hours all night just to keep from freezing was unnecessary, given the appealing option of spending the winter berthed on his son's sailboat tethered to a slip in Key West. He objected but with less conviction than he might have a year ago, and was helped along on his journey by those same friends who then saw that his house was drained and the water shut off just ahead of a deep freeze. Before he left, however, he managed something that suggested to many of us that we may have misjudged or at least misdiagnosed him, that maybe hauling in wood was no problem for him and that he only succumbed to humor us.
>
> Earlier this month, just as our first big snowstorm was getting underway, he expressed concern because a lady friend was driving from upstate New York, by herself, to visit him. We were concerned, too! A nine-hour drive in a blizzard would certainly be a struggle for a woman in her eighties. Next morning, after the big storm, I stopped in to see how he was doing and to see if his friend made it in one piece. I went in, wandering from room to room, calling his name and, hearing no response, opened the only closed bedroom door. She was lovely, about forty-five, and after she'd straightened her hair a little she graciously assured me I was not to feel embarrassed for having interrupted them.

I was reminded by a classmate of some trouble I'd caused decades earlier.

> Everyone who remembers the great Heart Fund Robbery is not yet dead. On a spring day in 1959, another boy and I, smitten by a lab class demonstration earlier that day of how malleable a thing is liquid mercury, conspired to get our hands on some of it. We deliberately misbehaved so as to be kept after school in detention and then, when dismissed from that onerous obligation, stepped into a nearby closet and remained there holding our collective breath while the teacher left the building and locked the door. I scurried up to the third floor lab. My co-conspirator unexpectedly offered to stay instead by the door and alert me if anyone was coming. In fact, he was not keeping watch at all; he was pilfering the Heart Fund money that had been collected earlier that day in the room where we'd endured detention. While I was plowing through the lab trying to find the mercury he came running up the stairs to report breathlessly, "Cubie is coming!" Cubie Winslow was the janitor, and he'd come to perform his usual chores but, hearing the commotion overhead, was now advancing slowly upward—he was a little overweight—while we flew down to a second story fire escape that led from a big double-hung window. We, as yet unidentified, ran down it. As we dis-

appeared into the nearby woods we looked back to see Cubie peering out the window while our mates, at ball practice just below, gleefully identified us. Hours later, after a massive manhunt conducted while we enjoyed pancakes at Coot Eaton's down at East Boston, we were taken into custody. The Heart Fund money, which it turns out my companion had hidden in the woods while pretending to relieve himself, was never recovered.

Restoration of the Old Engine House was about half complete. We hoped to present it to the town on the Fourth of July.

Reconstruction within and without the Old Engine Hall is past the halfway stage as we move forward. There's a little confusion about whether this is intended to be a historical restoration. It is not. Rather, it is intended to restore the building to usefulness while retaining its original elegance. When finished, it will be nearly identical but much more functional. The formerly dark first floor interior, for instance, is now bright and full of natural light and will be a sun-filled repository for our town's antique firefighting equipment and for memorabilia highlighting the town's proud firefighting history. Contributions continue to come in regularly, almost keeping pace with our obligations. The restoration of the Old Engine House is going to give our spirits a boost come this summer. We continue to rely on your generosity and pride in your community. If this project means as much to you as it does to us, please give your tax deductible contribution to Historic Downstreet, Inc., POB 209 or to the Town of Vinalhaven, POB 815.

Rehearsals, under the direction of Jessie Grant, had begun for a March production of *Noises Off*.

I was reminded, when I went to Rockland the day after a bad storm, of how fortunate we are to have a conscientious public works crew.

The day after the big snowstorm of early February, the one that left Magnus standing on a drift above the windows of the ARC, I walked to the ferry. Our sidewalks had been completely cleared, as had the roads, and it was an easy walk. When I disembarked in Rockland and walked up to Main Street I found a path that led generally toward town, one shovel width, next to the road. I couldn't tell whether the path was on the edge of the road or actually in the vicinity of the sidewalk. By the time I'd gone a block, the path ended and I had to climb over a snowdrift and down into the road to continue walking up Main Street against oncoming traffic. I thought Rockland must be experiencing labor difficulties or equipment failure, but then I went to the mainland again the morning after our most recent snowstorm. It had only stopped snowing in the middle of the night but at six a.m. our streets were bare, so were the sidewalks. Only a few ghostly figures were tidying up here and there; even the store entries had been completely shoveled out. I drove off in Rockland and didn't return till mid-afternoon. I left my vehicle at the terminal and then headed up Main Street to get a cup of coffee. Not a shovel full of snow had been removed from the sidewalks. A few shop owners had cleared a little in front of their doorways but each meager path simply led to the street and even then only lasted till the plow came by and filled it in again. Our crew might have gone over there after finishing up here.

Noises Off was another in a long, long line of wonderfully entertaining productions.

We've known (for too long) what Bill Chilles is capable of, but if we thought we'd seen the best of him we were shortsighted. His Selsdon Mowbray was—well, words fail me. Again! He was also largely responsible for the set, a singularly beautiful, mobile, and functional piece. Although no such instruction was credited in the program, Karen Burns choreographed the relentless action of this play as expertly as she directed the diverse and energetic characters who employed it. This was, with a couple of exceptions, a seasoned island cast that long ago set the bar high but who have now kicked it quite literally higher still. Rachel Noyes's Dotty was a genuine character, perfectly done, but then she's a Boyden and so can hardly do otherwise. Frank Morton's Gary was manic, certainly audible, and frighteningly athletic (I almost rushed the stage when he tumbled down the stairs). Jamie Thomas simply was an enormously frustrated director one minute, then a disconnected man on the make the next. Ellie Reidy was so appealingly distracted and oblivious she may still be on stage now, wondering what is going on. Francis Warren also did it again, so put-upon and so often foiled as his character tried and failed to consummate his stage debut that I still feel sorry for him. Then there's Jeff Aronson. When he and I first appeared on stage together I said to myself (certainly not to him), "this little fella's got potential." I was right, and he got this role not a moment too soon, because he was a little winded at the curtain call. Alison Thibault did a great job as the Stage Manager, playing off Francis wonderfully, and Jenn Gehnrich was a natural, never still (never winded, either), always in character, something only seasoned veterans usually manage. Everyone involved should be very happy with this production. It was a huge success!

Bailey is a little fellow who often visits his grandmother just across the street from my house. He's a fascinating and engaging kid.

When Bailey was just learning to walk he very courageously climbed up on the stone wall surrounding my lawn and walked along it holding his mother's hand. But he wouldn't speak to me, even though I sang his praises and told him how brave he was. That winter I threw a snowball at him but missed. The next year he walked along the wall without holding anyone's hand and I again congratulated him and complimented his prowess, but he still wouldn't speak to me. That winter I threw another snowball at him, missing again. Later still, when he was three or four, I had my winter's wood delivered and was stacking it in the garage. Bailey sauntered across the street and asked, "Want some help?" I said sure. He picked up a piece of wood and carried it into the garage, then another, then wiped his brow and headed back to his Gram's. I said, "Thank you," but he didn't say anything. That winter I threw a snowball at him. I missed, but he got quite excited and threw one back at me. The next year, when he was four or five, he came over again when my wood was delivered and asked, "Can I have one?" I said he could and he took a small piece and kicked it on down the road to his Gram's. Another kid showed up so he came back and got another piece for his friend. That winter I threw a snowball at him, but missed, and he threw several back. The next year he and his Gram made a huge pile of leaves in the fall. I ran across the street and jumped on it. Bailey covered me with leaves and howled with laughter but didn't speak otherwise. This winter I've ambushed him several times, nearly hitting him on several occasions. On one occasion he unleashed quite a barrage of return fire, but I don't usually give him the opportunity to throw one back because he's getting bigger and has quite an arm and could very well hurt me. Still, I plan on keeping up my attack till he says something.

OBSERVATIONS

I'd only just written a column praising the public works department when I found myself the subject of some derisive small talk. The blizzard that prompted it, though, also kindled a memory about an even bigger storm when I was a kid. As it turned out the storm happened before I was born but I'd made my memory of others talking about it my own.

> I'm way too sensitive to withstand having been the topic of disparaging chit-chat* on the town's very own CB radios. Imagine, then, my dismay and embarrassment when, having stopped in at Carver's for the evening's provisions, several friends hastened near to tell me that I had been the topic of precisely such unfavorable drivel. It seems certain of my town's snow removal workers or subs (paid with my taxes) took exception to my having put in an appearance at my own business on the day of the most recent storm, and they then ill-advisedly exchanged those scornful observations about not only me, but also about others whom they perceived to be underfoot while they went about their assigned duties. Of course, everyone was listening: First Responders and the many among us who keep a scanner monitoring things day and night. As I have pointed out, I am very sensitive, and, deeply troubled and hurt, I went home to pour my heart out to my beloved. I got much less sympathy than I'd expected and, instead, was reminded that I have spent my whole life in some sort of scandal or another and shouldn't let it get the best of me. I swallowed hard in acquiescence but pointed out that our grandson's love life hung in the balance since we'd both recently learned that Finn, now a year and a half, has taken a serious shine to the granddaughter of one of my critics. Whatever will become of family gatherings? Awkward.
>
> *chit-chat: mindless babble that customarily fills time that might otherwise be spent working.

> After last weekend's spectacular blizzard I read accounts of it having been the worst storm anyone alive can remember, but in the late 1940s the snow piled up so high on Main Street sidewalks that a tunnel was dug through it so we could access the stores. I remember walking across Main Street holding my mom's hand and stepping into a tunnel entrance near L.R. Smith (now Go Fish). We turned left into the tunnel and walked fifty feet or so to E.G. Carver's (Alternative Oil), navigating easily, the tunnel having been lit with a string of electric bulbs staked to the icy overhead, and passing others coming and going along the way. We popped in at Carver's and picked up a few things, then went on through the tunnel to MacIntosh Grocery (the ARC) for something else, then on to the Post Office at the Memorial Hall for our mail. The tunnel ended there because the wind screaming over the old Carriage House and down the alley between the Memorial Hall and the Masonic Hall (Carver's Harbor Market) swept the sidewalk bare right next to the drifts where the tunnel ended. On the way back we passed someone chopping window openings through the frozen snow wall so we could get a little natural light and see the street outside. Today I asked Louie, one of the decreasing number who might have shared that memory, whether his recollection matched mine. It did not. He pointed out that my memory of there having been a lighted tunnel was correct, but that it happened in the thirties, before he or I was born. I hate it when that happens.

When Barack Obama ran for president the first time I seized on several of his campaign promises. One was that he would close the Guantanamo prison camp. Now, years later, he hadn't managed it or even kept it on the front burner. I was ashamed, and remain so.

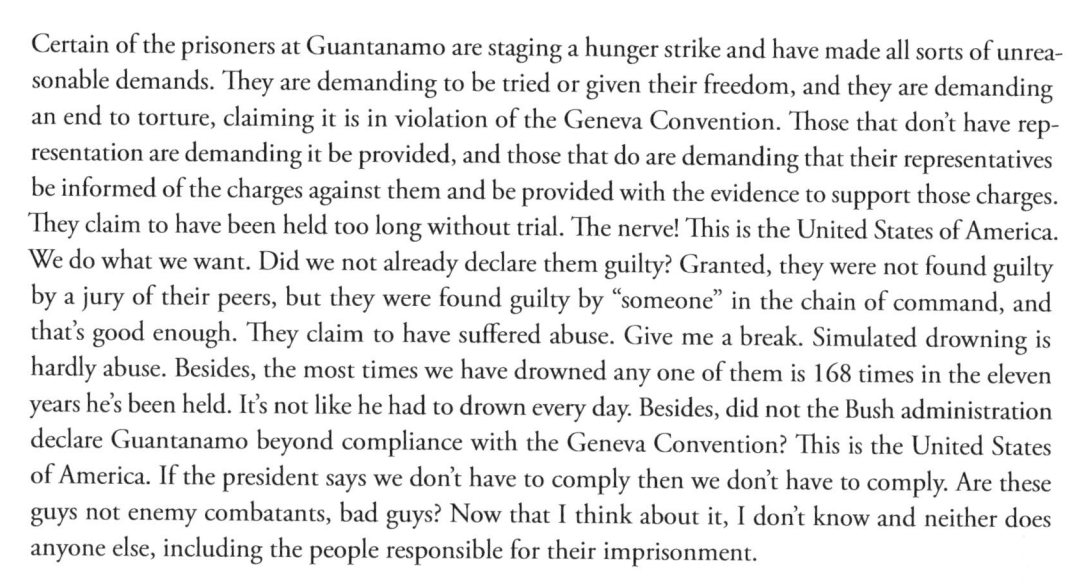

Certain of the prisoners at Guantanamo are staging a hunger strike and have made all sorts of unreasonable demands. They are demanding to be tried or given their freedom, and they are demanding an end to torture, claiming it is in violation of the Geneva Convention. Those that don't have representation are demanding it be provided, and those that do are demanding that their representatives be informed of the charges against them and be provided with the evidence to support those charges. They claim to have been held too long without trial. The nerve! This is the United States of America. We do what we want. Did we not already declare them guilty? Granted, they were not found guilty by a jury of their peers, but they were found guilty by "someone" in the chain of command, and that's good enough. They claim to have suffered abuse. Give me a break. Simulated drowning is hardly abuse. Besides, the most times we have drowned any one of them is 168 times in the eleven years he's been held. It's not like he had to drown every day. Besides, did not the Bush administration declare Guantanamo beyond compliance with the Geneva Convention? This is the United States of America. If the president says we don't have to comply then we don't have to comply. Are these guys not enemy combatants, bad guys? Now that I think about it, I don't know and neither does anyone else, including the people responsible for their imprisonment.

Work on the Old Engine House was moving along nicely and the kind of improvements that make an impression — roofing, siding, windows, and door — were about to begin. I continued to keep it in the public eye.

A couple of years ago at Town Meeting the issue of whether to take possession of the Old Engine House was a major topic. One of the issues was the cost of protecting it against further deterioration and then maintaining it. Soon a group of a dozen or so asked to be, and then were, appointed by the selectmen as the Engine House Committee and have since undertaken not only its stabilization but its restoration. After much discussion and some guidance from the board of selectmen and the fire department, the committee suggested and the selectmen approved a functional restoration rather than a historic one. Accordingly, the building would be saved from further deterioration and then, within certain practical considerations, and while retaining as much of its original appearance as possible, would be completely renovated and put to good use. Among those practical considerations were a fire resistant roof, removal of the unsafe and unsightly exterior stairway, the addition of two more windows to balance the appearance (fenestration), and upgraded wiring and plumbing. Otherwise the building was to look very much as it did in 1888 when it was built. The town raised $20,000 toward the project, and the committee undertook to develop plans, invite bids, raise additional funds on its own, and begin work. Its subsequent and ongoing campaign has brought in $67,000, with donations, ranging from $10 to $10,000, from seventeen seasonal and twenty-three year-round residents. Most of the inside work has been completed. Next month a new metal roof will be installed, then clapboard and other exterior repairs made, and the building painted. Finally Old Reuben and other pieces of the town's priceless antique firefighting equipment will be cleaned, polished, and installed inside for all to appreciate. An additional $60,000 is needed. The brand new and quite beautiful bay doors, already built and waiting, will open on the Fourth of July. Tax-deductible contributions can be made to the Town at POB 815.

OBSERVATIONS

I do hope you haven't wearied of hearing about the restoration of the Old Engine House. If that's not the case, however and you are, in fact, getting a little tired of it, do not despair. The end is in sight. After working for months on the interior, the inside is just about finished and work has begun on the outside. From now on the transformation will become quickly apparent. The hose tower has been completely rebuilt and painted. Take a look, because those are going to be the colors of the finished structure. By mid-month the Old Engine House will have a new roof and by the end of May it will have been completely painted and ready for the return of its antique firefighting equipment.

Over 175 of you have stepped forward and coughed up about $100,000. Thirty have given twice, nine gave 3 times, two gave 4 times, and two have given 5 times. We are enormously grateful to you all.

This is a restoration, but it's a practical restoration, not a historic one. In other words, it will resemble the original as closely as possible while making sense. It has two more windows than the original and the interior is now white instead of very dark stained wood, so there is a great deal of natural light within. It will have a metal roof instead of the original material. The removal of the exterior stair, which was not part of the original structure, revealed, just in time, a great deal of rot resulting from failed flashing.

Of course, this column would not be complete if we did not ask for more money. We need $47,000 more to finish up.

I found a place to lay the blame for my advancing years, and the spring behavior of a bevy of goldfinches attracted my attention.

I misplaced my keys a couple of weeks ago— keys to all the motel rooms, to my shop, to Island Spirits, to our post office boxes. Usually when this happens I can count on Elaine to find whatever I lost, to retrace my footsteps, methodically narrowing the options until she finds the errant item. This time, however, she was unable to locate the missing keys. I've seen this coming. Earlier this year I lost my Swiss Army knife, and it took her much longer than usual to find it, inside a bathroom fan, where I'd used its screwdriver blade to put things together. It was a week, maybe more, before she finally tracked it down, otherwise productive days lost to me because of her diminishing skills. I suppose it's to be expected; as time goes by some of us lose our edge although I haven't noticed it myself. Now I've lost my glasses. Perhaps recognizing her diminishments, she some time ago presented me with a little necklace with a ring in it that allowed me to hang my glasses securely in the loop while I did work that would otherwise have been handicapped by my short sightedness (or is it far?). At any rate, I remember recently having to do some close work and attempting to hang the glasses in the little ring, but it was gone. Frustrated, I put the glasses down somewhere and have not seen them since. Neither has Elaine found them, although she did find the necklace, which was around my neck, but with the loop hanging in back instead of the front. Not long ago, I'd have relied on her to notice that before I left the house.

Several goldfinches have been chasing one of their own, a female, around my pear tree recently. She keeps a couple of feet ahead of them and is afforded a brief respite now and then when they pause to try and intimidate one another. None is discouraged by the pugnacity of the others, however, and, having been thus briefly distracted, they all return their attention again to her. There is a great flurry of feathers as they scramble to catch up to her, although, while she might have availed herself of the distraction to make her getaway, she'd only stopped to preen herself while the boys sorted things out. This might have clued them that no urgency existed, other than the quite unmistakable and compelling one to which they'd all recently succumbed, and that she was not going anywhere. They might have noticed that, instead of flying away during this pursuit, she only ever hopped to the next perch to check her makeup and smooth the one or two feathers that had been ruffled during the pursuit as she fluttered from branch to branch, now and then glancing coyly back over her shoulder to fan the flames. It might have registered with them that she never moved more than a foot or two away. That this was lost on the competing flock does not surprise the observer. Rather, it reminds one of the enormous relief felt in not having to do that anymore.

Ellen Kingsbury, a legendary summer resident, passed away. My dad had worked for Ox and Ellen for years. They were among our favorites, everyone's favorites.

About fifteen years ago a small boat crossing the Thorofare struck a dinghy carrying several people, one of whom was ninety-year-old Ellen Kingsbury, known to most of us as Jerry. Jerry was knocked overboard. Jerry and Ox (Howard) owned Young Point on the Thorofare and were among the most gracious of our summer residents. Jerry's dad was a Major in the 35th Massachusetts Regiment in the Civil War. Ox had been a Gold Medalist in the 1924 Olympics. Of all the folks my dad worked for, Ox and Jerry were the two whose reacquaintance I anticipated each summer. Jerry tread water patiently as her frantic companions and the occupants of the offending boat maneuvered around to get her out of the water. The boat that had struck hers got there first and the captain reached over the gunwale to grab her. There is a right way and a wrong way, however, to retrieve someone — particularly a woman— from the water, and, as a counselor at Camp Wabenaki in the 1920s, Jerry was thoroughly acquainted with accepted procedures, and those did not include simply reaching into the water and grabbing whatever body part presented itself. Composed and paddling calmly, she took the time to politely instruct the captain on the requisite propriety and, when satisfied he understood, and entirely forgiving, suffered herself to be brought aboard.

My experience with restoring the Old Engine House reminded me of the generosity of many within our seasonal community.

While a small number of year-round residents often spearhead efforts — like the construction of our magnificent new school; restoration of the Union Church; the creation and funding of the Historical Society; restoration of the Washington School, where our Town Office now resides; preservation of land and environment for us all through the Land Trust; construction of our Fire and EMS Station; the creation of Vinalhaven Eldercare Services; the ongoing restoration of the Old Engine House; and so many other initiatives — none of it would get even one foot off the ground if it were not for the care and largesse of the well-heeled among our summer community or for the taxes paid by them all. Even the Ferry Service, Fox Islands Electric Co-op, the airstrip, and the landfill would not exist were it not for their involvement on some level. Those initiatives wouldn't get off the ground, either, if it were not for the fact that we who spearhead these things do so knowing full well that we can count on that generosity. Have we grown complacent, though, about how these projects are paid for and the degree to which we can absolve ourselves of taking as much responsibility as we might and instead rely on that summer community to do it for us? It seems so. Some among us have even adopted the lamentable attitude that the sort of help we've been getting from our summer people is the kind of help we should expect—a reasonable price they pay for the privilege of living here among us.

The Health Insurance Marketplace emerged from President Obama's Health Care legislation, and an outreach team operating from ICMS helped folks access and negotiate it.

The Vinalhaven Fire Department celebrated its 125th anniversary.

When Clyde Bickford, making his customary midnight rounds, came down over the hill by the Boyden driveway years ago, the back facades of the four buildings that comprised downtown Vinalhaven, then an architectural wonderland, came fortuitously into view across Carver's Pond. From his vantage a frightening glow could be seen where there should have been only darkness. The third floor windows of the Masonic Building, one of three magnificent Victorian mansards, were flickering orange and yellow. With the 125th anniversary of the Vinalhaven Fire Department upon us and celebrations of that event planned for this weekend it seems a good time to remind ourselves of one of their historic and astonishing achievements. A huge building, the Memorial Hall, the fourth spectacular edifice and four stories of dry tinder, loomed up even higher than the Masonic Hall, now ablaze, and only a few feet to the east, I.W. Fifield's, 2 ½ stories, was less than five feet to the west, so close that neither man nor equipment could even get between them. This was a fire of such proportions that the North Haven Fire Department was summoned and, carried across the Thorofare by the scow we used at the time, arrived in astonishing time. We marveled then, that after the Masonic Hall had been reduced to ashes, the two adjacent buildings still stood relatively unscathed.

An island wedding took place under cold and cloudy skies, but it was a great event.

I had the pleasure of attending an island wedding last week, a real island wedding, the kind that not only bestowed legitimacy, but that required a bride prove her mettle. It was to be an outdoor affair, out on the back deck overlooking a pastoral landscape. The Elder Bob Candage, an old hand at these things, knew beforehand how things would fall out. Very likely he had a hand in it. I'm talking about the weather. The couple had imagined an idyllic sunlit ceremony commencing with a beatific bridal promenade wafting elegantly up the hill from the tree line, through the wild blueberry, around the newly blooming columbine and aromatic bayberry, eventually turning a tranquil corner as they came into view of we who were gathered to lend our support and enthusiasm. For a while it looked promising, but just as the bride turned that corner, just as that lovely short-sleeved visage came into view, it began to get suddenly cold and to rain. Undeterred, the party continued to move gently in our direction, pausing at the chicken coop for the clearly rehearsed and thus perfectly executed approval of the Bridal Rooster, a nice touch. The creature's endorsement concluded, and shielded now by an umbrella, the bridal party continued up onto the porch and into the welcoming presence of Elder Candage. It was time to find out what this mainland bride was made of. And so, a ceremony that might have concluded, particularly in these wet and cold circumstances, more quickly, instead endured as Elder Candage invoked here a romantic admonition, there an exhortation for eternal happiness, now a prescription for the union finding favor with the Almighty, all the while watching the bride's bare arms for a sign that she was weakening. No such sign was apparent, and, after a fashion, we came to realize the groom had the genuine article on his hand: a formidable woman unlikely to pull her shawl up round her shoulders in deference to the weather or anything else.

Grandson Finn continued to provide me with material.

As many of you know, you who are on Facebook or are otherwise socially connected, my grandson, Finn, has cleared one of the most challenging obstacles — perhaps the most challenging to be overcome as one moves on from infancy. This is an enormous moment in a developing young life. We've been reminding him that Father's (and Grandfather's) Day is coming up and I like to think he had that in mind when, having emerged from his bath and with a "this has gone on long enough" expression on his mischievous face, he decisively deposited himself on the little potty his folks had been leaving on the bathroom floor and conspicuously in his path of late. And the deposits didn't stop there, either, as he settled in and did what was expected of him as if it was second nature. He did find it a little challenging to attend to both means of evacuation at the same time, but, no matter, no one was in the line of fire, and it was a fine beginning.

Memorial Day was approaching again and found me still struggling.

The years immediately following World War II were America's best. In spite of the horrors visited on millions of people, and the nearly irresistible appeal of revenge, the U.S. and its Allies chose, instead, to combine what resources they had left to save the starving people of West Berlin, enemies only four years earlier, and then to undertake the rebuilding of Germany's and the rest of Europe's economy and industrial infrastructure. The Berlin Airlift was our finest hour and an achievement of such miraculous proportions that had we (and Britain) not moved nearly three million tons of provisions by landing a loaded transport plane in West Berlin every three minutes, day and night, for a year and a half, few would have thought it possible. Many did think it impossible, and the suggestion that we risk World War III with the Soviets by running their blockade of the city or that we should be so charitable to people who just four years earlier had treated the world so badly was met with some derision. But others were possessed of the noble and determined spirit that, for so long, Americans proudly called our own. As a result, the remarkable combination of imagination, sacrifice (thirty pilots lost), and resources kept over two million of our former enemy alive until the Soviet Union finally capitulated. Today we routinely declare war all over the globe and fabricate justification for doing so; offer no assistance to those legitimately resisting brutality; manipulate or ignore the Constitution and international agreements to serve our own selfish or immoral ends; sweep up civilians in foreign countries, declare them enemy combatants, put them away for life, and offer no apologies or recourse. I hung my flag out — to see how it looked. It just hung there, and I can't imagine it wouldn't do the same thing if it were windy.

Visitors to the island, particularly those who return, pick up quickly — too quickly, sometimes — on the tendency we all have to wave to one another. I published a primer.

It concerns me that you folks who have visited the island once or twice, then fallen understandably in love with it and who then decide to move here for good, to uproot yourselves, maybe even your families and, on the spur of the moment, buy a house or get a rent here, may not have thought things through. There are the obvious obstacles, of course, along the idyllic course you've set for yourselves: stormy or cancelled boat rides, the fact that we will know much — perhaps everything — about you before you're even unpacked while you may never discover anything of consequence about the rest of us, the odd reception from some to your overwhelming enthusiasm and eagerness to help out. But the biggest challenge, by far, will be deciding who to wave to and with what degree of ardor or, more critically, who best not to bless with that acknowledgement at all. In between are myriad degrees of recognition, from a knuckle barely wiggling upward that says simply, "I acknowledge your existence and that you're new here and that my tiny gesture will make you feel better about yourself" to the gleeful and energetic greeting of someone you've met, perhaps your realtor. It's tempting, as a newcomer, to wave joyously to everyone from day one, even before you've absorbed the convoluted subtleties of island relationships, but the risk of taking to the road amateurishly, waving to all the wrong people or ignoring all the right ones, can set your immigration status back decades.

The drama department at school presented *Two Murder Mysteries*. It was another good production.

I went to the matinee performance of the two murder mysteries last weekend and was, for the longest time, mesmerized by the little old lady nodding off at stage left. I had to check and recheck the program to convince myself that the oldest character on stage was, in fact, Lily Warren, the youngest, or nearly so, kid in the cast. She was terrific. Emily Baird was similarly excellent, never out of character and rather a stunning presence. Bethany Candage, very circumspect as both the calculating Officer Occifer and the briefly wounded fiancée, was very convincing. Ivy Oxton did, in fact, know everything, just as she told us over and over, and just as she did when she came to the front of the school bus to help me navigate my way around town on my first day as driver several years ago. In each performance Ellie Reidy was the consummate distracted character we've come to appreciate ever since she stepped on stage. Everett Webster, cocky, brash, and continually in character, commanded everyone's attention. Hannah Noyes was very imperious and quite above it all, and Jason Moody, as the dog trainer, contrasted nicely with the rest of the assembled suspects. During the intermission I dozed off and might have remained thus had not Hannah Jo Moody screamed. That spectacular and regular element of the second mystery, and Hannah Jo herself, anchored the action as it lead from one frightening possibility to the next. Keaton Lear was great. Clearly, we can look forward to seeing a lot more of him in the years to come.

Dana Barton was reminded by an earlier "Observer" of an encounter he'd had decades earlier.

Car-Boat

A couple of weeks ago there was an article here in the *Wind* about a car that was also a boat! This story brought back some old memories of a few years ago for me. I was working my very first real summer job for Brud Carver at E. G. Carver & Sons Grocery. It was in the early '70s and my job was to deliver groceries up the island to the summer clientele. I would leave the store after lunch with a truck full of groceries packed up by the girls at the store of which Marion (Brud's wife) was in charge and spend the afternoon traveling the endless back roads to deliver my goodies. On this particular sunny afternoon I was driving down the Browns Head Light Road towards Fish Head when I met this little bright red convertible (car-boat)! I had never seen anything like it before.

> Behind the wheel was an older lady with a big white floppy sunhat (at the time I was told the lady was a Harrower, maybe Tina Harrower?). As we passed she motioned for me to stop. She wanted to know if I might have seen her propeller in the road. She had lost it somewhere along the way and it was crucial for her to find it so she could cross the Thorofare. I hadn't seen it, but told her I would keep an eye open for it. I don't know to this day if she ever found it or not! I just did a little research and found out that the boat-car was called an Amphicar, and only 4,000 were produced by 1965, with a Triumph engine. You can find more about it on the Internet. Very interesting!
>
> Dana Barton

By June, with the end of restoration in sight, I felt compelled to vent a little about the unhelpful handful who relentlessly took on the responsibility of criticizing the work we'd done on the Old Engine House.

> The old second floor meeting room in the Old Engine House is finished and the Vinalhaven Press will be moving back in soon, as will the Rockland Animal Hospital. We've had an astonishing number of helpful suggestions from sidewalk superintendents during the course of this project. Some have suggested we should not have installed a metal roof over the old one without first replacing the old sheathing, although an inspection beforehand revealed the old sheathing was sound. We were advised to jack up two corners of the building so the clapboards would be level, that we let the building remain in its settled condition but take off all the clapboards and straighten them, that we should have used pressure-treated material and that our perfectly clad doors will rot before the year is out, that we should have jacked up the entire building and installed a slab under it, that we were wasting time and money trying to save the beautiful vaulted ceiling when a suspended fiber ceiling would have sufficed, that the addition of a public restroom was a waste of time because it will be trashed, that there are too many people from "away" involved and we should have left the care of this island treasure to we who live here year-round, and, more recently, that the pink/grey now on the walls is hideous and we should have painted it the same lovely red that we applied to the hose tower. The grey being a primer, we will take their advice. Feel free to offer money, as well. $19,702 left to raise.

J.O. Brown, the legendary North Haven Boat Yard, celebrated 125 years in business.

The Maine Lobstermen's Union Local 207 was formed.

I appeared on a 2013 PIE sponsored authors' panel with Linda Greenlaw and Amy MacDonald.

The Water District began a substantial overhaul of the water distribution system — very impressive and efficiently done.

A first draft of the proposed Comprehensive Plan was made available for review.

I was asked if I read a great deal. I don't, but I enjoy it when I do. My daughter had read more books by the time she was five than I've read in a lifetime.

> I confess to a modest reading addiction. I read a book every day, not a different book, mind you, like my daughter does. Rather, I always have a book on my bedside table and I read it every night until I'm finished, which is often a month or more since I sometimes only read a couple of pages before being awakened by the sound of the book hitting the floor. Right now I'm reading *My Beloved World*

by Supreme Court Justice Sonia Sotomayor. I was supposed to have read it before last week's book group meeting, but I hadn't finished. I will, at this pace, by the end of the month. I read another four pages last night. I also read a couple of magazines faithfully. *The New Yorker* arrives weekly, and I read it all, except for the "Shouts and Murmurs" section and the poetry, neither of which make any sense whatever. The other, "Travels With Tessie Toodles," is a periodical in the truest sense. That is, it appears periodically, in a blog, whenever there's something to report. It's exciting reading, not unlike the vicarious thrill felt when reading the account of a hair-raising adventure, climbing Mt. Everest in a blizzard with a broken leg and having run out of food and water, maybe, the kind of thing that leaves the reader grateful to be simply reading about it because to be actually living that remarkable story would be beyond me, wouldn't it?

On Father's Day I received a gift — kind of — from Finn. It came with restrictions. In a few days he was to receive a gift himself, a new sister, and on July 14 that promise was fulfilled. My daughter Sarah's delivery coincided, to within a few minutes, with her first cousin Ariel's. These columns spanned several months but I've included them together for continuity.

A few days ago my grandson, Finn, became two years old and in a few more days he'll have a new sister. Brace yourself, boy! Being the oldest is undeniably satisfying to begin with but will eventually become a burden, one that will weigh heavily on your shoulders for the rest of your life as you struggle to fulfill your parents' expectations. The satisfying moments are many. Opportunities to frame and torment younger siblings present themselves continually and, while the rare quicker parents may catch on, it will likely take a while, time that can be profitably spent building resentment and nurturing rivalry. Perhaps, too, more will arrive, as they did in my family, as one brother after another, fresh fodder for their imaginative standard bearer, surfaced, as it were. The novelty of happy and successive torment will pass, though, as you and they grow older and the solemnity of your obligations crystalizes, freshened by continual and patently unfair reminders from your parents that you are to set an example. Once that transition takes place, and it will, your sobering role as elder will weigh heavily and remain thus forever or until they predecease and thereby free you from responsibility. As that is unlikely, better you simply resign yourself to looking after them in perpetuity, as I have, and take some comfort from knowing that, even in adulthood an occasional opportunity for harassment will present itself, and, free from the reproachful eyes of long-departed parents, you can now and then reap the rewards of being the oldest sibling.

My two-year-old grandson, Finn, presented me with a Father's Day gift this year. It was a tube, from a paper towel roll, I think, painted and decorated and to which were attached crepe paper streamers of various colors. He'd clearly been prepared to regard this as a special day, as a special occasion, and me as a special recipient. He came charging up the driveway full of purpose holding the fabrication out in front of him as if it were a sword. When the door opened he headed right for me holding it out as far as he could reach whereupon I accepted it, took it from him, all the while gushing with thanks and gratitude, praising its ingenious construction and lauding his creative genius. This, though — the likelihood that the thing would be taken away from him, that relinquishing possession was part of the giving process — had not been fully explained and he began to crumble, that heart-wrenching dissolve during which, in only an instant a happy face, full of life and love, transforms itself into grief-stricken despair. This was not the time for discourse, for explaining the joys of giving and receiving. I gave it back to him, and he mumbled thank you through his tears.

Honestly, if my family didn't continue to provide me with fodder I'd happily write about something else. Alas, however, this week was no exception — except that it kind of was — as my daughter and my brother's daughter, never seriously competitive till now, delivered babies within a few hours of one another. As the pregnancies progressed there was much speculation about how close the deliveries would be. It soon became clear, however, that the ladies would not indulge us in a race to the finish. Rather, they undertook to engage and eventually mesmerize the family in a masterfully orchestrated exercise intended to maximize and focus attention, and certainly the desired effect was achieved, although they didn't offer much variety — each a girl, each about eight pounds, each about twenty inches, each adorable, of course, and each healthy and happy. Ariel held off, as the due date approached, in a gracious albeit herculean concession to give Sarah, notoriously nonchalant about such things, a chance to wander onto center stage so they could perform as a spectacular duet. It was quite a performance. I wish my folks could have been here to welcome Harper Eden and Lorelei Angeline. They'd have enjoyed this.

Lorelei is different from her older brother, Finn. She's circumspect, for example. Finn is many things. Circumspect, however, is not one of them. Lorelei is a picture of calm and composure in the sea of commotion that is Finn's world, and that of their parents and household, for that matter, content to absorb and consider her options. And they are many. She was over for dinner the other night to celebrate her fourth week among us. While her family enjoyed dinner I took her to the living room and settled into a rocker to discuss some of those. But she did not share my sense of urgency, did not feel there was any need to hurry things. While I was prepared to talk about the future, about her prospects and the many choices that would present themselves, she seemed content to simply rock back and forth, gazing up at me and listening, now and then closing her eyes, to my renditions of "Up a Lazy River," "Moon Dance," "Sweet Georgia Brown," and a few others I'd worked up for just this occasion. She paid close attention, even smirking attentively when my voice cracked a little at the occasional high note and again when I sang the funny part about Georgia Brown having two left feet. I thought it remarkable that at just four weeks she could be so appreciative, and then a little gas escaped and she smiled even more broadly.

Last night our grandchildren were over for dinner. Lorelei is only six months old but has capably crafted a place on stage for herself, no small achievement when the other cast member is Finnley James. When Finn came into the world he had the stage pretty much to himself, and he adjusted to being a solo performer well and quickly, but he has adjusted well, too, to the need for accommodation and, while Lorelei must pick her moments, she has grown very adept at doing just that. She doesn't upstage him. That would be folly. When she wants attention she's happy to share the spotlight, if necessary, but when called for she can maneuver to center stage, too. Coyly casting an alluring

OBSERVATIONS

smile from her bassinet across the room in such a way as to stop not only the rest of us in our tracks but also Finn, she thereby cues him to call her onstage, whereupon he dutifully reminds us that "Ora eye" is "over there," as in "over yonder," and jerks a casual thumb in his understudy's direction by way of introduction. Then, if she has lines to deliver, he graciously steps aside and lets her take the stage. Sometime her lines are lengthy and challenging recitals. Other times she is only called upon to laugh and gurgle. She pulls off either convincingly, never out of character, and then, instead of exiting, simply fades a little and lets her brother resume his customary leading role. They're a delightful couple, growing more and more accustomed to and accommodating of one another. I predict we'll hear more about them.

The completely restored Old Engine House was presented to the town on the Fourth of July! In a nice ceremony attended by the fire chief, the board of selectmen, and the multitudes assembled for the Fourth, a ribbon was cut and the building was dedicated to Bodine Ames who had worked for so long to keep it from falling down.

If you were among the many in attendance on the Fourth at the Ribbon Cutting or have taken the opportunity to stop by and look at what's been accomplished, you are undoubtedly impressed and will, if you haven't already, contribute toward our modest $5,000 shortfall.

Our thanks and the thanks of the entire community go to Bodine Ames who has selflessly looked after this historic artifact (and much else) for the several decades preceding its salvation. Our thanks, too, go to the board of selectmen for having had the foresight to authorize its restoration, to the Vinalhaven Historical Society for agreeing to take the finished product under its wing, to the several contractors who gave rebirth to an otherwise terminal structure, to all of you who have contributed money or material, and to the fire department for helping restore Old Reuben and its companion antiques to their rightful place. May they rest now in peace (the antiques, not the firemen).

Your (really final) tax-deductible contribution to this project can be made to Historic Downstreet, Inc., POB 209.

Six Writers Read was again presented at the Windy Way Barn. This was the second annual event and featured Marian Godfrey, Sarnia Hoyt, Mia Mather, Dr. Jen Desmond, Janna Smith, and work by the late Max Ross (this read by Ruth Ripnitz).

I found myself in a romantic mood and composed a poem about a couple I'd encountered at a restaurant.

>A couple kissed,
>'twas just a peck,
>across the aisle from me.
>
>She was perched
>at the edge of her bench,
>poised for advantage.
>
>And she was lovely
>and cool and comfortable
>in her situation.
>
>And she was slim;
>most of her perfect hair
>gathered in a sloppy bun.
>
>And she wore a sleeveless top
>then a taut tan middle
>then jeans.
>
>Three silver anklets,
>then flip-flops
>then brown feet
>
>Her eyes were dramatic and
>their makeup subtle.
>Her thoughts were less so.
>
>He was eating sloppily,
>an adorable slob
>and in love.
>
>His hair was all over the place
>as if he'd toweled dry
>and thought it good enough.
>
>She leaned over to show him
>the necklace he'd coyly
>admired. His admiration
>wandered all around it.
>
>Each had a little overbite so
>their top lips met first,
>then the bottoms.

OBSERVATIONS

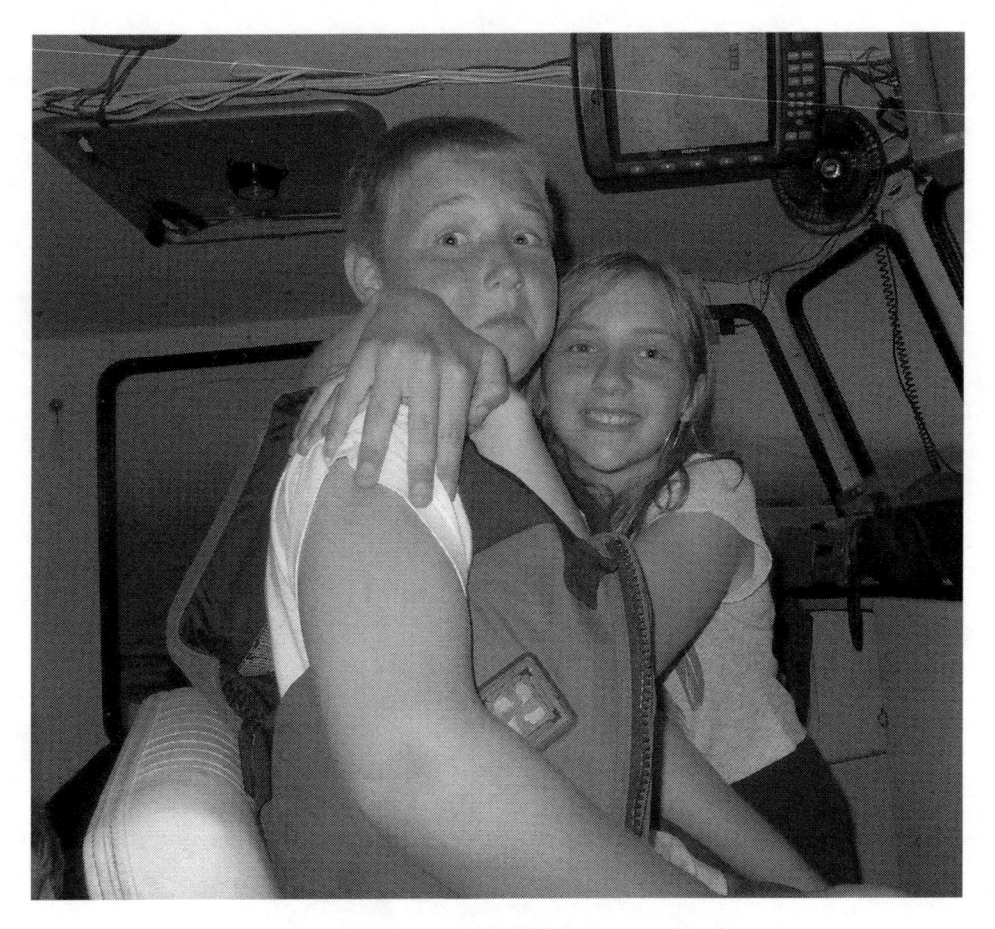

Photo credit: photo provided by the Lazaro family

A photo of a young man at the helm and his equally young admirer resulted in this short "Observer":

> There was a time when a sternperson could be reliably cast as a bad tempered, insubordinate, foul smelling adolescent. No longer.
>
> Here we have a captain, a young man with much responsibility, a lot on his mind and a little more gear to get up, stationed attentively at the helm. Suddenly his sternperson, a moment ago in oilskins and smelling of bait, emerges from below in a cute outfit and smelling quite the opposite and throws her arm around him. This is no impulsive gesture of appreciation for having taken her on. This is serious, and whether he should respond or pay attention to the tight quarters of Leadbetters Narrows just ahead is clearly troubling him.

The weather during the first half of July was awful: dreary, wet, foggy. I found it necessary to lie to motel guests to make them feel better about being here.

2013

It didn't come easily but a few weeks ago I found it necessary to lie to some visitors to the island, folks staying here at the Tidewater. It had rained for eight days in a row and the fog was so thick and low-lying you could sometimes only see half a person coming down the road. Often, unhappily, that was the bottom half. I found I needed to convince my guests that the dismal weather we were experiencing was actually quite pleasant compared to what we are accustomed to. I had to make them feel they'd done pretty well in choosing this soggy week to spend their vacation here, that it could be much worse, that they might have chosen a bad week, one with a high course tide that swept up across Main Street and carried away anything in its path, gale force winds that turned ferry rides into an agonizing passage with all hands hanging over port and starboard, the boat leaving a greasy green wake as it forged onward, or fog so fickle that it sometimes lifted enough to see the rest of the person they were now only seeing half of. I enlisted a couple of my employees to help persuade our more skeptical guests. When we saw one approaching holding onto her hat and straining to see, through the rain and fog, whether there were any cars coming, we would join with one another in a concert of gratitude for the lovely weather and broadcast our thanks that the bad weather that now and then visited itself on us seemed to be holding off and we were clearly in for another fine summer. Remarkably, or perhaps not, we were sufficiently persuasive to convince folks they were enjoying themselves.

By midsummer we were all rejoicing at the availability of fresh produce from several innovative island farms. It was a wonderful blessing and a tribute to the folks who made it happen.

When I was a kid there was a farm, Ross Grey's, I think, up where the airstrip is now. I remember Joe Goose and I were hired by Ross to heave manure into a big pile. We used pitchforks. Joe was in front of me — too close, as it happens. My pitchfork went into his ankle. It wasn't pretty; the fork, after all, had just been tine deep in — well, never mind. Dr. Earle saved him. Back then you could get a cucumber or a tomato if you went up to Ross's or to the one or two other humble operations around town, and those farmers would now and then come in to town and peddle their stuff or maybe sell it to the A&P. Today the freshest produce, right out of the ground, is continually available on the shelves of several island stores, at the weekly flea market, from farm stands, and, twice a week, through an enormously successful CSA (Community Supported Agriculture) that puts in a welcome and welcoming downtown appearance. Sparkplug Farm, Hall's, Peaceful Harbor, Creelman's, Adair's, Long Cove Farm, the Reach Farm and similar great operations on North Haven — all contribute to one degree or another to our access to unadulterated nutritious food, and as long as a rogue Monsanto seed doesn't waft across the bay on a westerly, we can look forward to that continuing.

The VLT was still engaged in raising money enough to purchase Big Tip Toe Mountain. I was embarrassed to admit I hadn't been up there since I was in high school so I went back. It was "high" time.

I went away for a few days to attend a funeral and Elaine took the occasion to go up to Big Tip Toe. She'd agreed to do some promotional artwork on the occasion of the Land Trust's imminent acquisition of that pristine and unique piece of Vinalhaven. When I returned she asked why, in all the time we've been here together, I'd never taken her to Big Tip Toe. "You've lived here all your life, known about this magnificent spot, and have never taken me there?" I'd forgotten! Even after having walked all the way around the island not long ago and passed by Big Tip Toe during the first of the four winters that adventure consumed, I'd forgotten what an extraordinary place that is. So

OBSERVATIONS

this morning I went up there before dawn and hiked up to the top to watch the sunrise. The sun reached Mt. Battie about seven minutes before it reached me and then the whole bay came to life, quite literally, as the dark patches that had, moments before, been Fox Rocks summit, Basin High Mountain, Isle au Haut, Stonington, Hurricane Island, and the water tower on North Haven came alive with light. As a kid I took this and everything else about this place for granted. I shouldn't have. Anyone might have purchased this and taken away the access we've assumed was ours. The Land Trust will take care of this gem and it will be ours in the truest sense.

I had no idea there were as many folks here on Vinalhaven who are as funny as I am, funnier even.

A couple of weeks ago I had a troubling thing, a wart or mole or something, removed from the lower right side of my neck. The resulting wound, requiring seven stitches, has caused speculation from all quarters. I'm grateful for the many who expressed genuine concern. The suggestion, however, that they might have gone all the way around and done us all a favor, that it might have been better for all concerned if they'd simply taken off my head, was a little jarring, particularly since it was made more than once. One asked if an undeveloped twin had been exorcised. Another guessed that I'd had a tooth extracted and that it had been easier to go in through my neck than to try and find a few minutes when my mouth wasn't running. Several asked if the bolt had fallen out and wondered at the absence of a hole on the opposite side. One inquisitive fellow marveled at the lengths to which I might go to achieve asymmetry. The best guess, though, was from those who supposed I was experimenting, for what all agreed were the obvious reasons, with having a facelift but had opted to just take a tuck in one side to begin with.

Every now and then, it seems to be cyclical, some yahoo goes on a rampage and tears around town in the middle of the night breaking things. Someone needlessly reminded me that I was once a yahoo myself.

It's been years since I suffered any vandalism here at the motel, quite a spell since anyone came staggering by and threw my bikes overboard, or busted into the office to try and steal money, or broke a window. I'd grown complacent. Sarah's mom, Janet, has been in residence at the cottage for the last week or so visiting our daughter and her growing family and it was she and her boyfriend, Peter, who noticed one of my canoes floating by upside down. Of course they assumed the worst but when they rushed to the shore to help someone in distress and saw another one emerging from under the bridge, but upright, they grew less concerned about boaters in danger and more suspicious that it was only the boats themselves that were in trouble. Between us we retrieved the canoes which had been thrown into the waterworks between the motel and the apartments the night before during the outgoing tide and, after banging around against the stone dam for a few hours, emerged into the pond when the tide turned. One of the culprits lost his wallet in the process. It had fetched up under one of the caned seats. There wasn't quite enough cash to make the needed repairs but it turns out the last four digits of Vinalhaven's zip code comprise his PIN, so I'll be OK.

Harold's father was Champ's caretaker and, like Champ, a home brewer. We'd overheard him telling about Champ's having made some beer when he'd arrived a week earlier and describing a too-hasty bottling process after which several cases had been stowed underneath Champ's back porch. Bigfoot,

> Staffie, and I turned down River Road after dark and parked about a quarter mile from Champ's cottage. There were several cars tucked into the bushes here and there, and, as we got closer, we could see that Champ was having a party. We headed down through the woods a short distance from the house, walked along the shore a ways, then came up toward the back side of Champ's place through the blackberry bushes. We found what we were looking for and, each carrying a case, crawled back through the thorns to my car. Just as we emerged from the woods, bloodied and bruised, a car came down the River Road toward us, and another from the opposite direction. Suddenly we were fully illuminated. I threw my case through the window into the back seat. Staffie turned back for the safety of the woods but ran into Bigfoot, and they both collapsed in a heap. Passing one another carefully on the narrow dirt road, the two cars, one driven by a fellow who worked for my dad and the other by Staffie's older brother, slowed to take it all in. We waved casually, Staffie and Bigfoot still sitting in the mud with a case in each of their laps, just as the first bottle exploded.

The Toughcats, a local band that was gaining some real recognition, was coming to the island to do a benefit concert for VES.

In several spots around the island honey bees were swarming and relocating with no apparent rhyme nor reason. One bunch chose a tiny hole in the soffit at my house. They're still in there.

> After Carver's Harbor Market closed on Sunday an employee headed for the back door, then remembered something and went back out into the retail area for a minute. A few minutes earlier I'd come home to find a Hitchcockian gathering of bees, thousands, on the inside of the bathroom window. I went to Fishy Friend for wasp spray, but they were out, so I went to Carver's to see if perhaps someone was still there, although it was nearly two hours after closing. Just as the aforementioned employee headed back into the store I pulled the back door open (to my surprise) and stepped in. The light was on in the upstairs office so I went up to ask about getting a few cans of spray. While I was going up the stairs the employee returned from the front, went out the door, and locked it. I was, and remained, unaware of her and she of me. I reached the top of the stairs and found no one in the office. I went back down and pushed open the swinging doors to see if someone was out in front but before stepping into the darkened retail area thought better of it, thought that perhaps I'd set off an alarm if I did. I went back upstairs and called the owners to alert them that the place was open and unattended. I got no answer so called the manager. I told her why I was there and that there was no one on the premises. She was astonished to think the place was unlocked and unattended but said that she'd be right down to lock up and I should go ahead and get what I needed. So I went on into the store and up toward the front where I know the wasp spray was kept. To her credit, Kim did not wet herself when I stepped out of the shadows. I wish I could say the same.

Robert Indiana enjoyed a major retrospective of his work, *Beyond Love*, at the Whitney Museum in New York City.

For the second time Elaine and I were suckered into playing croquet. Years earlier it was at Leo's Lane. This time it was up on Brighton Knoll.

> Chicanery has no place in cricket, fencing, coursing (look it up), or, it seems to me, in croquet. Neither should croquet be a "take no prisoners" competition. Outrage and deception have no place in gentlemanly competition, notwithstanding the loftily christened Brighton Knoll Croquet Park,

OBSERVATIONS

now in its second year of flimflam and treachery. The couple (from "Away") who brought this perfidy to the otherwise unadulterated Kingdom of Cabriplecot (formerly Carver, Brighton, Pleasant and Cottage Streets), while undeniably capable athletes and clearly in their prime, don't bring much else that is pure and righteous to their occasional invitationals. In the beginning the games were innocent enough, but as the summer wore on the host's clear unwillingness to accept an occasional defeat, or to acknowledge the existence — among the locals no less — of others who were their athletic equals festered until it became an obsession. We who are invited back as fodder do so with the full knowledge that at any moment and often throughout the match, balls will be moved, boundaries will become fluid, and imaginary offenses, conceived to fit the occasion and ensure they emerge victorious, will be called into play as needed, but folks, "wicketing" is not a verb and a boundary cannot be defined by wherever the dog chooses to lie.

I learned that a particularly resourceful islander, "Add" of the "Duck and Add" duo mentioned earlier, had thwarted the cable company.

Down on the east side, where a good deal of our skullduggery has been found to take place, Fairpoint, or whatever cable company is serving that area, is being cheated of taking the advantage they customarily take of the rest of us. Deep in the woods and fields, tucked in at the edge of the grid, and hidden from prying eyes, and certainly from the cable guy, a solitary island man has devised a means of getting clear TV reception. Perched on his stairs is a contraption that, while making it difficult to get upstairs to bed or to the bathroom, provides him with the clear picture the rest of us pay through the nose for. A straight-backed chair, tied off to the adjacent wall and railing, teeters on one leg on the landing, and impaled on its ear is a cardboard box that once contained the TV antennae, now balanced atop the box. Each of the prongs sticking out from the antennae is extended by many feet in all directions by continual rolls of tin foil, and from these, in turn, hang coat hangers, silverware, paper clips, kitchen utensils, pots and pans, a Swiss Army knife, etc., each bent or hung to point in a particular direction and gathered in well-established configurations. By sliding the Army knife down so the hanger tips to the west, and bending the foil roll on the uppermost prong downward, for instance, he can enjoy *Masterpiece Theater* as clearly as the rest of us.

Elaine and I took a fall vacation, renting a cabin up near Lake Megantic, site of the terrible train derailment and explosion a few months earlier.

Elaine and I spent the better part of a week recently in a log cabin up near the Canadian border, a lovely place on the northernmost of the Chain of Ponds that Benedict Arnold traversed on his astonishing and tragic trek to Quebec. The owner and I had bartered a week at her place for a week at the Tidewater. We certainly did not get the mellow end of that bargain. It was mid-October, the setting breathtaking, the foliage close to peak, and the cabin idyllic. So, with everything else so perfect, why, we wondered, would the cabin owner have so exuberantly misrepresented to us the existence of an abundance of wildlife? She'd forwarded extensive information about the area and the camp's idiosyncrasies, and scattered here and there throughout were bold exhortations about the creatures with whom we were about to share this neck of the woods. "WATCH OUT FOR MOOSE!" she wrote and in such big bold letters that we crept along up Route 27 toward her camp sure that at any minute a huge bull version of Bullwinkle, like the one we saw at Baxter a few years ago — or worse, his family — would appear, only to be struck down by we who had not taken our landlady seriously.

We made it to the camp without mishap, and for the next several days drove into town and back several times, but with nary a moose obstacling (many think it's not a word but the Freemasons know better) our passage. Her voluminous instructions also included a caution that we — I in particular — should wander freely around the cabin establishing a perimeter by "marking my territory" so the coyotes would be discouraged from challenging my dominance and would thus keep their distance. And squirrels!!! We were to dispatch the troublesome varmints with the loaded pellet gun she kept on the counter, lest we be overrun. "Also, take care to watch for mice. This is an old cabin; they love to scrounge around in search of crumbs and leftovers." She alerted us to the existence of mousetraps, baited and ready, throughout the camp. In addition, we were to pay particular attention to medieval contraptions, constructed so as to entice a hapless mouse to crawl up a lath toward something tasty, but in fact the lath leads to an empty and delicately balanced beverage can perched on the rim of a bucket of water. When the critter steps on the can, it rotates, causing the rodent to fall into several inches of water from which it cannot escape and in which it eventually drowns. Finally she thoughtfully called our attention to flies — cluster flies — that we might find an annoyance and to the several fly papers hanging from the rafters.

Excited about the prospect of encountering a moose but failing to have seen those promised on the highway, we embarked on canoe and vehicular expeditions deep into swamps and wetlands where we might reasonably expect them to put in an appearance. We did find piles of scat at a DOT sand lot next to a swamp and in such staggering quantities that we could only conclude they were not left by DOT employees but more likely by the elusive moose, unless, of course, the folks hereabouts— folks not unlike our landlady — were so hell-bent on convincing visitors that this was moose country that they imported the stuff from elsewhere to foster that ruse.

Otherwise, except for a few exciting moments during a hike, there was, while breathtaking beauty in every direction, nothing afoot/hoof/paw. Neither were there to be seen any coyotes and, while I am willing to concede that it was because I, having brought along plenty of beer, faithfully established a damp and regular perimeter, there were no squirrels either. Not a single fly disturbed our solitude. In short, not a creature was stirring, not even a moose, neither mouse.

While we were clambering up a rocky and steep trail toward Poplar Stream up near the Canadian border a while back, Elaine calling from ahead to encourage me to keep up, an oncoming fly mistook her open mouth for a refuge and flew in. Unfortunately for the fly, she swallowed just as it was settling in on an inviting warm spot. She was stopped in her tracks and compelled to try and dislodge the little invader, and I seized that opportunity to retake the lead. I slowed as I passed to remind her of its nutritional value and suggested she simply welcome and let her body make the most of it. She choked a response, but it was unintelligible, and I called out over my shoulder as I moved on by that many cultures in other parts of the world valued insects as part of their diet, and that they had recently become all the rage among the astute natural and organic food crowd in the States. She resumed walking but without her usual aggressiveness, and continued to struggle as she went; I think its little wings were tickling her throat on its way down.

The ARC organized a twenty-mile bike trip on North Haven.

OBSERVATIONS

A portion of the long awaited sidewalk from town to the ferry was completed.

> Kevin and Danny and the road crew have built a wonderful sidewalk, in conjunction with work being done on the water mains, from the fountain all the way up Water Street and Atlantic Ave. to the top of the hill, by Dick Healey's old place, overlooking the Lane's Island Bridge. Walking that stretch now is so much safer and so much more comfortable and enjoyable than navigating the rubble that preceded it. Meanwhile, there's been a great deal of turmoil and angst, as one anguished observer noted, about whether to accept the town's Sidewalk Committee (did you know we had a Sidewalk Committee?) recommendation that a similar sidewalk, but with granite curbing, reflecting the town's rich quarrying history, be constructed from the Legion Hall to the ferry terminal. The recommendation ran into opposition from here and there and was ultimately rejected, but we are encouraged to see that the town has agreed to install part of the recommended sidewalk, including the suggested granite curbing, from the Legion Hall to the crosswalk at Harbor Wharf. That work is being done in two sections. The first, from the Legion Hall to the fire station, is complete and looks terrific. The second half, on to the crosswalk, will be done in the spring. Imagine what it would look like if it extended to the ferry terminal as has been recommended, if we could steadily navigate that stretch instead of teetering along on the undulating remains of old asphalt or threading a path of our own where no obvious one exists.

Veterans Day was upon us again. That's all I needed. Then Thanksgiving: likewise.

> Uncle Mike is coming again. For several years now, since my dad passed away, his brother Mike and Mike's son Mike and Mike's son Mike have come up for a confusing weekend in November. Dad and Uncle Mike fought in Germany together. Dad was a gunnery sergeant in charge of launching artillery ahead of our advancing infantry. Uncle Mike was in the Battle of the Bulge. This year he is ninety-four years old and has reluctantly parted company with his beloved *Paper Doll*, a gaff-rigged sloop he's been sailing around the New England coast for sixty years. It's particularly fitting that he should be here this weekend. It's Veterans Day, after all, and he is among the few remaining of the last contingent of Americans sent off to fight for what can arguably be characterized as defending the United States of America. It wasn't much of a stretch to interpret the actions of the Axis powers as eventually representing a threat to our country. That was the last time we had a good excuse. Since then we've sent troops to Korea, Vietnam, Lebanon, Granada, Iraq, and Afghanistan, for all sorts of reasons, none worthy, some quite imaginative, some bogus, but none were to defend the United States of America. Veterans are veterans and certainly deserving of the same respect but some died for a noble cause and some died for nothing.

Having made such a troubling assertion, I was urged to visit a local lady who'd lost a son to the Vietnam debacle. She was very understanding.

> Lest anyone think I am content to simply rant I will take this moment, this Thanksgiving, to remind myself of how very fortunate I think I am to live in this country and, more particularly, in this place. Although I'm very unhappy about the direction in which this country is headed, I'm nonetheless thankful that I am free to say so till I am blue in the face. I'm aware that over three-quarters of the world's people are not free to say anything of the kind, and many of them are not free to say anything

at all about anything. Meanwhile, I can insist that my own government pay attention to me even though they don't. And then there's this island. When I graduated from high school I couldn't wait to get out of this place. When I got out of the service four years later I still felt that way and moved to a big city. Suddenly, and probably in the nick of time, I realized there was an empty place in my life and it could only be filled here on this island where I'd grown up (sort of). I know the same thing has happened to others; I see them go and then return all the time. And now I'm here and, in spite of my many attendant blessings, I know I have become complacent, both about being an American and about living here. This column has provided me with an opportunity to remind myself of my good fortune. There, I feel better.

A terrible fire, the worst we'd seen in years, left a local family homeless. Help poured in from all directions.

There are all sorts of ways to help out Hayley and Dana after this week's tragic fire, among those are through Vinalhaven Community Outreach. Ironically, Outreach was begun in 2001 to help, among other things, when Hayley and Dana's son, Isles, was badly injured. Community Outreach was begun by representatives of the island churches. Their purpose is to address the basic needs of families or individuals in times of crises by making payments directly to those institutions, such as utility providers and grocers, upon whom the affected family is dependent during an emergency. Donations can be made directly to Community Outreach, POB 331, at any time, of course, and will certainly be welcome, but they can also be made and earmarked for particular recipients such as this family. Donations can also be made directly through an account set up on Facebook by Beba Rosen. Search there for "Everything Vinalhaven," a wonderfully useful site created by Amy Lear, and follow the link to youcaring.com that is posted just below the fire photo. I'm sure donations of clothing and other necessities are also welcome, and a collection site will probably have been offered elsewhere in today's *Wind,* but failing that, feel free to drop off contributions of any kind here at the Tidewater.

One of the ladies employed at the Fishermen's Friend had been after me for years to rekindle the exchange of abuse that once had them all in stitches, so I did. It got the expected response the next week.

Last week, the fellow whose family lets him think he runs Fishermen's Friend was wheeling out several cases of Bud for his discriminating lunch crowd, when he nearly stumbled over four cases of really good beer and demanded, as well he might, given the pedestrian range of hops normally offered by the Friend, "What's this stuff doing here?" It turns out Island Transport, likely in the interest of raising the bar, so to speak, at the Friend, had delivered several cases of superior beer, otherwise destined for the uptown emporium known to discriminating drinkers as Island Spirits. Startled to learn that their beer had gone astray and might be contaminated by anyone or anything having to do with Budweiser, Spirits dispatched one of their lackeys to retrieve the four cases. Accustomed to exercising the same extreme care he'd been taught back at the shop, he began to carefully transfer the beer to his truck but was tripped — quite clearly it was intentional — by the aforementioned stock boy as he wheeled out another dolly, this of Bud Light. Stumbling, a case of fine Scottish ale hit the floor, breaking one bottle within. As he hurried out to the truck, the broken bottle draining through the cardboard, twelve valuable ounces of some of the best brew the world has ever and the Friend has never known left its aromatic trail from the back room to the door. Then, for hours, the usual Friend crowd — and this is testimony to the hope that the lives of even the most severely deprived can be improved upon — observed that the place never smelled so good. Even the girl behind the counter allowed that she wished her man smelled like that.

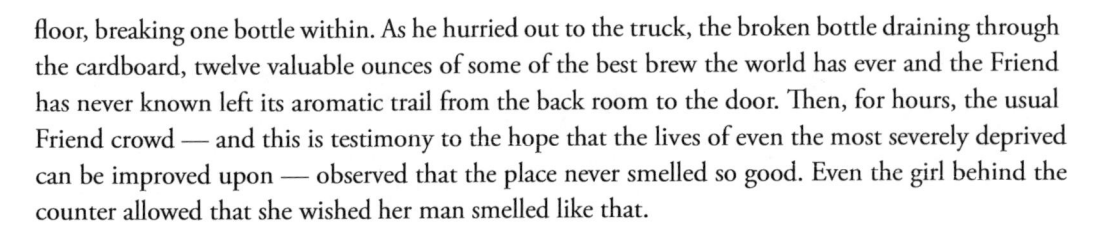

Fishermen's Friend's response

Early this summer, I received a phone call from a business partner at one of the beer companies whose products we carry. He told me he wanted to come out and "redesign" our cooler to include some ales and IPAs. I begged him to not put in too much because we needed the space for real beer. I told him that anyone looking for that caliber of drink would usually start at Island Spirits. He did indeed show up, and on July 3rd he gave our cooler a new look. My staff quickly told him that he had ruined America's birthday for them because he had moved the Budweiser from its assigned berth in the cooler. The following week when I got ready to order, I couldn't find any of the new products. I asked the girls if they had moved it somewhere. They informed me that it had all been sold over the weekend of the Fourth. Sales remained brisk for most of the rest of the summer. This week, while taking inventory in the walk-in, I stumbled over a 12-pack of one of the aforementioned IPAs. I couldn't help but notice that someone had been drawing "smiley faces" in the dust on top of it. The girls told me it had been in the cooler since the last ferry left on Labor Day. I chuckled warmly, and it was then that my faith in our PBR drinkers was renewed.

Jack Waterbury put in his annual appearance as Santa Claus, leaving us to wonder whether he'd be up to it next year. He might well. He is the "old sailor" referred to earlier, and he'd certainly been full of surprises that day.

As reported earlier, at Christmas I receive an amazing coffee cake. So do many others. It was time to say thanks.

When I came into the office the other day the usual big coffee cake was sitting on the counter. This happened last year, too. Come to think of it, the same thing happened the year before and maybe the year before that. This is an impressive cake, full of nuts and weighing about ten pounds. Elaine is allergic to nuts, and, while she is certainly appreciative of the gesture, I have the whole thing to myself and I'm quite content with that. So is she, for that matter, given her aversion to excessive consumption and my enthusiasm for it. There was no name on the cake, nor has there been in previous years. I wonder now if perhaps it was intended for Carol, always had been, and I just got to the office first. No matter. Carol would also probably applaud my having removed temptation. Better that than to consume the meager portions she brings to work for lunch or to snack on and which she forlornly hopes to have for herself. I've come to realize, however, that the coffee cake puts in an appearance elsewhere, too, and that the person responsible for it is probably not someone whose affections are for me alone but for the entire community. In fact, I now know that's the case and that, while the occasional cake may be gifts for a selected few, she is a gift to us all.

In 2013 one hundred and twenty-six million pounds of lobster were landed in Maine by 5,800 license holders, and the price was $2.89 per pound.

Brown's Head Light

Observations

2014

An amazing squirrel lives in our backyard and an amazing woman lives just across the way.

We have a few bird feeders just outside our back door. A couple of them hang on a line strung between two trees for that purpose. Another is attached to the middle of our kitchen window, where we can enjoy the considerable activity, particularly when there is deep snow and few alternatives. Two other creatures attend our feeders. One is an astonishingly acrobatic squirrel. I'm sure you are all impressed with the accomplishments of squirrels at your own feeders, but ours, I'm quite sure, are in a league of their own. Each of the line feeders is equipped with a little looping handle for handling and for hanging from clips on the line. The diameter of the half-circle created by those metal loops is two and a half inches and the feeder hangs on a line that is five feet from the deck rail. Philippe Petit strolls along the slippery vinyl deck rail as if it were sandpaper, stops abreast of the feeder, makes some obvious calculations, and then launches himself precisely through the loop, stops his trajectory by splaying his hind feet, then hangs upside down helping himself to the several little ports till he's stuffed. The other creature at our feeder is nearly as inventive and not much less acrobatic. She is our eighty-year-old (close enough) neighbor, who is so determined to leave hilarious little critters hanging from our feeders or glowering malevolently through our kitchen window that no amount of snow will keep her from her appointed rounds. Several times each winter we wake to find a little varmint—perhaps with a scarf, huge beak, a hideous grin, maybe goggles—gleefully astride a feeder or perched on the rail, and closely spaced laughing footprints trailing off across the backyard to Bodine's.

2014

I was reminded by watching my grandson watch my granddaughter of a short-lived relationship I had with a sister.

> I only had a sister for a year or so, when I was around fifteen and, while it was an eye opener, it didn't leave me with a deep understanding. An uncle's marriage had fallen apart and my folks took his lovely and flirtatious teenage daughter in to live with us in the Moses Webster house where we had plenty of room, and she could have one of her own. To her, the novelty of suddenly finding herself in the company of four curious boys was easily the equal of our astonishment and great interest in finding so intriguing a figure in our midst. She quickly became adept at maneuvering each of us to her advantage, particularly the three oldest, and pretty much had the run of the place. Suddenly our world was full of mystery. She didn't behave like us, didn't communicate like us, didn't resolve difficulties or disputes like us, and didn't play fair like us. Suddenly we found ourselves squabbling with one another without knowing why. The other night I watched as Lorelei's dad whirled from room to room while holding her aloft and naked (risky) on her way to a bath in the kitchen sink. Her older brother watched the aerials for the brief minute it held his interest and I wondered if everything about her was a mystery to him, like a little boy about his age I'd once overheard give voice to his confusion by asking, "Mom, how can she aim with nothing to hold on to?

The draft Comprehensive Plan was presented to the town for approval and approved unanimously before being sent on to the state for review.

I had the good sense to attend an amazing concert in Rockport.

> A brother sent us two tickets to a January 10 concert at Strom Auditorium in Rockport. We hadn't planned to go. It was to feature the Midcoast Community Chorus and we'd never heard of it. We figured we got the tickets because some little group was doing a concert and was desperate to have some folks attend (like when the Blanks sing). At the last minute, although I'd lost the tickets, we decided to take a day — it was like spring — and go to the mainland. We'd swing by the auditorium and if it looked worthwhile, maybe we'd stay for a few minutes. It was sold out. We had to make a very strong case for having been given tickets and lost them but were eventually led to the only two empty seats among the thousand-plus the auditorium held. It turned out to be the most inspiring event I'd seen, at least in recent memory. Given what recent memory is that's not saying much, but Elaine agrees, so I'm right. At the appointed time over a hundred singers, four-fifths of them women, from fourteen to ninety-one, filed on from the left, filled four tiers of walkways that swept around the entire wide stage descending from a height of ten feet or so, and a few stools downstage to accommodate those less athletic but certainly no less enthusiastic. Every face was a palette of joyous and contagious anticipation, and the reason for that blissful condition soon bounded on stage. Mimi Bornstein is the Founder and Artistic Director of the Midcoast Community Chorus, and clearly an inspiration. There followed two hours of exhilarating music. It could not be otherwise with her at the helm, not unlike our own Annie Boyden, and was over too soon.

OBSERVATIONS

A proposal to restore alewives to Old Harbor Pond was being discussed and was to be pitched to the board of selectmen.

Two Island Fellows from the Island Institute, Andy Dorr, who'd successfully sheparded the Comprehensive Plan to fruition, and Kelsey Byrd, now headed up individual initiatives. Andy — an economic development study, inviting participation from existing business owners and from those interested in starting new businesses, and Kelsey — the Wellness Coalition, whose focus was improving the health and well-being of this island community.

NASA announced an impending rendezvous that seemed impossible to me and I was reminded of an earlier event that seemed equally unlikely years ago.

> I was sitting in Gram J's kitchen on July 20, 1969 watching Walter Cronkite report that Neil Armstrong was standing on the surface of the moon. She abruptly got up and turned off the twelve-inch black-and-white console. I asked what on earth she was doing, and I turned it back on again. All this progress had happened too quickly and this, a man landing on the moon, was more than she could comprehend, and so she chose not to comprehend it. What would she think this morning? Ten years ago we launched Rosetta, a three-ton vehicle, into space and started it on a series of revolutions around the Earth and Mars, each revolution increasing in velocity so that, when slung from earth's orbit ten years later it would be going fast enough to make a prearranged rendezvous with a particular comet it will have had in its sights for the previous ten years. That meeting will take place in August, 500 million miles from here, when Rosetta, at a time and place arranged in 2004, will pull alongside the comet, travelling at fifteen thousand miles per hour or so, and get acquainted. Then on November 11 Rosetta will dispatch a lunar lander to probe the comet's surface and send back information about the origin and composition of the universe. It would most certainly send Gram J back to the kitchen.

The ferry service has to satisfy the needs of a lot of us and so is often the brunt of criticism. Not today.

The Call of Duty

An elderly lady, stalwart but winding down, indefatigable but not as sure on her feet as she once was, left home for the ferry. It was 6:20 a.m. She had ten minutes to get there. She slammed the door to close it tightly. It had swollen some, as usual this time of year. Her hand slipped from the knob as she tried to pull it closed and she fell over backward, striking her head on the floor. She nonetheless managed to get to her feet and, a little woozy, made it out to her car. She drove down and got in line, opened the door and walked, limping a little, to the terminal to pick up her line number. An alert ticket agent asked if she was OK, and while receiving assurance that she was, watched carefully as she headed back till she was safely in her vehicle, then called the captain on the bridge to alert him to her condition. The captain's wife happened to be a passenger and he sent a message down to her asking that she go out and invite the older woman to join her in the cabin. Her car was on the bow, winds were up, and she'd otherwise have a rough ride. That and her unsteady condition, he knew, would likely result in greater distress. The mission was a success; she was settled in the cabin and, after they were under way, a crewman, dispatched from the bridge, one assumes, arrived with an ice pack to ease the swelling and discomfort. It is, after all, the Maine State Ferry Service.

I took a quick trip to Florida to visit grandchildren.

Four days ago I was in Disneyworld, the Manic Kingdom to be more precise. My granddaughter and I wheeled her son through Sunday throngs, the magnitude of which made the Exodus of the Children of Israel seem like an event that had failed for lack of interest. I had purchased tickets in advance. The staggering cost, it was revealed, was for "preferred access" that would allow us to skip the long lines at each venue (electronic signs at every one announced the wait time— never less than an hour). It was, as I said, "revealed." Unhappily it was not revealed to me until, after having crept along through the brilliantly conceived and wondrously deceptive and serpentine lines, from Dumbo Ride, to It's A Small World, to the Mad Hatter's Tea Party in six hours, we exited the park with an exhausted and somewhat irritable two-year-old and with thousands of other equally miserable kids and their burned-out guardians who, like me, thought a day at the Manic Kingdom would be an event they'd remember all their lives. It was, of course, but for all the wrong reasons. I did wonder why such a fuss was made over us when we entered the park. Unlike the millions of others, we'd been asked to provide an electronic fingerprint which we were advised would be used to gain access to rides and events throughout the park, but I didn't deduce that our progress would thus be any quicker than anyone else's and so never went to the "express" line. Is it unreasonable to expect an allowance to be made for someone like me? I'm from Maine, after all.

I'm a little hard on my truck.

It's an '02 and because I'm hard on it and because it runs so well and has for so long, I'm content and happy with it and in no hurry to trade up for something newer I can destroy. The other day, I was plowing out a friend up-island and hit a little resistance. The truck stalled. It wouldn't start again.

OBSERVATIONS

It would turn over but no ignition. I called Todd and he came right up (I keep him on a retainer). He suggested it might be a fuel pump, but determined it was not, and then thought perhaps it was an ignition module. "How long will it take to get one?" I asked. "About two seconds; I have one in the Jeep." I was incredulous. "You have an ignition module for a 2002 Chevy in your jeep?" "I feel I need to be prepared for certain people," he answered tactfully.

Elaine has a very tidy and well-maintained little Subaru she's particularly fond of. It has an electric starter she can operate from the kitchen so it's warmed up, especially the driver's seat, by the time she climbs in to go to exercise class. It is perfect, babied, without a blemish, and scrupulously maintained. A week earlier she found it to be making a tiny, barely perceptible little clunk that no one else would have noticed and she took it to Todd, even after having earned a stern rebuke from his public relations person for having bothered him a week or so earlier with a malfunctioning seat warmer. While Todd was installing the module I asked if he had found the little noise the Subaru had been making. "No'" he answered, "and I couldn't hear it. She's a little fussier than you, I think," he observed astutely.

A snowplowing usurper showed up on the wrong side of the bridge.

Until recently I've been lauded as a hero by some of the single ladies in my neighborhood. I'd earned that accolade by being there to fix things, lift things, and plow and shovel snow. It was a great gig, sweetened by goodies. But all that came crashing down last week when, as was customary, I turned out early — well, fairly early — on the morning after a snow storm only to find first one then another of my dependents already neatly free of accumulation. The culprit, I learned from the nearly swooning ladies in question, was a usurper in every sense of the word. First, he was out of his element, an overcrosster on the wrong side of the bridge. Second, unable to manage on his own, he had an assistant, a young man, to take up his considerable slack (I'd never had an assistant). Third, he apparently does not linger to be admired or to receive goodies and so is setting a dangerous precedent for me as I step back into the fray. I suspect, however, he may be spreading himself too thin, that there are folks on his side of the bridge who were left high and dry as he tried to extend his meager resources. He should know, however, that I do not intend to stand idly by and be deprived of the fawning attention and treats to which I've become accustomed in favor of him and his helper (or helpers — who knows how many he'll need by then).

The annual Penobscot Bay Polar Dip was scheduled for a cold day in February, but dangerously bad weather postponed the event twice and it was then called off. Nonetheless three intrepid dippers, Anna Marie Lazaro, Anna Poe, and Durene Martin, indulged in the unthinkable after Joe Lazaro shoveled a path to the water. Supporters pledged contributions to the Vinalhaven Library.

Efforts were underway to raise money and contributions that would permit an Honor Flight for veterans to visit their memorial in Washington D.C., an event that took place on March 21.

Interest was by now mounting in joining the organizing efforts of a lobstermen's union.

By this time "Kindergarten Kids" had become a regular *Wind* feature, appearing weekly until each student in that year's class had been featured. The results were often appealing, such as this piece, but not always, given the fond hope expressed by others of them that they grow up to possess guns and shoot people.

CLASS OF 2025
Brandon Sean Philip

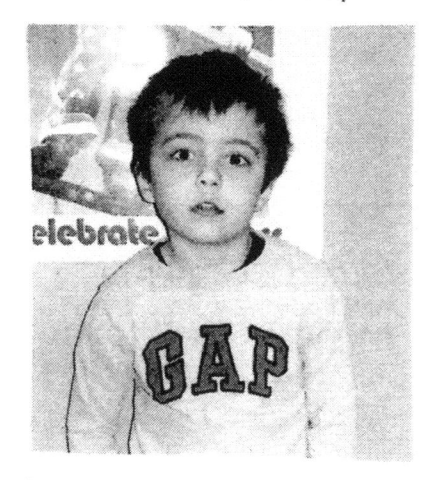

How old are you? five
When is your birthday? My birthday is June 29th
Where do you live? 9 Summer St.
Who is in your family? My dad, my mom, my sister. I have like a billion people in my family. My aunts, my cousins...
Do you have any pets? A dog, Capone he's yellow. My uncle has a cat Stewie, it's black.
What do you like best about kindergarten? Recess. I jump in the snow and PE because you get to run and climb.
Tell us the name of some of your friends. Anthony, Triton, Cooper...I think everybody is my friend!
What are your favorite toys? My cars, I did a jump with one and it almost went in the washing machine. I like a dozen toys in my house and you know what I like? Me and my sister climb over my bunkbed. Sometimes I sleepwalk. Sometimes I roll off my bed. Sometimes I even roll under my bed.
What do your parents do for work? My dad's a lobsterman and my mom works for Island Institute. She directs fellows on the mainland.
Tell us something about you that we don't know. I do pretty cool stuff. I smash my head into my snowman if I get angry. I can do a backflip. I can do a cartwheel. I weigh fifty pounds. **My sister weighs thirty. My mom is 33, my dad is 36.
What do you want to be when you are all grown up? A diver. I would dive for fish and money. I'll give people tuna fish. I will save the money for candy. I like candy! I will never stop liking it.

Bob Candage retired from being the active leader of the Community of Christ congregation. He and I have been friends since we were toddlers, but I'd have written about his retirement and all that he has been and done for his community even if that were not the case. I penned a related column and then had the privilege of offering a roast at the official ceremony.

> Elder Bob Candage is humble. I'd like to say, for a laugh, that he wasn't always, but the truth is he's always been humble, as was his dad. Bob and I lived next door to one another when we were teenagers. My memories of growing up here are few and not great, but my memories of being in Bob's company are good ones: up on Armbrust Hill playing good guys and bad guys, or cowboys or Indians on either side of the stockade fence that fortified his backyard. I have reminded you that he is humble by way of acknowledging that what I'm about to say is not going to sit well with him. That's not going to stop me, of course, but I do feel the need to at least recognize his resistance.

Last Sunday he presided, as the minister of the Community of Christ congregation, over his last Sunday service at the Pleasant River Chapel. The Blanks turned up to sing a couple of numbers. It was presumed, of course, that we were going to sing to him, so he sat down to see what we had up our sleeves. But he's a Blank and nothing we sing sounds as good without him as it does with him, so we asked him to join us. We did an innocuous number to set the stage for more unrelated tunes to follow, but then sang "Bridge Over Troubled Waters," whose chief lyric invites us, when we have pain or sorrow or are burdened, to "lean on me." I can't think of anything that so well describes the relationship of this town, we who have leaned so faithfully and so often for forty years, with and on Bob.

ROAST

When I was a teenager, I lived in the Moses Webster House, now the Paine Homestead. Bob lived next door. His dad was the Elder Ralph Candage. Bob continually reminded me that his dad was an Elder and mine was only a Bud. And furthermore, that it would ever be thus. His dad would always be the Elder and mine would always just be the Bud. And furthermore still, he had no compunctions about telling me that when he grew up he'd be an Elder just like his father and I would just be a regular man, and even that forecast he felt was optimistic. He said "the leopard cannot change his spots, Jeremiah 13:23." He talked like that, chapter and verse, and the Elder thing just never went away. When we were playing up on Armbrust Hill, Bob always had to be a cowboy and we had to be Indians. He said the cowboys were the good guys, and because they were the good guys, and because he was an Elder, God was on their side. The Indians were the bad guys. I had to be an Indian for what he felt were obvious reasons and because I would clearly never be an Elder.

So the ne'er do-wells— John Buteau, Bart Hopkins, and I — we'd be just ready to execute an Armbrust Hill ambush, when Bob's deep bass would ring out from behind a rock (he had a nice resonant voice, even then, and had been nurturing it along with the Elder thing since he was a toddler). "This is the Elder Candage. I am here behind this rock with God. You that dwell in the wilderness will now bow down before me and, as mine enemies, shall lick the dust, Micah 7:17." We would roll our eyes, but dutifully do as he commanded. He was easier to live with when we were compliant, and, frankly, he was a little scary when he spoke that way, like maybe God really was with him. On those rare occasions when we found him before he found us he would pompously bellow, "thou canst not see my face, for there shall no man see me and live, Exodus 33:20." It was quite sobering, particularly on a bunch of Indians whose grip on reality was tenuous at best. Gradually, as the years went by, we realized that God really was on his side. By then it was too late for us. Heading up to the hill during the last of our cowboy and Indian years we would whisper imploringly to God asking that he be an Indian for a change. But God whispered, "I'm on Bob's side. He is or will soon be an Elder. You are not and will never be. I'm sure you understand."

Later on, when our interests had shifted somewhat from cowboys and Indians to girls, Bob was unrepentant about using the Elder thing again to gain the upper hand. Although he was an underclassman, girls were taken in easily by his sonorous and certainly singular pick-up line, "Hi. I am the Elder Bob Candage. Those guys behind me are not elders and they never will be. Furthermore, the tall one is just a Crow and will never be anything else." That kind of doomed my hopes for the moment. I remember overhearing conversations between these very girls I'd been struggling, in vain, to impress. "So, you were out with the Elder Candage last night. I hear he doesn't smoke or drink. Couldn't have been much fun." To which came this unexpected response, "Judge not that ye be not judged, Matthew 7:1. We are going steady." "Do you call him Elder?" "Of course. He won't answer to anything else." "What does he call you?" "He said 'You at last are bone of my bones, flesh of my flesh and shall be called woman, Genesis 2:23.' I like it. It has a nice ring."

Later still, I came to realize that Bob was, in fact, with God and God was lucky to have him.

Jen Desmond, Nurse Practitioner, has been with us now for several years, and during that time she has won hearts and minds and gratitude in abundance — with good reason.

> A friend, an elderly man, was recently very sick. I called the Medical Center's answering service to ask that the provider on duty return my call. She did and asked whether I thought the patient could make it to the Medical Center or if he should come to his home. I told her I thought she'd better come over. (I'm mixing up my pronouns so you won't know who I'm talking about. I don't want to make her uncomfortable). He did come over and spent a lot of time, precious time, particularly for a woman on call on Sunday, with a two-year-old at home, and with other likely demands. When the exam was concluded he asked if the patient had eaten. He hadn't. She suggested he needed to have some nourishment and when he resisted was quite firm and offered to make him some oatmeal. The patient still resisted but barely and she set about making breakfast for him. I offered to do it so he could move on and fulfill what surely must be her many other obligations but he said no, that she'd be happy to help make my friend comfortable. I know from other firsthand experience and from talking to others that this is not unusual and that this particular provider is supremely caring and responsive routinely. I've only lived here for most of my life but assume this isn't the kind of attention one can expect to receive elsewhere.

Kirk Gentalen, who'd previously been doing this sort of thing all over the country, was now a resident steward and naturalist for Vinalhaven Land Trust and Maine Coast Heritage Trust. For the last seven years or so he has produced a wildly interesting blog (vinalhavensightings.blogspot.com) while conducting equally enchanting periodic nature walks. This spring it was a Woodcock Walk on Lane's Island.

The Community Lunchbox, a volunteer effort— now five years in existence — that provides hot delicious meals each week to walk-ins and shut-ins, served over a thousand such meals during the previous fall and winter.

The Maine Symphony Band performed a well-attended concert featuring two of our own young musicians — Ian Dyer on guitar and Danielle Newton on saxophone.

> There are posters all over town announcing the University of Maine Symphony Band Concert tomorrow at the school. Symphonic bands evolved from military band tradition, no strings, but plenty of wind, brass, and percussion. This band will perform for the kids during the day and then for the rest of us at 7:00 p.m. in the auditorium. I expect many of the students who heard them during the day will be there at night, as well. The band is that good. Those of us who know what a treat this is going to be will surely be there. Those of you who may be sitting on the fence should topple off and come, as well. Under the direction of Christopher White, these fifty or so enormously talented musicians will likely present a hugely varied program. Live music is better than Budweiser (but then what isn't?) and this evening will be better than most. You'll hear old jazz standards, Baroque classical

compositions, folk interpretations, marches, rock 'n' roll, waltzes, and, if guitarist Blade Ford takes the stage, an out-of-mind experience called "Chaos Theory" that, while certainly avant-garde, is not entirely chaotic. As an added treat, several of the musicians will sit in with our own school band, affording some of our kids the opportunity to play in a full-size dance band. A well-known jazz piece, "Killer Joe," will feature Ian Dyer on guitar and Danielle Newton will solo sax on "Moondance."

Grandchildren continued to provide fodder.

The other day Lorelei broke into a full throated lament and it was the first time in her eight months among us that I have heard her produce a sustained cry. And even then it was half-hearted. She is the singularly most laid-back little person I have ever known. She customarily greets each new situation, each new person and each reacquaintance with a delightful dimpled and welcoming smile and, when that person, me for instance, makes a silly face or even sillier noise or engages in some similarly mindless entertainment, she displays an endless capacity for delight and appreciation no matter how trifling and pathetic the effort may have been. The other night she came over for dinner with her older brother and her Dad. Mom wasn't feeling well. Dad was a little distracted and forgot to remove her from her carrier, left her on the table like the groceries. No matter. From that perch she surveyed with glee this moment's new surroundings as if she'd never seen them before, with a big-eyed appreciative smile of wonder and fascination. When Dad realized he'd overlooked her for a moment and returned his attention to her I think she may have told him to "chill." He gave her a green bean, in appreciation for which, for the next hour or so, she gazed up at him adoringly as she casually gnawed the thing into submission. A little later another bean was proffered. "Cool, whatever." She is so mellow she makes her older brother Finn, whom she also regards with fascination and applause with each day's incarnation, seem like a drama queen…which, in fact, well…never mind.

Red Cross volunteers tell us that Vinalhaven is one of the most receptive and giving communities. This year's blood drive — as every year — was no exception.

The Chamber of Commerce established an information booth at a small roadside building at Harbor Wharf.

Marjorie Stratton penned a particularly distressing "Town Manager's Corner" article.

Elections—There was an article that caught my eye in *The Week* magazine recently entitled, "Where people care about democracy." It was about the people of Afghanistan and the fact that 58 percent of eligible voters cast ballots in last week's election despite the Taliban death threats. 58 percent of eligible voters was the same as in our 2012 presidential election. Only 41 percent voted in our 2010 midterm elections to elect all 435 members of the House and 37 members of the Senate. We face no such threats and yet we stay home and choose not to participate.

I picked up the *Ellsworth American* last Friday and on the front page was the headline "Running from Office — Ballots Lack Candidates." This article caught my eye as well as it relates to our own open seats for Board of Selectmen. We have two open seats with no one running. At least, to date, no one has taken out nomination papers to obtain the necessary signatures to place a name on the ballot. The *Ellsworth American* article stated that "blank spots on the ballots were a common sight this town meeting season." Many towns hold their annual meeting in March. The article went on to ask, "Is it apathy? A poor economy? Unfamiliarity with Maine's town meeting form of government?

Lack of confidence? Or too much confidence in government?

It's hard to tell someone how rewarding public service is when I know that elected officials pay a price for contributions to their communities. In the best of cases the price paid is only in lost time with family and friends. Sometimes, however, the price is much higher. Long-term friendships are strained and perhaps a trip to the local store ceases to be routine. Your business can suffer from one controversial decision. Knowing that most of the community will respect you for your contribution is little comfort.

So how do we convince people to run for office? It is so important for any community to have strong, committed elected officials that can provide leadership and a common vision.

So how do I bring this to a conclusion? I set out to try and convince people to run for office and ended up talking them out of it. There is no sugar coating it. It can be very rewarding AND difficult. Someone once told me I was too honest to work in local government. Maybe they are right.

I had a beef as well.

Every state has designated a flower as its own. Maine is the only state not to have christened an actual blossom. The Pine Cone and Tassel (*Pinus strobus*) is the state flower of Maine. Not many towns have designated a particular flower as their own. We may be an exception, for, in allegiance to the state's having not chosen an actual blossom, we have apparently selected the empty Budweiser Can (*Chuckus emptius*) as our own town flower. It emerges reliably each spring just ahead of the crocuses, lending modest variety to the companionable and astonishing accumulation of debris that a few (but certainly enough) of us clearly feel perfectly free to toss out the window time after time, day after day, night after night. Those of us who think this is okay are exercising a proprietary contempt for their (and our) surroundings that is difficult to comprehend. And the rest of us have grown complacent about and accustomed to it. So habituated, in fact, that we muster all the kids in school, every spring, to go out and clean up after a handful of the rest of us. And they do it faithfully and well. Increasingly, certain adults join the effort, and this year was no exception. A group mustered for service last week and picked up a truckload of trash that will alleviate the burden on the kids who will soon be out on patrol again this year. And then there are Jim and Merry Boone, who have taken it upon themselves to clean up the entire downtown area, from the galamander to Old Harbor Road, every single morning. It's an extraordinary and consuming gesture of love and appreciation. Most of us are truly grateful for them and for the adults and kids who turn out year after year.

Phil 'n' the Blanks conducted an entire hour-long church service of Gospel music at the Pleasant River Chapel and at the Union Church, and Meals on Wheels ended another "off-season" having helped forty island seniors make it through the winter.

Lyme disease is caused by the bacteria, *Borrelia burgdorferi*, which in turn infect deer ticks, which in turn bite those of us who venture into the woods unprotected. It's not worth it! Continual warnings and notices full of useful information regarding protection and prevention were presented in the *Wind* all year long.

Elaine had taken up Zumba and the result was such a profound experience for me it became an "Observer" column.

OBSERVATIONS

A couple of years ago I emerged from The Green Elephant Bistro on Congress Street in Portland. Rhythmic and wonderfully compelling music came from a nearby building. I went to investigate. Behind huge street-level windows, in a space that must once have been retail, were fifteen or twenty women — a couple of teenagers, a couple of elderly ladies, and a dozen or so in-between—dancing in time to pleasantly loud and seductive Latin music — I think it was samba. Some were facing me, and the others, if not then, were within minutes. The music never stopped and the ladies never stopped moving, each in independent syncopation, and each with a universally rapturous expression. I can't recall ever having seen that much sheer joy expressed before, certainly not simultaneously by so many. Every woman was blissfully happy with what she was doing. I learned later it was Zumba. Elaine has always been in good shape and has always taken care of herself, but recently, in the last year or so during which she has been a Zumba enthusiast, her contentment with what she is doing has taken on a new and joyful dimension. She returns from each Amy Lear Zumba class feeling happy, good about herself, re-energized, eager for the next class days in advance, and grateful for the opportunity and experience. I am grateful, as well, and wish everyone could feel as good about themselves and what they are doing, or about seeing their partners enjoying themselves so much. And, of course, we can.

Efforts to fund a second Honor Flight, this time for veterans of all wars, was underway by spring.

A couple who had summered here for years retired, took up residence in town, and began right away to contribute positively to the quality of life here as so many other retirees have done and continue to do.

Last weekend, in spite of an earlier unpleasantness, we were invited back to Brighton Knoll Croquet Park. I thought, how lovely, this nice couple, presuming and determined to introduce the locals to the finer things in life (like croquet), did it badly, took some heat, but then determinedly took it upon themselves to do better. This time they even invited a lobsterman — always risky — and his better half, in a transparent effort to enlighten even the most unlikely and ingratiate themselves into the fundamental fabric of island life. The croquet of my youth used to be a simple game. Not anymore. We were divided into two teams, the men vs. the ladies, and provided mallets by the host. Each mallet had been curiously festooned with a hose clamp at each end, the clamps covered by white tape. A very lame explanation alluded to the need to hold them together in the face of so much aggressive play. I'm quite sure, in fact, that the inventive host had devised a way to handicap his opponents. I'm still not sure how — maybe they were little receivers to which electrical impulses were transmitted at critical points throughout the game (he's that inventive). We were also continually thrown off our game by the host's insistence that we carry around little butterfly clips, colored to match our mallets, and attach those to each wicket as we advanced around the course, as if we'd otherwise get lost. The bottom line, though, is that although I made it around first, my victory was ignored in favor of presenting victory ribbons to others whose accomplishments paled in comparison but whose favor was curried.

On June 1, the first of what are intended to be annual Lobsterman's Days took place, featuring boat parades, knot tying and trap heading contests, a tug-of-war, and a fish relay.

Vinalhaven Eldercare undertook the production of a new island phone book, and the results, a few months later, were quite beautiful and comprehensive. At the same time, Eldercare solicited support for a line item allocation in the upcoming town warrant.

The Maine State Ferry Service administration proposed a very badly considered new ferry line-up policy, with this result.

> A recent petition asks that the ferry service withdraw a badly conceived proposal for changing the line-up procedures in Rockland. It would prohibit the use of line cars, and provide for them TO BE TOWED AT THE OWNER'S EXPENSE. It would prohibit putting any vehicle in line for a ferry later than the very next one without permission, and would provide for vehicles found in line without permission TO BE TOWED AT THE OWNER'S EXPENSE. It would make it a violation to move people or goods in and out of vehicles in line any time during the thirty minutes prior to departure, make it a violation for someone in a vehicle to take delivery of a part for Hopkins Boat Yard, Todd's Garage, etc., if that delivery is made during the thirty minutes prior to boarding, make it a violation for an unoccupied vehicle to be found in line during the thirty minutes prior to departure, and provides for that vehicle TO BE TOWED AT THE OWNER'S EXPENSE. It would make it a violation for anyone to depart a vehicle in line during the thirty minutes prior to departure and provides for that vehicle TO BE TOWED AT THE OWNER'S EXPENSE. Taken literally, it says that if you are in line at 10 a.m. for a 10:30 departure but find, at 10:05, that you need to get out to pee, your vehicle will be TOWED AT YOUR EXPENSE during those few moments when you are experiencing relief, and, while I acknowledge that's unlikely, it's an indication of how badly considered this proposal is. Repeated emails to Manager John Anders (596-5422) asking that today's deadline for citizen comment, as posted at our terminal, be extended have been ignored.

The Island Institute invited business owners and those considering economic opportunity to a SUSTAINMe Conference on Chebeague Island. I was an invited speaker.

> When I was a kid, my friends and I went to great lengths to pick a secluded spot — or spots we thought were secluded — to smoke, drink, or otherwise misbehave, but the parents in this little island town of twelve hundred were an alert and conspiratorial bunch, and we often found our clandestine activities woefully transparent.
>
> One day in 1958, we picked up a pack of Camels from the Cascade Lanes and headed down the little six-foot-wide alley between L.R. Smith and Jerry Wadsworth's Restaurant to enjoy a smoke and to share a little bottle of vanilla extract we'd pocketed at E.G. Carver's, and a much larger bottle of Hafenrefer malt liquor we'd persuaded our customary adult resource to get for us at Tibb's Store. The resource ordinarily charged us a nickel per bottle, but on this day — sensing our eager - ness — soaked us for a dime.

The Cascade Lanes, where we got the smokes, was O.V. Drew's very busy bowling and pool emporium. League bowling took place every night, and the town was divided into imaginatively named teams of men and of women involving nearly all the town's adults. Similarly cyclical pool and billiard tournaments meant the place was jumping nearly every day and every evening. I was one of about a dozen adolescent pin setters who risked life and limb, certainly fingers, to return ten candlepins to their respective standing positions after each three-ball frame was bowled. A few of the aforementioned men found it more satisfying to knock the pins down with a ball that never touched the alley but rather sailed straight through the air to the pins, sending them flying in all directions. For ten cents a string, my fellow pin setters and I huddled on a little ledge above the lanes as deadwood flew in all directions. Three strings would give us the twenty-seven cents we'd need for a pack of Camels and a few pennies to spare. Proprietor Drew, a clinically calculating retailer, kept an open pack behind the counter and would make single cigarettes available for two cents apiece thus realizing a 33 percent profit beyond the profit he made from selling a pack for twenty-seven cents.

The little six-foot alley we navigated with our smokes and refreshments between L.R. Smith and Jerry Wadsworth's Restaurant led to an old abandoned carriage house where the town's drunks gathered routinely for their socials, often lasting all day. Though impolitic today, these few guys and one woman were called "the drunks," and they and the carriage house were as much a part of the fabric of town as any of the rest of us or of the other main street establishments.

The east side of the alley was the west wall of Jerry Wadsworth's Restaurant, which was really his mother Helen's, whose diminishing hope was that Jerry could be persuaded to step into her own shoes, which appeared increasingly unlikely, instead of stumbling over his own which, as a young alcoholic, he seemed doomed to do. Helen was famous for her codfish cakes, wonderful mouth-watering creations served three at a time with a little pile of homemade sausage patties and home fries that started out in the oven before being transferred to a huge stove top sauté pan to be finished off with peppers and onions. There were four or five tables, always full, particularly those at the window, and particularly around four thirty in the morning, when the restaurant opened, and from where the fishermen and lobstermen could tease Helen with crude language, see the harbor, and talk about weather conditions.

The west wall of the alley was L.R. Smith, a busy and bustling clothing store that sold oilskins and other foul weather clothing to lobstermen, but also all sorts of children's outfits and infant needs, men's and women's clothing, casual along with fine formal wear. It was run by Leo Lane, a shrewd and observant businessman, and by his son, Tim, then just stepping into his father's shoes and reflecting the same no-nonsense and profitable business savvy. Every piece of clothing I ever wore as a kid was procured there at L.R. Smith's, except for a Superman cape I got during a rare trip to Rockland at J.J. Newberry's (where the Island Institute is now).

Upstairs over the clothing store was the telephone exchange. A team of local ladies, all mothers, all members of the operator's guild, and all among the most well-informed of the aforementioned conspiratorial parents, handled every phone call made by anyone to anyone without exception. Our number, that of the Crossman household, was 137, three digits, but we hardly ever referred to them because everyone knew our number and we knew everyone else's. The only folks who needed to know our number were folks from away who called only once or infrequently. The operators — there were four of them — manned the switchboard, one at a time, twenty-four hours a day, and, except during the colder months, with the window open. Walking by on the sidewalk one floor below or coming and going from L.R. Smith you might hear "Operator."

"Hi, Mabel. Would you ring Cal for me?"

"Cal's not home, Clara. She's down to Isabel's knitting nets. Want me to call there?"

"Sure. Thanks, Mabel."

Mabel plugs Clara's 646 line into Isabel's 497 and the two begin chatting. "Cal, I thought we was gonna get together to play cards this morning."

"No, Clara, that's tomorrow down to Lucy's after I get done baiting trawl for Luther."

"Oh, goodness, that's right. I thought Luther was already gone seinin'."

Mabel never wanted to miss anything and so had never severed the connection. Now she jumps in, offering, "Luther's boat was gone at sunup."

That would have been a typical exchange, but on this day as we headed down the alley toward mischief, we'd have heard, had we paused long enough to listen, first the sound of ringing then Patricia Crossman's—my mom's—voice.

"Hello?"

"Pat, this is Mabel down to the switchboard. Phillip and Jo Jo just headed down to the carriage house and Phillip was smoking and carrying a bottle."

"Land sakes, Mabel, will it ever end? Thanks for calling. I'll send Bud right down."

E.G. Carvers, where I'd shoplifted the bottle of vanilla extract, was one of four very busy Main Street groceries. The others were an A&P, the Vinalhaven Grocery, and MacIntosh Grocery. It's difficult to imagine today, even during our busy summers, that this little town could support four full-service groceries, not more than a hundred feet apart, each with its own fish and meat departments, butcher, and support staff. Each, however, was always full of product, and full of people, and cumulatively they employed upwards of fifty people and profitably provided sustenance for twelve hundred during the off-season.

Tibb's Store was also within those two hundred yards that composed Main Street. It was kind of a grocery but only in a charitably inclusive sense. It was more like today's convenience stores, with snacks, lots of beer and soda, a few of the necessities like milk, butter, and eggs, and it stayed open later than the bigger groceries to serve the needs of the disorganized, the procrastinators, and those who only ventured out after dark. It's where we boys went to get prophylactics which we would then put strategically in our wallets so when the wallet was opened the little device in its plastic envelope would readily reveal itself to those assembled — other boys — so they would all know we were actively on the make. In fact, of course, they were invariably unused, dried out and shredded quickly, and had to be replaced with fresh ones from the little stash beneath the counter at Tibbs so that everyone would think we were scoring well.

It was the late fifties and early sixties, and Vinalhaven was jumpin'. Served by one wooden ferry that only carried one big car or two small ones, it could hardly be otherwise. One day Dick Poole bought a VW Beetle and drove it on board. The five-man crew and several of the male passengers picked it up and moved it forward to the bow. Then two cars, one big, one small, drove on and assumed their customary spots. It was the first time more than two vehicles had been carried on a Vinalhaven ferry. The ferry made two round trips a day. Going to the mainland for the day required a lot of planning. There was little point in going off island to do shopping. The logistics of getting a vehicle over and back were daunting, and the expense of riding around Rockland in a taxi was even more so. Besides, there was no need. This community of twelve hundred or so, captive because of logistics, was, on the other hand, thriving because it was captive. We had four or five gas stations. Admittedly they didn't bear much resemblance to today's filling station. Four of the five comprised one solitary pump in someone's front yard alongside a modest above-ground storage tank. We pulled up, leaned on the horn a little, and waited for someone to come out of the house and fill the tank or pump as much as we could afford. The more widely trusted pumped themselves then slipped the appropriate amount of money in a predetermined but not widely known hiding place, or came back the next day to settle up. There were little stores like Tibb's all over town. Each neighborhood had one. If you lived up on the Neck and ran out of milk you could walk down to Beatrice's, even at nine or ten, to get a jug. There'd probably be one or two bottles in the little cooler along with a pound or two of butter and some eggs. Beatrice didn't lock the door. You could just walk in, flick on the light and call her name. While you were retrieving the milk she'd come out of the back room where she and Ivan lived and take your money, or if they weren't home you'd leave it on the counter. The town sported three full-service automotive garages, this before there were even many cars or trucks, twine and net shops, several barbershops, a casket store, two cobblers, a tin knocking and plumbing repair shop, another pool room, four bakeries, two drug stores with companion soda fountains, a newsstand, two lumber yards, three hardware stores, a five-and-dime, dry goods store, three other restaurants, a tobacconist, movie theater, a fishing gear supply, a firewood business, photography studio, two maternity homes, and a mortuary.

Today the island is served by two big steel ferries. One carries sixteen or so vehicles, the other twenty-two or so, and together they make six round trips a day. The newsstand is about to close. The only remaining hardware store closed a few years ago. There is one grocery, no clothing store, no cobbler, no drug store, no soda fountain, no dry goods store, no movie theater, no five-and-dime, no conventional retail. There are several really nice restaurants, one spectacular gallery, a couple of nice gift shops, and a jeweler, but downtown is no longer the retail environment of a working community. It is a leisure market. This is certainly not to say Vinalhaven is a leisure community. We are home to the busiest and most profitable lobster fishing fleet in Maine, after all, and that critical element represents about 50 percent of the town's market value of goods and services. The other half comes directly or indirectly from the seasonal economy, an equally hardworking population, but what's left of our downtown serves those with more money to spend than needs to fulfill. The rest of us jump on the ferry with very little trouble, run around on the mainland getting all sorts of things done, and come back with a car full of stuff that afternoon, or simply sit down at the computer and order whatever we need, with hardly any exceptions, online.

Perhaps an active and realistic retail environment can be recreated in what used to be this architectural and marketing wonderland, but if so, it will only be because a comprehensive program of sustainability, one that will result in a kid emerging from high school with a perfectly clear sense of his or her relationship to this island community and their role in preserving not only its natural resources but its economy. That might be unrealistic. If so we'll have to find something else.

I was asked at the conference how I came to have in interest in writing and penned this explanation:

Stephen King and others caution against using too many words to say something that can be said with fewer. Although I doubt King is troubled (although he was the day I snuck up on him at Fenway Park and screamed BOO!), I disagree. I find beauty and continuity in well-constructed sentences and have an odd attachment to the semicolon. When I was a kid, I came under the spell of Gwendoline Greene, an iconic English teacher here at what used to be our Lincoln School. With one eye that wandered off to port and a singularly unattractive, if not scary, countenance, she was as untroubled by her own appearance as she was by the appearance each spring of another bunch of kids with bad attitudes and no interest in English. Why a stickler for grammar and language should have such a lasting effect or any effect at all on a teenager as angry and troublesome as I was a mystery then to the adults in my life and remains a mystery to me now. Still, I'm grateful for her lasting impression, one that was happily augmented by my mother's equally enthusiastic adherence to form and substance. Among those entrenched impressions was the admonition that I never begin a sentence with a connecting conjunction. Until recently — when I found myself momentarily swayed by changing convention, swallowed hard, and broke that rule in a piece I'd composed for the *Working Waterfont* it wasn't worth it. I could sense Ms. Greene standing next to my desk and looking over my shoulder disapprovingly and couldn't sleep for days.

Chris Guptill, a young man with his whole life ahead of him, or so we thought, took his own life, having succumbed to the ravages of drug addiction.

On the heels of town manager Marjorie Stratton's column lamenting the lack of interest in public service or even in voting, no one ran for the two vacant positions on the board of selectmen. Still, several write-ins were nominated:

The last time I ran for selectman, I ran hard and came in fifth. I didn't run at all this time and came in fourth, and, although I came in behind Karol Kucinski who also didn't run, and behind several who similarly did not run, I am encouraged, and have begun developing a strategy for my next non-candidacy. Since I came so close this time by not running, I intend to vigorously oppose myself next time around and expect that tactic to produce the desired victory.

I was trying to explain the nature of island politics to someone from Away the other day, someone who had read the election results, but lacked the requisite sophistication to understand the subtleties, the craft and cunning inherent in achieving election day victory. Pointing to the two top vote getters, Emily with thirty-eight votes, and Larry with seventeen, she naively pointed out that neither of them had run, and wondered if they would accept the position. I said that of course they would accept. She seemed surprised and wondered if they'd even been asked. "Of course, they haven't been asked," I said. "Why would we ask them? What business is it of theirs?"

Annual town meetings used to be well-attended popular and widely anticipated events that began with a pot luck supper. This year, as if to amplify Marjorie's lament, forty-three people attended; seven were under fifty. A few weeks later, Marjorie announced that she was leaving her position as town manager. Andy Dorr took her place as interim manager as a search for a permanent replacement got underway. Whoever steps in will have big shoes to fill. Marjorie was a strong and capable financial manager.

The Honor Flight volunteers announced a hugging and kissing booth fundraiser at the Fourth of July festivities to determine who was the sexiest man on Vinalhaven. I wasn't invited to participate.

The 23rd annual Great American Duck Race took place around the Fourth.

Another year, the twenty-third in fact, that I and my unsuspecting young assistants have pursued the elusive banner of wholesome activity known as the Great American Duck Race. I've volunteered at each of these, to paddle around in a canoe with one or another little kid in tow (this year it was my niece Hannah, a very capable duck retriever) in the fond hope that this year, perhaps, it will be a transparent exercise. One would think that after all these years I'd have learned that the game is rigged, the fix is in, and my duck or the ducks of the many other perpetually gullible participants will not be found to have crossed the finish line in first place, or at all for that matter, regardless of how obvious victory was. The truth is, not all duck retrievers share my noble sense of purpose. If a duck that does not belong to a member of the Michael family — or to whomever may have greased their palms — approaches the finish line it will inevitably be snatched from the jaws of victory, or held underwater till it expires, or squeezed so hard it displaces air with water by the ever-present and clearly deceitful other retriever, the one who surreptitiously launches downriver and out of view, the one whose companion retriever (Hannah's counterpart) jarringly refers to the stern as the back and the bow as the front. The result this year as it was eighteen years ago was that the Michaels' granddaughter Bethany was found to be the holder of the winning duck. How surprising.

The International Small Group and Tree Planting Program, a nonprofit run by Ben and Vanessa Henneke, was recognized as the Best Offsetting Project by Environment Finance, an agency reporting on sustainable development worldwide.

The Chebeague Sustainability conference resulted in convoluted logistics and dashed hopes.

A few weeks ago I published an invitation for others to join me in going down the coast to Chebeague

Island for the SUSTAINMe conference. Nine women responded. I'd like to think it was me. We left at five o'clock a.m. on a stunning moon-setting, sun-rising cruise across the bay aboard *Sea Breeze*. Captain Bobby arranged some comfortable seating in the cabin, warning of a chilly, maybe wet, ride across the bay. Ignoring our cautions and entreaties to join us in the cabin, the ladies all gathered in the stern and remained there for the duration. They seemed content without our company, unlikely though that may seem. When we boarded to return that evening around eight o'clock, the moon was rising and the sun setting. It was a good deal windier than it had been in the morning. Certainly that would work in our favor. Surely the women could be enticed to join us in the cabin and avoid getting seriously wet on the fantail. Bobby made the cabin even more appealing than for the morning trip: flowers, comfortable seats, drinks, soft music, and hors d'oeuvres. He even had Kirk Hansen on board as an added incentive. It was all for naught. He, Kirk, and I passed the moonlit cruise sequestered and alone in the cabin awkwardly enjoying the ambience and one another as the ladies huddled aft inexplicably content and appearing to enjoy their own company.

The Vinalhaven Community Wellness Coalition was by now in full swing, with regular gatherings to discuss all aspects of providing us all with "the tools and resources to live healthy and fulfilled lives."

I'd been diagnosed with an irregular heart rhythm, but perceived a practical solution.

By the time you read this I will have returned my heart monitor, a device I was directed to wear for a few days so my cardiologist could determine why my heart speeds up now and then, more and more recently, until it seems that, fed up with my inability to keep pace, it will explode out of my chest and run away. He suggested I might need a pacemaker, and my protestations that I was simply in love and these manifestations were to be expected, while apparently amusing, otherwise fell on deaf ears. Meanwhile, a friend stopped by for an early morning coffee, as he often does, and reported that his wife has opposite symptoms. Her heart now and then beats more slowly than it should, and she too is scheduled to visit a cardiologist who has already indicated, in spite of her conjecture that those symptoms too are nothing more than an amorous barometer, albeit more sultry than my own (it could hardly be otherwise) she may be a candidate for a pacemaker, as well. It seems to me that the perfect solution is right here in front of us, and a good deal less expensive and time consuming. If my heart is racing excessively and in eager anticipation, and hers is doing the same thing but simply being coy about it, perhaps we could just get together and hug now and then when the symptoms overwhelm us and hold that pose till our hearts have syncopated. Just a thought.

A young fisherman, Jeremy Philbrook, was lost at sea, and left behind a wife and three daughters. I was to have given a Vinalhaven Land Trust talk but we postponed it till next year. Instead, I wrote a column about a common phenomenon that attends tragedies like this.

Several folks, each needing to talk about what they were experiencing after last week's tragedy, stopped by. Each had been at Greet's Eats just before the news of Jeremy's loss became known. Each made the same observation. Each described the happy atmosphere at the wagon, waiting to order, the comradery inside and outside while considering their options, ordering, the smiling and happy faces behind the counter and at the grill, waiting for their name to be called, good-natured chatter with others, and finally, after a perfectly reasonable and understandable wait, lunch presented and eaten. Each recalled nearly the same delightful sequence and each clearly felt the need to relate it, to relive it, as if they could reconcile their happiness and enjoyment then with the dismay they felt now,

OBSERVATIONS

only a day later. What can be gained by such an exercise, by talking over and over and over about the pleasant circumstances of one day in the grim reality of the next, by reliving the excitement and positive energy of Wednesday within the gloom and desperation of Thursday? What profit can be found, after absorbing such a loss, in reminding oneself, again and again, of how much better things had been so recently? And what benefit is there in sharing those pleasant memories with another who has precisely the same recollection? Clearly, a great deal.

Once again we solicited the very generous service time of folks from outside the community to do for us what we might have expected to do for ourselves. This time twelve Bowdoin college students accomplished a great deal in our town parks, the Owen Webster playground, and elsewhere, under the typically magnanimous direction of Bodine Ames.

A visit to the Historical Society reminded me of the drawbridge that used to span Indian Creek at Lane's Island.

When I was a young kid, I lived on Lane's Island. We rented the smaller of two houses up on the hill from Harold Vinal, Vinalhaven's Poet Laureate, who owned it but lived Around the Mountain. The drawbridge was being dismantled at the time — a sadly misguided decision, not unlike tearing down the Memorial Hall, that seemed prudent at the time, but which rendered to history a component of the stunning reality that was sailing ships travelling directly between the East Boston Quarry and, via Carver's Harbor, the rest of the world. I admit that the quarry being no longer in business and there being no more sailing ships were contributing factors. During the dismantling and reconstruction of the bridge as we now know it, I walked to and from school each day with Nate and John Hall across a single plank with a rope railing. Each day I approached with mounting trepidation as the workmen there admonished me to hurry along because a troll lived under the bridge and was particularly fond of kids about my age. Nate always stopped to challenge that troll. "Bring it on" was his general attitude toward danger in any form, but the terrifying prospect of having to avoid that creature when I returned home that afternoon haunted my school day. I was sure that someday the troll, thus challenged, would consume us both.

An announcement in early September called our attention to International Hope Day, a hastily arranged event whereby limited editions of Robert Indiana's Hope prints, signed by the artist, were to be offered for sale, the proceeds to be given to P.I.E. and the Medical Center. On the appointed day prints were available for sale at 200 dollars each but they were neither numbered nor signed. It was a fiasco, with sales taking place right outside Bob's Star of Hope residence, but with him resisting calls to acknowledge pleas from both the organizers and the press to come out and sign the prints or even give his blessing to the event. Nonetheless, forty or so were sold, apparently in the hope that they would eventually be assigned numbers (thereby giving some legitimacy to their being one of a limited editions), and signed by Bob.

The beginnings of a sidewalk from the village to the ferry terminal were begun prompting this enthusiastic endorsement.

There's been more construction in and around the village this year than since the municipal sewer, and it's all been good. Smoothly paved roads have replaced rutted and heaved byways, and comfortable, level sidewalks now exist where there had been nothing worth walking on. Now underway, the most recent of these, interestingly, is precisely where the town's Sidewalk Committee last year recommended it be installed, a suggestion that was rejected at the time. But that's another story. The price of all this construction — and it's easily been worth paying — has and continues to be the ungodly sound of Danny's Kobelco Excavator as, each day at dawn, the monstrosity creeps along toward its eventual and routine consummation with Kevin's Zim Cement Mixer. Screeching imploringly for its mate, as well as for lubrication, those of us who've been thus awakened each morning — nearly everyone in the village area — by that unearthly sound are reminded, if we're old enough to remember the fifties and sixties, of the great old horror flicks of that period. Godzilla and Rodan — huge wanton creatures that stomped across the landscape turning buildings and bridges to rubble, and people, women in particular, into fainting apparitions with each contemptuous step — were gleefully frightening, and the bone-chilling shrieking noises they made, particularly Rodan, were nearly identical to the Kobelco's imploring call to the Zim Mixer for attention. Later, when that union is finally achieved, the satisfied grunts of the Zim Mixer can hardly be misinterpreted.

The second Honor Flight, this one open to all veterans, took place in September, and those returning veterans were treated to a marvelous display of patriotic appreciation.

Elaine and I went to New York City to see John Wulp's *Red Eye of Love*, an off-Broadway production of the play he'd co-written in the 1950s and produced on North Haven in 2013. During that road trip we used my GPS and when we returned home I became a fashion consultant.

Parking on the West Side Highway in New York City is severely limited. If one can find a space one had better pay attention to the signs that call for limitations and restrictions. Failure to do so will result in one's car being towed off even if one is asleep in the back seat and wakes up to protest. For example, all vehicles must be elsewhere on Mondays and Thursdays between nine and eleven thirty a.m. so the street can be cleaned and curbside trash picked up. That means that the thousands of folks who own those cars pile out of their apartments and, in some cases, just drive around Manhattan for a couple of hours before descending like mad prospectors on the same or a nearby spot. At the northern end of each block is a fire hydrant. There is no parking within twenty or so feet of the hydrant. I parked our 2012 black Subaru in the last spot before the hydrant on the corner of 104th Street. In the morning I went out to move it before nine a.m. I walked a block north from our apartment and, while I remembered it being further, found the Subaru and pointed my ignition gizmo to unlock it. Nothing happened. I began to imagine having to break a window and drive all the way to Maine with cardboard in its place. I looked at the car — right color — Maine plate (I made a note of the number — LR3056). I looked inside — not our stuff. Confused, I walked up a block and there in the last spot before the hydrant on the corner of 105th was another Subaru. It responded to my gizmo. Six hours later we passed LR3056 on the Maine Turnpike headed north.

The other day my sweetheart came into my office wearing a nice outfit — I think it was a dress — and asked if I thought she should wear it that night — we were going out somewhere — or if she should wear the outfit she'd worn at her last gallery opening, an event now over a month past. Moments like these are a little awkward. On the one hand, I know perfectly well that on some level she knows I do not remember what she wore at that opening, and yet she asks. If I say I think this outfit looks great — an easy appraisal because it did — she will ask if I like it better than the one she wore a month earlier. If I say yes, I will be asked why. If I say no, I will be asked why. It's not an intentional trap and it's not a test to see how much attention I pay when attention is certainly the natural and prudent course. It's just something that has to play out. On this occasion I allowed that I liked this one better because it flowed more naturally and because it moved with her instead of in spite of her. Further, I considered, the garment accentuated her most appealing features — which I then eagerly illuminated — and was just the right color to complement her eyes and went well with her shoes, which I also praised. A fellow can get a lot of mileage from complimenting shoes. I wasn't looking for leverage that evening but it is worth noting that the subject of shoes can be used to great advantage — to warm a moment or to simply change the subject, for instance. We've developed a nice repartee. We both know she gets better input from another woman, but I'm all there was for the moment and she made the best of it.

For a while now there's been a little tension between two of the most important ladies in my life. It needed airing.

Years ago Elaine got me a GPS to help me find my way, as it were, but its male voice was annoying. He was quite full of himself and clearly felt he should be behind the wheel and I should be plugged (or not) into a distant power source. Recognizing my irritation we traded him in for a more agreeable model whose persona was that of a woman with a gentle English accent. As she only came to life in the car we named her Carmela. On those rare occasions when I find myself on the road without Elaine, Carmela is quick to snuggle up next to me on the front seat. While she reluctantly accompanies us when we are a travelling threesome, she's clearly more at ease when it's just the two of us. For that matter though, Elaine is also more relaxed and herself when we can find our way without Carmela, i.e., when she is shut up in the glove compartment. Before long, however, Carmela became a little possessive of me and quite clearly resentful when Elaine was with us. And, to be truthful, the reverse was just as true. On our last trip, typically, the two could not agree on whether I should take the first or second exit from a roundabout in Boston. The discussion got quite heated, ending when Elaine called Carmela hysterical and threatened to throw her out the window if she didn't shut up. Carmela, in turn, got in quite a huff and refused to even offer an opinion when the next navigational quandary presented itself and, while she did not have the gift of gab, instead employed one of her stock phrases, "lost satellite reception," to make it quite clear that she had no interest in what Elaine had to say and that her own regard for Elaine was no less contemptuous. During a more recent solo sojourn I plugged her in to give her a chance to be herself. It was a nice drive. She seemed to breathe a sigh of relief and grew quite coy.

A visitor to the island was impressed with the vagaries and assortment of waves he encountered and submitted this column.

The Vinalhaven Wave
as seen by someone from Away

My family and I recently had the pleasure and privilege of spending two weeks on the humble island of Vinalhaven. We were guests in the house of a friend who grew up there, and whose father was from the island as well. To protect his character I'll not give a name, or further hints of who this might be. But let's just say, like nearly every local, he has a nickname, and it's a play on his last name. I'll leave it at that. Of all the unique, and sometimes quirky, things that make Vinalhaven a special place, perhaps my favorite is the ubiquitous wave from behind the windshield of nearly every driver passing along the roads.

Having grown up in Vermont, and visited other parts of Maine countless times, I was already familiar with this habit. However, nowhere else have I ever witnessed it as acutely as on Vinalhaven. After a few days, I began to change my own wave habits. At first, I found myself often initiating the wave to the oncoming driver. Then, days later, it occurred to me, that with my out-of-state plates, perhaps this could be viewed as irritating, or even rude — a "tourist" making someone who may not have felt like waving raise a hand or a few fingers. So, out of courtesy, I stopped being the first to wave, only waving after having been waved to.

Having fallen comfortably into this pattern after three or four days, and learning that it was best to drive with my right hand atop the steering wheel to afford the least amount of effort to respond to an oncoming gesture, I began to observe more closely the wave habits of my fellow drivers, and occasionally, nearby pedestrians.

Following are my findings and assumptions:

> More men than women wave.
> Wave styles fall into at least these several categories:
> – a full hand wave, raised completely from the wheel
> – a half hand wave, while still holding the wheel
> – the middle, ring, and pinkie fingers raised slightly off the wheel
> – the index finger wave (which my island friend employs)
> – a slight luffing of some of the fingers
> – and my island friend tells me there is one fellow who, instead of waving, simply gives a stiff sort of backwards nod of his head and upper body. Many of you reading this perhaps know who he is referring to.

I later decided that some folks might have several different uses of the above-described waves reserved for varying circumstances. For example, if one is passing a close friend, or family member who hasn't been seen or spoken with in a few days, I'm guessing that occasion calls for a more generous wave, like a full hand. On the other hand (couldn't help myself) if one is passing a tourist, like me, who is a stranger, maybe the index finger is enough to compete the task. And so on. The style I adopted was the half-hand wave while still holding the wheel.

The most vexing thing for me was, upon returning to the relative metropolis of a certain New England city that begins with B, is known for its traffic, and is home to several beloved professional sports teams, I had the itchy impulse to wave to oncoming drivers, which due to the aforementioned traffic, was an impossible feat.

I look forward to politely waving back to each and every one of you next summer. Should you care to wave to me first, that is.

Robert M. Sturtevant

There were other idiosyncrasies worthy of comment as well.

> I used to marvel at the ability of Jane Goodall to tell one chimpanzee from another. She'd been with them for so long that she could flawlessly distinguish among hundreds of animals that, to me, looked

OBSERVATIONS

the same. Little distinctions like posture, markings, gestures, and even facial expressions and sounds that made one critter different from another had imprinted themselves on her brain. The same thing is true out here on these islands among the herd of inhabitants and among the longtime summer visitors who arrive each spring following the exhausting summer migration from their winter grazing and breeding grounds to the south. Living our lives in the context of others, as we must unavoidably do on an island, we are similarly familiar with one another and can, as well as Jane Goodall, identify individuals from afar before their distinctive faces become visible. Like her we employ posture and its attendant elements, particularly one's gait and wave, affectations that are entirely individual. Just this morning, driving into town, I came up behind a familiar truck, familiar because there are several of them out here. Still, I didn't have to wonder who was behind the wheel. The torso was shifted toward the driver's door while the head was cocked a little to starboard—unmistakable. And just ahead I knew who was striding, as only she does, around the Sands, still a quarter mile away. And behind her a summer resident who undertakes long walks daily and who has an unusual but signature hitch in his stride.

Louie granted me another of his sporadic interviews. They are customarily all over the place and I have given up on presenting them in an orderly fashion. On the other hand, he is an island icon and I intend to put these excerpts of his life in whatever form he chooses to give them to me.

Louie Lives Here

This is another in the sporadic series of Louie's remembrances. He sat down with me, as he usually does, and simply began reciting events and naming folks—no particular context—from the distant past as if it was all yesterday. In earlier columns I'd tried to organize his thoughts but to no avail and it's his voice after all. Some names have been changed:

Spider, Edith, Grace, and Fred were siblings who lived across the street. My sister cooked for them long ago. Spider and Fred bought and dried fish down where Fishermen's Friend is. Now and then I'd steal a piece to chew on. E.G. Piper lived in a house right there where the chamber's information booth is now. He kept hens and they lived right in the house with them, even slept with them. His daughter, Georgie, taught at the White Schoolhouse. One day we put eggs in the gutter over his door and tilted it when he came out—the eggs landed on his bald head. Jimmy Calderwood had a lumberyard next to Piper's, between there and Hopkins Boatyard. He had a planer. Bob Kelwick was his delivery man and I helped some when I was around fifteen. Plato Arey sold firewood—they cut and split all day—across from the Co-op. He was father to Goose and Harold. There was a bench down near the water and some men used to set there and run on about things like they did in the hardware store later on. One of them was Wiggle Room. His brother Knotty was there too. They each had different fathers. Neither was the one married to their mother, and who fathered their brothers and sisters—I think.

In October a handful of islanders secured from eBay the return of an original E.P. Walker fireman's helmet, a piece of protective gear that had originally been at home on our 1872 fire engine.

In November a historical photograph and explanation appeared citing as its source "The Bleak House Archives." I hope this feature continues because the originator is an island historian and his contributions would certainly enhance the *Wind's* appeal.

*Harold Chillis
At Roger Young's
Summer 1998*

Harold S. Chilles 1931 – 2005 (73)

After giving me a lift home Harold and I sat, in his truck, reminiscing about people and events we had known. I had never talked to him, before, about anything. In the caption on the right of my snapshot Chilles is spelled wrong. This, you might say, provides a symbolic example of how little we knew about each other: even in the "Hot House" environment of a place like this...

Source: **BLEAK HOUSE ARCHIVES**

Manhattan again proved to have more in common with Vinalhaven than each being the same size.

> I've often compared Manhattan with Vinalhaven. They are the same size after all, and each has eight bridges, but there's at least one big diference: Folks from Manhattan can come here and get away from it all but the reverse is apparently not true. Last week I took a walk up West End Avenue and then cut across to Broadway on 105th Street. There, coming toward me, was a man with an expression on his face not unlike my own — one of astonishment — as we recognized one another. Elaine and I were on our way to D.C. to see a play and— amazingly — this guy composed the music for the show. The next day down at the other end of Manhattan, walking in Greenwich Village, we found ourselves gaining on a tiny woman we thought familiar. As we passed, Elaine prepared to glance discreetly down to see if it was who we thought it was and noticed she was carrying one of my sister-in-law's netted bags. Sure enough, it was a long-time summer resident and friend in town visiting relatives. Similar astonishments were exchanged, and then we headed back to our host's apartment. On the way I noticed an ad announcing the appearance of another friend, a jazz trombonist, at a venue just a few blocks away, so I put in an appearance there about a half hour ahead of time. When I entered, he was setting things up and wearing the familiar expression of astonishment.

Observations

Veterans Day was upon us again.

President Obama bestowed the nation's highest honor on a Civil War soldier — Alonzo Cushing, undeniably a hero of the Battle of Gettysburg. The ceremony took place a week before Veterans Day. It's nice, on occasions like that, to indulge our patriotic fantasies. The fantasy, of course, isn't that Cushing was a hero. That was no fantasy. He certainly was and so were all the other recipients of the Medal of Honor in the decades of war since then. The fantasy is that the glory and honor outweighs the misery and despair visited on combatants and on the families of those who are lost or simply absent for prolonged periods. The fantasy is that it's somehow more meaningful for our government and for many of us to focus our attention on waving the flag and honoring the fallen instead of giving treatment and comfort to the veterans who desperately need it and who are still among us. The numbers of those veterans who take their own lives each year, each day, is staggering. It always has been but it's much worse now, and we hear very little about it. Many of those have simply come to the end of their rope trying to seek the treatment they need from a badly dysfunctional Veterans Administration. There are legions of folks at the VA who are compassionate and devoted but not enough. The thousands of veterans who are hopelessly stalled in their efforts to get treatment suffer at the hands of VA staffers who care more about fabricating their own achievements in pursuit of performance bonuses than about giving veterans the attention they have earned.

The Philae lander rendezvoused with Churyumov comet, an astonishing achievement that left me running metaphorically amuck.

The European Space Agency's Philae Lander united with the comet Churyumov-Gerasimenko

Ten years ago a boy became enamored with a young woman and, singularly obsessive, settled on a date ten years hence to win her heart — the second week in November — last week. He paid close attention, not stalking her exactly — well, I guess he did in fact but not threateningly, just smitten and determined. As the unwavering trajectory of her life carried her steadfastly onward, he struggled to keep up a parallel, albeit erratic, course he intended would converge with hers on that distant November date. She may have noticed his pursuit. In either event she was not dissuaded from her own course. If he cared enough he'd keep up, if not—well, whatever. He did, as it happens, care enough. His determination to catch up equaled her own to keep going and, while he continually found himself having to adjust his own less precise course, he began gaining on her. During the ten year pursuit he often had to stop and rest, sometimes for long periods, before again taking up the chase. When that happened he had to avail himself of extremes — energy supplements, propellants and such — in order to catch up. But he was closing on her— and last week circumstances were such that he found himself at her side, breathless, not only with the excitement of being near her but from having worked so hard for so long. Since then her course has not wavered but she has succumbed to his advances and, for as long as he can cling to her, seems willing to have him along for the ride.

Louie visited again and we agreed to do this weekly for as long as we could each stick to it.

Louie Lives Here

George MacDonald and Eva had a son Byron and a dog named Goofy. Eva was sister to Oscar Waterman of North Haven. Young Curtis Webster walked Goofy often, for the thrill, because each time it saw a cat it pulled Curtis off his feet. Curtis and I were both short-legged. A goat roamed on Skin Hill and used to chase us. My shoes had clips on them and sometimes, when running away from the goat, my feet would get tangled. Then the goat would catch me and ram me in the butt and knock me over. Once it hit Harry Stinson really hard — really hard. One day I was in the loft of George's barn with Arthur Philip. We were smoking. George saw the smoke and called the fire department. They came and stuck a hose up in the loft and turned it on. I think they knew it was us. After that I always teased, "Georgy Porgy, puddin' and pie, kissed the girls and made them cry. When the boys came out to play, Georgy Porgy ran away."

Around Thanksgiving a summer resident expressed his gratitude for the refuge this place is for some.

For as long as I can remember, my family and I have traveled to the place where I am most content, a place I consider my second home. Every year, the same familiar feeling overtakes me, when we start to plan our annual visit to these islands. A longing for the solitude and tranquility they exude comes over me, as I think of where we will soon be. After much anticipation, the day finally comes, and the long drive begins. We always start our journey as early as possible, in order to catch the first ferry. Although the drive is long, it is always exciting with its special landmarks. As we pass over the bridge in Bath I spot the huge shipyard below me with massive boats being built, while others silently bob up and down on the water. I know that once we are over this bridge we are almost at our destination. I can barely sit still in the car anymore, thinking of the simple joy of hitting golf balls into the water, and seeing which of us can hit one closest to the brightly colored buoys.

Everything about these islands is so distinct: the salty smell of the ocean, the soft roar of a motorboat, the persistent whistling call of the osprey, and the ever-present, cool sea breeze. All these images never fail to fill me with a sense of serenity and contentment. The combination of a familiar place, its breathtaking beauty, and the fact that I'm able to detach myself from my daily life is magical, and makes me feel truly at peace. With limited cell reception, no internet access, and no television I have the freedom to isolate myself with my family and friends. I realize that every part of a teenager's life, nowadays, is so entrapped in fleeting trends, which at best scarcely last a season. On Vinalhaven I'm always able to focus on enjoying the things I want to do. Nothing can compare to a walk through the woods on the winding, narrow path to the boathouse. Our dogs lead the way, darting back and forth through the trees, constantly disappearing in the woods, loving the surroundings as much as I do. I live for the nights when we go out for a boat ride in the setting sun. The cool night air and the gentle sound of the foaming wake fill me with feelings of calm. I treasure this atmosphere which gives me the opportunity to be carefree and savor my surroundings without distractions.

These islands are the place where I am without any conflicts. I have become keenly aware of the value of this spot, as we have been unable to visit it over the past two summers. The absence of this place has shown me how special it is. I used to take the islands for granted, because they were part of my life for longer than I can remember. The first summer when we did not take our accustomed trip to Maine is when I realized the value of this place. However, I find that I can transport myself to this heavenly spot by merely closing my eyes and thinking of it!

OBSERVATIONS

I feel blessed that we spent our summers on these islands and that I have experienced a place with immeasurable natural beauty. A place where I know I can be in touch with myself and relax. The serene atmosphere of Vinalhaven and North Haven will always be an integral part of me.

By Sawyer Tracy (submitted by Richard E. Byrd)

I was delighted to see another installment from Roger Young's Bleak House Archives.

RAYMOND LAFON WALLS WITH PHOTO OF HIS BROTHER RICHARD IN ROGER YOUNG'S KITCHEN, OLD HATBOR RD. MAY 2004

Vinalhaven born Raymond Walls (1935-2009) came to borrow a shovel to bury his brother's ashes. Without hesitation I volunteered. "There are two shovels... want some help?"

Returning from City Point we sat in the kitchen having coffee, donuts and a discussion of some of our entwining family photographs. In the great scheme of life, Raymond's father was my father's uncle. I felt honored that morning when he came to borrow a shovel! (November 23, 2014)

BLEAK HOUSE ARCHIVE

Marge Conway had by now begun an interesting column: Marge Remembers

Marge Remembers

A good time for this story as the holidays are here. The girls were married. Neither Edward nor Herb would go Christmas tree hunting. I finally said to myself, I'll get one. I grabbed the trusty saw and started out back of the school house. Well, I walked and walked, hunted and hunted, and finally got discouraged. Russ Wortinger was the janitor at the school at the time. He was outside bringing out trees that the school had used for their parties. He asked me if I was looking for a Christmas tree. When I said yes he said take one of these, they won't be saving them. I took one I thought looked pretty good. When Herb and Ed came home, they asked did you find this tree out back of the school house? I was pretty proud of myself. Me, cutting down a tree. Then I spoiled it by telling them what happened.

Now Louie was making a regular appearance.

Louie Lives Here

When I was little I used to visit Grace Barker. She and Fred lived where Geno and Laura live now and Fred had a boat shop there. I would sit with her for hours. One of the things she always said was, "You're no one's fool. You're smart, have a good personality and a good memory." She also told me if something wasn't worth working for I didn't need it and also that if mischief wasn't necessary — don't do it! One day Grace gave me the multiplication tables to study. I studied them each time I visited and one day she took them away and said, "Now, let's see what you've learned." I knew them all. Fanny Ames lived just down the little hill from Grace and Fred. She was a teacher on North Haven and was Clyde Ames's sister. Clyde's wife Ruth ran Seabreeze. One day Fanny gave me a book to read and told me to write something of my own when I was through with it. She gave me a long fountain pen that had to be dipped in ink. She said, "If I can do it, you can do it." So I did. My Aunt Marion Martin taught kindergarten. She read what I'd written and couldn't believe it. She asked Grace who wrote it and Grace told her I did. Ruth Billings, Ethel Doughty, and Dot Melin were my other teachers at Washington School, grades 1-3. One day Aunt Marion asked me to help her teach the kids to learn the multiplication tables and I did. I said, "If I can do it, you can do it," and they all learned the tables.

An acquaintance had won a Pulitzer Prize for critical writing and had been a book critic for the *New York Times* but I didn't know it.

About ten years ago I had the chance to have a collection of essays published by Dartmouth College Press. I was excited about the chance to see them in book form and I began to gather and edit the components. Before long I had them ready for submission and several friends offered to read them and write reviews. One of these was Richard Eder. He read it, told me he loved it, and offered to write a review for the back cover. I knew Richard as a casual friend but knew nothing of his credentials or even if he had any credentials. I was skeptical. Privately I thought it sounded a little risky. I didn't want just anyone to write a blurb for the book. What if it was amateurish or badly written and I found myself having to reject his friendly offer? He was so sincere, though. I resisted quizzing him about whether he had any writing or review experience and, a little reluctantly, accepted Richard's offer although I already had a perfectly wonderful review that Capt. Ivan Olson had provided. I hoped, if Richard happened to submit something worth publishing, that he wouldn't be intimidated at finding himself in Ivan's company. Before long Richard presented his flattering review. It comprised seventy words, a few of which I had never seen in juxtaposition or even the same proximity. I submitted the two reviews. The publisher called as soon as he received them. He wanted to know if my reviewer was THE Richard Eder. "I don't know," I replied. "How many are there?"

Just as the year ended and 2015 got underway, a dear friend to us all passed away.

I don't know if she was simply determined not to be a burden and it had become clear to her that was what she would soon become or if she was just too uncomfortable with the particulars of what would be required to keep her alive, but a little more than a week ago, Rhoda Boughton decided to forego further nourishment and let nature take its course. This extraordinary and gifted woman, who had given and only given for her entire life, had no interest in enduring — for the time remaining — the care and attention of others. During a lifetime among us, Rhoda has given of herself with a generosity that knew no bounds and with an equally boundless and remarkable, even at eighty-nine, energy. Whereas most of us entertain at least a little superficiality — I certainly do — Rhoda did not. Everything she gave she gave from the depths of her heart and soul and when she gave of herself it was without qualification. When she asked about something or someone it was with a depth of genuine interest that left no doubt where her heart was at that moment. Bill Chilles, who has been largely responsible for so many successful stage sets over the years, gives Rhoda glowing credit for having taught him so much about color, composition, and accomplishing illusion in set design. An acquaintance, one of many at her bedside and in her humble presence during those last few days, told me she felt she was in the presence of greatness. Certainly no one who knew her would deny that.

~

I could go on, I suppose, add a new "Observer" column and a little more about what's going on as each week passes, as each new edition of the *Wind* hits the streets, but, as a dear acquaintance pointed out, I could also decide to publish what I have assembled now, while I am still upright, rather than simply taking it with me, week by week, as I advance toward the grave. That makes sense.

This, then, is the conclusion. It's been over one hundred and thirty years since Owen Lyons and Charles Healey undertook the creation of the first *Wind,* and forty years since Ray Blaisdell gave the breath of eternal life to the *Wind* as we now know it. During those forty years, hundreds have assembled the contributions of thousands. Those volunteers have further ensured the timely delivery of over two thousand issues comprising over twenty thousand pages to us in the village and to others around the country and the world who care deeply about what is going on here on Vinalhaven.

Today's assembled volunteers, putting together the Wind.

Today's distribution volunteers, putting out the Wind.
Photos by Mike Seif

Design by Joanna Young

TALKING CROW

Vinalhaven, Maine

Made in the USA
San Bernardino, CA
10 August 2016